SIGILL : COLL : CARLETON
DECLARATIO SERMONUM TUORUM ILLUMINAT
NORTHFIELD, MINN. A.D. 1866

Fighting Napoleon

Fighting Napoleon

Guerrillas, Bandits and Adventurers in Spain, 1808–1814

CHARLES J. ESDAILE

Yale University Press
New Haven and London

For information about this and other Yale University Press publications, please contact:
U.S. Office: *sales.press@yale.edu* yalebooks.com
Europe Office: *sales@yaleup.co.uk* www.yaleup.co.uk

Set in Ehrhardt by SNP Best-set Typesetter Ltd, Hong Kong
Printed in Great Britain by St Edmundsbury Press Ltd, Bury St Edmunds

Library of Congress Cataloging-in-Publication Data
Esdaile, Charles J.
Fighting Napoleon: guerrillas, bandits, and adventurers in Spain, 1808–1814 / by Charles J. Esdaile.—1st ed.
p. cm.
Includes bibliographical references and index.
ISBN 0–300–10112–0 (Cl.: alk. paper)
1. Peninsular War, 1807–1814. 2. Guerrilla warfare—Spain—History—19th century. 3. Spain—History—Napoleonic Conquest, 1808–1813. 4. Wars of Liberation, 1813–1814—Spain. 5. France—History, Military—1789–1815. 6. Spain—History, Military—19th century. I. Title.
DC231.E833 2004
940.2′742′0946—dc22

A catalogue record for this book is available from the British Library

For Alison, in love and gratitude

Contents

Illustrations

Preface

In both Britain and Spain the most well-known aspect of the Peninsular War – the great struggle that convulsed the Iberian Peninsula between 1808 and 1814 following its invasion by Napoleon Bonaparte – is beyond doubt the participation in the fighting of large numbers of irregular bands of armed civilians. Renowned for having given the English language the word 'guerrilla', these forces are generally agreed to have inflicted huge damage on the invaders, and it has often been argued that their activities rendered the conquest of the Peninsula a task that was beyond the capacities even of Napoleon. Yet in neither England nor Spain (nor, indeed, anywhere else) has any attempt ever been made to write a detailed analysis of the guerrilla war. Nor, meanwhile, has any systematic attempt ever been made to make use of the wealth of material that exists on the subject in the Spanish archives (indeed, it has rather been assumed that the 'people's war' cannot have left a footprint in the documents in an age when the vast majority of the populace was illiterate). In brief, this work seeks to remedy both wants, and at the same time to take account of the growing body of scholarship that has led the academic community to question traditional arguments in respect of popular responses to war, occupation and mobilisation in other parts of Napoleonic Europe. As such, it may certainly be deemed an exercise in revisionism: for too long has treatment of the subject been dominated by myth and propaganda. That said, it is only a beginning: extraordinary riches remain untapped in the Spanish archives (not to mention those of France and Portugal), whilst there is clearly much scope for regional studies of the sort that Jorge Sánchez Fernández has so admirably pioneered in respect of Valladolid. Whatever else may be said of it, then, let us hope that this work is never called the last word on the subject.

As usual, the acknowledgements are by far the nicest lines that I have to write. At the top of the list, of course, come the various sources of research funding on which I have drawn – in this case, the Leverhulme Trust, from whom I was lucky enough to obtain a two-year research fellowship for the period 2000–2, and the University of Liverpool, which provided me with considerable assistance from its Research Development Fund. In this context, however, I should also like to mention two institutions in Spain in the form of the Universidad Autónoma de Barcelona, whose kindness in inviting me to present a staff seminar funded a productive visit to the Catalan archives, and, above all, the Real Colegio de San Albano in Valladolid, whose boundless hospitality enabled me to make full use of the vital materials housed in the Archivo General de Simancas. At the head of the list of people, perhaps, comes Christopher Allmand, whose wise counsel and gentle prompting during his years as my Head of Department at the University of Liverpool constitute the spark that gave life to this work. At A.M. Heath Literary Agents, Bill Hamilton has been a loyal friend who has worked tirelessly to ensure its appearance on the market, whilst at Yale University Press I should like to thank Robert Baldock. The staff of all the libraries and archives at which I have worked have without exception been kindness and helpfulness themselves, but in this context I should particularly like to thank Christopher Woolgar, Karen Robson, Sue Donnelly and Mary Cockerill at the University of Southampton; Ian Jackson at the University of Liverpool; Nieves Sánchez Hidalgo, Estrella Valentín-Fernández Fernández, Inmaculada Martín Muñoz, Amalia Jiménez Morales, Ana Sanz Robles, Jesús Rodríguez Izquierdo, Maribel Baenas Pérez, Paqui Mateo Macias and Yolanda Ruiz Esteban at the Biblioteca Nacional; and Pilar Bravo Lledó of the Archivo Histórico Nacional. Also pivotal was the generosity of a number of people who helped me stretch my limited resources by receiving me into their homes, amongst whom I should especially like to mention Esther and Mari-Cruz de Carlos, and Francisco Varo and Araceli Muñoz. Other good friends have included, as before, Leopoldo Stampa of the Ministerio de Asuntos Exteriores, Concha Bocos, Rafael Agasagasti, William and Sonia Chislett, Emilio de Castro, Dolores Schilling, Jo Klepka, Enrique Mardones, Fernando Fanjul, Antonia Rodríguez, Jesús Maroto, José María Espinosa de los Monteros, Santiago Nistal and Maribel Piqueras. My fellow researchers David Alonso, Azucena Pédraz Marcos, Leonor Hernández Enviz, Grahame Harrison, Susan Lord, Marta Ruiz Jiménez and Satoko Nakajima have provided me with insight and relaxation alike. And, finally, amongst my fellow *peninsulares* and Napoleonists, I should like to thank Rory Muir, Arsenio García Fuertes, Jorge Sánchez Fernández, Vittorio Scotti-Douglas, John Tone, Alicia Laspra Rodríguez, Esteban Canales, Lluis Roura, Antonio Moliner Prada, Francisco Carantoña Alvarez, Antonio Carrasco Alvarez, Javier Maestrojuan, Herminio Lafoz Rabaza, Mike Broers and Alan Forrest, all of whom have at one time or another offered me help and encouragement. Of these good people, I should like to make particular mention of Rory Muir, who has, as with all my works, subjected every word of this manuscript to a stern eye. Needless to say, however, such errors as may have crept into its pages are the fault of no one but the author.

It is, of course, to my family that my debts are greatest. Over the past two years Alison, Andrew, Helen, Maria-Isabel and Bernadette have endured absences on my part that have been as continuous as they have been prolonged: that I am grateful, they know, but it is always good to record the happy home background that lies at the heart of any success I may have achieved.

Liverpool, June 2003

The Iberian Peninsula, 1808–1814

I

The Guerrilla in History

The guerrillas who opposed the Napoleonic conquest of Spain have occupied a central role in the historiography of the Peninsular War ever since 1814. For Spanish historians of all shades of opinion they have been at one and the same time proof positive of the heroism that the people of Spain had displayed in fighting off the armies of Napoleon, clear evidence that the conflict had been a 'national' war that had seen an entire people confront an alien invader, and a sure defence against wounding British accusations that the Spaniards had played little part in their own liberation. For French historians eager to defend and attack Napoleon alike, they fulfilled an important function, for they could be used to argue both that the emperor's every step was dogged by ignorance and superstition, and that he was in the end brought down by his refusal to take account of the will of the people. And finally for British historians they provided a means of paying lip-service to the Spanish struggle that subtly emphasised the superiority of British arms and of the British national character: peasants skulking in the shelter of rocks and bushes might be useful allies, but gallant soldiers standing shoulder to shoulder in the famous 'thin red line' conveyed a much more manly image; equally, whilst the raids and skirmishes of *la guerrilla* killed more Frenchmen than ever perished at the hands of Wellington, they could hardly match the drama of such victories as Salamanca and Vitoria.

If emphasising the importance of the guerrillas fitted in with a variety of national needs and preoccupations, it was also convenient in another sense, for it dovetailed all too neatly with the laziness and incapacity that have often characterised the historiography of the Peninsular War. Let us take, for example, the many British writers who have essayed accounts of the conflict. With some exceptions – the outstanding examples are Robert Southey and Sir Charles Oman – either mere hacks or military men with little interest in anything other than the campaigns of the Duke of Wellington, they have frequently been either unfamiliar with Castilian or unable to travel to Spain. Restricted to British and French sources alone (and very often only published ones at that), they found that the only aspect of the wider conflict on which they had plenty of material was the guerrilla war, and in consequence persuaded themselves that the gaps in their account could be filled in by this alone. This attitude, meanwhile, was reinforced by a certain unwillingness to delve beneath the service of the Spanish war effort: even Oman, it may fairly safely be said, confined his researches in this respect to such obvious secondary sources as the Conde de Toreno and José Gómez de Arteche. For the Spaniards themselves, of course, the position was somewhat different, but even so, particularly for academic historians unwilling to get to grips with the nuts and bolts of military history, emphasising the importance of the guerrillas was an attractive option that got them off a variety of 'hooks' and fitted in with changing historical perceptions (it was, for example, easy to ally the guerrillas' role with the strongly Marxist currents of thought prevalent by the 1960s).

The ability of modern Spanish historians to reconcile traditional views of the guerrillas with Marxian theories of history is most ironic, for the insurgents' appeal is in fact deeply bound up with images of Spain that are strongly romantic – that are, in fact, the work of Romanticism. Thus, *la guerrilla* of legend is the Spain of the bandit, the bullfighter and the flamenco dancer at war, just as its protagonist is the Spaniard as untameable individual and natural anarchist. Visually, too, the guerrilla that we know is a Romantic creation, as witness, for example, such French paintings as Lejeune's depiction of Espoz y Mina's victory at the Puerto de Arlabán in 1811. Amidst a mythologised landscape of soaring peaks and shady groves the Spaniards are rushing forward clad in shirts and breeches, with scarves tied round their heads and brandishing daggers and blunderbusses, when sober reality would have had them fighting in lines and columns, dressed in army-style uniforms and armed with muskets and bayonets.[1]

In short, the traditional view of *la guerrilla* is a creation that is deeply artificial, if not wholly spurious. In fairness to the Romantics, however, it must be said that they did little but embellish the propaganda characteristic of the war itself. In innumerable pamphlets, newspapers and works of commentary and analysis the guerrillas were established as heroes of the struggle against the French. Typical, perhaps, were the efforts of an Augustinian friar named Salmón, who between 1812 and 1814 produced what may be regarded as the very first general history of the Peninsular War. Thus, angered by French efforts to decry the guerrillas as bandits, Salmón was determined to show that they were, rather, legitimate combatants who had the right to be treated as soldiers should they be taken prisoner by the enemy. Underpinning his work, however, there was also a strong political purpose. Bitterly hostile to the maxims of the French Revolution, he also wanted to prove, first, that the Spanish people were unanimous in their rejection of liberty, equality and fraternity; second, that they had thrown themselves into the struggle against the French absolutely wholeheartedly; and third, that they had throughout remained loyal to the established political and social order. The result was a picture of the guerrillas that is wholly positive. The product of action on the part of the Spanish state – in this respect great importance was accorded to the various decrees issued by successive governments with respect to the formation of guerrilla bands – the guerrillas had, it was claimed, 'truly kept up the enthusiasm of the nation, whilst doing more damage to the enemy than . . . large armies'.[2] As Salmón continued:

> They were . . . true defenders of their fatherland . . . who had been authorised by their government to harass the common enemy subject to the captain or commandant-general of the province in which they resided . . . *partidas* that religiously . . . respected the humblest peasant, constantly persecuted . . . all those who strayed from the path of right . . . spared no means to avenge the . . . orphans and widows who wept for the fathers and husbands torn from their sight by the insatiable ambition of the most inhuman hangman . . . and ravaged the enemies of humanity, making head against them . . . in such terms that no convoy, dispatch rider or senior officer could move a step without an escort of hundreds or even thousands of soldiers.[3]

In this conflict, moreover, many thousands of Spaniards took part, Salmón talking of the participation of 'immense multitudes' of heroes 'from every corner of the . . . peninsula'.[4] As for the commanders of the individual bands, he could not be more complimentary:

> In every history of the world the name of El Empecinado will be famous. An obscure man with . . . no more knowledge than the sort to be expected of a poor artisan, he . . . kept the whole of the enemy's Army of the Centre in constant movement and did not allow it a moment's rest by day or night. What glories will not be told . . . of the imperturbable Espoz y Mina, that other military genius . . . who overnight abandoned the plough for the battlefield? Is there any praise of which the sometime sergeant Brigadier Julián Sánchez is not worthy? Is there any honour which the doctor of Villaluenga, Don Juan Palarea, does not merit?[5]

From all this it followed that to call the guerrillas bandits was unjust in the extreme, and all the more so as they had proved to be a great help when it came to upholding law and order. As Salmón wrote, indeed, 'They clean the roads and countryside of the vile rabble . . . that infest them with more energy and success than do the French themselves, and ensure that they pay with their lives for their robberies and other excesses.'[6] Needless to say, meanwhile, their contribution to the war effort had been enormous:

> It is not possible to paint a full picture of the debt which the nation owes to these valiant *partidas*. Although they cannot decide its fate with a single blow, they keep up its hopes and . . . inspire those who are afraid or in despair . . . with strength, constancy and patience. At the same time, they never cease to fatigue the enemy, destroying him little by little in petty combats and reducing his domination to the ground which he physically occupies. Who can number the dead, wounded and prisoners that they have inflicted in the short time that has gone by since their . . . organization?[7]

Such an impression was commonplace. Let us take as a further example the anonymous *Historia de la Revolución Española*, published in Valladolid during the brief period when it was occupied by the Allies in the summer and autumn of 1812. Thus:

> In the year 1809 there began to appear the famous guerrillas, the units of mounted and dismounted volunteers who, aided by their perfect knowledge of the terrain, have made themselves so feared by the enemy on account of their valour and indefatigable activity. Amongst the large number who have seen action, the most important have been those of El Empecinado in the vicinity of Madrid . . . Mina in Navarra . . . Longa in Alava . . . the Marquesito in Asturias, Don Julián Sánchez in the province of Salamanca . . . Starting with only a handful of men, many of these commanders in less than a year managed to raise divisions of between 2,000 and 4,000 men . . . Attacking small detachments and weak garrisons and intercepting convoys . . . and dispatches, they have so troubled the French that for a long time they have not dared to travel even main roads except in caravans escorted by at least 1,000 men.[8]

The impact of this hero worship was beyond doubt very great, a good example being the attention that was heaped upon the famous Juan Martín Díez. To quote Salmón, for example:

> To the astonishment of some and the dread of others, the name of El Empecinado began to resound in every province of the Peninsula and even in Paris and London. So much was this the case, in fact, that in both London and Cádiz subscriptions were opened to provide this valiant leader with uniforms, saddles and armament, whilst many English ladies made a point of adorning their . . . bosoms with his image.[9]

If El Empecinado became the centre of a major personality cult, it is hardly surprising. Typical of the effusions of which he was the subject was the following ode that appeared in the Cádiz newspaper *El Conciso*:

> Who is this who rides so proudly by,
> Bathed in the blood of Spain's enemies . . .
> Armed with pistol, blunderbuss and knife . . .
> And ready to kill Frenchman, Saxon, Italian, Bavarian
> . . . Swiss, Russian, Pole or Spanish renegade?
> Is it . . . another Duke of Alba?
> Not a bit of it: it is someone quite different,
> The immortal and most worthy El Empecinado.[10]

As early as 1811, meanwhile, there appeared a life of El Empecinado of whose tenor the following is an excellent example:

> His memorable actions inspired the French with such fear that they ceased to hope for any success whatsoever unless they managed to capture this gallant leader. Yet El Empecinado mocked their efforts, and punished their foolhardiness every time they tried to surprise him: though all the resorts of their perfidy were set in motion, they were facing a brave Spaniard who did not know how to turn his back on a fight and wrecked the miserable schemes dreamed up by their treachery . . . The rapidity of his marches and counter-marches never ceased to amaze the legions of the tyrant. Over and over again they would think that the troops of El Empecinado were far away, only to find that they were suddenly set upon and destroyed. Nothing, indeed, got in the way of his daring.[11]

Thanks to such efforts, there were by 1812 parts of Spain in which all the guerrillas were referred to as *empecinados*.

Another leader who became a living legend, meanwhile, was Francisco Espoz y Mina. About him, too, bad poetry was soon being written, whilst his native cunning enabled him to exploit the enthusiasm of the liberals who dominated the *cortes* of Cádiz and win much support for his demands for greater government recognition.[12] For a good example of how he was seen we have only to turn to the work of José Clemente Carnicero, a resident of Madrid who recorded his experiences of the war in a three-volume chronicle published in 1814. Writing, for instance, of the reports from the battlefronts that reached Madrid in the course of 1811, he remarked that 'those which had most impact . . . were the ones that spoke of the famous Mina', and remembered that he and his friends were particularly impressed with the manner in which, having captured a large French convoy near Vitoria, Espoz y Mina contrived to march all his prisoners to the sea through the very midst of the enemy armies and load them aboard British ships.[13]

Amongst British observers, too, there was much excitement about the guerrillas. As a somewhat unusual example, we might cite Robert Brindle, a young seminarian who was caught by the events of 1808 at the English College in Valladolid, and the following year escaped on foot to Portugal with the aid of El Empecinado. Thus:

> An insurrection . . . sudden and universal baffled every stratagem of the French. Even their vast armies were found insufficient to restore quiet. If small parties were detached, they were infallibly cut to pieces by the Spanish peasantry. If large bodies marched out, they found no enemy to encounter. The lawless conduct of the French had frequently excited the just anger of the Spaniards, and before the quarrel became national, hundreds had fallen in the perpetration of the most enormous crimes, victims to the stiletto. But when something like a pretence for violence was offered, they gave full scope to their wantonness and brutality, and the activity of the stiletto increased in proportion. The Spaniards, at length aware of the treachery and base designs of the French, thought no mode of extermination unlawful. A French commissary general declared that they lost 500 men every week by private assassination, exclusive of those who fell in the field or were kidnapped by the guerrillas. Hence we may form some estimate of the enormous waste of French troops in Spain, which according to the most exact calculation amounted during the whole war to at least 700,000 men.[14]

Particular testimony to the influence of Espoz y Mina, meanwhile, may be found in the memoirs of the cavalry officer William Bragge:

> Navarre is a most delightful province and . . . certainly the most loyal and patriotic in Spain. Their great leader is [Espoz y] Mina, who is a wonderful man. About three years since this man (who was then a farmer) adopted his nephew's name, took the command of a battalion which he had raised and by a continual succession of bold, skilful and daring enterprises has worsted the French . . . increased his own force to a legion of 10,000 or 12,000, who are all volunteers, and the best-organised troops in Spain, well-paid, fed and clothed.[15]

And lastly one might cite the words of Edward Cocks, an intelligence officer who spent much of the war on missions that took him deep into occupied Spain: 'The Spanish guerrillas have annoyed the enemy very much; they are very useful because they oblige the enemy to form so many detachments in order to secure his communication and command in some measure the resources of the country.'[16]

By 1814, then, a very positive image of the guerrillas had been created in Britain and Spain alike, and in both countries it was this current that came to dominate the historiography. In Spain, for example, their cause was given solid support by the Conde de Toreno, a leading liberal who played a major part in the *cortes* of Cádiz and went on to serve as prime minister in 1835. Founded as his *Historia de Levantamiento, Guerra y Revolución de España* was on a determination to justify the *gaditano* revolution and identify it with the cause of the Spanish people, it was only natural that the guerrillas should have played a major part in his story. Indeed, Toreno himself remarked on the amount of time that he had given to the myriad skirmishes of such figures as El Empecinado and Espoz y Mina. For this, however, he made no apology:

> These actions will to some people seem as boring as they are unimportant. It is quite true that, viewed in isolation, they at first sight look trivial, but . . . taken in the round they in large part produced the marvellous . . . defence of Spain's independence that will forever serve as a guide for all those peoples that wish to conserve their own freedom.[17]

Somewhat later in the nineteenth century, meanwhile, the only history of the War of Independence that has ever been written with the guerrillas as its main theme struck an even more positive note. Thus the message of Enrique Rodríguez Solis' *Los Guerrilleros de 1808: Historia Popular de la Guerra de la Independencia* is absolutely unequivocal. Napoleon, Solis claimed, had lost some 500,000 men in Spain, of which only some 200,000 could be accounted for by the war's formal battles and sieges; the 300,000 that were left had, by implication, fallen to the guerrillas. Looked at in this fashion, he maintained, it could be argued that these 'popular heroes of eternal memory' had actually won the war, whilst it was certainly true that the decisive factor in the conflict had been the absolute refusal of the Spanish people to abandon the struggle. And, if they had refused to surrender, it was because they were inspired by dreams not just of independence but of political regeneration – a point that allowed Rodríguez Solis to claim for the guerrillas the revolutionary politics which he himself espoused (the son of a radical who had been banished for his part in the rising of 1848, Rodríguez Solis was active both in the overthrow of Isabel II in 1868 and in the establishment of the First Republic in 1873).[18] But if the guerrillas were a revolutionary phenomenon, they were also a Spanish one, and Rodríguez Solis went so far as to maintain that 'it is no exaggeration to affirm that with the Spaniard there was born the guerrilla', and, further, that much of Spain's military history had in fact been centred on guerrilla warfare (thus we learn that even Rodrigo Díaz de Vivar, better known as El Cid, had to all intents and purposes been a guerrilla!).[19] Entirely spontaneous in their origins, the irregulars had no other purpose than to fight for the fatherland, in which capacity they proved to have no equal. In short:

> The guerrillas were the nation in arms. They fought in the morning and worked in the afternoon. They were both soldiers and citizens. . . . The guerrillas were the champions of our independence for seven years of incessant struggle . . . Though beaten from time to time, they were never tamed . . . They had no other roof than the heavens, no other bed than the ground. They did not . . . tire; they did not sleep. They were the eternal shadow of the invader, his constant nightmare, an ever-present menace. They abandoned family and home and gave their lives for the fatherland with . . . joy in their hearts. They left their homes with the loving kisses . . . of their beloved wives still warm on their lips . . . to die a few hours later on some lonely road, all that they asked of their fatherland . . . being a tender memory, a patch of earth and a simple cross.[20]

In Britain no less than in Spain historians were inclined to laud the guerrillas. First in the field was Robert Southey, whose account of the Peninsular War is larded with visions of popular resistance. Beginning with his account of the uprising, this stresses the role of the people and is adamant that they acted spontaneously, without direction, and with no other idea than to fight for their king, their independence, their religion and their ancient traditions. For themselves, by contrast, they wanted nothing. Angered by the submissive attitude of most of their superiors, the populace, it was true, turned on them, and the result was a short period of 'dreadful anarchy' in which 'the unreasonable people were sometimes hurried into excesses by their own blind zeal, sometimes seduced into them by wretches who were actuated by the desire of plunder or of private revenge'.[21] Yet what occurred was no revolution. Thus:

> The people had no desire to break loose from the laws and the habits of subordination; the only desire which possessed them was to take vengeance for their murdered countrymen, and to deliver their country from the violent usurpation which was attempted. If any obstruction was offered to this generous feeling, they became impatient and ungovernable: otherwise, having always been wont to look to their rulers . . . their very zeal displayed itself in the form of obedience; they were eager to obey any who would undertake to guide them, and no person thought of stepping beyond his rank to assume the direction.[22]

So much, then, for the general character of the Spanish insurrection. With the populace united in its detestation of the French, it followed that there was immense enthusiasm for the war. Large numbers of recruits came forward for the new armies being formed by the assortment of provincial authorities that now ruled Spain; the new levies clamoured to be led against the French; the inhabitants of Gerona, Zaragoza and Valencia stood to arms and repelled a series of assaults on their walls; and, above all, the first stirrings began to be witnessed of guerrilla warfare. Particularly important in Catalonia, where the existence prior to 1808 of the local home guard known as the *somatén* facilitated the emergence of this phenomenon, it was also witnessed in La Mancha and Andalucía. As Southey wrote of the march of the two divisions dispatched to reinforce the column of troops that had been marching on Cádiz when the uprising broke out:

> In passing through La Mancha they found that the sick, whom Dupont had left at Manzanares, had been killed. . . . When the advanced guard attempted to pass the Sierra Morena, they found an irregular force well posted and entrenched in the tremendous defiles of that great line of mountains, and they were compelled to fall back upon the main body. Notwithstanding this warning, the French entered upon the pass without precaution. . . . The first brigade and the cavalry were allowed to pass an ambush, which was laid among the trees and rocks in advance of the entrenchment; a fire was then opened upon the second; and the French suffered three discharges before they were ready to act in return.[23]

Faced with the problem of explaining the dichotomy between the supposed enthusiasm of the first days of the war and the apathy that characterised the period that separated the Spanish triumph at Bailén and the onset of the great French counter-offensive in November, Southey attributed the situation to the misguided tactic of boosting the confidence of the populace by minimising the threat posed by the enemy.[24] Examples of popular resistance at the moment of occupation, meanwhile, were cited as evidence that the people were in fact as staunch as ever, whether it was the inhabitants of Villacañas fighting off the forage parties that had descended on them for five days or those of El Escorial going down bravely in a desperate struggle outside the gates of the town.[25] Not until he comes to his account of the second siege of Zaragoza and the Galician insurrection, however, is Southey able finally to rid himself of the problem. Thus, with regard to the former much is made of the continued patriotism of the inhabitants, who are claimed to have refused to leave the city, to have been utterly convinced that the Virgin of the Pillar would grant them victory over the enemy, and to have fought with the utmost gallantry (it is claimed, indeed, that no fewer than 600 women and children died fighting the French).[26] Of more importance for our purposes, however, is the account that Southey gives of events in Galicia. Invaded by the French as they followed up the retreat of the army of Sir John Moore, the Galicians had initially, as Southey admits, remained quiet. However, in the weeks that followed the arrival of the imperial forces, moved by 'true feelings of loyalty and patriotism . . . honest, enthusiastic ardour [and] cool and determined courage', the countryside erupted in revolt.[27] There followed a bloody conflict:

> Into whatever town or village [the French] entered, not a living soul was to be found, except those who from infirmity were unable to follow their countrymen. They who had arms had gone to join the army; the others, with the women and children, had taken refuge in the wild parts of that wild region and were on the watch for every opportunity of weakening their invaders by putting a straggler to death. . . . That sort of war was kept up which . . . tended to the sure destruction of the invaders. The Spaniards never exposed themselves, and never lost an opportunity of harassing the enemy. They availed themselves of their perfect knowledge of the country to profit by every spot that afforded cover to their marksmen; and, leaving their fields to be ravaged, their property to be plundered, and their houses to be destroyed, they applied themselves with a brave recklessness of everything except their duty to the great object of ridding the country of its invaders. . . . The utmost efforts of the French were ineffectual against the spirit which had now been raised in Galicia . . . Accustomed as the invaders were to the work of destruction, they were baffled by a people who dispersed before a superior force could reach them, and reunited as easily as they had separated.[28]

And, it is implied, thanks to this war, Galicia was evacuated, it being claimed that the French became 'eager to get out of a province where the people were able and determined to take such vengeance as their invaders had provoked'.[29] Important though events in Galicia were, Southey is careful to show that they were in no sense isolated or out of the ordinary. The inhabitants of the mountainous Valles district of Catalonia, for example, are singled out for the courage which they displayed in bidding defiance to the French, whilst those of the Señorio de Molina, we are told, 'took arms, trusting in themselves and the strength of the country: for want of better weapons some of them used slings . . . and they made wooden artillery, so light that a single man could carry one of these pieces up the heights and yet strong enough to bear from fifteen to twenty rounds'.[30] Most weight of all, however, is placed on events in Navarre, where Mariano Renovales, one of the erstwhile defenders of Zaragoza, is described as having effected his escape from French captivity and, in the company of a group of fellow fugitives, raised the inhabitants of the Roncal valley in revolt and beat off two attempts to suppress his insurrection. Eventually overwhelmed though he was, he nevertheless put up a fierce fight that supposedly cost the French over 1,000 casualties and at the same time won much renown by the suitably defiant answers that he returned to the attempts of the French authorities to get him to change sides.[31]

For Southey, however, 1809 was chiefly important as the moment when 'that system of warfare began which soon extended throughout Spain, and occasioned greater losses to the French than they suffered in all their pitched battles'.[32] Amongst the first leaders to be noted are Juan Díaz Porlier and El Empecinado, but the most successful and effective as far as Southey was concerned was clearly Martín Javier Mina, of whom he remarked, 'It was in vain that the French made repeated efforts to crush this enterprising enemy; if his troops dispersed upon the appearance of a formidable detachment, it was only to reunite, and, by striking a blow in some weak point or distant quarter, render themselves more formidable than before'.[33] If guerrilla warfare spread, meanwhile, it was because it touched a chord in the popular psyche. Thus:

> Frustrated as [the people's] expectations of immediate deliverance had been, their confidence was not shaken; the national temper led them to think lightly of every disaster, but to exaggerate every trifling success; and the defeats at Arzobispo and Almonacid were less felt or thought of by the body of the people than the successful exploits of those predatory bands who, under the name of guerrillas, were now in action everywhere. The government partook of this disposition, and . . . the official . . . journals published every adventure of this kind more fully and circumstantially than some of those actions wherein their armies had disappeared. The example which Mina and the Empecinado had set was followed with alacrity and tempting success, rich opportunities being offered by the requisition of plate from churches and from individuals which the intrusive government was at this time enforcing.[34]

In the face of this offensive the French are portrayed as being helpless. Efforts to form bands of counter-guerrillas proved a universal failure, whilst reprisals of the sort that General Marchand threatened in León in the face of the raids of Julián Sánchez – another commander whom Southey singles out for early mention – merely provoked indignant letters of defiance. As for the wholesale executions in which the French engaged, they were utterly ineffectual: the victims went to the *garrote*, scaffold or firing squad with a mixture of pride and indifference. Nor were the invaders' periodic *battues* any more successful, since these were frustrated both by dispersion and the guerrillas' keen knowledge of the countryside and of their enemies' movements.[35] As we shall see, Southey was by no means unaware of the problems thrown up by the guerrillas. However, all such nuances are lost in his overall assessment of the subject. As an example, we might quote his assessment of their motivation:

> Many were influenced by the deepest feelings and strongest passions which act upon the heart of man: love of their country which their faith had

elevated and strengthened; and hope which that love and that faith had rendered inextinguishable; and burning hatred, seeking revenge for the most wanton . . . injuries that can be inflicted on humanity . . . [And] the greater number were men who, if circumstances had permitted, would have passed their life usefully and contentedly in the humble stations to which they were born; labourers, whom there were none now to employ; retainers who partook of the ruin of the great families to which they and their ancestors had been attached; owners or occupiers of land, whose fields had been laid waste, and whose olive yards were destroyed; and the whole class of provincial tradesmen, whose means of subsistence were cut off, happy if they had only their own ruin and their country's quarrel to revenge, and not those deeper injuries of which dreadful cases were continually occurring wherever the enemy were masters. Monks, also, and friars, frocked and unfrocked, were among them: wherever the convents wre suppressed . . . which was done in all the provinces that the French overran, the young took arms.[36]

As for the importance of the guerrillas, of this too he had no doubt:

The French were no sooner masters of the field than they found themselves engaged in a wearing, wasting contest wherein discipline was of no avail, and, by which, in a country of such extent and natural strength, any military power, however great, must ultimately be consumed . . . They were never safe except when in large bodies or in some fortified place. Every day some of their posts were surprised, some escort or convoy cut off, some detachment put to death. Dispatches were intercepted, plunder was recovered, and, what excited the Spaniards more than . . . all other considerations, vengeance was taken by a most vindictive people for insupportable wrongs . . . There was nothing in their dress to distinguish them from the peasantry; everyone was ready to give them intelligence or shelter; they knew the country perfectly; each man shifted for himself in time of need; and when they reassembled at the appointed rallying place, so far were they from being dispirited by the dispersion that the ease with which they had eluded the enemy became a new source of confidence.[37]

Beyond this, of course, the guerrillas served also to restrict collaboration. Southey reported several cases where prominent *afrancesados* were seized and executed or where the populace was threatened with the most savage punishment if they obeyed any orders issued by the French authorities.[38]

In order to give substance to all this, recourse is chiefly had to the story of Espoz y Mina, whose exploits are regaled at great length and whose leadership is praised to the skies.[39] Curiously enough, however, little attempt is made to draw a direct link between the operations of the guerrillas and Wellington's victory at Vitoria, and it was left to William Napier and, above all, Sir Charles

Oman, to make the connection. An officer of Wellington's army who had fought in the famous Light Division, between 1828 and 1840 Napier published a six-volume history of the Peninsular War whose chief characteristic was rooted hostility to the Spaniards. As we shall see, this work was extremely sceptical about the early history of the guerrillas, but, viewing the activities of Espoz y Mina in particular, even Napier could not deny that by 1813 some of the *partidas* had become a major force in the struggle. As he wrote of the French situation at the end of 1812:

> The French troops were . . . only relieved from the crushing pressure of Wellington's operations to struggle in the meshes of guerrilla and insurrectional warfare. Nor was its importance now to be measured by former efforts. The chiefs . . . possessed fortified posts and harbours, their bands were swelling to the size of armies, their military knowledge of the country and of the French system of invasion were more matured, their depots better hidden, and they could at times bear the shock of battle on nearly equal terms . . . The [French] contributions could no longer be collected, the magazines could not be filled, the fortresses were endangered, the armies had no base of operations, the . . . troops, sorely pressed for provisions, were widely disseminated and everywhere occupied, and each general was averse to concentrate his own forces or aid his neighbour. In fine, the problem was become extremely complicated.[40]

Although it is impossible not to draw the appropriate conclusions from his account, to the end Napier remained unwilling overtly to admit the contribution made by Espoz y Mina and the other guerrillas of northern Spain to Wellington's victories. To establish their importance, we therefore have to turn to Oman. Writing his *History of the Peninsular War*, as he did, over a period of nearly thirty years, Oman was naturally influenced by the changing circumstances of his times. A military historian, he could not have been unaware of the theories of the 'indirect approach' that were circulating in the wake of the First World War. By the 1920s – the period when he was writing the volumes of his history that cover the later years of the Peninsular conflict – he may therefore have been predisposed to stress the importance of the guerrillas.[41] At all events, in his sixth volume, published in 1922, Oman waxes lyrical about what he called 'the northern insurrection', and makes it the very *sine qua non* of Wellington's victory at Vitoria (whereby the French forces were evicted from the whole of Spain with the exception of part of Catalonia and a few scattered fortresses in the Basque provinces, Navarre and the Levant), arguing that so many troops had to be pulled back from the Portuguese frontier that not enough were left to hold back the Anglo-Portuguese army.[42] Yet even in earlier volumes Oman is much kinder in his judgements than Napier. Time and again the guerrillas are given credit for starving the French of information, hampering them in their operations or diverting forces that might otherwise have been used against Wellington or the regular Spanish armies. The praise showered upon the guerrillas, indeed, is anything but sparing. For example:

> Old Castile, Navarre and the lands of the upper Ebro were kept in a constant turmoil by a score of guerrilla chiefs . . . On the whole, there were probably never more than 20,000 *guerrilleros* in arms at once in the whole region between the Sierra de Guadarrama and the . . . Bay of Biscay. They never succeeded in beating any French force more than two or three battalions strong, and were being continually hunted from corner to corner. Yet despite their weakness in the open field . . . they rendered good service . . . by pinning down . . . twice their own numbers of . . . French troops.[43]

In so far as the Anglo-Saxon historiography was concerned, Oman's magisterial conclusions set the seal of approval on the guerrillas. On all sides the many populists who chose to write about the Peninsular War leapt to acknowledge the exploits of the guerrillas. To quote Longford, for example:

> Spain was to be saved . . . not by grape-shot, greybeards and grandees, but by hardy guerrillas and the sudden flash of the knife. These peasants spontaneously organised themselves into small do-or-die bands . . . headed by folk-heroes . . . Even the basic force of 200,000 veterans which Napoleon was compelled to keep, year after year, in Spain would never be safe from the noon-day ambush and things that went bump in the night.[44]

So enthusiastic were these writers that they were soon seeing the entire Spanish war effort in terms of the guerrillas, as witness the extraordinary account of the battle of Bailén – a wholly conventional field action fought entirely by regular troops of the old Bourbon army – that we must now quote from Richard Humble:

> As soon as Dupont put his demoralised troops on the march out of Andújar the Spaniards closed in and harried them. A running fight escalated into a full-scale engagement at Bailén . . . Dupont's soldiers had been all right during the march on Córdoba, but now they were on the receiving end against an enemy who did not bother to attack them when they formed square, but only when they were least ready.[45]

Curiously, this refusal to believe that Bailén could be the work of regular troops resurfaced in the course of the Spanish Civil War. To quote the Austrian journalist Borkenau:

> The French general Dupont . . . was stopped on his way to Andalusia, forced to retreat, and finally surrounded and forced to capitulate by the peasants at

> Bailén. The Spanish general Castaños claimed the glory of the day. But, in reality, one look at the battlefield, a large open plain of olive groves, is convincing as to the real situation. It was impossible to surround the French there with a small army. Only a rising of all the villages could and did bar the way.[46]

It was not just the writers of popular history who echoed the general refrain, however. Amongst British historians Oman's theories have been accepted without question and even pushed to fresh lengths. 'It was above all', wrote David Chandler, 'the interaction of Wellington's operations with those of the guerrilla bands that . . . made the French problem wholly intractable . . . Even with 320,000 men the marshals could not both contain the diffuse . . . "war of the flea" and . . . meet Wellington's latest foray deep into their territory.'[47] So enthusiastic, indeed, is Chandler that he sometimes makes it appear as if the guerrillas were among Wellington's first concerns. Thus:

> As for Wellington, he appreciated that he had to preserve England's only field army and at the same time give maximum possible assistance to Portuguese and Spanish resistance – especially the popular kind. Having established a safe base at Lisbon . . . he conducted forays into enemy-held territory to divert French attention and thus ease the pressures on the . . . partisans; then, in 1812 . . . he began a systematic reconquest of Spain by conventional means.[48]

Nor have British historians been the only ones to underline the guerrillas. Since the 1960s, for example, a succession of American and Canadian historians have laid great stress on their contribution to the struggle. For Gabriel Lovett

> The War of Independence did not produce on the Spanish side great generals . . . The true giants . . . must be sought elsewhere. They could be found . . . in the craggy mountains, among the barren hills, in the forbidding gorges . . . They were the leaders of those intrepid bands that almost from the very beginning made the war in Spain a nightmare for the Napoleonic armies. Swooping down from their mountainous hideouts . . . they never let the invaders forget . . . that Spain had not given up the fight. It is not an exaggeration to say that these bands . . . made history. They carried on the war . . . when there were few regular Spanish forces left to continue the struggle, and . . . must be given a large . . . share of the credit for the emperor's failure in the Peninsula.[49]

In his detailed account of the 'little war' in Aragón – a study rendered the more valuable by the fact that it rests on detailed research in the French archives –

Alexander argues that the 'combination of conventional resistance, galvanised by Wellington's army, and the irregular opposition of the *partidas* proved irresistible'; that 'the *partidas* could probably have sustained resistance indefinitely'; and even that 'the partisan leaders were able to forge from the spirit of opposition an army that managed to exploit French military difficulties and liberate Aragón'.[50] And, finally, for John Tone, whose study of the guerrillas of Navarre is by far the most detailed work that the English language boasts on the subject:

> Armed peasants made chaos of French communications and performed other tasks of value to both English and Spanish regular forces. Partisans scoured the countryside for French spies and sympathisers and brought a continuous stream of information to the Allies. The guerrillas also effected a kind of psychological warfare in which the French had to be constantly on the alert, while the Allied armies could rest securely in the midst of a vigilant peasantry. The guerrilla war was a long and demoralising nightmare for France. In the regions of insurgency, where each peasant was a potential guerrilla, there could be no campaigning season, no safe havens, no truces. Everywhere and always there existed the possibility of a hostile encounter . . . In guerrilla country, the French governed only where they could actually have troops in place. When these troops were withdrawn, the territory reverted to the guerrillas, becoming valueless to the French, if not a positive drain on their resources. War in Spain did not pay Napoleon as it had in other parts of Europe. On the contrary, guerrilla action made the occupation of Spain a constant burden and made the Spanish war unwinnable.[51]

Less inclined towards military history in their treatment of the subject though they have been, Spanish and French historians have been no less appreciative. For Miguel Artola, for example, 'An analysis of the war which attempts to give more weight to the death and destruction inflicted on the enemy than to the description of field battles cannot but suggest very strongly that the guerrillas were more important than the regular armies of either Britain or Spain.'[52] Equally, for Manuel Espadas Burgos:

> The guerrilla war was an undoubted success. It did not have the momentary brilliance of a great victory in the open field like . . . Bailén, but its constant action kept up year after year without a moment's rest, without a moment's dismay, ended up by grinding down the morale of the French army. For all of Europe the *guerrilla* was an unbeatable lesson in resistance.[53]

As representatives of modern French historiography, meanwhile, we may cite Jean-René Aymes, Gérard Dufour and Richard Hocquellet. 'The more the mass of the population was alienated from political affairs, the more it participated in the war against the invader, its concrete enemy', wrote Aymes. 'The regular army being a matter for nobles and professional soldiers, through their independent instincts and ignorance of the traditions of the art of war the people invented a genuine form of struggle: *la guerrilla*.'[54] For Dufour, too, the 'little war' was crucial:

> The many French soldiers who wrote their memoirs after the conflict all coincided in underlining the decisive role of *la guerrilla*, whilst Napoleon himself . . . confessed that he had been beaten in Spain by the people rather than by the army . . . Its first characteristic was that it was . . . a war fought by the people and with its complicity: those who did not fight . . . assisted the combatants when they had to flee pursuit.[55]

Last but not least, we have Hocquellet:

> As a result of their diffuse character, the guerrillas never engaged the imperial columns. No decisive battles can be attributed to them, but the state of permanent insecurity with which they imbued the Napoleonic armies had such an impact on morale that the high command was forced to take them very seriously. The memoirs of soldiers of the empire who served in Spain all insist on the constant air of menace: they could never be certain of their surroundings.[56]

Such, then, is the traditional version of events. From the very beginning, however, there was another side to the story. Whilst the French and their supporters were quite prepared to acknowledge the impact that the 'little war' had had on their operations and activities, they attempted to assuage their bitterness by denigrating the partisans as cowards, savages and murderers.[57] Linked to this was an insistence that the central problem had been one of brigandage. 'Brigand', indeed, was a term habitually used by the invaders to describe bandits and guerrillas alike – a habit that greatly complicates the task of the historian – whilst they generally insisted that the bands either stemmed from the swarms of bandits and smugglers with which the Iberian Peninsula was so afflicted prior to 1808, or were made up of deserters from the armies of the French and their opponents. Hatred of the invaders was recognised by some writers as a motive for resistance, whilst others believed that the cruelty and greed that they held to be inherent in the Spanish character had been inflamed by a clergy desperate to forestall the religious reforms certain to be imposed in the wake of French conquest; but the possibility that the guerrillas might be inspired by genuine political or ideological motives was in almost every case denied.[58] As for the propaganda of the *josefino* state, it never ceased to ram home the message that the *partidas* were the enemies of not just property and the social order, but also of life and limb. To quote the *Gazeta de Sevilla*, for example:

> The guerrillas commit all the robberies imaginable: nobody is free of their plundering. Spanish, French, English, all alike are victims of their wickedness; priests, mayors, labourers, muleteers, nobody is spared . . . Such are the instruments that presently serve perfidious Albion . . . Not being able to conquer, by means of these men [the British] oppress those whose independence they feign to protect.[59]

This sort of thing is exactly what one would expect from observers favourable to Napoleon: the emperor, after all, always maintained that his rule stood for the defence of landed property, and, further, that he was the champion of a civilising mission whose central aim was to eradicate the violence, ignorance and superstition of the masses.[60] Yet this line has still proved remarkably influential. For one thing it was impossible to deny that the subject threw up serious difficulties. Writing of the aftermath of the French evacuation of Galicia, for example, Southey remarked, 'Men who had done their part in driving out the enemy, having now no means of providing for themselves, roamed about in armed parties, so that the condition of the helpless inhabitants was little better than when they were under the French yoke.'[61] Equally, he admitted that attempts to regulate the guerrillas were only observed 'where the government had sufficient authority to enforce them, which was only where they had armies on foot'.[62] And, if this was so, it was in part because 'some were mere ruffians, who if the country had been at peace would have lived in defiance of the laws, as they now defied the force of the intrusive government', and others men 'attracted by the wildness and continual excitement attendant upon a life of outlawry and adventure, to which in the present circumstances . . . honour, instead of obloquy, was attached'.[63] As he wrote, indeed:

> For, as in times of pestilence and earthquake, wretches are found obdurate enough in wickedness to . . . enrich themselves by plunder, so now, in the anarchy of Spain, they whose evil disposition had been restrained . . . in some degree by the influence of settled society, abandoned themselves . . . to the impulses of their own evil hearts.[64]

Some of the worst offenders are named by Southey. There was, for example, José Pedrazuela, a sometime actor from Madrid, who embarked on a reign of terror in Extremadura; Echevarría, whose band was largely composed of German deserters; and Martina, a woman of whom no other details are given, who led a gang of bandits on the frontiers of Vizcaya and Alava.[65] Southey was in no doubt that the consequences for Spanish society in the long term could not but be dreadful:

> The restraints . . . which the soldier is compelled to learn . . . counteract the demoralizing tendencies of a military life, and compensate for its heart-hardening ones. The good soldier becomes a good citizen when his occupation is over, but the guerrillas were never likely to forego the wild and lawless course in which they were engaged, and, therefore, essential as their services now were, thoughtful men looked with the gloomiest forebodings to what must be the consequence of their multiplication whenever this dreadful struggle should be ended.[66]

Despite these doubts, Southey in the end refused to let them colour his judgement of the guerrillas. Other writers, however, have been less charitable. A great admirer of Napoleon, for example, Napier was uncritical in his acceptance of the imperial line. The guerrilla bands, he wrote, 'were many, because every robber who feared a gaol or could break from one . . . was to be found either as chief or associate in a *partida*', whilst, not satisfied with this, he saw one of the chief reasons for their initial emergence as 'the hope of intercepting the public and private plate which under a decree of Joseph was being brought to Madrid'.[67] Napier being profoundly prejudiced against all things Spanish, his views are only to be expected, but doubts were also entertained by Spanish historians. We come here to the views of the nineteenth-century writers José Muñoz Maldonado and José Gómez de Arteche. Beginning with the former's *Historia Política y Militar de la Guerra de la Independencia contra Napoleón Bonaparte desde 1808 a 1814*, we find much praise for the guerrillas. For example:

> Nothing was safe from the activity, audacity and perseverance of . . . the *partidas*, and . . . they harassed the French armies so incessantly that the latter were forced . . . to be always on the look-out. Even if it could not bring decisive results, implemented with constancy and, above all valour, this form of warfare ended up by weakening the enemy very considerably.[68]

Muñoz Maldonado, however, was by no means the uncritical observer that these words suggest. At various points, for example, he was keen to stress the importance of regular troops in *la guerrilla*: the partisan operations that so harassed the unfortunate Dupont in the campaign of Bailén are ascribed to the flying columns of Murgeon and Valdecañas, both of which were composed of troops who were, if not regulars, then at least men who had been formally embodied under the command of regular officers.[69] Just as interesting is the fact that Muñoz Maldonado mentions a number of incidents in which guerrilla bands resisted the imposition of a greater degree of militarisation, as, for example, when the followers of Juan Díaz Porlier mutinied rather than allow their commander to march them to Galicia for a period of intensive training.[70] As he also provides an account of the uprising in Galicia that is devoid of all mention of the *alarmas* and speaks of popular participation only in connection with occasions when the people-in-arms could clearly be shown to have been acting under the command of the army, it is clear that Muñoz Maldonado too, was driven by an agenda that dictated a cautious approach with regard to the guerrilla.[71]

None of this is at all surprising. A staunch supporter of Fernando VII who was possessed of close links with the court, Muñoz Maldonado was writing at a time when the monarch and his administration were increasingly being challenged by the so-called *apostólicos*. Soon to become known as Carlism, this ultra-traditionalist movement drew its rank-and-file support from an agricultural populace that was in many areas ever more disaffected and mutinous. In 1826, indeed, there had already been a serious insurrection in Catalonia known as the *guerra de los agraviados*. With many of the likely leaders of revolt men who had led guerrilla bands, to draw attention to the populace's ability to organise itself was hardly politic, and it is notable that in his account of the emergence of the guerrillas Muñoz Maldonado laid much stress on the role played by the Junta Central and its agents in bringing the phenomenon to fruition. Nor was the darker side of *la guerrilla* forgotten: guerrilla warfare, the populace was reminded, was likely to involve them in terrible sufferings, especially as the *partidas* were a force that might all too easily turn on its own progenitors. A graphic description, therefore, is provided of the manner in which Burgos was pillaged by undisciplined irregulars in September 1812, and it is specifically pointed out that at the end of the war many guerrilla bands had to be hunted down and tried as bandits.[72]

José Gómez de Arteche, meanwhile, was even more hostile. A general regarded as the leading military writer of Restoration Spain, Arteche's view of the Peninsular War was at the very least ambiguous. However much he praised Spanish heroism – the fourteen-volume history of the conflict that he penned between 1868 and 1903 is very much the story of how Spain won the war with some incidental help from the British and Portuguese – Arteche the soldier could not forget that in reality the Peninsular War had been something of a calvary for his forebears. From the very beginning the army had come under attack from civilian society, and its operations had constantly been impeded by a whole range of factors, not the least of which had been the guerrillas. These had challenged the army's monopoly of armed force, undermined its strength and provided the anti-militarism that was a powerful element in the politics of Patriot Spain with much useful ammunition. In consequence, Arteche put forward a view of the war that stressed the military's political priorities (maintenance of order and national unity, and the defence of the army's prestige) emphasised the role of regular soldiers in the defeat of Napoleon and downplayed the contribution of armed civilians. In part, such a stance was reinforced by the political context. Like most of the senior officers of his day, Arteche was deeply enmeshed in the highly conservative political order that had grown up in Spain since the 1840s. Centred on the protection of property, this could not but look askance at the disorder that had been such a feature of the uprising, not to mention the manner in which contemporary radicals found inspiration in the struggle against Napoleon. For Arteche as for many others, then, the Peninsular War was a *deus ex machina* that had injected Spain with 'discord' (by which was meant a threat to the ruling classes).

The result of all this was a strong prejudice against the guerrillas. Much praise is heaped on the popular heroism of the first days of the war, and considerable detail provided on the achievements of the *partidas*. Yet from an early point Arteche appears anxious to point out that the picture was not quite as flattering as his extravagant language might have suggested. Thus, his praise for the *somatenes* involved in the famous French defeat at El Bruch (in which a column marching on Lérida was ambushed on a mountain pass and forced to retreat) was qualified by allegations that much more might have been achieved if only they had combined their operations and been prepared to operate outside the immediate vicinity of their home villages.[73] Driven, one suspects, by deep suspicions of the Catalan nationalism that had begun to emerge in the late nineteenth century, Arteche returned to the issue of the *somatenes*' reliability again and again.[74] His disapproval, however, was not directed just at the Catalans; and in his treatment of the revolt that took place in the Serranía de Ronda following the invasion of Andalucía in January 1810, the various *cabecillas* of the district are portrayed as having fallen out not only with one another, but also with the army officers sent from Cádiz to organise the inhabitants and the junta that had been established at Jimena. Serious though the difficulties posed by the revolt remained, the result was that the Serranía remained 'unable to realise the results that might have been expected from the enthusiasm of its inhabitants and the difficulties imposed on the enemy . . . by their inability to take Cádiz and their need to guard their flanks and rear against the armies of La Romana and Blake'.[75]

Mention of the regular armies brings us to another theme in Arteche's work, in that it is clear that for him much of the 'little war' was not to be attributed to civilians at all, but rather to Spain's much maligned soldiers. As he pointed out, many of the so-called guerrilla leaders were regular officers and their bands organised commands of regular troops, with the result that they could not really be regarded as guerrillas at all, if 'guerrilla' was taken to mean only a fighter sprung from the people.[76] Still more, for Arteche there was no difference between the host of minor campaigns engaged in by the regular army and, say, the attacks of Espoz y Mina in Navarre. Indeed, as far as he is concerned, such disturbances as the revolt of the Serranía de Ronda were clearly of far less import than the operations of, say, General Ballesteros, whose division of regular troops was currently harassing the French in the more remote parts of the present-day province of Huelva.[77]

Not content with redefining *la guerrilla* so as to reduce its popular content, Arteche also drew strong links between irregular resistance and the breakdown of law and order. The guerrillas, he stressed, had played a very important part in the defeat of the French. As he remarked:

> The genuine representatives of people's war for the most part belonged to the classes who, for want of education, were those that were most hostile to the ideas of order and military discipline, and, at the same time, those whom the strength acquired through work in the fields had made most fitted to endure hunger, fatigue, bad weather and the horrors of war. To look to such people for harmony and subordination is the purest chimera: when they do not have an enemy to fight, they quarrel amongst themselves . . . whilst their patriotism is manifested chiefly through the pursuit of vengeance.[78]

This, of course, is not quite the same as saying that all those guerrillas who were not regular soldiers, or who did not at least adopt military forms, were brigands. Indeed, great emphasis is placed on the efforts that were made by such commanders as Espoz y Mina to put down any band that overstepped the bounds of discipline.[79] But for Arteche evil was never far away. The provocation, true, was great but, even so, popular resistance had 'a savage character' that was 'truly extraordinary and on every count lamentable'.[80] And, as he was not slow to suggest, efforts to impose discipline were not always entirely successful, since many of the bands that had to be suppressed by Espoz y Mina and the rest were composed of guerrillas who had run away rather than submit to the imposition of military discipline.[81]

At the heart of all this was Arteche's belief that the guerrillas reflected the individualism that he saw as being central to the supposed Spanish national character. Content to fight the French, Spaniards wanted to do so alone, or, at least, as masters of their own fate.[82] In doing so, moreover, they naturally gravitated to environments and procedures which they understood. As the general remarked: 'The better to execute this individualistic strategy, patriots took the hills as their favourite haunt, rocks and scrub as their best shelter, the roads as their battleground, and shepherds' huts as . . . their headquarters.'[83] But from this there flowed a number of alarming consequences, as the lowliest Spaniard had been presented with a model of resistance that he could twist to his own purposes. The most obvious beneficiary of this development being the Carlist movement, it followed that *la guerrilla* had done much to precipitate the civil wars of the nineteenth century, but there was also the question of social revolution. In the mid-nineteenth century republican *partidas* occasionally appeared, whilst lurking beneath the surface of the general's thoughts was also undoubtedly the rise of the anarchism that was to prove so powerful a strand of the Spanish labour movement: hence his denunciation of the guerrillas' encouragement of *personalismo* and resistance to authority, and his veiled criticisms of the way in which the war against the French had raised certain leaders above their station in life and fuelled their personal ambition.[84]

Explicit in the historiography of *la guerrilla*, then, is an important debate that was perplexing observers even at the time of the conflict. As the British diplomat Thomas Sydenham put it:

> It is very difficult to know what to say about the guerrillas. That some of them have been of eminent use during the progress of the war cannot be denied. They obliged the French to fortify themselves in every village and town in the country; they harassed the parties who were spread through the provinces either to subsist themselves, or to procure supplies for the enemy's magazines; they murdered all stragglers and sometimes intercepted convoys of prisoners and stores; they rendered the communications of the enemy very difficult and hazardous, and often cut them off for weeks together and finally they assisted in keeping alive the spirit of resistance against the invaders. On the other hand they doubled the calamities inflicted by the French. The inhabitants were compelled to feed the enemy with one hand and the guerrillas with the other. They plundered many towns with as little mercy as the French, and where the French preceded them, they generally carried off all which the French left. Many of them under the pretence of patriotism and of serving against the enemy became regular freebooters and subsisted on the pillage of the country. It will probably become necessary one of these days to establish a new Santa Hermandad to clear Spain of these bands of robbers. They prevented the recruiting of the regular armies, for every Spanish peasant would naturally prefer rioting and plunder and living in free quarters with the guerrillas to being drilled and starved in the regular army. While some of them kept alive the spirit of resistance . . . others compelled the inhabitants to look to the French for protection, for the inhabitants would at length prefer the systematised pillage . . . of the enemy to the wasteful, capricious, uncertain and merciless plundering of their own countrymen. On the whole, therefore, it may be said that the guerrillas did as much mischief to the country as they did to the French, but, in as much as they certainly did considerable damage to the enemy, they were on the whole useful to the common cause.[85]

Lengthy as this quotation is, it admirably sums up the problem faced by the historian. Were the guerrillas heroes who fought their country's enemies and played a major part in expelling them from the Peninsula, or were they, by contrast, bandits whose real interest lay in personal gain, and who merely used the struggle as a cover for their depredations? To put this another way, was their motivation ideological or was it economic? That the question is an important one, there is no doubt, as witness the extensive literature that has emerged with regard to brigandage and rebellion in France in the same period.[86] With regard to the comparable Spanish example no such literature exists, however: what is striking, indeed, is the extent to which the whole issue has been allowed to fall by the wayside. Analytical articles by Artola and Aymes that might have been looked to as a launch pad for debate are disappointing: the former confines itself to theory, whilst the latter's interesting discussion of the efforts of the Patriot authorities to subject the guerrillas to their control is spoiled by its failure fully to examine the problems that gave rise to the regulations that resulted, not to mention its stubborn refusal to abandon the notion of a popular crusade against the French.[87] As for the questions raised by the current author in several attempts to address the issue, they have largely gone unanswered – Hocquellet's recent book, for example, claims to be about resistance and revolution in Napoleonic Spain but, in fact, spends the bulk of its time looking at such issues as the composition of the provincial juntas, the concept of *la patria* and the establishment of the *cortes* of Cádiz. By contrast, all that Hocquellet can spare for the armed struggle that might have been expected to constitute the heart of his work is a mere eight pages.[88]

Hardly discussed as yet, the revisionist view still awaits its day: indeed, the prominence of authors writing a century or more ago in this discussion is itself suggestive of the failure of the academic community to address the issues raised by the guerrillas. However, the penetrating analysis offered by Sydenham quoted above is quite enough to suggest that the doubts of writers such as Napier, Muñoz Maldonado and Arteche cannot be ignored. The fruit of positions that were clearly *parti pris*, they nevertheless were – as will be seen – founded on a reality for which there is abundant evidence in the archives. At the very least further debate is wanted, whilst there is clearly a need to address many of the gaps in the existing literature. Who, for example, were the guerrillas? Why, too, were they fighting? And was the image of a Spanish crusade against Napoleon reflected in the grim realities of recruitment and mobilisation? All these questions remain to be answered, as do many others, but it is not to be expected that finding a satisfactory response will be easy. As Avesty has written:

> The eagle . . . is perplexed. The peace of the high mountains has been shattered. . . . Some men have come and startled her from her nest. Who are these men? None of the animals knows. . . . Are they smugglers trying to save

> their goods . . . bandits fleeing some robbery . . . or guerrillas defeated in a skirmish . . . Who are these men? Guerrillas, smugglers or bandits? Nobody knows, and they do not stop to provide us with the answer.[89]

For all Avesty's whimsy, the fact that the guerrillas are shrouded in ambiguity cannot be denied. Generally portrayed as either villains or heroes, they were in reality an extremely complex phenomenon. Thus, bandits who preyed on the French and their supporters might legitimately assume the status of freedom fighters, just as the most patriotic guerrilla leaders might find themselves at the head of men who aspired only to pillage and highway robbery. As Goya captioned the engraving in his 'Desastres de la Guerra' showing the execution of eight *malhechores* by the garrotte, 'One cannot find out the reason.'

Even working out who the guerrillas actually were is a problem: not only was the *guerrilla*, as we shall see, a phenomenon that embraced forces that ranged from entire divisions of the regular army to handfuls of armed civilians, but the very nomenclature of the period often makes it very hard to pin down exactly what is being referred to in any given document. The word *guerrilla*, for example, can refer to a guerrilla band or to irregular operations, but it can also mean a picket of regular troops or be used to describe the use of skirmishers on the battlefield; by the same token, the word *partida* can stand not just for a guerrilla band but also for a detachment of soldiers.[90]

To add to the problem, the guerrillas – or, to be more precise, the phenomenon of the Spanish people in arms – were recorded far more from outside their ranks than they were from within. Many of the better-known leaders left much evidence of their activities in the archives (it is therefore incorrect to speak of *la guerrilla* as an episode beyond the reach of empiricism). But it is the case that, beyond those elements of the movement that were both literate and possessed of links with the Patriot authorities, there was a much wider circle of individuals whose activities were only recorded by the representatives of property and order, whether French or Spanish. The consequence, of course, is that the archives tell a story that is weighted by a whole series of prejudices and value judgements. On the whole this may be assumed to have worked against the guerrillas, but, against this, we have the boasting and exaggeration engaged in by those *cabecillas* who did document their own activities. In short, no source is entirely to be trusted: we can no more, say, accept the words of Francisco Espoz y Mina as gospel than we can those of his opponents Reille and Abbé.

The difficulties thrown up by the skewed nature of the documentation relating to the guerrillas lead us on to another question. On the whole, those who have expressed doubts with regard to the 'official' version of *la guerrilla* have been historians of a progressive bent whose strong desire it is to re-insert the people into the historical process. Eager to extol popular heroism, they have accepted unreservedly the idea that the Spanish people flung themselves into the struggle against Napoleon, and have interpreted all moves to regulate or control the *partidas* as attempts to protect the social order. Inherent in this view is the issue of the 'primitive rebel', the armed peasant who sought redress for the grievances of both himself and his neighbours through forms of violence traditional in rural society. With Spain the home of anarchism – the earliest movement of organised agrarian protest in European history – there is clearly a strong desire to identify the guerrillas with social revolt. To quote the Marxist J.S. Pérez Garzón, for example, the guerrillas were 'disinherited peasants . . . plunged by a disamortizing bourgeoisie into an implacable process of proletarianization'.[91] Such views, meanwhile, have been echoed by the equally Marxian Eric Hobsbawm, whose *Age of Revolution* observes that 'the spontaneous movements of popular resistance against French conquest cannot be denied their social-revolutionary component, even when the peasants who waged them expressed it in terms of militant church-and-king conservatism'.[92]

Since no archival evidence has ever been presented to support these claims, yet another area of the subject presents itself for exploration and debate. Given the obvious tensions that mark the historiography of *la guerrilla*, the conclusion is obvious: in the absence of any up-to-date analysis of popular resistance in Napoleonic Spain, a new study is needed that will re-examine the issues raised in this chapter in the light of the contents of the Spanish archives. Yet the prospect is a daunting one. As we shall see, when Thomas Sydenham remarked that it was very difficult to know what to say about the guerrillas, he never wrote a truer word, the difficulties that face the historian being such as to give the expression 'the Spanish mousetrap' a whole new meaning.

2
The Guerrillas at War

The military history of *la guerrilla* is not a subject for the faint-hearted. For some five years those parts of Spain that were in the hands of the French witnessed an incessant series of marches, counter-marches, raids and skirmishes that are almost impossible to document in their entirety.

Even were it possible to chronicle all the operations of the *guerrilla*, the result would be less than satisfying for, wherever one looks, the picture is more or less the same: whether it was in Castile or Catalonia, Aragón or Andalucía, the guerrillas – according to the traditional version, at least – spent their time ambushing French couriers, convoys and foraging parties, attacking French posts and encampments, and pouncing upon, dodging or fighting off the French columns sent to hunt them down. Given the see-saw nature of events, indeed, the general effect would be to confuse the reader, and obscure the main outlines of the subject. Recognising this problem, all previous writers who have sought to go beyond broad generalisations have attempted to resolve matters by focusing on the narratives of the most prominent guerrilla commanders. Yet this approach does not help either. Setting aside the risk of hagiography arising from the myth-making and self-aggrandisement typical of many memoirs and contemporary accounts, the result must inevitably be to reinforce a variety of stereotypes and undermine both context and perspective.

Elaborating an alternative treatment of the conflict will not be an easy task, but it is one that cannot be shrunk from, for it is only by subjecting the military history of the 'little war' to close analysis that the way can be cleared for fresh thinking. Putting the issue at its most simple, it is impossible to dodge the fact that the French faced an abnormal situation in Spain. In the campaigns of 1805–7 French armies had swept across Germany, Austria, Bohemia and Poland with scarcely a thought for the safety of their couriers, foraging parties and lines of supply, whereas in Spain Napoleon's troops had to garrison every square inch of the territory they conquered and even then could not sleep safe in their beds. Unless this issue is addressed, there is no room for revision, for any challenge to the image of the guerrillas as the heroic defenders of *dios, rey y patria* ('God, king and fatherland') would have an obvious riposte. Find an answer to this question, by contrast, and the picture changes dramatically. Hence the need for a chapter that is unashamedly military in its preoccupations.

Before proceeding with our analysis of *la guerrilla*, let us first devote a little time to thinking about the geo-strategic problems faced by the French in the conquest of the Iberian Peninsula. As is constantly restated, both Spain and Portugal are countries ideally suited to guerrilla warfare. Not only are there wide regions that are extremely rugged, if not downright mountainous – one thinks especially here of Galicia, León, Navarre, Catalonia, the Maestrazgo, south-eastern Andalucía and Beira – but chains of mountains such as the Sierra Morena, the Montes de Toledo and the Sierra de Guadarrama criss-cross Spain in particular, thereby ensuring that time after time even main roads are forced to cross precipitous mountain passes or to run through lengthy gorges of the most terrifying nature. Perhaps the most well-known of these defiles, and one of the ones most feared by the French, was that of Pancorbo, between Burgos and Miranda de Ebro, where the main road from Madrid to the French frontier wound its way between towering saw-toothed peaks, but similar spots were to be found in many parts of the Peninsula. Indeed, many mountain *pueblos* can only be reached via defiles that are miles long, walled in by sheer cliffs and only a few feet wide. Competing with such places as potential bases, meanwhile, were the many monasteries perched on towering crags in the *sierras*, of which a prime example was the Catalan fastness of Nuestra Señora de Monserrat. It is not just a matter of mountains, however. Even where the country is not particularly elevated, it is in many areas covered with the dense scrub known as *matorral*, or thickly dotted with pines and holm oaks. And, last but not least, in many parts of the country human settlement is relatively infrequent, with the result that it is difficult to establish an adequate network of garrisons and police posts.

Staying with notions that have already been widely publicised, we next come to the condition and habits of the populace. Nineteenth-century writers, of course, were all too ready to see the origins of the *guerrilla* in some invented Spanish national character. Thus, for French observers, Spaniards were cruel, savage and xenophobic, just as for Spanish ones they were proud, noble and heroic, the point being that, whichever the case, they were likely to hurl themselves upon an invader with the utmost ferocity. From the twentieth-century point of view this is so much dross, but there are still strong grounds for arguing that there were environmental factors that gave the idea of partisan activity a peculiar resonance. Thus, large parts of the populace were either habituated to violence or long familiar with notions of irregular resistance. Across wide regions of the country the intense poverty of the rural masses ensured that banditry was commonplace, whilst the many internal customs barriers and state monopolies encouraged the emergence of powerful bands of smugglers. To deal with this problem, the Bourbon authorities had raised a variety of local security forces, which were known collectively as the *resguardo*, and the result was that many provinces witnessed incessant skirmishes which schooled both sides in the techniques of raid and ambush. As if this was not enough, meanwhile, certain parts of the country – above all, Galicia, the Basque provinces and Catalonia – possessed home guards consisting of all the male inhabitants, who were supposed to turn out in the case of invasion under the leadership of local notables (in Galicia officers involved in the War of Independence included *señores* such as Juan Bernardo Quiroga, Diego Núñez de Millaroso and Joaquín Tenreiro, magistrates such as Ignacio Herbón and Manuel Cordido, and local officials such as Cayetano Limia and Joaquín José Márquez). Known in Galicia as *alarmas*, in the Basque provinces as *migueletes* and in Catalonia as *somatenes*, in the last two instances they had even seen much service against the French in the course of the Revolutionary War of 1793–95. Of this conflict there were bitter memories in most border districts, but throughout the country its effect had been to confirm views of the French as 'the other' that were strengthened by the inflammatory language used in sermon and pamphlet during the war against the Convention.[1]

A country that was both physically suited to guerrilla warfare and accustomed to its concepts, Spain was therefore conditioned to hate the French. Also important was the pattern that military operations in the Peninsula were certain to take. Thus, thanks to the Pyrenees, there were only two roads across the French frontier that were practicable for large armies, of which the first entered Spain at Hendaye on the Bay of Biscay and the other at Port Bou on the Mediterranean. Of these, however, the second was of only limited utility, for it in practice led only to Barcelona (there were, of course, roads from Barcelona to the rest of the country, but they were for many reasons not very convenient). In consequence, the main axis of conquest was always likely to be the Hendaye road, especially as Bayonne was a much better depot than Perpignan. Yet from this followed certain consequences. As this highway led to Madrid, in all likelihood the French would find themselves having to conquer the Peninsula from, so to speak, the inside out. With the Spanish army unlikely to be able to stop them at the frontier or on the Ebro, the French would in effect be sucked deep into the interior. Madrid would fall soon enough, doubtless, and with it the plains of Old and New Castile, but the invaders would be denied immediate control of the coast. Strike out for it in all directions they certainly would, but for most of its length it was protected by high chains of mountains. As for

Portugal, she was hard to penetrate, for the main routes across the frontier were all covered by imposing fortresses. All round the northern, western and southern periphery of the country, then, there would be the potential for small forces of regular troops to sally out and attack the French. At the same time, of course, the deeper the French advanced into the Peninsula, the more vulnerable they became to such attacks, whilst even breaking through to the coast did not resolve the problem, in that there was always the chance of raiding forces being landed from the sea.

Viewed in detail, the matter appears even more complex. Thus, a French invasion based on the Hendaye road would be unlikely even to overrun the whole of the interior of the country. With the two Castiles and the capital would almost certainly go much of Aragón, for there was little to stop Napoleon's armies pouring down the valley of the Ebro and overrunning the steppes that surrounded Zaragoza. Separating Old Castile and La Mancha from central Aragón, however, is a broad strip of hills and mountains that all but runs from the Bay of Biscay to the Mediterranean. At its northern end its proximity to the French frontier and the fact that it was pierced by the Madrid–Hendaye road meant that it could be kept under some semblance of control, but to the south and east it was a different matter. There being little likelihood that it would be penetrated straight away, Spanish forces would therefore be able to maintain themselves deep inside the hinterland of the country. The problem was not insuperable – if the invaders could take Tarragona and Valencia, the region might ultimately be isolated and overcome – but it nevertheless made an already difficult situation still worse.[2]

All this was, as we shall see, to become a matter of some importance in *la guerrilla*: above all, in fact, the scene was being set for a scenario in which the French would be harassed not just by bands of guerrillas but also by substantial forces of regular troops. At the beginning of the war, however, it was seemingly the stereotype that ruled. Thanks to the divisions in the Spanish court and Napoleon's own astuteness, the French did not have to fight for Madrid and Barcelona: rather, they were let in unopposed, still other forces being allowed to march all the way to Lisbon. No fighting was expected – it was assumed that the armed forces would rally to the Napoleonic takeover – but in case of British raids a division was sent to occupy Cádiz under General Dupont. At this point, however, revolt broke out all round the country, and Dupont's division found itself cut off from Madrid by parties of insurgents who fell upon the convoys, detachments of soldiers and hospitals it had left scattered in its wake. All the inmates of a makeshift hospital at Manzanares were massacred, for example, whilst a band of peasants led by the *alcalde* of Montoro, Juan de la Torre, overpowered the seventy-strong guard that Dupont had left to hold the Puente de Alcolea. Other attacks took place at Santa Cruz de la Mudela, where the escort of a convoy of biscuit was put to flight after losing a third of its strength, and La Carolina, where the French general René was taken, along with his wife and secretary. Very soon, indeed, the whole district between Córdoba and the Sierra Morena was swarming with guerrilla bands led by such figures as the priest Ramón Argote. Indeed, sent down from Madrid to assist Dupont, the divisions of Vedel and Jacques-Nicholas Gobert only got through the Sierra Morena, as we have seen, by dint of some hard fighting. And everywhere murder was commonplace, French soldiers being pushed down wells, poisoned or knifed in their beds.[3]

According to all accounts, the attacks were accompanied by scenes of the utmost cruelty. Doubtless the tales grew in the telling, but it is clear that a number of those who fell into the hands of the insurgents met a horrible end. Perhaps the most often repeated of these stories concerns René, who was stabbed to death by a mob at Las Correderas after being taken prisoner some days earlier, but there are also reports of men being stoned to death, boiled in oil, sawn in half or buried up to their necks in the ground and left to die of thirst.[4] Nor was La Mancha the only setting for irregular resistance. In Catalonia the *somatenes* routed an enemy column sent to occupy Lérida at the pass of El Bruch (as we have seen), seriously molested the operations of other French forces and blockaded Barcelona, whilst the Junta of Gerona took into its service a friar named Francisco Rovira, who had formed a number of peasants armed with fowling pieces and pitchforks into a guerrilla band.[5] Near Aranda an obscure peasant named Juan Martín Díez led his three brothers and a number of other men in a series of attacks on French couriers and distinguished himself by capturing the wife of Marshal Moncey at the village of Carabias, whilst the road from Toledo to Madrid became the beat of a young doctor from Villaluenga de la Sierra named Juan Palarea.[6] In the vicinity of Madrid itself, a resident of Carabanchel named Pedro Serrano formed a *partida* and attacked a number of couriers.[7] In Aragón a wealthy clothier from Illueca named Fidel Mallén established a 100-strong band that harassed the French rear during the first siege of Zaragoza.[8] And finally, in Navarre still more *partidas* were raised by Andrés Eguaguirre, the lawyer Luis Gil and the priest Andrés Galdúroz.[9]

By the summer of 1808, then, guerrilla warfare was firmly established as a feature of the Peninsular War. With much of Spain evacuated in the wake of the battle of Bailén and the remaining pockets of French occupation crammed with troops who had been pulled back from Madrid, Burgos and Zaragoza, there was for the time being little scope for *partidas* to operate. However, in Catalonia such irregulars as Rovira, José Mansó and Francisco Miláns del Bosch continued to play an important part in events, with insurgents blockading Figueras, harassing the imperial forces sent to take the defiant fortress of

Gerona and even raiding the French frontier. Typical were the activities of Miláns del Bosch, who in September alone attacked the French at the Coll de Moncada, Badalona and San Feliú.[10] Nor was it long before *la guerrilla* was back in the limelight. Furious at the setbacks suffered by his troops, Napoleon poured heavy reinforcements into Spain, and in a whirlwind campaign defeated most of the Spanish armies and recaptured Madrid. Yet his very success meant that the French were once again vulnerable to guerrilla warfare. All around them, indeed, there swarmed bands of fugitive Spanish soldiers, not to mention angry civilians who had seen their homes plundered and destroyed and their families murdered, the French counter-attack having been marked by conduct of the utmost brutality. To quote just one example, from December onwards a time-expired soldier from Pozal de Gallinas named Jerónimo Saornil launched a number of successful attacks at such places as Madrigal de las Torres and Fuentesaúco.[11] Also active at this time, meanwhile, was a guerrilla band that had been established in the Tagus valley under Pablo Morillo, an erstwhile sergeant of the regular army who had been commissioned as a sub-lieutenant in a new regiment entitled the Voluntarios de Llerena.[12]

In memoir after memoir, indeed, we find evidence that isolated Frenchmen were even at this early stage going in fear of their lives, whilst there were stories that men who fell by the wayside out of exhaustion were shooting themselves rather than take the risk of falling into the hands of the Spaniards.[13] For a good example of the nightmares that plagued the invaders we have only to turn to the experiences of the aide-de-camp Marbot. Carrying the dispatches from Tudela to Madrid in December 1808 via the present-day province of Soria, with a small escort, he first encountered a French cavalry officer who had been nailed head downwards to a barn door and left to roast over a slow fire, and was then attacked by a party of armed civilians. These were driven off without difficulty, but a further attack was launched on Marbot and his men by five soldiers, and the Frenchmen were only saved by the providential arrival of a rescue party. Wounded and exhausted, a chastened Marbot later recalled the affair as 'one of the most terrible experiences of my military career'.[14]

If things were bad in 1808, in 1809 they got still worse. Faced once again with enemy troops, such early *partidas* as those of El Empecinado emerged from the shadows in which they had spent the summer and autumn of 1808, whilst many new bands also began to appear. In alliance with that of El Empecinado, for example, there came that of Jerónimo Merino, the semi-literate parish priest of the tiny village of Villoviado, near Lerma, who was soon attacking French couriers and convoys travelling between Madrid and Burgos, and making life uncomfortable for the garrison of Lerma.[15] Also active in Old Castile, meanwhile, were Bartolomé Amor, an erstwhile private in the Burgos provincial militia regiment, and the friars Lucas Rafael and Julián Délica.[16] Joining them in the north of the region were Juan Díaz Porlier, a young officer of marines who had obtained a command in the provincial militia following the uprising and escaped with a handful of his men into the hills in the wake of the Spanish defeat at Gamonal in November 1808; Francisco Longa, a blacksmith from Puebla de Arganzón who had got into trouble with the occupying forces; and Juan López Campillo, who in 1808 had been an officer in the *resguardo* in the province of Santander. And finally, in the east, Soria and Logroño saw a host of minor bands take to the field under such leaders as the noted smuggler Ignacio Alonso (known as Cuevillas) and the Benedictine monk Jácobo Alvarez.[17]

Nor was Old Castile alone in being affected by *la guerrilla*. On all sides, indeed, the French found themselves in similar difficulties. In the Tagus valley and La Mancha the chief leaders – not counting Palarea, who had initially confined himself to sporadic sallies from his home village – were Toribio Bustamente, a postal courier from Medina de Río Seco; Camilo Gómez, who was a wealthy *labrador* with lands in the vicinity of Talavera de la Reina; and José Pedrazuela, who had originally been an actor in Madrid. In Vizcaya and Guipúzcoa there emerged *partidas* headed by such figures as the *labrador* Juan Fernández Echevarrí, the law student Juan José de Abecía (who had fought as a volunteer in the defence of Zaragoza before managing to escape capture and flee to his home town of Marquina), and, most interestingly of all, a young woman named María Martín de Ibaibarriaga, whom family legend holds to have taken to the hills following the murder of her parents by French soldiers.[18] In Aragón we see the formation of bands under such figures as the prosperous *labradores* Miguel Sarasa and Fidel Mallén, the erstwhile smuggler Anselmo Alegre, and the mule contractor Miguel Domper.[19] In Catalonia there were bands led by the wealthy customs official Sebastián Gotti and the friar Francisco Rovira, who had now got together a group of refugees from the occupied district of the Ampurdán known as the Battalion of Expatriates.[20] And finally, in Navarre, at least a dozen bands were roaming the province in the spring of 1809. That of the priest Galdúroz we have already met, whilst the leaders of the others included another parish priest, named Hermenegildo Garcés de los Fayos, a bandit who had escaped from gaol in the confusion of the uprising named Andrés Ochotorena, a schoolteacher named Francisco Antonio Zabaleta, a smuggler named Félix Sarasa, a butcher named Pascual Echeverría and a day-labourer named Juan Lizárraga. By the autumn, meanwhile, they had been joined by a still more dangerous foe in the person of the university student Martín Javier Mina y Larrea, a young man who was not only energetic and talented but also enjoyed the full support of the military and political authorities (commissioned to take on the task of fomenting resistance in Navarre by the Spanish general Areizaga, Mina had won vital financial backing from the improvised provincial junta that had been established at Ujué under the leadership of its parish priest, Casimir-Javier de Miguel e Irujo).[21]

All this was the source of much trouble to the French. On 25 June 1809 Délica scored a considerable coup by capturing the French general Franceschi in an ambush, whilst on 28 June Merino massacred the guard of a French convoy at Quintana del Puente. On 6 July Miguel Sarasa attacked a French force at Fuentes de Sarsa; on 19 July the same commander attacked Sangüesa; and on 28 July Ignacio Alonso and Juan López Campillo wiped out a French detachment at Santo Domingo de la Calzada. On 6 August Logroño was temporarily occupied by the *partidas*; on 8 August Haro was raided and a foraging party destroyed at Maella by Santiago Pérez; on 14 August a large party of Spanish troops who had been taken prisoner the day before at the battle of Almonacid was liberated by Isidoro Mir and Ventura Jiménez; on 18 August a column of 150 Frenchmen that was marching from El Burgo de Osma to Soria was ambushed at Villar del Ciervo with the loss of a third of its strength; on 20 August Pérez beat 600 Frenchmen betweeen Alcañiz and Caspe; on 23 August Sarasa fell on another force heading from Zaragoza for Navarre; and on 24 August Porlier demonstrated against the walls of Palencia, inflicting a number of casualties on a party of French troops sent out to chase him off. On 5 September Toribio Bustamente and Mariano Ricafort swept into Torrejoncillo in a surprise attack that cost the French garrison fifteen dead and twenty-six prisoners; on 6 September Rovira routed a French column near Montaut; and on 16 September El Empecinado beat another one at Fontanar. Striking again at Casar de Talamar on the penultimate day of the month, the same commander killed seventy of the enemy, and was driven off only when the survivors opened fire with a cannon and badly wounded his second-in-command, Saturnino Abuin. On 5 October Francisco Sánchez overwhelmed a party of eighty Frenchmen at La Guardia, and Merino overcame a small French force at Santa María del Campo six days later; still other columns were attacked by Sarasa at Lasiero on the 17th and Abecia at Marquina on the 28th. On 5 November Sarasa infiltrated the walled town of Sos under cover of the fact that it was market day and, in a sudden *coup de main*, drove out the garrison and seized a large quantity of plate, grain and livestock. On the 7th Merino won another victory at Quintana de la Puente; and on the 8th Mina attacked Tafalla. On 12 November El Empecinado raided Guadalajara and retired with a large quantity of woollen cloth; on 13 November Domingo Sabirón seized 400 goats from their French guards near Cariñena; and on 15 November José Velasco took prisoner a party that had been sent to reconnoitre the mines of Almadén. On 18 November Mina gained what, for the guerrillas, was a major success at Sansol; on 26 November Abecia captured a French courier at Armiñón; and on

29 November Mina raided Tudela in company with Alonso and López Campillo.[22]

'This small-scale warfare', wrote Joseph Bonaparte's friend and confidant Miot de Melito, 'quietly undermined us. We only possessed the ground actually occupied by our armies, and our power did not extend beyond it. The business of administration ceased, and there was neither order, nor justice, nor taxation.'[23] For the invaders actually caught up in the fighting, meanwhile, the impressions left by the insurrection were still stronger. Among the garrison of Aragón, for example, was the Prussian officer Heinrich von Brandt, who was serving in the French-organised Polish force entitled the 'Legion of the Vistula', and who later recorded his impressions in one of the first serious attempts at an analysis of *la guerrilla*. Thus:

> Local causes, added to hatred, revenge and other passions . . . brought the mountaineers together . . . From corps thus formed . . . the boldest and most determined stepped forward as leaders . . . As long as the guerrillas were thus constituted, they made no appearance as a body, but were nevertheless extremely dangerous to the French. They formed the basis of an actual armament of the people, and were soon upon every road and path . . . and eagerly seeking for plunder . . . They rushed with the utmost rapidity upon their booty, or placed themselves in order of battle according to the nature of the undertaking . . . As soon as the enterprise was completed everyone went his own way, and armed men were scattered in all directions . . . Thus the communication on all roads was closed. Thousands of enemies were on the spot, though not a single one could be discovered; no courier could be dispatched without being taken; no supplies could set off without being attacked . . . At the same time, there existed no means of striking out against a combination of this kind. The French were obliged to be constantly on their guard against an enemy who, while continually flying, always reappeared, and who, without actually being seen, was everywhere. It was neither battles nor engagements which exhausted their forces, but the incessant molestations of an invisible enemy who, if pursued, became lost among the people, out of which he reappeared immediately afterwards with renewed strength. The lion in the fable, tormented to death by a gnat, gives us a true picture of the army at that period.[24]

Serving with the Second Hussars, meanwhile, was Albert de Rocca:

> In these mountainous provinces in the north of the Peninsula the French, although always conquerors where the . . . Spaniards showed themselves in battle, were not . . . the less assailed by clouds of armed mountaineers, who, never coming near to fight in closed ranks, or body to body, retreated from

position to position, from rock to rock, on heights, without ceasing to fire even in flying. It sometimes required entire battalions to carry an order . . . to another distant one. The soldiers wounded, sick or fatigued who remained behind the French columns, were immediately murdered. Every victory produced only a new conflict. Victories had become useless by the persevering and invincible character of the Spaniards, and the French armies were consuming themselves . . . in continual fatigues . . . and anxieties.[25]

Things did not get any better for the French in 1810. In the first place, it seemed that they were powerless to make any headway against the guerrillas. Here and there one *cabecilla* or another was picked off and his band scattered: examples include Délica in Old Castile, Francisco Sánchez in La Mancha and Mina in Navarre. But no sooner had one leader been dealt with than another sprang up to take his place: Mina, for instance, was replaced by his distant kinsman Francisco Espoz Ilundain, and Sánchez by his neighbour Manuel Hernández. Equally, by dint of very great efforts, it sometimes proved possible to force back the *partidas*, and all but clear them from a province. By the end of 1809, for example, the French commander in Aragón, Louis Suchet, had succeeded in defeating many of the bands that had been threatening his dominions. But unless action was co-ordinated with the garrison of neighbouring provinces victory was never final, for there was nothing to stop the guerrilla leaders from slipping across the frontier in search of both a quieter life and fresh targets. And it was useless simply to mount great sweeps against the insurgents: territory had to be cleared, certainly, but it also had to be thoroughly garrisoned, and this the French rarely had the troops to manage. Ordered to launch an offensive against such strongholds as Lérida and Tortosa in an attempt to pave the way for the conquest of Valencia, for example, Suchet saw the bulk of his Aragonese conquests overrun by the *partidas* once more.[26]

For the French, then, campaigning against the guerrillas was as exhausting as it was frustrating, as witness, for example, Bigarré's account of his experiences as temporary governor of Aranjuez in 1811:

The guerrilla leaders Morales and El Abuelo [i.e., Manuel Hernández] were constantly making incursions in the vicinity . . . One extremely hot day the sentries stationed at the Ocaña gate were taken by surprise, and these two chieftains . . . galloped down the street that led to the main square . . . shouting, 'Long live Fernando VII!', followed by 500 of their men. Warned of what was going on by one of the sentries, I jumped on my horse, and charged them with such impetuosity that they took flight . . . and dispersed in the countryside . . . Seeing that [El Abuelo] was only a short distance ahead of me, I rode out to get him followed by my aides-de-camp and about twenty chasseurs . . . With my horse going at top speed, I suddenly found myself faced by a canal eighteen feet wide. This I attempted to leap, but my horse was not good enough to make such a jump, and I was thrown right into the middle, along with my aides-de-camp and four of the light horsemen . . . I felt the effects of the fall for some months, but I was not going to let El Abuelo . . . get away with it . . . On 6 June I heard . . . that El Abuelo and his guerrillas were going to spend the night of the 7th at Uclés . . . At a quarter to ten, 400 infantry . . . and twenty-five light horse . . . arrived outside the town . . . Charging into the town, they met no resistance . . . Having been shown the house where El Abuelo stayed whenever he spent the night at Uclés, I ordered it to be surrounded. Several shots were fired at us . . . but in the same instant the doors were forced by some *voltigeurs* . . . Rushing inside, they killed four guerrillas . . . but El Abuelo, who had been in bed with his wife, saved himself by scrambling out of an attic window in his nightshirt and jumping down into the garden. Although more than twenty shots were fired at him, he then managed to gain the safety of the open country.[27]

Nor was it just that fighting was incessant. If anything, the problem was inclined to get worse rather than better. Every French advance, for example, created fresh guerrillas. Thus, the arrival of the French in Andalucía in 1810 sparked off a new wave of resistance. None of the leaders is as well known as those that had appeared in the previous two years in the north and centre of Spain, but they were nonetheless extremely numerous. In the province of Seville the men involved included Pedro Zaldívar, Miguel López, Antonio Veas, Salvador Sierra and two anonymous *cabecillas* known only as Palmetín and El Mantequero. In Córdoba we find Lorenzo Díaz, Juan Antonio Mármol, Juan Lorenzo Rey and Mariano Rodríguez. And in Jaén prominent names were Antonio Calvache, Jerónimo Moreno, Pedro Alcalde and Mateo Gómez. In the same way, when Suchet finally conquered Valencia in 1812, he was challenged by such figures as the peasant Gregorio Martínez, the well-known bandit Jaime Alfonso and the Franciscan friar Agustín Nebot.[28]

As the war went on, then, the number of guerrillas may be said to have multiplied dramatically. But it was not just that there were more opponents for the French to face; the fact is that there was also a steady intensification of the challenge. Thus, in the beginning most *partidas* consisted of no more than a handful of men, whilst their members were equipped with whatever weapons they could improvise or capture from the enemy, dressed in civilian costume and entirely ignorant of the art of war. The free and easy spirit of the first days is captured extremely well by Francisco Espoz y Mina:

In the beginning, and for some time afterwards, the guerrillas of Navarre . . . operated as they wished . . . The only tactic was to go wherever enemies

> were to be found that could be attacked with some hope of success . . . and these expeditions were captained by the wisest and most valiant.[29]

In many bands this situation remained unchanged throughout the war, but from fairly early on there was a tendency for at least some *partidas* to grow in size. In part this was the result of a process of concentration: not only were the more ambitious *cabecillas* eager to take over the forces of rival commanders, but it was soon found that a multiplicity of small *partidas* was a recipe for chaos. Thus in 1810, for example, most of the guerrillas in the province of Soria were united under the command of a colonel of the regular army named José Joaquín Durán y Barazábal, who had escaped imprisonment at the hands of the French.[30] But, in part, too, it was also simply that success bred success, for the more dynamic the band the more recruits it got, and the less likely it was to suffer from desertion. And, by the same token, the more recruits a band got, the more likely it was to be successful.

More men, however, meant that for both logistical and operational reasons it became necessary to adopt structures that reflected the new situation. Battalions of infantry and squadrons of cavalry therefore began to supplant the *partida*, and these in time multiplied and allowed commanders who had started out with a handful of followers to lay claim to the command of brigades and even divisions. And, very soon, the picturesque style of the early days was being abandoned. Uniforms – generally brown breeches and jackets topped off with round black hats – took the place of peasant dress; muskets and bayonets replaced knives and blunderbusses; and lines and columns supplanted the crowd of individuals fighting as the fancy took them. Let us quote, for example, the account of Espoz y Mina's forces given by a prisoner of war rescued by them in 1811:

> His cavalry are chosen men and . . . are dressed as hussars in blue . . . His infantry . . . wear rope-soled sandals, half-gaiters, breeches and jackets; their muskets . . . fire well, whilst their bayonets are kept very sharp . . . The soldiers receive one *real* per day, together with an abundant ration of bread, meat and wine . . . Their tactics are confined to firing on the enemy and then charging home in various combinations of line or column.[31]

Underlying this transformation was in part the combination of the military superiority of the French and the sheer efficacy of conventional models of tactics and organization. Thus, as *partidas* grew bigger and more permanent, they presented the French with an easier target, and, what is more, one on which it was easy to inflict terrible damage. Caught in the open at Belorado in La Rioja in November 1810, for example, Espoz y Mina's infantry were overwhelmed by a force of 7,000 Frenchmen and all but destroyed.[32] Shocked by this defeat, the Navarrese leader, who only escaped death or capture on account of an earlier bullet wound in the leg, which had forced him to abandon his command for the safety of his native hills, responded not, as Tone claims, by limiting himself to guerrilla-style operations but by demanding that his men should learn to fight as regular troops. As he says, 'This was the moment when the regiments began to receive military instruction . . . From then on the greater part of their time . . . was spent doing drill.'[33] And, once the decision to fight in a regular style had been taken, there was no space for a specific *táctica guerrillera*. Espoz y Mina had already learned that sniping at the French from the hillsides was to be avoided in favour of charging home, and his troops were now schooled in methods of fighting similar to those of Wellington's army. When three of his infantry regiments were attacked at Aibar in December 1810, for example, they were ordered to give the enemy a single volley at close range and then launch a bayonet charge.[34]

It was not just the pressures of operating against the French that drove the larger *partidas* to adopt military forms, however. For commanders with neither military training nor formal education it was a vital means of legitimising themselves in the eyes of hostile generals of the regular army, whilst for all *cabecillas* it was a way of cementing their own positions by invoking the principles of hierarchy and giving themselves access to important sources of patronage, not to mention fresh recruits. This could result in recognition from the government and that brought with it shipments of arms and supplies, the prospect of regular pay, access to the privileges of the military estate and the possibility of further promotion. As members of the armed forces, they could free themselves of the political interference sometimes engaged in by such provincial juntas as managed to maintain themselves in the occupied territories. And, last but not least, possession of a regular commission or membership of a regular-style unit offered some protection, for captured soldiers were granted prisoner-of-war status rather than simply being executed out of hand.[35]

Many bands went through this process of development. As early as the end of 1809, for example, Porlier's *partida* had been organised into the Primer Cántabro and Castilla infantry regiments and the Husares de Cantabria cavalry (also under command was the Laredo infantry regiment, but this was in fact a unit of the pre-war army that had been assigned to Porlier to bolster his forces). Other northern guerrilla bands transformed in this fashion eventually included those of Longa, with the First, Second, Third and Fourth Iberia infantry regiments, and the Husares de Iberia cavalry; and Jáuregui with the First, Second and Third Guipúzcoa infantry regiments. As witness the record of Durán's 'División de Soria', these forces often developed into powerful opponents. Thus on 28 May 1812 Durán stormed Tudela and pillaged a large convoy that had stopped in the town for the night, whilst on 14 June he launched a surprise attack on Aranda de Duero that saw his forces scale the walls and force the defenders to take shelter in the bishop's palace. Having been equipped with a number of 12-pounder guns by Wellington, meanwhile, in the autumn of 1812 Durán and his men twice beat the French at Fuenmayor, besieged Calatayud and, deprived of victory by a French relief force that evacuated the garrison in the nick of time, vented their spleen on the castle of Borja, which was quickly bombarded into surrender.[36]

However, the powerful force-multiplier that the combination of increased strength and militarisation represented is best studied through the medium of Francisco Espoz y Mina's 'División de Navarra'. Thus, in 1810 the then Francisco Espoz Ilundaín was a volunteer serving in the *partida* of his kinsman Martín Javier Mina. After escaping from the disaster that saw the capture of his commander on 31 March 1810 – an episode to which we shall return – he set up as a *cabecilla* himself, and, though initially supported by only a handful of companions, succeeded in uniting many of his old comrades under his leadership, in part because of his crafty assumption of the name Espoz y Mina. A series of minor successes brought in many fresh recruits, whilst the new commander was careful to give his forces a sound logistical base by levying customs duties on all goods crossing the French frontier and, later on, securing control of the administration of the properties expropriated as *bienes nacionales* by order of the *cortes* of Cádiz. In this manner the need to live off the civilian population was reduced to a minimum, whilst Espoz y Mina earned further plaudits by suppressing many bandits. Establishing a monopoly of armed force – any *partida* that resisted his authority was crushed without mercy – he was able not only to establish an efficient civil administration but also to create an effective army that was able to offer the civilian population at least some measure of protection.[37] All this brought growing military success, most notably at the Puerto de Arlabán on 25 May 1811. Thus, a large French convoy that had just left Vitoria *en route* for France was wending its way through the pass when it was attacked from both sides by Espoz y Mina's men. As one contemporary account had it:

> The battle began between five and six o'clock in the morning, and Espoz y Mina's troops loaded and fired with such skill that two or three volleys threw the French into consternation . . . The fruit of this brilliant action . . . has been the death of 300 Frenchmen . . . the capture of 700 or 800 more and the release of some 800 . . . Spanish prisoners who armed themselves there and then with the muskets of their oppressors . . . The booty also included more than 4,000,000 *reales*.[38]

Such successes were often exaggerated: in his own report Espoz y Mina more than doubled the size of the escort, for example. But, skilfully publicised, such victories secured recognition in Cádiz, and with it further authority, with the consequence that Espoz y Mina was able to form still more units, of which many were recruited from beyond the borders of Navarre. By 1813, indeed, his forces had grown to nine regiments of infantry and one of cavalry. Repeated French attacks proved unavailing, and eventually the situation got quite out of hand. With the garrison of Navarre and Aragón stretched unmercifully by the need to make up for the losses of the Russian campaign, and Espoz y Mina armed with artillery landed by the British from the sea, the French position became impossible. Strongpoint after strongpoint was taken by the guerrillas; the forces of two or three thousand men that were all that the harassed French commanders could scrape together to take on the guerrillas in the open field were repeatedly beaten; and those few garrisons that remained too strong to be attacked were blockaded and threatened with the spectre of starvation (for a more detailed account of these operations, see pp. 135–6). To say that Espoz y Mina liberated Navarre on his own would be to go too far: had the French been able to concentrate all their forces against the Navarrese commander, there is little doubt that they would in the end have overcome his troops. Yet the fact remains that militarisation and dictatorship had between them created a situation that had no equal.[39]

By the end of the war forces such as those of Durán and Espoz y Mina had obviously come a long way from the tiny groups in which they had their origin. Yet on the surface the guerrillas remained a popular phenomenon. Even when they could lay claim to the status of army officers, for example, most of the chieftains affected nicknames that at first sight both perpetuated and asserted their civilian status. Thus Espoz y Mina was 'Uncle Frank' (Tío Francisco) or the 'King of Navarre' (Rey de Navarra); Mina was 'the lad' (El Mozo); Merino 'the priest' (El Cura); Alegre 'the potter' (El Cantarero); Délica 'the Capuchin' (El Capuchino); Porlier 'the little marquess' (El Marquesito); Palarea 'the doctor' (El Médico); Juan Martín 'Stick-in-the-Mud' (El Empecinado); Rodríguez Valdés 'the cook' (El Cocinero); Orué 'the little lawyer' (El Abogadillo); Abad 'Jerkin' (Chaleco); Abuin 'One-Hand' (El Manco); Alonso 'Caves' (Cuevillas); Príncipe 'Bourbon' (Borbón); Bustos 'the brigand' (El Brigante); Fernández 'Two Hairs' (Dos Pelos); Gastón 'Titch' (El Chiquito); Jaureguí 'the shepherd' (El Pastor); Marañón 'the Trappist' (El Trapense); Manuel Hernández 'the grandfather' (El Abuelo); Francisco Sánchez 'Frankie' (Francisquete); and Santos González 'the black' (El Negro).[40]

With nicknames common in popular parlance – even today Spanish footballers and bullfighters often use such *apodos* – no statement could be clearer: the guerrillas were, quite literally, the people in arms. If anything more was needed to make the point, meanwhile, it is the image that they frequently affected. As Robert Brindle wrote of his meeting with El Empecinado in the summer of 1809, for instance:

> Though elevated at this time to the rank of colonel, [El Empecinado] had not cast aside the dress of the peasant. His hat was the same as that worn in many places by the peasants, with a small crown and broad brim, and was fastened under his chin by an old ribbon . . . A carbine was fastened to his side by a silk handkerchief and he had a sword on the opposite side [and] a brace of pistols . . . and a large knife in a sash tied round his middle.[41]

A year and a half later, meanwhile, it seems that his persona was but little changed: all his letters were signed 'El Empecinado', whilst an archdeacon who met him in Cuenca in February 1811 compared him to the proverbial 'rough diamond'.[42] Such an image, meanwhile, is very much that conveyed by Dennis Dighton's 1813 painting of 'the brigand Croza', one of the very few contemporary pictures of a *cabecilla* drawn from the life that has come down to us. It shows a ferociously moustachioed figure with a sinister face, clad in peasant costume, complete with broad-brimmed hat and rope-soled sandals, who is pointing out some unseen enemy to two equally grim-looking followers with a dagger.[43]

And, beyond doubt, even the unmilitarised bands gave the French much trouble. Patrols and forage parties were likely to be set upon, and stragglers to be murdered out of hand. To get through to their destinations, couriers had to be escorted by hundreds of troops, whilst, by the same token, the transport of supplies had to be undertaken through the medium of convoys that were as large as they were well protected. And even the strongest parties could experience serious difficulties, for many *cabecillas* evolved ways of fighting that were suited to the capacities of their men. It was, for example, Espoz y Mina's boast that, to make up for their lack of training, ammunition and proper firearms, he encouraged his men to fire a single volley and then to charge home immediately.[44] Most of the Navarrese guerrillas fought on foot, but on horseback the irregulars were even worse. To quote an aide-de-camp of General Hugo:

> They appear . . . at the gallop, disorder our columns with their murderous blunderbusses, and then take advantage of the confusion to ride in and cut down the men. If they see that our forces are too strong for them, they fire a single volley . . . and then ride to the rear whilst they load their arms, which they can effect with great speed even on the move. If we follow them, they turn back and fire at us again, causing us still more casualties . . . and in this fashion they make their escape, whilst laughing all the while at our efforts to catch them.[45]

As a result of all this, immense resources had to be devoted to dealing with the problem. Amongst the more ingenious strategies adopted was to hide small cannon (in fact, probably over-sized muskets designed to be fired from special pivots built into fortress parapets) in covered wagons in the style of the famous 'Q-ships' of the First World War.[46] Along some main roads, too, the French built chains of blockhouses in which squads of soldiers and *gendarmes* could be housed and victims of guerrilla attacks take refuge.[47] But above all the issue was one of manpower. For reasons that will become clear, the large garrisons that the French had to maintain in all the provinces which they occupied were not there solely to maintain law and order. That said, however, if the situation was not to get completely out of hand, thousands of soldiers had to be dispersed across the country in 'penny packets'. Still worse, meanwhile, many units found themselves deprived of reinforcements: sent across the frontier from Bayonne and Perpignan in temporary detachments known as *bataillons du marche*, thousands of conscripts found themselves seized upon as garrisons and convoy guards by the overstretched governors of such towns as Pamplona and Figueras. To deal with the situation, Napoleon created a large force of *gendarmes*, and encouraged the formation of civic guards and anti-guerrilla units of various sorts. As early as April 1809, meanwhile, the *comisario regio* responsible for the Basque provinces ordered the formation of no fewer than seven companies of coast guards to prevent raids on the coast of Guipúzcoa. But there were never enough of the *gendarmes d'Espagne* to go round – though the initial establishment alone consisted of twenty squadrons – whilst the various *juramentados* were by no means wholly reliable. And of course the programme added greatly to the costs of occupation, thereby increasing the pressure on the populace and propelling them further in the direction of resistance.[48]

There is, then, no smoke without fire: there was a popular guerrilla movement that fought the French in Spain between 1808 and 1814; not only that, meanwhile, but it also secured much success, and developed tactics that were very effective. But this is not the whole story of *la guerrilla*. Even popular resistance to French occupation is not to be measured solely by reference to *partidas*. There were many spontaneous acts of individual resistance, such as that which took place in Yepes on 30 December 1809, when a *juramentado* who had had too much to drink and started boasting about the money he was getting from the French was shot in the back in the main square.[49] And in Vizcaya in August 1808, Galicia in February–June 1809, the Navarrese valley of Roncal in March–August 1809 and the Serranía de Ronda in March–August 1810 resistance rather took the form of peasant revolt. In each case the pattern was the same, improvised local militias taking up arms under a variety of leaders – in Galicia and Vizcaya local notables, in the Roncal escaped prisoners of war, and in Ronda a mixture of local notables and agents dispatched by the central authorities – and harassing the French columns sent against them. Some of the tactics used by the insurgents were reminiscent of those of guerrilla warfare – the Roncal even witnessed the formation of a number of *partidas* – but on the whole the phenomenon was quite different, the combatants remaining close to their villages and dispersing to their homes after every combat. As Southey noted, their efforts were 'more properly a national than a guerrilla warfare, the work of destruction being carried on less by roving parties than by the settled inhabitants who watched for every opportunity of revenge'.[50]

To illustrate what Southey means, we can do no better than turn to the account of the French cavalryman Rocca, whose unit was part of the garrison of Ronda:

> The most popular pastime among the labourers of Ronda was to sit on the rocks among the olive groves . . . and smoke cigars while they fired upon our vedettes. In the morning they would go out of the town with their tools as if they were going out to work in the fields, but there or at the farmhouses they found their guns, and returning them at night they would come back to the town and sleep in the midst of us. It not infrequently happened that our hussars recognised their hosts among their enemies . . . The women, the old men and even the children were against us, and served as spies for the enemy.[51]

It will be noted that there is no mention of any guerrilla band here. This is not to say, of course, that there were no *partidas* in the region. The first opposition the French met in the district of Casares, for example, came from a group of goatherds who armed themselves with fowling pieces and attacked a party of thirty-six Frenchmen who had come looking for horses, whilst the *serranía* in general became the haunt of such *cabecillas* as Vicente Moreno, José Fajardo, José Ruiz Falcón, José Aguilar and José Villalobos.[52] But the model described by Rocca was very different, what we see rather being an *ad hoc* home guard tied to its own *pueblos*. As he implies, there was at first no organisation, but as time went on, so the men of each village were grouped into loose companies, and these in turn were eventually organised into four infantry battalions known as the *cazadores patriotas* of Casares, Jurique, Gaucín and Cortés.[53] Called out, as these were, only in times of danger, what we see is rather a reliance not on guerrilla bands but on people's militias in the style of the *alarma* and the *somatén*.

The value placed on this model of military organisation is evident from events in various parts of Spain. Thus, threatened by the forces of Marshal Victor, on 21 March 1809 the Junta of Extremadura ordered the enlistment in a militia of every man between the ages of seventeen and fifty, the intention being that this force should engage in guerrilla operations against the French.[54] However, as was only to be expected given its long traditions of self-defence, it was Catalonia that proved to be the chief exponent of this home-guard model. As witness the events of the autumn and winter of 1809, the *guerrilla* was at least as vigorous in Catalonia as it was in other parts of Spain: on 16 October Juan Clarós attacked a French convoy at Monroig; on 26 November José Mansó chased the French from San Boy; and on 18 December 1809 no less a person than the commander of the French forces in the region, Marshal Augereau, was attacked near Figueras whilst returning to his headquarters following a brief visit to France.[55] Whilst there were, as we have seen, a number of Catalan *partidas*, in all of these operations most of the irregular element of the Patriot forces was provided by the *somatén*, for which each community was expected to raise and maintain a certain number of its inhabitants.

The *somatenes* remained in action throughout the war. In the summer of 1811, for example, large numbers of them were used to harass the forces besieging Tarragona.[56] But not all the Catalan forces, and still less those which were engaged in guerrilla-style operations, were composed of irregulars. Even in 1808 many of the most active resistance fighters had in fact been soldiers from the garrison of Barcelona who had fled the city after it was taken over by the French: the first recruits of Juan Clarós, for example, included men from both the Spanish and Walloon guards and the Extremadura line infantry regiment.[57] In 1809 much of the south and west of Catalonia was still in the hands of the Spanish Army of the Right, commanded by General Blake, and it was in fact troops from this force that bore the brunt of the fighting in the operations we have mentioned. Many of them, it is true, were little more than irregulars in appearance and attitude, especially in the case of the forty regiments of *migueletes* that the Junta of Catalonia had raised as a gesture to local feeling in preference to imposing conscription to the regular army. In brief, these units were enlisted wholly from volunteers, paid a substantial bounty, allowed to elect their own officers and guaranteed their liberty at the end of the war.[58] Prominent among them were such supposed guerrillas as Juan Clarós, Juan Baget, José Mansó and Francisco Miláns del Bosch but, despite the fact that they had all been civilians in 1808, to none of them can the term really be applied. Their troops may have been of poor quality – at the beginning, indeed, arms were in such short supply that many of the men had to be armed with pikes – but they fought alongside and in the same style as the regulars, and cannot be separated from them. And, in the same way, the regulars cannot be separated from the *guerrilla*. For example, a particularly prominent role in the incessant raids and skirmishes that took place around the besieged city of Gerona was played by Enrique O'Donnell, a brigade commander who in 1808 had been an officer of the Ultonia infantry regiment. Thus, having broken into the city with a supply convoy on 1 September, twelve days later he broke out again in spectacular fashion, storming the sleeping camp of General Souham, running off all his horses and baggage animals and forcing the officer concerned to take flight dressed in his nightgown.[59]

Events after the fall of Gerona on 11 December 1809 demonstrate still more clearly the vital role played by the regular army in the 'little war' in Catalonia. With the siege out of the way, Marshal Augereau's next objective was the relief of Barcelona, which had been closely blockaded by Catalan forces (both regular and irregular) and was facing starvation. Moving on the capital via the roads that ran through Vich and Hostalrich, the French troops that had been concentrated around Gerona found that their every movement was harassed by clouds of sharpshooters, that passes such as that of El Grao could only be cleared by heavy fighting and, further, that Rovira and other commanders continued to be active in their rear: at the Arroyo de Masanet, for example, General Verdier, who was responsible for the district between Gerona and the frontier, lost some 400 men in an ambush.

Worse was to come, however. The Army of the Right had just been placed under the command of the energetic O'Donnell, who proceeded to launch a series of attacks on the French. On 12 January 1810 a French reconnaissance was routed at the pass of Collsuspina, just north of Centellas. Reinforcements having been called up, O'Donnell hastily fell back on Manresa, only to reappear suddenly ten days later and fall upon a French brigade stationed around Granollers. Taken completely by surprise, the invaders lost 1,000 men, and, whilst the survivors, who had barricaded themselves in a convent, were rescued by a relief column led by Augereau himself, the Catalan troops got clear away. There followed a brief lull in the fighting, but on 19 February O'Donnell appeared yet again, this time attacking the French division that had been left to hold Vich and badly wounding its commander.[60] Thanks to the superiority of the French cavalry, the Spaniards were in the end defeated at Vich, but O'Donnell was undaunted. The Spanish general first thwarted an attempt on the part of Marshal Augereau to capture Tarragona by attacking the garrisons that had been dropped off at Villafranca and Manresa to keep open communications with Barcelona (both were all but destroyed), and then joined with the local *somatenes* in harassing the would-be besiegers' retreat on the capital. Much aided by Augereau, who to Napoleon's fury decided to pull most of his troops back to Gerona on the grounds that the population of Barcelona could not be fed at the same time as a large field army, O'Donnell then marched west to assist Lérida, which had in April been besieged by troops dispatched from Aragón under Suchet. In this he failed – over-confidence and want of caution led him to march into a clever trap at Margalef that cost him several thousand casualties – but the French were too preoccupied with the siege of Lérida (and, after that of Mequinenza and Tortosa), not to mention the perennial task of getting convoys of food into Barcelona, to follow up their success. As a result, the Spanish general was accorded a breathing space, which he used to rebuild his battered army, whose divisions were deployed in a great horseshoe in the mountains of central Catalonia in positions that allowed them to keep up the blockade of the capital, harass convoys moving along the high road from Gerona to Barcelona and impede Suchet's attempts to move on Tortosa and Tarragona from the west.[61] At the same time, meanwhile, the *somatenes* were called to make a major effort. Thus:

> All the inhabitants of the districts of Tarragona, Tortosa and Lérida capable of doing so should leap to arms. Having elected experienced commanders of proven courage and patriotism, they should mass at Falset and Tibisa . . . and intercept the enemy's communications. And let no *pueblo* provide our perfidious foe with aid of any sort: any that does so will be treated as an enemy by its own brothers.[62]

There followed a further spate of minor actions, with small forces of regular troops attacking the enemy at such places as Tibisa and Balaguer, the guerrilla bands of Narciso Gay and Francisco Rovira operating along the main roads and raiding such garrisons as that of Besalú, and the *migueletes* of Clarós, Mansó and other commanders skirmishing with the French around Barcelona and Gerona and even striking across the border into France.[63] In September, meanwhile, O'Donnell attempted his most daring operation yet: picking up his northernmost division from its base of Cardona, he struck eastwards towards the sea, and fell on a German brigade whose task it was to watch the coast in the vicinity of Gerona. Aided both by further troops that had been sent up from Tarragona by sea and a number of irregulars, the Spanish commander gained a complete victory: taken by surprise, the Germans were overwhelmed and taken prisoner.[64]

As the war went on, meanwhile, the tendency of the Catalan forces to engage in small-scale operations increased still further, particularly in the wake of the fall of Tarragona in June 1811. The defenders of Catalonia, now known as the First Army, had suffered terrible casualties, been cut off from the sea and driven back into the poor and thinly populated hinterland of the province. In this situation all that could be done was to launch the occasional raid, a good example of which was the attack launched by the First Army's new commander, General Luis Lacy, on a large French convoy that was travelling from Gerona to Barcelona near Igualada on 7 October 1810. The details of this affair are of some interest, for they are little different from those of, say, Espoz y Mina's attacks on similar convoys travelling along the main road from Madrid to the French frontier. Thus, it was decided that a strong force of troops under the Barón de Eroles should attack the column from the front whilst Lacy cut the road in its rear and, further, that the attack should go in at night whilst the French were in camp. The Spaniards having spent the previous day holed up at Manresa, the first the French knew of the attack was when some 300 enemy cavalry charged into their encampment at three o'clock in the morning. Many French soldiers were killed or wounded in the first rush, but the remainder fled into a nearby convent, where they held out stoutly. Unable to take this redoubt for want of artillery, Lacy eventually had to retreat, but it had still been a very successful raid: at least seventy Frenchmen lay dead, whilst the Spaniards' booty included 150 mules loaded with flour and 700 head of cattle.[65]

The Catalan example has been discussed at some length because it shows not just how local militias could be just as important in *la guerrilla* as partisan bands, but also how the regular army played an integral part in its operations. Indeed, this was a feature of the fighting in a number of provinces. In Galicia, for instance, the uprising of the first months of 1809 was lent added bite by the presence of the Marqués de la Romana's Army of the Left, which, though much battered after the campaigns of the autumn and winter of 1808, remained in being and in March 1809 sallied out to capture the French strongpoint of Villafranca del Bierzo.

For an even better example, however, we might turn to Asturias. Isolated behind its mountains, that province had been stripped of most of its regular troops in the summer of 1809, and in early 1810 seemed ripe for invasion. On 31 January, then, the division of General Bonnet occupied Oviedo. The mere occupation of the capital did not put an end to resistance, however. Most of the garrison had fallen back to positions in the west of the province, and from there a number of officers sallied out to raise the populace, who had previously been organised into an *alarma* modelled on that of Galicia. At the same time, meanwhile, the forces of Juan Díaz Porlier, which by this time consisted of a flying column of regular troops, moved into a position from which they could threaten Bonnet's communications with León. There followed a series of minor actions: Porlier, for example, attacked a French detachment near Infiesto and captured many prisoners; Bárcena, the regular commander, defeated another small force at Puente de Soto; and various small groups of irregulars closed in on the capital. With his communications completely cut – many of his dispatches fell into the hands of the Spaniards – on 12 February Bonnet was constrained to evacuate the capital and start to fall back on Santander.

At this point, however, the Spaniards behaved in such a manner that the French general was afforded the chance of a counter-stroke. Unable to resist the temptation of staging a triumphal entry into the city, Porlier and Llano Ponte (the commander of the division that had originally held the eastern part of the province) descended on Oviedo, along with large numbers of irregulars, and settled down to enjoy the fruits of victory. Realising that he was not being pursued, Bonnet turned back and, taking advantage of snow and thick fog, inflicted a shattering defeat on the Spaniards two days later. With Oviedo once more occupied, the Asturian forces again fell back on the River Nalón, where they were reconstituted with the aid of a small force of regular troops dispatched from Galicia under a Lieutenant-Colonel Luis Díaz. With Bonnet soon in exactly the same straits as before, by the middle of March the way seemed open for a counter-offensive. Some 5,000 troops were therefore placed in motion for Oviedo, and on 19 March the latter's outnumbered garrison was defeated in a sharp action at the Puente de Peñaflor, with the result that Bonnet once again abandoned the capital and retreated, this time, to Cangas de Onis.

Barely a week had passed before he was back again, however. Having received reinforcements from Santander, he retraced his steps and attacked the Spaniards, who had re-entered Oviedo. Largely composed of raw troops, badly armed and lacking in cohesion – one of the battalions sent from Galicia was a provisional unit composed of fragments of no fewer than four different regiments – the defenders fled with little resistance, leaving the French to enter Oviedo for the third time in two months. Yet this profited them not at all. Bonnet lacked the troops to force the line of the River Nalón, to which the Spaniards had once again withdrawn, and from the safe base that this afforded them detachments of partisans and regular troops were soon sallying out to harass the French. Not, indeed, till the fall of Astorga permitted the dispatch of substantial reinforcements to Bonnet in late April was the stalemate broken. Only then were the French able to cross the Nalón and occupy much of the west of the province.[66]

Yet the French offensive of 1810 did not bring the fighting in Asturias to an end. Whereas it had previously been used merely as a base for guerrilla warfare, the principality now became a theatre for its operations. Once again, however, we see that the *partidas* were not alone in the struggle. Porlier, it is true, for some months held out in the mountains in the south of the province, whilst other irregulars continued to raid Bonnet's lines of communication with León and Santander, but other elements also played their part. Amongst these were the *alarma*, who took part, for example, in Porlier's raid on Santoña in July 1810 (see below).[67] But from the summer onwards naval power played an increasingly important part in the equation. Thus, the month of July saw Porlier come down to the coast, take ship with the British squadron stationed in the Bay of Biscay and seize the town of Santoña in the neighbouring province of Santander. Forced to abandon this conquest in the face of overwhelming numbers, he then spent some time cruising up and down the coast harassing the French and picking up recruits for his command. Returning to Asturias, on 17 October he attacked Gijón, where he was joined by a brigade of regular troops that had been dispatched from La Coruña under Mariano Renovales along with 800 British marines. The French troops in the vicinity being heavily outnumbered, Oviedo was quickly retaken in addition to Gijón, but it was not to be held, for a vengeful Bonnet was soon bearing down on the city with every man that he could muster. Whilst Porlier headed for the hills once more, Renovales therefore re-embarked and sailed for Santander; further mischief was put a stop to only when a violent storm wrecked the expedition, sinking many of the Allied ships and resulting in the death of some 800 troops.[68]

By the end of 1810, then, the fighting in Asturias had settled into a pattern that blended regular and irregular warfare. Nor did 1811 bring much change, the importance of the guerrillas being, if anything, inclined to decline. An attempt on the part of Mariano Renovales to establish a force at Potes on the lines of that commanded by Porlier in the hope of raising the Basque provinces in revolt went badly wrong, whilst the first part of the year saw the latter commander experience not only repeated defeats, but also a major mutiny amongst his men.[69] August, it is true, saw Porlier redeem himself by making a forced mach on Santander, which enabled him to raid the city and take most of the garrison prisoner; but, if Asturias was evacuated in June, it was not because of the guerrillas, but rather because the Spanish forces in Galicia essayed a cautious offensive that secured a minor victory at Cogorderos and forced all the French troops in north-west Spain to march against them. This in turn gave renewed life to the *partidas* of Old Castile and León – it was at this time, for example, that one Lorenzo Aguilar de Toro, an escaped prisoner of war who had got back to his home territory of Zamora, is supposed to have killed no fewer than seventy-one Frenchmen in just four days – but again it is clear that the regular army was as much a combatant in *la guerrilla* as the *partidas*.[70]

If this was true of the north of Spain, it was also true of Andalucía. As we have seen, when the French moved south in January 1810 they soon encountered much irregular resistance. To quote an anonymous intelligence report sent to the Patriot government from Seville, for example: 'In a word, the ferment is spreading to every *pueblo*: war is following the French like a fury, and death and destruction are mounting by the day.'[71] On occasion this resistance reached considerable heights: an ill-judged raid on Murcia that required the use of most of the troops used to garrison the kingdom of Granada allowed the 'mountain flies', as the French called them, to threaten many minor posts and even temporarily to occupy Málaga. The serious nature of the problem is suggested by the draconian decree issued by Marshal Soult (the head of the French forces that had invaded southern Spain) on 8 May 1810. According to this, *pueblos* that failed either to establish a civic guard to defend themselves as the French had ordered, or to put up a fight in the event of the arrival of a *partida*, were made liable to heavy fines, and it was further announced that all those taken in arms would be shot out of hand.[72] Meanwhile, Algodonales and Grazalema were singled out as particularly troublesome centres of resistance and, having been occupied by punitive columns, subjected to sack and massacre – so thorough was the destruction of the former, indeed, that Joseph's *comisario regio* in Seville boasted that it would forever after be a desert.[73]

Yet the real threat to the invaders came not from the efforts of the *serranos* but rather from the regular forces that continued to be scattered around the periphery of the region. Of the forces that had been defeated in the Sierra Morena when the French had burst through the passes there was little enough to be feared (though a few fugitive units ended up in the *serranía* and supported the insurrection there). However, a division of veteran Asturian troops had been sent down from the headquarters of the Army of the Left at Badajoz into the present-day province of Huelva and, under the enterprising leadership of its commander, General Ballesteros, it was soon causing major problems for the French. Thus, defeating columns under Beauregard and Gazan at Ronquillo and Valverde, Ballesteros moved to attack the French forces who had occupied the Condado de Niebla. Furthermore, although he was himself defeated at Zalamea la Real on 15 April, he got away without any great difficulty and established himself in the wilds of the Sierra de Aracena, from whence for many months he was to continue to harass the French. Nor were his men alone. A 700-strong detachment of troops consisting of fragments of half a dozen different units that had managed to escape capture when the French took Seville had succeeded in reaching Ayamonte, where it was taken over by General Francisco Copons y Navía, who had been sent round from Cádiz. Aided by some hastily organised local militias, these men embarked on a series of raids and skirmishes in the Condado de Niebla. And, having again landed from the sea, a full division under General Luis Lacy first struck into the Serranía de Ronda from San Roque, and then re-embarked and sailed round to Huelva, where it drove off the French garrison and advanced some way inland before returning to Cádiz.[74]

All these troops were regulars: Lacy's division, for example, consisted of the line infantry regiments of Murcia and Canarias, the light infantry regiments of Valencia and Campo Mayor, the Ciudad Real regiment of provincial militia and a composite battalion drawn from the Spanish and Walloon Guards.[75] Yet it is clear that their activities belonged entirely to the realm of *la guerrilla*: the Spanish attack at Valverde, for example, had been launched at midnight. As Salmón wrote of Copons' activities in the Condado de Niebla:

> There were . . . no pitched battles between full-scale armies because such forces did not exist, but raids and skirmishes were to be found in abundance. Fiercely contested and very bloody, they showed the French that the spirit and valour that has always characterised Spaniards were not dead . . . As for

> taking control of the district, the enemy could never do so, there being no point within its bounds where they could post themselves without being immediately set upon, harassed and overcome.[76]

For a good example of the sort of action to which Salmón was referring, one might cite the attack launched by Brigadier Miguel de Alzega at the *pueblo* of Castillo de las Guardas on 21 August 1810. The commander of the light infantry regiment known as the Cazadores de Barbastro, Alzega marched his men through the night and fell upon the French at dawn. Bursting into the streets, the Spaniards chased the garrison into the castle, but the defenders showed no signs of giving in and so Alzega ordered a withdrawal, having lost one man killed and another four wounded.[77]

The situation in Andalucía in 1810 is especially interesting because it again raises the question of the limits that can be set to *la guerrilla*. On the frontiers of Galicia we have already seen the deployment of an entire Spanish army in a role that is at the very least closely related to the guerrilla war. And, as for Galicia, so for Andalucía. Around Badajoz there remained in being the Spanish Army of the Left under the Marqués de la Romana. Renamed the Fifth Army in the course of 1810, it engaged in frequent skirmishes with the French troops facing it and in August and September twice struck southwards in the direction of Seville, only to be beaten in minor combats at Villagarcía and Fuente de Cantos. Similar demonstrations, meanwhile, were engaged in by the Spanish forces – the Third Army – that had gathered around Murcia under Blake, at first with rather greater caution, but eventually with an over-confidence and carelessness that produced a substantial defeat at Baza on 4 November.[78] Such petty campaigns are hardly to be equated with the great strategic movements of the war, but they are intimately related to the doings of the *partidas*, the marches and counter-marches of the Third Army once again affording great freedom of action to the insurgents of the Serranía de Ronda and the Alpujarras. Thus, in the absence of the large numbers of troops who had to be sent to deal with Blake, the *serranos* captured Almuñécar and Motril, thereby opening fresh communications with the sea, and even went so far as to attack the city of Granada. More typical of their activities, however, were those engaged in by the followers of José Ruiz Falcón, José Aguilar and José Villalobos: on 3 September Falcón captured a small convoy on the road to Málaga; on 21 October Aguilar defeated a French force outside Ronda; and on 30 October Villalobos wiped out an outpost of forty Polish troops at Alameda de Baza.[79]

To make matters even more complicated, at this point British troops also became involved in *la guerrilla*. At the suggestion of the prominent Spanish general and nobleman the Duque del Infantado, a number of British officers had already been sent into the interior in an attempt to produce a greater degree of organisation among the peasantry. But now the governor of Gibraltar, General Campbell, agreed to a request from the Spanish government to provide troops for an expedition to the coast of Málaga. Along with a Spanish regiment from Ceuta, one and a half battalions of redcoats of the Gibraltar garrison were therefore embarked, together with a provisional battalion of foreign deserters, the plan being for them to land at the little port of Fuengirola and then to seize Málaga. Commanding the whole was Lord Blayney. With a little imagination and foresight on Blayney's part much might have been achieved, but he allowed himself to get bogged down in the siege of Fuengirola's insignificant castle. To make matters worse, rather than hastening to take ship again as soon as the large force of troops that the French sent to relieve the garrison hove into view, he stood and fought, despite the fact that his only complete British battalion had still not landed. With the enemy consisting of some 3,000 men, not to mention the garrison of the castle, which also joined in the fight by means of a violent sally, the result was never in doubt: outnumbered and outfought, Blayney and 200 of his men were captured.[80]

Disastrous though it was, the Fuengirola expedition was the harbinger of many other British raids on stretches of coast occupied by the French. Of particular note in this respect was the naval component of the campaign of Salamanca in the summer of 1812. Whilst aware of the actions of the Spanish guerrillas, Wellington was not inclined solely to trust to their assistance when it came to reducing the considerable numerical superiority that the armies to which he was opposed always possessed in relation to his own forces. To tie down the French Army of the North, he therefore took up the suggestion of the British naval officer Sir Home Popham, that a seaborne *guerrilla* should be waged against the enemy garrisons that dotted the coast of Santander and the Basque provinces. On 17 June 1812, then, a squadron of warships put out from La Coruña under Popham with two battalions of marines. Aided by the forces of the Spanish Seventh Army – the name that had been given to the irregulars of the region – for the next two months Popham launched attack after attack on the French. Lequeitío, Guetaría, Castro-Urdiales, Portugalete, Santander and Bilbao were all assaulted, and in most cases taken, whilst the enemy troops in the region were exhausted by endless marches and counter-marches, for Popham could easily appear before one stronghold, bombard it for a few days and then take ship for another as soon as a relief force hove into view. Despite the occasional defeat, meanwhile, Allied casualties were minimal and, in a development vital for the campaign of 1813, Santander was retained as a permanent base.[81]

Nor were amphibious raids of this sort the only occasions when British forces fought in the 'little war'. In the period 1811–12, indeed, entire divisions were employed in raids that took them deep into the hinterland of Spain. The first of these was the surprise of Arroyomolinos de Montánchez of 28 October 1811. Hearing that a reinforced French division commanded by General Girard had advanced to the Extremaduran town of Cáceres, and thus placed itself far beyond the reach of any possible support, the British General Hill, who was guarding the southern frontier of Portugal with a much larger force, resolved to take the enemy napping. Supported by a few troops from the Spanish Fifth Army, he therefore led 8,000 British and Portuguese regulars across the frontier in a forced march on Girard's communications. In the event the French commander escaped being surrounded, as Hill had hoped, for, discovering that Allied troops were in the area, he withdrew from Cáceres in the nick of time. However, the invaders' retreat was not quick enough, and in the early morning of 28 October they were attacked in camp at the village of Arroyomolinos de Montánchez. Taken completely by surprise, the French were routed with the loss of many prisoners and all their baggage.[82] Meanwhile, it was Hill, too, who was the chief protagonist of the Anglo-Portuguese army's other great raid: it was he who, in May 1812, led a powerful striking force to destroy the vital bridge across the River Tagus at Almaraz, an operation that he accomplished with consummate skill.[83]

In one way or another, then, considerable forces of both Spanish and Anglo-Portuguese troops were drawn into *la guerrilla*. In most instances this was on a purely temporary basis: Hill's corps, for example, had by the autumn of 1812 once more adopted a role that was purely conventional. But amongst the Spaniards in particular, circumstances led a number of regular soldiers to acquire a place amongst the ranks of the guerrillas that was all but permanent.

We must here in the first instance turn once again to the division of General Ballesteros. This force we last met fighting a long series of actions in the mountains of western Andalucía in the first months of 1810, and it in fact continued to engage the French in this district for the next year: early in 1811, for example, Ballesteros seriously embarrassed Marshal Soult by suddenly appearing on his flank and rear just as he was marching northwards from Seville to attack Badajoz. Large forces were detached by the French commander to hunt him down, but the Spanish general – in 1808 a mere officer of the customs guard – skilfully evaded them and drew his pursuers nearly as far as the Portuguese frontier before finally stopping to fight at Villafranca de los Castillejos. The action that followed was no disgrace to the Spaniards, and they then slipped away to Alcoutim, leaving their weary opponents no choice but to retrace their steps in search of Soult, whose attack on Badajoz had in the meantime been much delayed. No sooner had they gone than Ballesteros reappeared, this time defeating the small French garrison left in the Condado de Niebla and briefly threatening Seville.

May 1811 saw a brief return to full-scale campaigning when Ballesteros took part in the bloody battle of Albuera, but his presence there was purely fortuitous, its only reason being that a French force under General Maransin had driven the Spanish general far to the north and forced him to take refuge with the Allied army that had come up to retake Badajoz (Soult's attack had been successful and the fortress had surrendered on 10 March). Returning to Andalucía with the rest of the Spanish forces that had fought at Albuera, Ballesteros then sailed from Ayamonte to Algeciras, where he plunged into the Serranía de Ronda and embarked on a fresh series of raids and skirmishes. Large numbers of French troops being sent against him, he then took shelter at Gibraltar, only to sally out again as soon as the danger was past and pounce on one of the retreating French columns at Bornos, forcing the surrender of an entire battalion of *juramentados* in the process.

After wintering on the coast, having been reinforced by two extra divisions, in April Ballesteros struck north again and again headed for Seville, only to fall back in great haste at what turned out to be a false report of superior French forces heading his way. Self-respect having been restored by the destruction of a small French column at Alhaurín on 14 April, he then again returned to Gibraltar, this time with the enemy very much in hot pursuit. Within weeks, however, he was on the march again: as the French had fallen back for want of provisions, he first engaged in some skirmishes around Ronda and then marched north-west to Bornos, where he fell on the reserves of the troops engaged in the fruitless blockade of Cádiz and gave them a very considerable fright before finally being driven off with some loss. Falling back on his usual refuge of Gibraltar, he licked his wounds for a while, and then set out on a long march through the mountains to Málaga, whose garrison he took completely by surprise and drove into the castle. Tarrying for just long enough to strip the town of such recruits, money and supplies as it could offer, he then tried to get back to the shelter of Gibraltar, only to find that the way was blocked by a large force of French troops. With more enemies coming up in the rear, there was only one hope and that was to head west towards the valley of the Guadalquivir, which move he turned to his advantage by launching a surprise attack on the garrison of Osuna. Having secured yet more plunder, he then marched for the sea again and, getting round the flank of the troops sent to cut him off, by 1 August he was back in touch with Gibraltar.[84]

As Andalucía was evacuated by the French very soon afterwards, the rest of Ballesteros' military career need not concern us. But his operations in the period 1810–12 have been discussed in some detail because they are in reality almost impossible to distinguish from the operations, say, of the division of Espoz y Mina in Navarre. Ballesteros rarely commanded more than 5,000 men, after all, and his tactics throughout were those associated with guerrilla warfare.

Ruses, dawn attacks, surprises, night marches, petty combats, ambushes and the use of rough terrain all figured in his campaigns, and it is also very much the case that he fought only when he enjoyed the advantage of superior numbers. It is, indeed, almost impossible to count the number of times he fell back into Portugal or retired on Gibraltar rather than risk battle with a stronger enemy. Although the soldiers Ballesteros commanded were all regulars, his operations therefore occupy a definite place in the history of the 'little war'. Lowly customs guard as he was, he also had far more in common with many guerrilla commanders than with most of his fellow generals. Indeed, in Juan López Campillo, a fellow *resguardo* officer from the neighbouring province of Santander, he possessed almost an exact counterpart in their ranks, whilst his own elevation to the ranks of the *generalato* was entirely owing to the prodigality with which the Junta of Asturias had showered commissions on its adherents in 1808. And, last but not least, both the general and his men shared many of the proclivities that we shall come to associate with their more irregular counterparts. To quote a British liaison officer who served with Ballesteros' division:

> Of all the unworthies produced by Spain during this war (and God knows there were plenty of them), this man was the greatest impostor and charlatan . . . He certainly kept a body of men together, but they proved only a curse to the inhabitants . . . [and] appeared to be composed of the debris of defeated and dispersed armies, men who would not fight, yet reassembled to obtain food because they were too idle or too dissipated to work. Whenever the French retired, the Spaniards followed, composing and reciting songs of victory, but at too respectable a distance to disquiet the enemy. If the French . . . attempted to pursue them, they soon found how vain was the undertaking.[85]

To separate Ballesteros from the 'little war' is therefore impossible, but, for all that, neither he nor his men can really be described as guerrillas: regular soldiers, they had simply been detached from their normal duties for a while and, with the French gone from Andalucía, they were soon to return to more conventional operations. And even in the course of their normal duties, soldiers might easily become involved in guerrilla warfare. In a few instances, such as the case of Juan Díaz Porlier, who received the assistance of the old Laredo provincial militia regiment, regular units were formally assigned to the command of guerrilla commanders in an attempt to boost their potential.

But let us look at the far more common experiences of the sort encapsulated by the skirmishes that took place in the district of Extremadura known as the Tierra de Barros in May 1810. On 9 May a detachment of soldiers drawn from the garrison of the town of Feria ambushed a French force that had been sent to pick up a consignment of supplies from the town of Fuente del Maestre. Caught unawares and attacked from both sides, the Frenchmen beat a hasty retreat, leaving the road strewn with their dead and wounded.[86] In response the French drove the Spaniards from Feria, but the commander of the garrison, Pablo Morillo, immediately counter-attacked, forcing the enemy troops to withdraw into the castle and burning such of their supplies as he could not carry away, before finally beating a hasty retreat in the direction of Jerez de los Caballeros.[87] With the French making no effort to pursue him, a week later he attacked again with much the same result.[88] A month later Morillo was back in action again, this time at Burguillos, where he attacked a French column advancing from Zafra and succeeded in forcing it to retreat.[89] And finally, after a long night march in pouring rain, at dawn on 7 September Morillo attacked Fuente Ovejuna at the head of two battalions of line infantry. The details of this fight are worth recording as they show the similarity between the *modus operandi* of the guerrillas and that of the regulars. Morillo and his men charged into the town to discover that the French garrison of 108 men were barricaded inside a large house and the town's granary. Unable to storm the buildings, Morillo piled numerous barrels of wet straw against them and ordered them to be set on fire. Driven out by the choking smoke, the French then made a dash for the parish church and managed to get inside, only for the latter to be fired as well, whereupon they surrendered, having lost fourteen dead and sixteen wounded.[90]

At least Morillo did at one point early in the war command a band of irregulars. Many other figures who are generally represented as having been guerrillas, however, never merited the description at all. Pride of place here must probably go to the Leonese leader, Julián Sánchez García: in frequent contact with Wellington's army, he is inevitably the *cabecilla* who figures most prominently in British memoirs. A peasant from the *pueblo* of Muñoz on the road from Ciudad Rodrigo to Salamanca, Sánchez was thirty-four in 1808 and had served from 1793 to 1801 as a soldier in the Mallorca line infantry regiment. For reasons of which we know nothing, on 15 August 1808 he enlisted in the militia that had been raised to defend Ciudad Rodrigo in the aftermath of the uprising. Soon promoted to the rank of sergeant, he was given command of a small picket of cavalry. The arrival of French troops in the vicinity of the fortress early in 1809 therefore involved him in a series of minor skirmishes that brought him a commission as an *alférez*. By the summer he was in command of a full squadron of cavalry – the genesis of what was to become the First Regiment of Lancers of Castile – and at the head of these men on 21 June he defeated a much stronger party of French dragoons at Almeida de Sayago. Many other such raids followed, with Sánchez, who was now a brevet captain, undoubtedly enjoying a great deal of independence.

Range far and wide though he and his men did, however, there was never any question as to Sánchez's dependence on the army that was now based at Ciudad Rodrigo under the Duque del Parque: indeed, when Del Parque went on the offensive in October, Sánchez and his lancers were called in to assist with reconnaissance and outpost duty. Badly beaten at Alba de Tormes, Del Parque then went into winter quarters on the borders of León and Extremadura, and Sánchez in the meantime busied himself with such tasks as rounding up deserters, gathering in supplies and skirmishing with the French forces based at Salamanca. In the spring, though, Del Parque was replaced by La Romana, who took the army south to Badajoz. Left behind, Sánchez and his men were formally attached to the garrison of Ciudad Rodrigo, in which capacity they fought a series of actions with the enemy troops now closing in on the city. Here and there minor successes were obtained, but no amount of skirmishing could prevent the French from commencing siege operations. As cavalry were of only limited use in this situation, the governor, Andrés Pérez de Herrasti, ordered Sánchez to break out of the city, which he did by means of a sudden charge launched at one o'clock in the morning on 23 June 1810.[91]

The army to which he had belonged having completely left the area, Sánchez was effectively a law unto himself for most of the next year, and as such it might be thought that he now had to all intents and purposes become a guerrilla. He took part in no regular campaigns, but rather confined himself to harassing the communications of the French army that had invaded Portugal under Marshal Massena following the fall of Ciudad Rodrigo. To quote an anonymous staff officer attached to the headquarters of the Spanish Fifth Army in the spring of 1811, for example: 'The bands that are at the orders of Don Julián Sánchez in Castile have made . . . a continuous massacre of the unfortunate Frenchmen who have been trying to escape from Portugal.'[92] Raids and ambushes were very much the order of the day, whilst the troops whom the Anglo-Portuguese army encountered when they arrived back on the frontier in March 1811 had all the appearances of being an irregular force. 'A more verminous-looking set of fellows you never beheld', wrote William Bragge, whilst Charles Boutflower remarked, 'A Spaniard well-known by the name of Don Julián was here yesterday . . . His followers sometimes amount to 1,000; at others he cannot muster fifty. They make a great deal by plunder, and absent themselves for the purpose of spending their money, which having done they again join his standard.'[93] Such, too, is very much the impression that is obtained from French accounts. Marbot, for example, describes his men as 'irregular bands . . . who were quite unfit to resist troops of the line'.[94] But the reality was rather different. Whilst Sánchez's style was certainly that of an irregular – nicknamed El Charro, he affected a French shako with the imperial eagle worn upside down – he throughout remained both an officer of the regular army and an agent of La Romana, who in fact ordered him to raise a second regiment of cavalry, provided him with a troop of horse artillery and eventually secured him the rank of brigadier. At the same time, the independent role of earlier years vanished: although outpost duty and reconnaisance remained the roles in which his troops were most commonly employed, Sánchez's brigade fought with Wellington in the Salamanca campaign and ended the war as part of the garrison of Ciudad Rodrigo.[95]

If the forces of El Charro constitute the best-known example, various other *partidas* also turn out in reality to have been composed of troops belonging to the regular army. For two further examples we have only to turn to Aragón. Set up in the summer of 1809, for example, the band of Pedro Villacampa is at first sight hard to distinguish from, say, those of El Empecinado or Espoz y Mina. Typical of its actions, for example, was its attack on Teruel on 8 March 1810, together with the fighting that followed. Suddenly appearing outside the town, Villacampa drove the garrison back into the complex of fortified convents that it had converted into a makeshift citadel. Leaving some of his men to pin down the defenders, he then turned north and annihilated a small relief column that he encountered at Caudé, before finally pouncing on the garrison of Alventosa.[96] Villacampa even referred to himself as a guerrilla, as witness, for example, a call for volunteers that he issued in the spring of 1810.[97] Yet in reality he was a regular officer who had been taken prisoner in the siege of Zaragoza. After managing to escape, he had been sent out by the local Spanish commander, General Blake, to foment popular resistance in Aragón. His forces consisted of the regiment of which he was himself colonel, the remnants of the line regiments of Soria and La Princesa, which had escaped a Spanish defeat at Santander and made an epic march across occupied Spain in search of safety, and a unit of new levies raised by the Junta of Molina.[98]

Even more dubious, meanwhile, is the case of another Aragonese commander, Felipe Perena. Villacampa might just qualify as a guerrilla – he was sent out specifically to conduct irregular operations – but the same cannot be said of Perena. Perena was a regular officer who had in 1808 been chasing bandits, and had been appointed by José Palafox to be the governor of Huesca. Although he joined *la guerrilla* in the wake of the fall of Zaragoza, it was for want of strength to do anything else. In the raids and skirmishes that followed he showed some talent – true, it was forces under his command that in May 1809 succeeded in capturing 600 French troops who had become trapped on the wrong side of the River Cinca by a sudden flood – but his 'band' turns out to have been none other than a regiment of volunteers raised in 1808. Indeed, it was as regular troops that his men met their end: caught up in the French offensive against Lérida in 1810, they were overwhelmed at Balaguer, and the few men who remained in the ranks after this defeat were marched into captivity when the fortress finally surrendered.[99]

The distinction between the regular and irregular elements of *la guerrilla* is often blurred. For example, regular units involved in the struggle might very easily pick up recruits from the same sources as the *partidas*. This was particularly true of units that disappeared into the hills for long periods. As a senior official in the Ministry of State wrote to his chief, Bardaji, 'A great part of Zayas' deserters are with the insurgent Ballesteros.'[100] Yet such points of congruence should not be exaggerated. By 1812 Ballesteros' division may have come to resemble that, say, of Espoz y Mina, but in essence they remained different phenomena. On the other hand, however, they were also engaged in the same struggle. Nor is this surprising, for by 1811 the regular army had been so ground down that, as one British officer put it, it was 'unfit for anything more than mere guerrilla warfare'.[101] From this point – the realisation that *la guerrilla* was the work not just of bands of armed civilians, but of a wide range of forces that included elements of the regular armies of Britain, Spain and Portugal alike – it follows that it is possible to reassess the popular struggle against the French without being constantly tripped up by arguments that the guerrillas played a vital role in the defeat of the Napoleonic invaders. Favoured by factors of strategy and geography that rendered the French zone of occupation uniquely vulnerable to attack, the 'little war' *per se* may well have played such a role, but proof of the involvement of many different forces in the struggle means that it is no longer necessary to pay unreserved homage to all its different participants. No longer can it be taboo to suggest that Espoz y Mina, El Empecinado and the rest were anything but pillars of Spain's independence. And, by the same token, no longer can admirers of the guerrillas bolster their arguments by reference to actions for which in reality their heroes can take no credit. If room has thereby been created for a reassessment of the guerrillas, the doubts, concerns and divisions of opinion that have already been revealed in our survey of the historiography suggest that that reassessment cannot come too soon. Add to these the many contradictions in the Spanish struggle against Napoleon that will be revealed in the next chapter, and the need for such a reassessment will come to seem still greater.

3
The Guerrillas in Context

> Patriotism . . . resounds from the high Pyrenees to the coasts of Andalucia . . . Thousands of combatants are coming forward . . . greed and egotism have been silenced, and a thousand sacrifices are providing riches for the needs of the state.[1]

These words encapsulate one of the abiding images of the history of modern Spain: the idea that when Napoleon overthrew the Bourbon dynasty in 1808, he found himself confronted by the resistance of the proverbial people numerous and armed, and, what is more, a people numerous and armed that threw itself into battle with a ferocity and determination that have rarely been surpassed. To quote Gabriel Lovett, 'All the energies of unoccupied Spain were directed toward one objective, beating back the invaders.'[2] So often has this idea been repeated, indeed, that it is impossible to find a work on either Napoleon, the Peninsular War or the history of modern Spain that does not simply take it as read. At the same time, it is, of course, the very foundation of the 'heroic' view of the guerrillas, for, without total popular support for the struggle, the *partidas* would neither have come into being nor survived for very long. And, by the same token, like the operational history of the 'little war', it is a theme that must clearly be opened up for discussion if the guerrillas are to be properly reassessed: if the Spanish people really were panting for war and revenge, it would clearly be difficult to bring into question the patriotism of the *partidas*. Yet it would be surprising if the traditional view were to prove convincing. Indeed, in line with developments in the treatment of other areas of Europe, the historiography of Napoleonic Spain has begun to undergo something of a revolution. Thus, a new generation of writers has already begun to generate a picture of the struggle against Napoleon that is very different from its traditional predecessor.[3] According to such authors, popular enthusiasm for the war was minimal, although as yet their work has largely been confined to regional analyses. What is lacking is a study on a national scale, and it is this that the following chapter will seek to provide.

In embarking on a critical reassessment of the Spanish war effort, the historian is immediately faced with a major problem in that the struggle began with a series of episodes that appear to confirm the idea that the populace rushed into battle against Napoleon. In La Mancha, for example, the invaders found themselves assailed on all sides by bands of angry peasants who committed the most appalling atrocities against any Frenchmen unlucky enough to fall into their hands. In Catalonia the popular militias known as the *somatenes* flocked to arms and inflicted an embarrassing reverse on the French at the pass of El Bruch. And, above all, at Zaragoza the armed citizenry manned the walls, beat back a major assault and refused to give in even when the French finally penetrated their defences.[4] Images of heroism, then, were to be found in abundance, but, whilst the problem cannot just be ducked, it would be wrong to allow these episodes to stand in the way of attempts at revision. Particularly helpful here is what Raymond Carr called 'a political great fear'.[5]

The origins of this phenomenon may be traced to the revolt of 2 May 1808 in Madrid. In this affair it was the Spaniards who struck the first blows, but this was not the story that reached the rest of the country. Carried by terrified fugitives seeking shelter with friends and family in the provinces, the tale grew in the telling until it was believed that the French had not only slaughtered thousands of innocent civilians, but also that they had deliberately set out to massacre the populace. For an example of the spirit in which the news was received, one might cite the city of Zaragoza, whose experience of the first three decades of the nineteenth century was chronicled in great detail by one Faustino Casamayor. Thus for 5 May 1808 his journal read as follows:

> Today's post brought the disagreeable news of the misfortunes suffered by the gallant inhabitants of Madrid on account of the inhuman fury of the French commander, Murat . . . No sooner had it arrived than there was an extraordinary meeting of the town council, at which it was decided to warn the public of what had taken place and in addition to take precautions against the chance of anything of the sort happening at Zaragoza. All this plunged the populace into great fear, and whipped up great anger against . . . the French.[6]

With many people already unsettled by the absence of the royal family (in whose protection the humbler elements of the population reposed much faith), taking up arms seemed an immediate necessity. Typical, perhaps, was the response of Ciudad Rodrigo, where news of the Dos de Mayo led the populace to man the walls in panic in expectation of an immediate attack. When nothing happened, the excitement subsided, but even so, the junta formed in the wake of the uprising had no difficulty in becoming a new militia consisting of five battalions of infantry, three companies of artillery and a regiment of cavalry.[7]

This Spanish 'great fear' was reinforced by a number of other factors. Not the least of these was the influence of religion, the atmosphere of crisis producing outbreaks of veritable hysteria. Thus, in the Asturian shrine of Covadonga large drops of sweat were seen to trickle down the face of Our Lady of Battles, whilst at Santiago de Compostela the shrine of Saint James was heard to ring with the clash of arms.[8] It is, however, Zaragoza that provides us with the most direct evidence of the phenomenon:

> At about twelve o'clock [on 17 May] . . . a number of people began to say that they could see a palm tree surmounted by a crown in the sky above the dome of the shrine of Nuestra Señora del Pilar . . . At this stupendous news everyone began to invoke Our Lady and cry, 'A miracle! A miracle!', whilst at the same time it was claimed that a similar sight had been seen inside the shrine itself. At this the excitement grew even greater, and the *santa capilla* was soon resounding to the cry of people imploring the powerful assistance of the Virgin.[9]

As the days passed so the hysteria grew, reaching its climax in the wake of the national revolt provoked by the news that Fernando VII had been dethroned by Napoleon. Fear of massacre was not the only cause, however. In Manresa, for instance, the rising was precipitated by fears that 'we were going . . . to end up not only stripped of Church and King but serving [Napoleon] God knows where'.[10] Also instrumental was the Spanish Church, much of which was bitterly opposed to Revolution and emperor alike. As the French apothecary Sebastian Blaze remembered:

> The monks skilfully employed the influence which they still enjoyed over Spanish credulity . . . to inflame the populace and exacerbate the implacable hatred with which they already regarded us . . . In this fashion they encouraged a naturally cruel and barbarous people to commit the most revolting crimes with a clear conscience. They accused us of being Jews, heretics, sorcerers . . . As a result, just to be a Frenchman became a crime in the eyes of the country.[11]

Although the sermon was probably mightier than the pen when it came to lambasting the French, mention should also be made here of the blizzard of pamphlets, letters, poems, odes, manifestos, exhortations, proclamations and calls to arms that was called forth by the insurrection. The themes of this campaign – hymns to Spanish heroism, panegyrics on Fernando VII, denunciations of Napoleon and the hated royal favourite Manuel de Godoy, mockery of

Joseph Bonaparte, promises of rapid victory and stories of French atrocities – are so well known that to detail them here seems pointless. But, in brief, there was plenty to stir the fear of the populace, Napoleon being portrayed as a new Attila the Hun, the French army as a bloodthirsty rabble and the Dos de Mayo as the acme of massacre. The mamelukes of the Imperial Guard who formed Murat's personal bodyguard, for example, were supposed to have stripped eleven prisoners naked, thrown them in a pit and then hacked them to pieces.[12]

Not surprisingly, then, by the end of May the streets and squares had been gripped by panic. At Ronda the house of the nephew of the victor of Bailén, General Castaños, was stormed on the pretext that a guillotine had been hidden there; at the Galician town of Villalba, 8 June saw rumours suddenly surface to the effect that 8,000 Frenchmen were marching on the town, burning and killing everything they came across, with the result that the entire population stood to arms with whatever weapons they could muster; at La Coruña news that the French were landing from the sea brought an attempt to lynch some prisoners incarcerated in the town's gaol on the grounds that they were traitors; and at Ribadeo stories that 6,000 enemy troops had sacked nearby Castroverde produced threats that the mob would burn down the homes of the local junta unless it was allowed to kill a solitary French aide-de-camp who had just arrived in the town.[13] Spy mania, too, was common: an unfortunate Italian mercenary was thrown in prison for no better reason than the fact that he had served the French as an interpreter. Meanwhile, one officer, sent to raise the upper Pisuerga valley in revolt, only saved himself from being lynched by the mob by climbing on to the roof of the inn in which he was staying, from which predicament he was somewhat ignominiously rescued by the fortuitous arrival of a French cavalry patrol.[14] Enemy citizens, too, were put to death, as, for example, in Málaga, where the French consul was killed on 20 June 1808, and Valencia, where an ambitious friar named Baltasar Calvo instigated the murder of no fewer than 380 French merchants and their families.[15] Most revealing of all, though, are the demands that confronted the *alcalde mayor* of Almaraz:

> We want to kill someone, Sir. They have killed one person in Trujillo, one or two more in Badajoz and someone else in Mérida, and we do not want to be left behind. Sir, we want to kill a traitor.[16]

With feelings so inflamed, we do not need to look very far to explain the desperate resistance that the French encountered when they first appeared before the walls of certain towns (caution is needed with regard to such stories, though: the heroic attempt to defend Zamora in January 1809 mentioned by both Gómez de Arteche and Oman was in 1913 shown by a conscientious local historian to have been a fabrication got up by the *ayuntamiento* to ingratiate itself with Fernando VII[17]). Thus, the populace genuinely thought that their last hour had come, whilst the defence of their own homes was a cause that was easy to understand and identify with.

It is worth pointing out, however, that such acts of mass resistance were often carefully choreographed: in Zaragoza – by far the most dramatic case – as dictator of the city José Palafox from the start adopted a demagogic manner that became ever more accentuated, whilst he was careful to surround himself with popular heroes such as Jorge Ibort, Santiago Sas and Agustina Zaragoza Domenech. At the same time mention might be made of the persistent stories that were in circulation concerning the use of terror to keep the defenders at their posts. In addition, the scenes witnessed in Zaragoza became increasingly rare as the war wore on, for the terror that the French evoked in the first months of the war proved short-lived. Despite desperate efforts on the part of the Junta Central to organise every *pueblo* for house-to-house defence in the style of Zaragoza, when the French stormed across the Sierra Morena in January 1810 the response was almost everywhere one of apathy. A call for volunteers to defend the town of Huelva, for example, produced just thirty-six men, whilst in Jaén a similar appeal failed to secure a single man.[18]

Even when there existed a willingness to defend hearth and home, this was not the same as identification with the war. There was some voluntary enlistment in the ranks of the army and the new regiments being established by many of the provincial juntas, but neither patriotism nor fear seems to have played much part in bringing in recruits. The only exception to the rule were students: in Santiago de Compostela, for example, the entire university presented itself to the town's newly formed junta and asked to join up, whilst other cities provided many individual recruits (examples include a young Galician studying in Madrid named José Salgado, a doctor's son from Leciñena named Matías Calvo, the future Carlist leader Tomás de Zumalacárregui and, most famously, the guerrilla commander Martín Javier Mina y Larrea).[19] But most of the men who came forward did so for reasons that had nothing to do with the political situation.

One factor was clearly compulsion on the part of the *amo*. On 21 July 1808, for example, the Junta of Vigo reported that it had issued a call for volunteers that had secured 147 young men, of whom many were dependants of leading citizens of the town.[20] Also important was poverty. Spain, as we shall see, was in desperate straits in 1808, whilst the rising had occurred at a point in the agricultural year when most day-labourers were out of work. Nor did it help that in March and April unseasonably heavy rain had reduced the work available in the fields and done much damage to the crops. Military service was therefore a welcome opportunity to earn a few days' pay, especially as the money on offer was frequently extremely generous. As Sir Brent Spencer observed of Seville, for example, 'The pay allowed these new levies . . . is perhaps imprudently large. I understand they have daily . . . four *reales*, which is more than double what the old regular troops receive.'[21] Nor was this an end to the largesse available, for recruits were also sometimes paid a substantial bounty. As Casamayor noted in his journal on 14 November 1808, 'Today saw the publication of an order issued by the new Duke of Hijar in which he promised the sum of two *reales* to any of his vassals who would take up arms.'[22]

But taking up arms was clearly an activity embarked upon only with certain provisos. Service was envisaged in the first place as being only a short-term commitment, in the second as something that would very much be restricted to hearth and home, and in the third as an experience that would not put the recruit on the same level as the despised and hated soldiery of the Bourbon army. There was, indeed, a sense of play-acting about the whole business. Let us quote, for example, the *comandante de armas* of Marín, Eugenio Iglesias:

> On the morning of the 4th the post arrived with the news . . . that on all sides volunteers were coming forward . . . to fight in the war that had just been declared against France. At about ten o'clock a group of inhabitants appeared in front of my house with a drum and a flag bearing the arms of Spain, and obliged me to accompany them to the fort of San Fernando, where they raised the flag with due ceremony . . . Leaving it flying there, they then marched out . . . to the sound of the drum amidst repeated cheers for Fernando VII, having told me that they would come back at four o'clock . . . Just as they had said, they came back in the afternoon armed with muskets, fowling pieces and blunderbusses, and, taking the flag, asked me to place myself at their head, after which we marched through the streets to the church of the Virgen del Pilar, where the flag was laid upon the altar and the rosary recited by all those present with the greatest devotion.[23]

All too soon, however, the excitement began to wear off. To the horror of the volunteers, indeed, they discovered that fighting the French meant something other than drawing their pay, parading through the streets of their home towns and hunting down spies and traitors – that, in short, the unspoken assumptions concerning their enlistment would not be honoured. In consequence, the war had hardly started before desertion became an issue.[24] In any case, there were never enough volunteers, particularly in provinces such as Galicia, where military service was habitually identified with local home guards (in June 1808, for example, the *alarma* of Orense alone amounted to 15,680 men organised into 147 companies; by contrast, so few recruits came forward for the army that it was only possible to raise two new regiments[25]). As a result, the new authorities who had emerged from the uprising were very quickly forced to move to conscription. Broadly speaking, all men between sixteen and forty were declared to be eligible for military service, regardless of status (an important concession since, as we shall see, the existing conscription regulations exempted all Spain's million-strong nobility). However, it was promised, first, that married men would not be taken until the supply of bachelors and widowers without children had been exhausted; and second, that any volunteers produced by a *pueblo* would be set against its quota.[26] As for the number of men that were needed, as one example we might take Galicia, where 4 June 1808 saw the announcement of a *quinta* of 40,000 men.[27] Nor was relief to be sought from the new central government formed at Aranjuez, known as the Junta Central, for in October it announced the call-up of an unprecedented 400,000 men.[28]

These measures place the massive propaganda campaign that accompanied the war against Napoleon in a new light. Thus, the populace was not just being energised to fight the French, but also conditioned to accept measures that the Bourbons would not even have dreamed of. As Godoy wrote of the war against France of 1793–95, for example, 'The idea of a general levy of troops was not adopted and could never have entered a rational mind, first, because no civilised nation had set such an example and, second, because the encumberance and enormous expense of such a multitude set in motion would have at one and the same time paralysed them and endangered their efficiency.'[29] Recognising the extreme nature of their demands, the Patriot authorities therefore did everything that they could to encourage support for the struggle. Their propaganda was often tailored, however crudely, to a popular audience – one might cite here the use of the style known as *costumbrismo*, and the constant stress that was placed on the idea that Napoleon's chief intention was to conscript all Spain's young men into his armies – whilst events of public importance called forth large-scale celebrations that included comic operas, bullfights and firework displays.[30] On occasion, such was the largesse displayed by the authorities that it amounted to almost open bribery: on receipt of the news of the victory of Talavera, for example, the governor of Ayamonte ordered the distribution of 20 *reales* to every prisoner in the town's gaol, threw a dinner for twelve beggars, had his staff give 4 *reales* to every member of the town's poor and threw money from his balcony to the crowd.[31]

According to the official line, all was well: the people were lined up behind the struggle and incapable of riot and disorder.[32] But, in fact, the authorities were living a nightmare. As Salmón put it, 'When the populace is out of control, there are no reins that can control it, the contagion of licence and disorder spreading with such speed that the common people come to be the sole dictator. What ills did we not suffer as a result of this upset!'[33] Thus, in many regions the rising was accompanied by outbreaks of rioting that, whilst ostensibly the result of hatred of the French, were redolent of a more general attack on wealth, privilege and authority. 'Very soon', warned one observer, 'the poor will be sovereign, and eliminate rich and French alike.'[34] Indeed, the panic that marked the first days of the war was often a cover for, or at least intimately connected with, something else altogether. Arrested as a traitor after the battle of Bailén on the specious allegation that he had plotted with one of Castaños' divisional commanders to effect the escape of the French, the *alcalde mayor* of Mengíbar was found by an official enquiry to have been persecuted on account of 'an excess of the . . . temerity and pride [typical] of a man of wealth and prominence'.[35] And in Galicia the *ayuntamiento* of El Ferrol complained, 'On the pretext of a variety of rumours, both real and invented, [the mob] has reached the extreme of attacking and insulting the chief authorities, and committing robberies, murders and other lamentable actions of the sort that are always produced by any outbreak of tumult.'[36] In the words of the Junta of Santiago de Compostela, meanwhile:

> On a number of occasions when rumours have gone round that the French were about to attack us . . . the people have rioted. We have no doubt that a number of these stories, all of which have been both silly and unfounded, had their origin in Spaniards who are French at heart and by these means wanted to frighten the populace and spread disorder.[37]

Such stories of French agents deluding simple countryfolk might have comforted some of the more vapid members of the juntas, but they hardly reflected the truth. In fact, the populace was on the move. Examples of unrest are widespread, but perhaps the most dramatic comes from Castellón de la Plana:

> On 19 June [1808] . . . a gang of malcontents assembled . . . in the town, and ran through the streets, shouting, 'Long live the King, the Fatherland and the Faith! Death to the traitors!', and disturbing the public peace. Having murdered the governor, Coronel Don Pedro Lobo, and a landowner named Félix de Jiménez, they followed these execrable excesses with an attempt on the life of the commissary, Don José Ramón de Santi . . . In addition, the insurgents broke into the Capuchin nunnery, and freed all the prisoners in the public gaols by force.[38]

Nor did the troubles subside. To take just two examples, in Oviedo and Don Benito the autumn saw fully fledged agrarian risings. Of events in the latter *pueblo* we have a particularly interesting description:

> The town of Don Benito . . . has been in the most deplorable condition ever since . . . a number of discontented porters, day-labourers and artisans – men whose ignorance and immorality always incline them to the worst – launched a furious attack . . . on the . . . town council at the very moment

> when the list of those eligible to be chosen for the defence of the fatherland was being drawn up, demanding land and crying that only the people with anything to lose should go to war. This outrage, which ended in the precipitate flight of the . . . council, which would otherwise have been murdered, has been followed by others which have caused respectable inhabitants the utmost consternation. Continually insulted . . . by these malignants, they have had to watch them . . . occupying the pastures rented out by their neighbours in the most disorderly fashion . . . These they have ploughed and harrowed, whilst in the meantime threatening anyone who opposed them with death.[39]

To understand these issues, we need to think a little more about both Spanish society at the end of the *antiguo régimen* and the background to the struggle against Napoleon. Radicalised by a disastrous war that had wrought considerable damage on large sections of the economy, a series of epidemics and natural disasters, a variety of structural problems that were undermining the livelihood of different segments of its ranks and a programme of reform that had not only produced much disruption in the countryside but also threatened a wide range of popular customs, the populace had been becoming more and more restive prior to 1808. This was particularly the case, given the fact that the lot of the common people was extremely harsh at the best of times: in the countryside, for example, the vast majority of *campesinos* were either landless day-labourers who earned miserable wages, endured long periods of seasonal unemployment and were in general utterly at the mercy of the *caciques*, or desperately poor tenant farmers who suffered from a range of problems embracing such issues as usury, rack-renting and insufficient land. Particularly in Valencia, where the tensions that it provoked were especially strong, *señorialismo* was being challenged by many communities, whilst there had been numerous bread riots and peasant risings.[40] In consequence, the sudden succession to the throne of Fernando VII in March 1808 had been greeted with great excitement, just as his overthrow by the French had caused genuine dismay, but this did not in itself mean that the *populacho* were necessarily devoted to the person of the new monarch, nor to the *antiguo régimen*. Fernando having been presented to them by Godoy's opponents as a kind of latter-day Prince Charming who would put all things to rights and usher in a golden age of peace and prosperity, their real loyalty was rather to a paradise in which they would no longer be subject to the demands of Church, state and *señor*. Willing enough to riot against the representatives of *godoyismo*, they therefore had no desire to be marched off to fight against the French, especially as military service had always been particularly hated.[41] Indeed, as one perceptive British officer noted of the Spanish peasantry, 'had they been permitted to live in peace, it would have been a matter of the greatest indifference to them whether their king was Joseph, Ferdinand or the ghost of Don Quijote'.[42] As for the propertied classes, they had become so alienated that on occasion the rest of the populace actually joined with the French soldiery in the sack of their homes, an excellent example of such an incident occurring after the battle of Medina de Río Seco in July 1808.[43]

What made this situation all the more dangerous was the fact that the Patriot authorities were drawn almost entirely from *los de siempre*. Thus the structure of power and authority had been little altered by the uprising. Indeed, in local and provincial juntas alike, the Bourbon élites remained firmly in control: in Murcia, for instance, the junta consisted of the bishop, an archdeacon, two priors, seven members of the old *ayuntamiento*, two of the city's magistrates, five prominent members of the local aristocracy and five serving or retired army or navy officers, all of them of high rank. In Ciudad Rodrigo the junta comprised nine serving officers, including the pre-war deputy governor and the commanders of all the units that had made up the garrison, five retired officers, of whom two were brigadiers and one an erstwhile *regidor perpetuo*, a local nobleman possessed of a position at court, the local Intendente del Ejército, two officials of the old *consejos* and eighteen members of the local clergy, including the bishop. And the junta in Zamora comprised two representatives of the *ayuntamiento*, the three most senior officers of the garrison, the dean of the cathedral, the prior of the monastery of San Jerónimo, two representatives of the nobility and two representatives of the *vecinos honrados*.[44] In a few places lip-service was initially paid to the need to grant some representation to the populace through the co-option of *de facto* 'tribunes of the people', but the figures who secured the positions concerned were for the most part unsavoury adventurers, and within a matter of weeks they had almost all been picked off and in some cases imprisoned.[45]

Absolutely terrified, the élites embarked on a programme of repression: indeed, it is quite clear that in a number of cities the only reason that they had established juntas was fear of the mob.[46] All round the country, then, we see frantic efforts to maintain order, as in Galicia, where the juntas established police commissions and armed security forces, and issued strict orders that no one should be allowed to travel without first obtaining a passport; in Granada, where a proclamation of 24 June 1808 banned all public gatherings, forbade the carrying of arms of any sort and threatened anyone who challenged the authorities with the death penalty; and in Valencia, where special militia companies were set up to maintain order, the existing anti-bandit company increased by 400 men, the use of firearms banned except on official service, and all householders admonished to make certain that no one for whom they were responsible disturbed the public peace.[47] At the same time even tiny numbers of regular troops were regarded as valuable allies, several of Galicia's local juntas making desperate efforts to hang on to detachments of soldiers that happened to be near by at the time of the uprising.[48] And finally, the Junta Central not only ordered the formation of a nationwide *milicia honrada* that was recruited from the propertied classes, placed under the control of the local authorities and charged with the task of patrolling the countryside, guarding the streets and repressing outbreaks of disorder, but issued the most draconian orders with respect to the treatment of rioters.[49]

Whilst trying to overawe the populace, the new authorities at the same time made great efforts to force it to accept its station in life. Nowhere is this more visible than in Cádiz, where one observer decribed 'the lower class of the people' as 'layabouts who are lacking in industry and . . . much inclined to disturb the peace'.[50] Thus, in a proclamation of 16 January 1809, whilst enjoining the population to be assiduous in the practice of its religion and the education of its children and moral in its lifestyle, the junta announced that '*habitués* of prohibited games . . . layabouts . . . women of no pride . . . blasphemers, malcontents, drunks, and those who constantly engage in indecent talk' would be fined, imprisoned or sent to penal colonies.[51] Following serious riots in February 1809 (see below, p. 76), meanwhile, the ecclesiastical authorities were instructed to enlighten 'the common people of this town, which is . . . governed on the one hand by agitators and on the other by drunkenness, robbery and other detestable disorders'.[52] Some days earlier, meanwhile, the *alcalde mayor* had issued an order stating, first, that all minors of either sex who were found alone on the streets on whatever pretext, begging included, were to be arrested, and with them their parents, and, second, that any woman who was involved in any sort of disorderly gathering was to be placed in solitary confinement, the very fact that she had seen fit to be present clearly showing that she could not be 'a lady worthy of appreciation and respect'.[53] And, last but not least, we have a very similar proclamation that appeared in July of the same year that ordered the immediate arrest of not just all 'idlers, layabouts, vagrants . . . women of no repute, and suspicious persons', but also 'all those who try to hide their vagrancy by pretending to be peddlars or hawkers'. As if all this was not enough, meanwhile, blasphemy, indecency, seditious talk, gaming and the possession of knives and pistols were all strictly prohibited; the strictest regulations imposed on such activities as letting rooms; and taverners enjoined not to let their customers sit around for too long.[54]

In a country where many regions were characterised by chronic underemployment, and where normal economic life had all but broken down, this programme was at the very least dangerously provocative: to attack pedlars and vagrants, for example, was to attack some of the few means by which the poor could hope to make a living. But, as if all this was not bad enough, fuel was added to the flames by the use that the *pudientes* made of their power. Perhaps typical was isolated Paymogo, of which a commissioner sent by the Junta Central wrote:

> Governed by a number of young men . . . at the say-so of those elements who can play the role of *caciques*, the town has been reduced to the most dreadful chaos . . . Your Majesty must understand that the original sin of such places consists of three points: who is going to rule, who is going to rob the most, and who is going to pay the least.[55]

Had the *caciques* proved willing to sacrifice themselves for the *patria*, then, some of the edge might have been taken off the situation, but this was not the case. On the contrary, in many *pueblos*, such as Socuéllamos, there were complaints of 'the bad example that has been set by the . . . *poderosos*, who . . . are living . . . a life of leisure and . . . impropriety'.[56] By all accounts, indeed, abuses of power were widespread. The commonalty could, for example, be blackmailed: one officer involved in the recruitment process was arrested for demanding 64 *reales* from one of the inhabitants of Osuna, on pain of conscription.[57] There were many instances of corruption: at León the father of a fugitive Guardia de Corps sold his son's horse – the property of the Spanish state – to the local provincial junta for 2,000 *reales*; at Molina de Aragón the local junta was accused of embezzlement; at La Coruña the secretary of the Junta of Galicia was supposed to have obtained up to 1,600,000 *reales* from the sale of public offices by October 1808 alone; and from Alhaurín el Grande it was reported that the deputy *corregidor* was skimming off public funds, engaging in wholesale extortion, selling off the grain reserves kept for years of dearth, making huge profits from fraudulent public works contracts, appropriating intestate property that should have passed to the state, imposing illicit levies on the populace and extracting sexual favours from pretty girls whose husbands, brothers or sweethearts had been conscripted.[58] And, at least as far as those who could pay were concerned, place-seekers had a field day: on offer were hundreds of commissions in the new regiments being formed by many of the Patriot authorities and thousands of administrative posts and special commissions of all sorts, the men concerned often giving cause for great scandal. To quote one complaint that was sent to the Junta Central from Cádiz, for instance:

> A change in the senior personnel of the Customs House . . . would save the state many millions . . . The officials concerned . . . get rich with no other source of income than their salaries, have balconies at the playhouse . . . keep fine tables . . . and enjoy every sort of luxury . . . How can there not be some sort of malversation going on?[59]

Not surprisingly, then, the most colourful language was soon being used in connection with the juntas. Let us take as an example, the following description of the Junta of Badajoz:

> It being clear that the spark that . . . lit the flame of patriotism throughout the kingdom was the work of divine providence, all good Spaniards accepted the juntas that were formed in all the provincial capitals . . . But that of Badajoz has been abusing its powers . . . Many of its members are vain, ignorant and vicious egotists, and from this there stems . . . a multitude of excesses. It is very frequent to find military ranks and enormous salaries heaped on the unworthiest of people, and all to accommodate relatives and clients. Sometimes the motive is money, but sometimes even darker forces are at work: it is said that ranks have even been given to prostitutes in exchange for members of the junta being allowed to enjoy their favours.[60]

All this caused immense offence. Of all the abuses of the juntas, however, by far the most serious were those relating to the recruitment of the army. Before going any further, we ought first to consider the system of conscription that was in use in Spain. Known as the *sorteo* or *quinta*, it had been introduced in 1770 with the intention that it should be imposed on an annual basis. Such was the hostility with which it was regarded, however, that in 1777 it had been decided to use it only in emergency. Since then, indeed, it had only been employed in 1793 and 1795, and the army had instead relied on voluntary enlistment and the impressment of criminals and the destitute. In theory, the *sorteo* worked by setting an overall target for the country as a whole, whereupon each *pueblo* was assigned a quota in accordance with its population. This having been done, a list of eligible recruits was then drawn up, and the men required selected by ballot (recruits were to be aged from sixteen to thirty-six, unmarried, in good physical health and with a minimum height of 5 feet). So far so good, but the whole system was in fact shot through with unfairness. The nobility and clergy were exempt, together with the inhabitants of various regions with special privileges, such as the Basque provinces, students, professionals of all sorts, university graduates, town councillors, magistrates, *alcaldes*, officials and couriers of the postal service, clerks in government offices and men engaged in a wide range of specialised activities (examples include sailors, gunsmiths, stockbreeders and skilled workers in most aspects of industry and agriculture). Not all the exemptions were quite so privileged in character – a real attempt was made, for example, to protect sole breadwinners – but the general effect was to ensure that the brunt of the burden fell on the poorest sections of society and, in particular, the agricultural labourer. The inherent injustice to which all this gave rise was reinforced by the numerous possibilities that existed for men with money and influence to subvert the system and buy themselves out of trouble.[61]

In theory, 1808 brought radical change. Whilst the existing regulations were retained in so far as the actual administration of conscription was concerned, the provincial juntas suppressed all grounds for exemption other than those designed to protect sole breadwinners, whilst generally extending the upper limit of the age range to forty or even forty-five. Accepted and codified by the Junta Central, these reforms gave Spain a system of universal military service. In theory, this was both fair and humane, but in practice the reality was very different, since the *pudientes* were quite shameless in their determination to avoid having to go to war. The *ayuntamiento* of Murcia, for example, requested that its members be exempted even from service in the *milicias honradas*, whilst one proposal for the introduction of the principle of substitution maintained that *herederos* made very cowardly soldiers on account of the fact that, unlike the poor, they had something to lose.[62]

Let us here look at some concrete examples of the sort of fraud in which the propertied classes and their allies engaged. The first priority, of course, was to ensure that they and their sons were never entered in the draw. As the Junta Central put it, 'There have repeatedly been very serious complaints . . . on account of the many men who have been escaping service in the army by claiming that they are exempt.'[63] Thus, in Córdoba it was noted that there were many men falsely passing themselves off as the only support of aged parents, whilst in Vivero and Cuenca others got off on grounds of nobility.[64] Such dodges implied the use of bribery – in Granada the cost appears to have been between 300 and 400 *reales* – though it may be that blackmail was also employed.[65] Just as illicit, meanwhile, was the common practice of openly buying exemption by means of patriotic donations (in 1808–9 the going rate was a fully accoutred horse and a minimum of 4,000 *reales*, whilst by 1811 it had risen to 20,000 *reales*).[66] And finally, there was a rush to obtain bolt-holes of one sort or other. In Valencia, for example, there was an increase in admissions to the university, whilst the rush for public office was partly explained by a desire to 'avoid going off to fight'.[67]

Most of the time such devices were enough to get the *pudientes* out of trouble but, on the rare occasions that they failed, all was not lost: at Sallent, for example, there were allegations that the presiding tribunal had refused a request from the men who had been declared liable for service, to check that the names of all the potential conscripts had actually been put in the urn. The point of such complaints is revealed when we discover that at Puebla de Guzmán several men had been omitted who had no exemption whatsoever.[68] And should things still go wrong, there were always grounds for appeal: named as *somatenes*, José Viladerau appealed for exemption on the grounds that he had already given generously to the cause and sent two of his employees to join up; Francisco Felíu claimed that he was nearly blind in his right eye and had only been put on the list 'in consequence of the intrigue and enmity that characterise small towns'; and Francisco de Paula Aragonés argued that service in the field was incompatible with his job.[69] And, lamentably, when combined with bribery, such tactics often worked: conscripted into the army in the autumn of 1808, a prosperous inhabitant of Turienso named Francisco Castellanos suddenly reappeared in his native village claiming that he had been released from the ranks.[70] 'Half of those who are called up are allowed to go free,' wrote one observer, 'some thanks to money, others thanks to blackmail, and still others thanks to a thousand different tricks and frauds.'[71]

As examples of the sort of thing that went on, let us cite a few individual cases. To return to Alhaurín el Grande, great anger was caused by the case of one Eusebio Guerrero. The nephew of the corrupt deputy *corregidor* whose crimes have already been outlined, Guerrero was beyond doubt liable for conscription. Yet, although conscripted in the *sorteos* of both 1808 and 1809, on each occasion he escaped, the first time by submitting a totally false statement of his circumstances, and the second by deserting. Still worse, despite the fact that he was known to have taken refuge with his parents, no attempt was made to round him up and send him back to his regiment.[72] In Cumbres de en Medio (a village situated in the north of the present-day province of Huelva), meanwhile, the two *alcaldes*, Juan Domínguez and Juan de Barajar, had managed to save their three sons from the *quinta* by pretending that one was already serving in the army, having the second one claim that he could not bite open cartridges because of problems with his teeth, and hastily arranging for the third one to get married.[73]

With money, indeed, it was even possible to play at being a soldier without ever having to experience the rigours of life in the field. One variant on this theme was the formation of 'guerrilla bands' in areas that were hundreds of miles from the nearest Frenchmen, a good example being the 'company of mounted smugglers' extolled by the Junta of Ayamonte as being 'the terror of the French' in August 1809.[74] Another was the numerous corps of 'distinguished volunteers' that sprang up all over Patriot Spain. Thus, in exchange for paying the cost of their uniform and equipment, men could enlist in units whose only duties were to mount guard on city walls, inject civic life with a certain degree of military pomp, add a degree of lustre to the new authorities and maintain the prerogatives of the propertied classes. Hardly surprisingly, these units soon acquired an evil reputation. The Voluntarios Distinguidos de Cádiz – a force later lauded to the skies by liberals eager to find a model for a new army – was described as 'battalions of cupids' composed of 'a multitude of infamous men of evil habits who . . . possess neither merit, nor subordination, nor inclination to the true object for which their arms were created'.[75] As for the Junta Central's personal guard – the grandiloquently named Voluntarios de Honor de la Universidad de Toledo – it was written:

> If it is wished to put things right . . . these soldiers . . . should be expelled from the city . . . There is not a married woman who because of them has

not fallen out with her husband, not a widow who has not emptied her house to take up with them, not a maiden who has not abandoned . . . honour at their instigation . . . They have neither king nor religion, and spend day and night alike in the tavern.[76]

Even service in the privileged conditions that these units offered, it seemed, was too much trouble. There is much evidence that many of the men involved tried to avoid such commitments, paid substitutes to do their duties for them or quickly tired of the whole business altogether.[77] If the *milicia honrada* failed to get off the ground in most provinces, then, we need hardly be surprised.[78] As for fighting, as one cynic remarked, 'These *caciques* are only brave . . . in the main squares of their home towns.'[79] Indeed, fearing that they might be sent to the front, in February 1809 the Voluntarios Distinguidos de Cádiz even instigated an insurrection whose main goal was to extract a promise that they would never have to serve beyond the walls of the city.[80] And, of course, the Patriot authorities themselves were most unwilling to see the departure of their protégés and bodyguards, as witness the bitter protests provoked by the arrival of orders stripping Catalonia's local juntas of the special companies of *migueletes* that they had kept back to quell the mob.[81]

The impact of the *pudientes'* behaviour on the structure of the Patriot army was all too predictable. In theory universal, liability to military service in practice fell on precisely the same groups as before. Thus, if we look at the 152 men called up in Manresa in 1810, we find that 141 of them are listed as being either of little fortune or of none at all, and that of the remaining eleven, only four are deemed as being wealthy: and, equally, observing a column of prisoners taken by the French when they defeated Joaquín Blake at Baza in November 1811, the captured British general Lord Blayney observed that 'one third of the privates were . . . half-starved boys from fourteen to sixteen; another third infirm old men, just able to crawl; [and] the last third . . . men of a tolerable appearance, [who] could alone have opposed . . . the French'.[82] And when, later in the war, desperate efforts were made to find fresh troops by combing out the lists of those who had earlier been exempted, in Santa Coloma de Queralt, at least, the only men taken were five artisans of various sorts and twelve peasants.[83]

In the Spain of the early nineteenth century nothing could have been more unfortunate than the perception of injustice that all this produced. To quote a retired army captain who dispatched an angry protest to the Junta Central:

It is obvious that nothing can be more damaging to our sacred cause than . . . angering the people by extending undue favours and privileges . . . on account of family relationships, clientage or bribery . . . The mass of the populace is convinced of the need to fight for its freedom, but when it sees

> the multitude of conscripts who, on account of private favour, are released, allowed to remain in their homes, or posted to positions that could be filled by men who have been exempted from service, the danger that it must suffer . . . becomes repugnant to it, and it loses its enthusiasm.[84]

To understand why feelings of patriotism could not hope to overcome such resentment, we need to turn to some recent works on the growth of national consciousness. In Spain, as we have seen, the Patriot authorities made great efforts to swing the populace behind the struggle against Napoleon. But, as Linda Colley has shown in her seminal work *Britons*, modern nationalism depends on the completion of a series of social processes, including historical acculturalisation, urbanisation, the collapse of rural insularity and the spread of popular literacy.[85] As Broers has pointed out, meanwhile, in their absence the demands of modern war were certain to be faced with massive resistance.[86] Spain, however, was very much a 'backward' state, on which the impact of enlightened absolutism and the processes analysed by Colley had alike been minimal, whilst, even in the narrow confines of the intellectual élite, the idea that a Spanish nation even existed had hardly ever been mooted.[87] In consequence, it would always have been hard to persuade the *pueblo* to make the gigantic efforts called for by the war against Napoleon. Thanks to the *pudientes*, however, the task was all but impossible. Always likely to be hostile, Spanish society reacted with immense violence, and matters were made worse still not only by the fact that the authorities' efforts to keep control, hunt down bandits, round up deserters and render the *quinta* effective were often exploited as a means of escaping military service, but also by the fact that the special forces raised to achieve these goals became ever more oppressive and burdensome.[88]

Given the problems caused by these improvised security forces, they are worth considering in more detail. Of particular interest in this respect is the situation that pertained in Málaga. Since the countryside was overrun by deserters and bandits, the authorities eventually sanctioned a proposal that, in effect, a thief be set to catch a thief, and allowed its author to go round the local gaols picking out repentant bandits to act as the nucleus of a force of poachers turned gamekeepers. Only later, however, did somebody notice that the enterprising *pretendiente* whom they had just taken on was none other than a renowned local chieftain named Matías Hispano, and, still worse, that the men he had selected were all members of his old gang who had been caught by the local justices.[89] This, perhaps, was an extreme case, but even so the general reputation enjoyed by these forces was very poor. From Llerena, for example, came complaints that the security patrol Manuel Muñoz Vaca had been permitted to establish by the Junta of Badajoz had proved to be little more than a scheme aimed, first, at securing him a substantial salary; second, at allowing him to escape front-line service; and, third, at giving him the power of patronage (service in such anti-bandit patrols was for obvious reasons very popular).[90]

The evidence of violent hostility to authority is overwhelming. In the words of one of the numerous *comisionados* sent out by the Junta Central to whip up patriotic feeling, round up deserters and draft-dodgers, and accelerate the *quinta*, for example:

> When I arrived at Paymogo I found the most horrible picture that I could possibly outline to Your Majesty. I did not dare to do so from there, because my letter would inevitably have been intercepted, thereby putting me at risk of falling victim to the . . . violence of a populace that has never known either subordination or respect for authority. All my fiery spirit had to be exchanged for humility, sweetness and generosity . . . The whole area presents the most lamentable sight. It is a confused anarchy in which the entire body politic is undone. On every side one sees ferment, disorder, intrigue and the spirit of faction.[91]

In Asturias, meanwhile, General Ballesteros was complaining of the 'disobedience of the . . . inhabitants of this territory, unaccustomed as they are to being punished for their crimes', whilst from Málaga a despairing official told the Junta Central's secretary-general, Martin de Garay, that the 'insubordination . . . of these *pueblos* has left me so frustrated that I have no option but to trouble Your Excellency in the hope that your intervention might reduce them to submission and respect'.[92]

There were, doubtless, other factors in the equation, not least among them the outrage and despair that were felt at the inability of the Spanish army to hold back the French in the campaign of the winter of 1808, and, prior to that, the false hopes engendered by the boasting and vainglory that had filled the Patriot press following the battle of Bailén.[93] Nor did it help that lack of foresight in the expansion of the army in 1808 had given rise to many supernumerary officers.[94] Left with nothing to do, such men naturally gravitated to cities such as Seville and La Coruña, where they were joined by still other men who had simply abandoned their regiments, and, as one British officer put it, together they 'served only to make a military appearance in the streets and gaming houses'.[95] Even when they were with their units, meanwhile, Spanish officers had an evil reputation. The Duke of Wellington remarked, for example, that 'Subordination and habits of obedience . . . can be acquired by soldiers only in proportion as they have confidence in their officers, and they cannot have confidence in officers who have no knowledge of their profession . . . have no subordination among themselves, and never obey an order.'[96]

All this, of course, only served to swell the mood of social unrest, not least because many of the more exalted liberals fanned the flames by trumpeting demands for a renewal of the officer corps on the basis of 'new' men made in the revolution. How far such radicalism awoke a popular echo, it is hard to say, but there is no doubt that it reflected feelings in the *pueblo*. In the words of one anonymous letter sent to the Junta Central:

> With the exception of a few of the better commanders, all the officers of our armies are loud-mouthed braggarts . . . If we are to win, we must make our privates into sergeants, our corporals into captains, and our sergeants into colonels.[97]

In certain parts of Spain, too, even among the common people there may have been traces of an incipient regionalism. For a variety of reasons – not least folk memories of armed revolt – this was particularly strong in Catalonia. As the Marqués de Lazán warned General Blake, for example:

> Garrisoning Lérida . . . with the Catalan legions that are being formed would be very dangerous. It is not for me to meddle with your . . . plans, nor still less change them . . . But, even so, I know the Catalans, and, for all its walls and towers, I would not answer for Lérida if it was held by Catalan troops . . . The people of the area are most barbarous, and the soldiers would certainly take their side if there was any sort of riot.[98]

As the years went by, growing anti-British feeling amongst men of letters and the civil and military authorities may also have rubbed off on the people. Following the abortive campaign of Barosa, for example, quarrels in Cádiz between the British commander, Sir Thomas Graham, and his Spanish counterparts produced rumours that the British had seized Cádiz and decapitated Generals Zayas and La Peña, whilst there were many stories to the effect that the British intended either to commandeer the Spanish army for their own purposes or to force the populace to enlist under Wellington.[99] But the central issue remained conscription. Throughout the eighteenth century this had always been hated and feared by all concerned. Few young men relished being torn away from the bosom of the families to an uncertain fate, and few families could contemplate the loss of their labour with any equanimity. Meanwhile, military service was associated with vice and ultimately beggary, since those men who eventually returned to their homes generally did so as drunken misfits. The Patriot régime having utterly failed to awaken an echo among the populace, there was no chance that these feelings would be swept away by the events of 1808, and, by the same token, every chance that the populace would seek to defend itself.[100]

In this situation resistance took many forms. Crudely written, poorly spelt and very often anonymous, denunciations of the local authorities were soon being received by the Junta Central by the sackload. For example:

> The Junta . . . of Ciudad Real . . . is not the work of . . . the people . . . Its members are Godoys, traitors, egoists and thieves who clubbed together so that the people would . . . not get at their money . . . The province is scandalized, for everybody knows that they are malignant rogues.[101]

Also well to the fore were complaints on the subject of conscription. One correspondent from Guadix demanded the formation of a *cuerpo preferente* (literally, 'regiment of the privileged') that would bring together all those who had managed to have themselves exempted on fraudulent grounds, together with all public employees under the age of fifty, and a number of letters may also be found calling for the immediate conscription of all members of the clergy apart from those who were absolutely indispensable for the celebration of the sacraments.[102] Typical enough is the following example from Galicia:

> Is there any reason why every single noble . . . should not be sent off to war in the space of three days? Is there any reason why they should not be followed by all priests, friars and clerks in minor orders under the age of forty . . . by all tax officials of whatever rank . . . by all writers of whatever sort?[103]

For most families, however, the action to be taken was more practical. Patriot Spain therefore began to experience precisely the same problems visible in Revolutionary and Napoleonic France. All over the country men tried desperately to avoid being subjected to the *sorteo*. There were, for example, hundreds of petitions for exemption.[104] Meanwhile, as the British officer John Patterson noted, 'Married men being . . . exempt from the contributions required to fill up the ranks, all the youthful fellows in the neighbourhood espoused themselves in order to avoid the Junta's levies' (in one *pueblo* in Córdoba it was reported that there were nineteen marriages in a single day).[105] In the coastal districts of Catalonia a frequent dodge was to obtain false papers stating that the holder was enrolled in the navy's list of sailors, and therefore in ordinary circumstances exempt from conscription to the army.[106] Another favourite choice was to flee or go into hiding. 'In this city', complained the Junta of Santiago, 'the young men who have been conscripted into the army can often be heard complaining of the large number of their fellows who have fled to . . . Portugal in order to avoid being enlisted.'[107] Even more interesting, meanwhile, is the situation in Ecija, where flight from conscription clearly meshed with agrarian discontent. Thus: 'A considerable number of the young men who are eligible for service have fled into the countryside, where they have pillaged many properties and estates without their owners being able to do a thing about it.'[108] And, last but not least, it was always possible to fake illness or physical handicap: the village of Paymogo saw eleven men redeem themselves in this fashion in the period 1808–9.[109] For most of those who took this way out, the basis of their claims lay in childhood accidents or illnesses that had supposedly left them unfit to fight, but the really desperate might pull their front teeth out, chop their trigger fingers off so as to make it impossible for them to fire a musket, or, still worse, simulate the effects of syphilis by applying caustic substances to their genitals.[110]

The impact of such tactics was immense. In many parts of Spain the prevalence of migrant labour meant that for much of the year the number of potential conscripts in any given district was much smaller than was theoretically the case. Ordered to find sixty men for the *somatén* in December 1809, for example, the chief magistrate of the mountainous district of Tosas reported that most of the young men in the area who had not already been called up were absent working at jobs in the fertile coastal plain.[111] This phenomenon was bad enough, but in some areas so many men were exempted from service that the burden on the remainder became quite intolerable. Of this a good example may be found in the Catalan district of Arens de Mar, which in June 1811 was ordered to find 450 fresh conscripts. At first all seemed well, as there were reported to be 2,780 men of military age in the area, but of these 1,939 were either married men or widowers with children, 324 medically unfit and 390 disqualified from serving on account of having been declared to be sole breadwinners. This left just 126 men out of the 841 bachelors and widowers without children who formed the first category of the call-up. In some of the district's *pueblos*, indeed, the situation was even worse. Overall, something less than one man in every seven of those theoretically available for service would have to take his chances in the *sorteo*, but of Malgrat's sixty candidates just one was left in the draw, of Palafolls' twenty-nine just one, and of Arens de Mar's thirty-four just four.[112] Hardly is it surprising, then, to find that the Junta Central as early as May 1809 agreed to reduce the minimum height required of a soldier from the already diminutive 5 feet to the still more tiny 4 feet 10 inches.[113]

Such problems, of course, served only to stiffen the resistance of the populace. As a *miguelete* officer sent to Arens de Mar to get things moving complained, 'Without armed men, it is impossible to obtain a single recruit . . . The only means of making oneself obeyed is to use force.'[114] The populace, however, was undaunted. As in Don Benito, the ballot that actually determined who should serve in the army might be disrupted by riot or mutiny: on 8 June 1808 proceedings at the Galician town of Mesía had to be abandoned when a shout went up that the French were coming; on the very same day three miles east of El Ferrol an angry crowd stormed the courthouse at Neda at the very moment that the ballot was taking place, before going on to force the arrest of a number of alleged spies, ransack the tax offices and pillage the homes of various local notables; and in October 1811 Arens de Mar's conscripts refused to leave for the army unless they were accompanied by one Miguel Buch, who they claimed was being protected by relatives with positions on the Junta of Gerona (which was at that point based at Arens).[115] Meanwhile, there were also periodic attempts to coerce the authorities. In La Mancha, for example, the mayor of Miguelturra was murdered. In Catalonia the first day of 1809 witnessed a violent revolt in Lérida whose victims numbered the commander of one of the *tercios de miqueletes* which the Catalan authorities were currently trying to form as a substitute for recruitment to the regular army. In Jerez de la Frontera on 27 February 1809 a large crowd gathered on the main square to protest at the way in which many men were being unfairly exempted from the *quinta*. And, finally, in Murcia the provincial junta's efforts to round up deserters provoked a major rising that was used by its enemies to bring about its overthrow.[116]

Nor did resistance cease once men had been drafted into the armed forces. Given the reverential treatment that has customarily been accorded to the resistance put up by Catalonia even by British historians, the evidence that we have from that province is particularly interesting. Far from being the heroes of legend, the *somatenes* and *migueletes* proved to be extremely reluctant to do their duty. It is particularly indicative that in March 1809 the Junta of Granollers was forced to reissue the orders alerting the local *somatén* to be ready for action and laying down the procedure under which they were to be called out.[117] From all sides, indeed, there came complaints of every sort. The *somatenes*, wrote Enrique O'Donnell, 'impede the army's recruitment and get in the way of its operations', whilst the Marqués de Portazgo blamed the fall of Olot on the failure of the garrison's many men of this sort to put up a fight.[118] Rather than face battle, many men 'break their muskets . . . whilst others throw them away . . . or sell them'.[119] And still others simply went home. On 19 January 1810, for example, Francisco Rovira reported that it was useless sending him groups of *somatenes* as they disappeared as soon as they arrived, whilst much the same sentiment had been expressed some months earlier by Joaquín Blake:

> Only a little while ago General Casamayor saw 2,000 of these armed peasants disappear the moment that the assembly was sounded . . . whilst a few nights back 3–4,000 fled from the command of Lieutenant-Colonel Juan Clarós. Let them come and give new proofs of their constancy by all means, but, when it comes to attacking the enemy, I will place no trust in such people.[120]

As if this was not enough, the Catalan militias also took out their wrath on the homes of the more prosperous inhabitants. To quote one petition sent to the Junta of Catalonia:

> With the greatest regret, the justices of the Valles district cannot avoid informing Your Excellency of the many disturbances, robberies, assaults and other crimes that the *migueletes* are committing in the homes of the *labradores* . . . the number of their crimes being as numerous as that of the houses which they come across. As for the owners, they can do nothing to stop this execrable behaviour, for . . . the men . . . threaten to shoot them unless they are allowed to have their way.[121]

Such complaints were widespread. On 16 September 1809 Blake told the Junta Central that the only reason the *somatenes* came together was 'to devastate the province'; and on 31 December of the same year one José Roset wrote from Tarrasa:

> The *somatenes* think they have the right to engage in insubordination and libertinage, whilst at the same time having first call on the precious resources that could save us from the slavery that threatens us. Enormous gangs of men . . . pass though this town all the time. Most of them are armed, and the majority with muskets at that. What they are up to, I do not know, but I fear that putting such weapons into the hands of the mob is tantamount to turning each one of them into an enemy who is far worse than any Frenchman.[122]

But most scathing of all was a young Andalusian officer named Francisco de Paula Guervos, who had been sent to Catalonia with a division of reinforcements. Thus:

> Every day I hate these people more: they have no God but money, and for it would sell their fatherland, their families, their saints and anything else that comes to hand . . . Much vaunted though it is, the Army of Catalonia is nothing but a collection of bands of thieves who under the name of *somatenes* enter the towns and villages in almost the same manner as the French . . . the only difference being that they are rather more skilful when it comes to robbing them.[123]

As we have seen, resistance to the war effort in Catalonia may have been intensified by a variety of factors that were peculiar to the province. Yet there is no reason to believe that things were much better anywhere else. In Jaca, Santander and Oviedo officers who attempted to bring their troops to order and subject them to the rigours of drill found that they were accused of trying to stifle their patriotic spirit.[124] And throughout Spain soldiers engaged in various forms of evasion. As in other conflicts, one means of escape was the self-inflicted wound, but by far the most popular was desertion.[125] As early as 31 May 1808 the Junta of Seville was complaining that many of its *alistados* were seemingly unwilling to serve even as local militiamen, let alone regular soldiers, and further that the substantial regular army that it had been able to amass was experiencing serious desertion, whilst on 24 June the Junta of Zamora had to give orders for the conscripts of the *pueblo* of Argusino to be placed in the charge of an armed guard.[126] Moving on, in January 1809 it was reported that there were many deserters in the district of Rubia in Galicia; in March that over 100 men had deserted in a single night from one Galician regiment; in April that *infinitos dispersos* were hiding in the rough country that lined the south bank of the River Tagus; in May that no fewer than forty-eight deserters had been picked up in the city of Málaga alone in the course of the past three months, and that in Galicia many men were hiding in their homes; and in June that the district of Socuéllamos was full of deserters who ignored every attempt to appeal to their better feelings and had to be dragged back to the army by force.[127] Losses often peaked when regiments were marched away from their home provinces, but such issues were merely incidental: even when in their own part of Spain the men kept running away. Catalonia, for example, saw at least one third of its soldiers desert, despite the fact that Catalan regiments rarely served beyond the boundaries of the principality.[128] Rounded up by detachments of loyal troops sent out for the purpose, most *dispersos* – the crowds of fugitives and stragglers who escaped from the ranks after every battle – simply absconded again as soon as their captors' backs were turned.[129] And, still more extraordinarily, there were cases of men who had been captured by the French refusing to effect their escape when they were offered the chance of doing so, on the grounds that they would rather be prisoners of war than go on facing life in the army.[130]

That desertion was so prominent a phenomenon is hardly surprising. Above all, it was an easy option. The lack of marching discipline off the battlefield and the frequent routs upon it made it simple for a soldier to slip away from the ranks. Runaways could pass unnoticed because clothing shortages meant that many units were dressed in a style little different from that of the civilian population.[131] A proclamation of 3 January 1809 had laid down the most savage penalties for deserters and all those who helped them, but there was a marked reluctance to shoot men who had gone absent for no other reason than the fact that they were starving.[132] And there was always somewhere to run to: just as town councils and justices in the Patriot zone were often prepared to turn a blind eye to the presence of deserters, so the French were quite content to let men whose *pueblos* lay in areas that they happened to control live quietly in their homes, always providing, of course, that they had no truck with the insurgents.[133]

In traditional accounts of the war the act of desertion has often been portrayed as having stemmed from a desire to perpetuate the struggle by means that were more efficacious than those being employed by the regular army. To put it another way, deserters were patriots whose only crime was to decide that they could serve the *patria* more effectively as guerrillas than as regular soldiers. This, however, is dangerously disingenuous. That there were deserters in the ranks of the guerrillas is obvious – out of 1,166 men identified as having served in their ranks thus far, forty were either certainly or almost certainly deserters – but at only 3 per cent the number uncovered is surprisingly small, whilst several of the men concerned only joined the *partidas* in which they served some time after they deserted and as a result of either poverty or *force majeure*. Most deserters, then, may rather be assumed to have fled their posts in order to go home or, alternatively, to have found some means of subsistence that was more profitable and less burdensome than the army (an intention, as we shall see, that was by no means incompatible with a decision to join some band of insurgents). All the more was this the case, meanwhile, given the terrible conditions endured by many soldiers, the army being notoriously ill-paid, ill-clothed and ill-fed.[134]

And, as in Catalonia, hand in hand with the question of resistance to the war effort went that of law and order. Thus, from the vicinity of Cádiz one *comisionado* reported that the whole area was swarming with 'bad Spaniards, who, having either deserted or fled from the draft, have necessarily become thieves and wrongdoers, robbing passers-by . . . sacking farms, and [oppressing] the [inhabitants] with more inhumanity than the . . . French', whilst the military governor of Santiago complained of 'a plague of deserters who march from crime to crime'.[135] Even when they returned to their native *pueblos*, indeed, many deserters had no option but to resort to extortion: from La Carolina, for example, came complaints that a group of soldiers from the area were hiding in the hills outside the town and bombarding the *ayuntamiento* with demands for food and clothing.[136]

In the face of all this violence even the more responsible local authorities felt completely helpless. To quote the Junta of Villafranca:

> Given . . . the general scorn with which our measures are looked upon, not to mention the fact that the town has neither garrison, nor governor, nor commandant . . . we do not know . . . what to do. Despised, surrounded by wrongdoers . . . [and] continually threatened with fresh incursions on the part of the enemy . . . we can neither fulfil our own obligations, nor make anybody else fulfil theirs: our authority is neither respected nor feared.[137]

Confronted with a populace that was armed and mutinous, and with roving bands of outlaws who were not only wreaking havoc on all sides but capable of taking the most savage revenge on anyone who crossed them, many juntas were understandably prepared to let sleeping dogs lie. As the bishop of Ciudad Rodrigo complained:

> We are in what approaches a state of anarchy here . . . because the junta and its president are obsessed with fear of the people, and do not dare to dispense justice with regard to either delinquents or deserters . . . In eight months of horrible events we have not seen a single punishment . . . and as a result . . . it is the people who are in command.[138]

Desperate not to provoke any more trouble than they could help, the local authorities therefore often themselves resisted the *quinta*. Thus, the Junta of Vizcaya refused to form any regular units at all, and chose instead to rely upon bands of irregulars in the style of the Catalan *somatenes*; the Junta of Molina alleged that one of the town's ancient privileges was to provide for its own defence (which meant, of course, that no men could be sent to the army); the Junta of Cartagena took refuge in both an outbreak of yellow fever and the fact that much of the male population was either registered for sea service or employed in the city's important naval arsenal; the Junta of Mallorca blamed the absence of the captain-general of the Balearic Islands on the campaign in Catalonia; the *ayuntamiento* of El Ferrol made out that all of its men were needed for the defence of the town; the Junta of Ayamonte seized on ambiguities in the conscription legislation to pretend that all married men and widowers were completely exempt from conscription; and, finally, the Junta of Galicia tried to impede progress by querying a number of minor contradictions in the orders that it had received.[139] Alternatively they sought to concentrate their efforts on marginalised groups within the community – in Andalucía, for example, it appears that many migrant labourers were pressed as tramps and beggars – or ensured that the men who were sent were the weak, the unfit and the undersized, and therefore those whose labour would be least missed by their families.[140] Finally, still another scheme, and one that had the added benefit of killing two birds with one stone, was to offer free pardons to every convict, bandit, smuggler or deserter who would agree to join up, or even to conscript men directly from the gaols: in Zamora, for example, on 21 June 1808 the junta voted to send off to the army the convicted murderers Juan López, Manuel López, Diego Salvador and Baltasar de la Torre.[141]

The central authorities were not, of course, unaware of these problems. Indeed, as the war went on, they made strenuous attempts to force their provincial counterparts to implement conscription in a fair and efficient manner through the dispatch of *comisionados* in the style of the *représentants en mission* of the French Revolution. Rather more tepidly, perhaps, some of the provincial juntas adopted the same expedient with regard to the *juntas de partido* and local justices: on 28 October 1808, for example, the Junta of Zamora sent out a circular to no fewer than fourteen different *pueblos* informing them that an inspector would be visiting them with a view to discovering what had happened to a large number of missing conscripts.[142] But, whilst a few individuals were deprived of their positions, in the end little was achieved, for the intervention of outsiders was often met with resentment and obstruction, if not open hostility.[143] And that the local authorities were right to be careful, there was no doubt, for efforts to hurry things along often led to still more violence.[144] Recognising the weakness of their position, the *comisionados* sent by the Junta Central therefore often backed off in their turn, in some cases indulging in more or less specious excuses and in others admitting that they were just plain beaten.[145]

In consequence, recruitment languished. By November 1808 the number of men under arms had risen by fewer than 100,000 men, whilst wide areas of Patriot Spain presented an extraordinary spectacle. As one British observer wrote of Granada:

> In this province there is positively nothing: one squadron of cavalry is forming, and one battalion of foreign infantry is doing duty in the town, but beyond that there is not a soldier, no depot of recruits, no provision of any sort for keeping up the armies at their present force, or in any way carrying on the war. All seems at rest. The hordes of deserters that are known to be about are not meddled with, and indeed the encouragement given to deserters by that means is so great that . . . numbers of families are sending for their sons from the armies, assuring them that they will not be punished.[146]

For the troops of the Duke of Wellington and Sir John Moore, all this came as a great shock. To quote the commissary Augustus Schaumann, for example:

> The more one sees of the Spaniards, the more discouraged one gets. Everything that has been so blatantly trumpeted in the papers about their enthusiasm, their great armies and the stampede to join them is simply lies. It often looks as if Spain were not even willing to defend herself. In all the hamlets, villages and towns, the inhabitants . . . lounge about in their hundreds, completely apathetic, indifferent and gloomy, and sunk in their idleness. Is this the daring, patriotic and impetuous race about which the press have raved so bombastically?[147]

What the solution to the problem was few could envisage. It is all too easy to state the obvious: that the people of Spain had to be given something tangible to fight for, or, to put it another way, that the millenarian hopes that had been awoken by the accession to the throne of Fernando VII should be translated into reality. Reform of the sort that was needed, however, was something that was far beyond the imagination of most of the leaders of Patriot Spain, and, in the case of the liberals – the force that dominated its politics between 1810 and 1814 – directly contrary to their ideology. Anxious to drive through their agenda, the liberals did repeatedly make use of the argument that the enthusiasm of 1808 had been squandered by the failure of the Junta Central to consolidate the revolution of that year.[148] However, with the exception of a few far-sighted individuals, they did not interpret reform in terms of the interests of the populace, and persuaded themselves that their own private objectives were consonant with those interests. Indeed, even the *cortes* of Cádiz's much-vaunted abolition of feudalism proved a bitter disappointment, as the peasants had in many cases to go on paying the dues that they had owed to their old *señores* in the form of rent. Only very rarely, then, do we find a recognition of the truth. One such instance comes from General Abadía, who, sent to the Campo de Gibraltar in 1810, decided that the only way to put an end to the agrarian discontent that was rocking the area would be to parcel out plots of uncultivated land and distribute them amongst the local *yunteros*, and another from José O'Donnell, who as commander of the Spanish forces in Valencia and Murcia in March 1812 issued stringent orders against grain speculation.[149] However, even such initiatives as these did not make very much difference to the overall picture, for, whilst liberal support for disamortisation ensured that much land changed hands in the course of the War of Independence, very little ended up in the hands of the rural lower classes (in theory, half the lands of the municipalities were set aside for distribution to veterans of the war, but the principle was not acted upon). Amazingly, meanwhile, not until the very end of the war did the *cortes* think to make any provision for men who had been incapacitated in the fighting, and even then its thinking on the subject was hardly generous: all that was done was to order the establishment of a *depósito de inutilizados* in each province and to lay down that the men concerned should be assigned the same pay as they had been receiving at the time that they were wounded.[150]

It may, then, be taken as read not only that the bulk of the population had little interest in the war, but also that such little interest as it possessed was squandered by the corruption and short-sightedness of a local élite that had maintained its position intact in the face of the so-called Spanish revolution. Inspired by a mixture of panic, millenarian excitement and black propaganda, the populace was initially prepared to lend itself to acts of mass resistance, and particularly so when the élites flattered its vanity and reached out to it through the use of interlocutors capable of speaking the language of the streets. But, for all that, all is not what it seems. Despite a massive propaganda effort that has to this day created the impression that the Spanish struggle against Napoleon was a new people's crusade, the populace on the whole wanted nothing to do with the war. Far from rushing to the colours, indeed, they had rather to be forced to take up arms, and even then did so with the utmost unwillingness. At the same time, terrified by popular violence, the authorities themselves backed away from the idea of employing the nation-in-arms against Napoleon. For the reasons why all this was so we must turn to the 'want of patriotism' so complained of by British observers. Patriotism in the modern sense did not exist in Spain, and, what is more, could not exist, for the country had not gone through the processes that were the *sine qua non* of such feelings. But if this is the case, then, we must also seek alternative explanations for the decision of many men of humble origins to take up arms against the French. *Partidas* there may have been, but in the light of the conditions that we have discussed in the present chapter it would be absurd to argue that they were activated solely by love of *dios, rey y patria*. Having established, however, that *la guerrilla* was a phenomenon that rested on a far broader spectrum of forces than just the people in arms, this presents us with few difficulties: if bands of armed civilians were only a small part of the 'little war', there is obviously room for an alternative agenda of the sort that will now be opened up for discussion.

4

The Origins of the Guerrillas

From what has gone before it is quite clear that the way is open for a complete re-evaluation of the guerrillas. Many of the men we know by this name, it turns out, were not armed civilians at all, but rather regular soldiers who were either detailed to carry out irregular operations or forced by circumstances to make them their *modus vivendi*. As for the populace, though hardly enamoured of the French, it was at best uninterested in the war effort and deeply hostile to the *caciques* who everywhere had a monopoly of political power. There were areas of Spain, clearly, where the arrival of the invaders or the experience of French occupation proved sufficiently traumatic to overcome this initial ambivalence. At the same time, fighting in a guerrilla band close to home and family was not the same as being marched off to the other end of the country as a conscript, just as fighting to defend home and family was a concept that carried more weight than fighting to defend the fatherland, the Church or the rights of Ferdinand VII. Yet, for all that, it is no longer possible simply to accept the bald claim that *la guerrilla* was a popular crusade. That some men – many men, even – took up arms is certain, but the reasons why they did so are open to question. Just as interesting, meanwhile, are the issues of identity, organisation and leadership. Who, we may ask, were the guerrillas? How did the phenomenon of guerrilla warfare actually emerge? And, finally, how far did the *cabecillas* who headed the individual guerrilla bands genuinely spring from the Spanish people?

The importance of these questions is reinforced by the manner in which they have often been answered by reference to examples of dubious value. Let us take, for instance, the case of Navarre. Well documented and superficially attractive, the figures of Martín Javier Mina y Larrea and Francisco Espoz y Mina seem the very epitome of popular *caudillos*. As for the resistance movement they headed, on the surface it was both very strong and deeply ideological. Over and over again, then, we find Navarre used as an epitome for the *guerrilla* in the whole of Spain. Yet, in fact, Navarre is a very special instance that has little relevance to the rest of the country. In Francisco Espoz y Mina, in particular, it had a military commander of some talent. Able to win battles against the French, he at the same time possessed both the utmost ruthlessness and considerable political acumen: whilst he stopped at nothing to eliminate all his rivals in the province and unite the resistance movement under his leadership, he also strove hard not just to live off the backs of the inhabitants. Aided by the numerous mistakes made by the occupying forces, the growing numbers of recruits brought in by his successes, the social structure of the Navarrese *montaña* and the rugged terrain by which he was surrounded, he was also able to offer the people a greater measure of protection against enemy reprisals and requisitioning than was generally the case elsewhere. But, above all, the socio-economic situation was all but unique. Unlike in most of the rest of Spain, in northern and central Navarre – the areas that provided both Mina and Espoz y Mina with the bulk of their support – the populace were reasonably satisfied with their lot. Homes were generally owned rather than rented, whilst the substantial farmhouses that characterised the region were positively palatial when compared with the miserable cabins and tenements that were the usual lot of *campesinos*. With land easy to obtain, smallholdings were large enough to keep a family and were either owned outright or held on reasonable terms (rents, indeed, were extremely low, and had generally not been raised for generations). Farming was mixed and labour-intensive, thereby ensuring employment throughout the year, whilst good rainfall and rich soil kept yields high and food prices low. Social divisions were limited, and feudalism all but non-existent thanks to the fact that up to 80 per cent of the population could claim noble status. As for the Church, it was no burden. Given the relative absence of great religious houses in the mountains of Navarre, the clergy owned few estates and had almost no feudal fiefs. The parishes were small and their priests recruited from amongst the villagers whom they served, and such land as the Church did possess was rented out to the peasantry for sums that were for the most part purely nominal. Thanks to the province's traditional *fueros*, too, taxation was low, whilst customs of village democracy ensured that it was imposed on a reasonably equitable basis. And, last but not least, the *fueros* – an immediate target, be it said, for French reform – were also economically beneficial to the peasantry, enshrining traditions of paternalism, protecting the common lands and ensuring that there was no obstacle to the export to France of wool and hides that was an important part of the *montaña's* economy and offering many possibilities for smuggling (the key factor here was Navarre's exclusion from the Spanish customs frontier).

Unlike, say, on the great estates of Andalucía, the populace therefore had something to fight for, but at the same time they also had something to fight against. Hard up against the Pyrenees, they could not but entertain notions of the French as 'the other', whilst they had also bitter memories of the war of 1793–95, in which the armies of the Convention had stormed across the province. Close to their clergy, they were in addition more likely to be influenced than many other Spaniards by pamphlets and sermons excoriating the French as the spawn of the devil (it may also be of significance that many of the French priests and religious who had fled to Spain had settled in the frontier provinces). And, on top of all this, they also had a tradition of taking up arms in their own defence, having always been required to form irregular militias in time of war and invasion (farming techniques and practices in the hillier parts of Navarre were such that young men could be spared for part-time military service with relative ease).[1]

With these conditions mirrored only in the Basque provinces, if at all, there is no way that the example of Navarre can be regarded as a model for the whole of Spain. Indeed, even in Navarre they did not hold good for the entire region: in contrast to the *montaña* of the north, the *ribera* of the south – a land of rolling steppes, clerical dominance, great estates and densely populated 'agro-towns' such as Corella and Tudela – was marked by the poverty, feudalism and deep-rooted social division characteristic of a region in which the majority of the populace were either day-labourers or tenant farmers burdened by high rents and constant insecurity. So great were the problems experienced by the *ribera* that the residual benefits conveyed by the *fueros* could do little to offset them – there were, indeed, arguments that they were an obstacle to its prosperity – and it is in consequence no surprise to find that recruitment to Espoz y Mina's forces was far less successful there: of 3,477 men listed in a census of the volunteers who joined his forces commissioned by the provincial authorities after the return of Fernando VII in 1814 only one quarter hailed from the *ribera*.[2] From such areas, too, come reports that make it clear that the guerrilla commander's relations with the civilian population were not always as smooth as was the case in the north of Navarre. 'The guerrillas', wrote Heinrich von Brandt, 'cared even less about their compatriots than we did and certain chiefs held sway over the countryside by terror alone. When they intercepted requisitioned cattle, it was in order to confiscate them for their own profit. When they themselves requisitioned something, it was usually upon pain of death.'[3] Elsewhere, meanwhile, Von Brandt was even more scathing, writing, 'The country was made to suffer dreadfully to satisfy this man's absolute will and selfish ambition.'[4]

The question of Espoz y Mina is one to which we shall return. Much more important for the time being is the identification of positive engagement in the struggle with a satisfaction with pre-war society suggested by the case of the Navarrese *montaña*. The claim that enthusiasm for the guerrillas was strengthened by possession of a reasonable degree of security and status is reinforced by reference to the social composition of the guerrillas. Extensive work in primary and secondary sources has produced a list of some 322 members of guerrilla bands whose occupation in 1808 is known. Of these, no fewer than 204 may be said in one sense or other to have been the representatives of property, power and social success as students, professionals, landowners or wealthy tenant farmers, serving or retired army officers, or members of the clergy (the remaining 118 include taverners, butchers, stall-holders, municipal employees, muleteers, peasants, day-labourers, artisans, common soldiers, smugglers, bandits and deserters from the imperial army).

Too much emphasis should not be placed on such figures, for members of the Church, the army or the propertied classes were far more likely to leave a trace in archive or written record than members of the *populacho* but the figure is still an arresting one. In all, 1,166 individual guerrillas were identified in the research that produced this work, and, even if every single one of the 844 names whose occupation remains a mystery were to turn out to be peasants, day-labourers, servants and the like, we would still have a situation in which groups representing fewer than 10 per cent of the population provided 17 per cent of the guerrilla movement. Also significant, meanwhile, is the identity of men who at one time or another commanded a *partida*, for, out of the 371 such leaders who have been identified, 103 came from the middling or upper echelons of society, and only 37 from the *populacho* (the remaining 222 were unknown).[5]

We therefore have a movement that appears to have had strong support amongst groups that were in one way or another beneficiaries of the *antiguo régimen*. At the same time, when *hacendados* such as the Marqués de Barriolucio or Esteban Pascual y Casas took the field, there seems little reason to doubt that they did so to uphold the old order.[6] That said, however, the mere fact that 137 members of the clergy have been identified amongst the 322 guerrillas whose occupations we know is in itself meaningless, and certainly not enough to sustain the traditional French charge that *la guerrilla* was the work of a Church intent on blocking enlightened reform. If the famous Jerónimo Merino – in 1808 parish priest of the tiny village of Villoviado, near Lerma – was to become a convinced defender of absolutism and, in his latter days, a Carlist, the Valencian leader Agustín Nebot was a rebel who began his career by running away from his convent and was to fight just as determinedly for the liberals. And what, too, is one to make of cases such as those of the friar Julián Crespo, who fought under Espoz y Mina as a corporal, was imprisoned following the rising of 1814, sought secularisation under the liberal régime of

1820–23 and, when this was denied, ran away from his convent to join an absolutist *partida*? Then there was Nicolás Uriz, a Navarrese friar whose chequered career under first El Empecinado and then Espoz y Mina culminated in his going over to the French rather than face charges of corruption, and the parish priest of Fuentespina, Bernardo Mayor, who formed a *partida* of fifty men but behaved in so oppressive a fashion that he was arrested by Empecinado, only to escape from custody and go over to the French. And, finally, we might here also cite Antonio Temprano, a friar of the Order of Mercy who early in 1809 joined a band commanded by one José Armengol, only to abscond and set up his own band, at the head of which he committed numerous misdeeds (these he later tried to excuse with the engaging remark that the time had arrived 'when one can do whatever one likes').[7] Notable here, too, are complaints of the drunkenness and disorderly conduct of young ecclesiastics who had been given permission to join guerrilla bands, whilst, even when ideological motives were seemingly paramount, closer observation frequently suggests a different story. Merino started killing Frenchmen not because he feared what Napoleon might do to the Spanish Church, but rather in revenge for being pressed into service as a porter by some French soldiers in January 1809; furthermore, he might not have become a *cabecilla* at all but for the fact that he was a harsh and unbending character who was unlikely to suffer insults lightly, and a keen huntsman who was used to life in the open air and knew the local countryside like the back of his hand.[8] Indeed, would any of the many monks and friars to be found amongst the irregulars have taken up arms but for the fact that the closure of their convents by the French had left them homeless and without support? For a pattern here we might take the figure of Antonio Jiménez. A monk from Medina Sidonia who headed a *partida* in the Condado de Niebla in 1810, Jiménez makes it quite clear that he fled to Cádiz and sought a career in the employ of the government only because of the dispersal of the community of which he had been a member.[9]

Similar problems are to be found with regard to most of the other explanations that have been put forward with regard to the motivation of the guerrillas. Many *cabecillas*, we are told, took up arms out of sheer disgust at the events of the Dos de Mayo and the overthrow of Fernando VII: examples of such men include Juan Palarea and Juan José de Abecia, a student at the University of Zaragoza who fought in the defence of the city in 1808 and 1809 and then returned to his home town of Marquina to form a *partida*.[10] And such at least was the reason put forward by many of the men involved themselves.[11] However, a desire to defend the fatherland might easily mask other interests. Thus Martín Javier Mina may or may not have been a sincere patriot, but he was certainly the very archetype of the nineteenth-century *pretendiente* – the young man anxious to secure patronage and preferment in government service.

If he threw himself into liberal politics after 1814, it was not just out of conviction but because there was no other way for him to make his way in the world, and the impression of opportunism that one is left with after considering his career is strengthened still further by the fact that his captivity in France at one point actually saw him offer his services to Joseph Bonaparte. For such men the guerrilla bands offered a golden opportunity, and it is worth turning aside to consider two of them in more detail.[12]

Of these, the first is the fascinating figure of Mariano Renovales. A junior officer in the colonial militia, he had just returned to Spain after many years in America when the war broke out. After joining Palafox at Zaragoza, he had quickly secured a commission as a brigadier, and gained some repute in the defence of first Zaragoza and then the Valle del Roncal, to which he managed to escape whilst he was being sent to France as a prisoner of war. After travelling to Cádiz in 1810, he had then succeeded in persuading the government of the virtues of a wild scheme to raise the inhabitants of the Basque provinces in revolt. As he wrote to the captain-general of Galicia, Nicolás Mahy:

> My command . . . extends to the Basque provinces, La Rioja and Santander, and in so far as these points are concerned, I have already sent orders to the soldiers and guerrillas stationed in them . . . to molest the enemy without risking a general action . . . Colonel Miguel Eraso is in the province of Burgos with 1,500 men; there are 2,000 Navarrese in the area of Vitoria under the command of their chiefs . . . Gastón and Hosca; the commandant, Miguel Horno, is near Bilbao with another thousand men; and there are strong *partidas* lurking in the vicinity of . . . Santander.[13]

When this scheme proved so much hot air, Renovales soon fell out of favour with the commanders of the Spanish forces of Galicia and Asturias, whilst the cadre of professional officers attached to his command became so disgruntled at his posturing and incapacity that they eventually placed him under arrest.[14] Thoroughly disgraced, Renovales then took no part in the war until Allied forces threatened the French hold on Biscay in 1812, whereupon he rushed to claim his satrapy, only to fall by sheer ill luck into the hands of the enemy (a fate that he turned to good account by striking an attitude of such defiance that he was eventually confined in the fortress of Joux – the Napoleonic equivalent of being sent to the Second World War German 'bad boys' camp' of Castle Colditz). After going into exile in 1814 rather than return to the Spain of Fernando VII, he drifted into liberal politics in London and, as we have seen, became involved in a scheme to raise a revolt in Mexico. Supposed to be its leader, he lost heart at the last minute and betrayed the whole scheme to the authorities, at whose behest he agreed to turn *agent provocateur* so as to ensure a clean sweep of the conspirators.[15]

Few sensible observers would ever claim that Renovales was much of a hero, but this was not the case with our other example, who is none other than Francisco Espoz y Mina. According to the Navarrese leader's own account of events, outraged at the French invasion in general, and the behaviour of the French soldiery in particular, he rushed to enlist in the Patriot army, in which he served as a private in a newly raised Aragonese unit entitled the Tiradores de Doyle. Stationed in Jaca as part of its garrison, he then found himself in danger of becoming a prisoner of war, for the town's governor decided to surrender without a fight as soon as enemy troops arrived following the fall of Zaragoza in February 1809.Having slipped away in the nick of time, he then returned to Navarre, where he enlisted in the *partida* of his distant relative Martín Javier Mina y Larrea, with whom he served until the latter's capture in March 1810.[16]

There are, however, a number of problems with this account. Let us set aside the fact that Espoz y Mina's enlistment in the Tiradores de Doyle did not follow the uprising against the French quite as swiftly as he makes out (there is a story that for a while he actually took service with the French as a groom). Much more important is the fact that he claims to have heard of Mina's activities when he was at Jaca, although the latter did not take the field until several months after the fortress surrendered, and, even more important, that a later aside suggests that he only joined his relative's band after he killed a bandit-cum-guerrilla who had tried to pillage his home.[17] If patriotism was absent from his decision to enlist, self-interest most certainly was not. To judge from his later conduct and public persona, Espoz y Mina was a deeply ambitious man determined to throw off the shackles imposed on him by his position as a younger son of a peasant household in a remote hamlet in Navarre. No record exists of his inner thoughts at this time, but Von Brandt describes him as an 'excellent macchiavellist', whilst a remarkable pamphlet written in 1813 paints a picture that is all too plausible. Thus, this suggests that the then Francisco Espoz Ilundaín was inspired by the model of Napoleon to seek his fortune on the battlefield, and, in particular, to form a 'legion of the damned' composed of outcasts of all sorts – smugglers, bandits, fugitives from the Spanish armies and the urban and rural poor – that would provide him with a loyal power base and make him a power in the land.[18]

If this seems a little fanciful, it can only be observed that all of Espoz y Mina's actions after succeeding to the command of the forces of his predecessor conformed to just such a programme. As we have seen, all his rivals were wiped out, usually on the pretext that they were behaving like bandits and causing more harm to the populace than they were to the French, whilst in at least one instance even emissaries of the central government appear to have been eliminated.[19] Also got rid of was the self-proclaimed leader of the insurrection in Navarre, Casimir de Miguel e Irujo, who in 1810 had travelled to the new capital of Cádiz, and, on the strength of having been of some assistance to Mina at the time he had been organising his band, secured the grandly named position of 'commander-in-chief of the guerrillas of Navarre'.[20] And before all this there is the question of just how Espoz y Mina came to take command of the band originally commanded by Mina. Well before the end of the war rumours were circulating that the latter had been betrayed, and, whilst nothing can be proved against him, the account that Espoz y Mina gives of the affair is at the very least deeply suspicious. Thus:

> Hardly had we arrived in Labiano when a column of 3,000 enemy troops appeared in the vicinity. Seeing what was going on, I rode out with a few horsemen to take a look at them, whilst my nephew [*sic:* see below, note 21] had a rest. Seeing that they were heading straight for the village, I sent a message warning everybody who was there to get clear, and tried to slow down the enemy by having my men fire at them with their carbines, only galloping clear when the French had got within pistol-shot of us. Believing that [Mina] had by now got clear away, I then retired . . . only to find that . . . he had either believed that the danger was not as immediate as was actually the case, or wanted to give an example of courage, and been betrayed by his own daring. When he finally mounted his horse, the French had already entered the village . . . Shooting his mount, they quickly surrounded him, and took him prisoner.[21]

Reading between the lines of this account, it is impossible not to suspect that Espoz y Mina either deliberately provoked the French into attacking Mina at a moment when he knew that the latter could be taken unawares, or simply betrayed him outright.[22] Whatever the truth of the matter, there is little doubt as to what happened next. As Espoz y Mina himself provides few details as to how he persuaded the survivors of Mina's forces to accept his command, let us quote the harangue cited by the anonymous author of the pamphlet cited above:

> Well, lads, if you are not careful, you will find that the French will have left you no option but to get an honest job, for, what with requisitioning, looting and imposing fines, they will soon have grabbed all the swag. . . . All the gold, all the silver, all the jewellery, in fact all the good things in life, will end up in their hands if you do not . . . resist them to the death. Do not be afraid: I will be your leader, and if you obey me you will . . . cover yourselves in glory. Unable to show your face in any town, until now you have had to work by night and make do with lonely roads and isolated houses as your targets. Lacking a legitimate reason to live off . . . other people's property, meanwhile, you have been persecuted by all and sundry. But from now on you will be respectable. As the French are the enemy, if you kill them you will be able to enrich yourselves not just with their money, but also with everybody else's

> . . . You will be called defenders of the fatherland, and as such seen as men of honour. You will be able to enter without fear not just small places, but also towns and cities, whilst you will be able to . . . demand all the food you could eat and all the money you could possibly desire . . . And if anyone resists you, you will be able to deal with them . . . Indeed, you will be able to flog the very justices who once persecuted you without anyone daring to say a word for fear of being . . . punished as a traitor . . . At the beginning Bonaparte was no more than a lowly [junior] officer . . . and yet now he is an emperor who is . . . troubling the entire world. All I ask for is obedience: for the rest you may rely on me.[23]

What this says about the nature of Espoz y Mina's forces is something that is best left to another moment. The important point here is simply to note that we cannot trust most stories about why individual guerrilla commanders took up arms. For another example, let us look at the issue of revenge as personified by the unknown combatant who figures in the memoirs of the British officer Joseph Sherer:

> In a village about three leagues from Pamplona . . . I met with . . . a guerrilla . . . I asked him where he lived and under whom he served. 'Señor,' said he, 'I have no home, no relations, nothing save my country and my sword. My father was led out and shot in the market place of my native village; our cottage was burned; my mother died of grief; and my wife, who had been violated by the enemy, fled to me, then a volunteer with Palafox, and died in my arms in a hospital in Zaragoza. I serve under no particular chief: I . . . feel too revengeful to support the restraint of discipline and the delay of manoeuvre . . . But I have sworn never to dress a vine or to plough a field till the enemy is driven out of Spain.'[24]

All this seems plausible enough, especially as British, French and Spanish observers are agreed that the appalling behaviour engaged in by the invaders played a major role in stirring up popular resistance. As a British general captured in an unsuccessful raid on Fuengirola wrote of an incident that occurred whilst he was passing through Jaén, for example:

> The fact . . . is that at the commencement the Spaniards were lukewarm in their own cause, and would probably still have remained so had not the cruelties and excesses of the French roused them to resistance and revenge. . . . While at dinner I learned that Major Ropach had been sent with a detachment to destroy a village about twelve miles distant where some French soldiers had been murdered the preceding night, for it is a general order that the inhabitants of the place where such a crime is committed are put to the sword, without exception of age or sex, and their habitations

burned to the ground . . . By this system of terror and extermination the French have created the bands that they name brigands, for the inhabitants of a village who are fortunate enough to escape from these military executions, having no place of refuge, join the first armed party they meet, and, urged by revenge and desperation, commit the greatest cruelties on the enemies who fall into their hands.[25]

To back up this observer, meanwhile, we might cite the Frenchman Captain Elzéar Blaze and the Spaniard Salmón. Referring to the plunder of Spain's churches, for example, the former wrote, 'Had some of our amateurs of fine art . . . been picked out and shot, the war would not have become national . . . These dilapidations were the cause of the war to the death that the Spaniards waged against us.'[26] And finally, it was Salmón's view that the 'cruelty and terrorism that the French saw as the most effective means of limiting the growth of the *partidas* served only to multiply their numbers and give them greater vigour'.[27]

To substantiate these arguments, case after case may be cited of *cabecillas* who are supposed to have joined the struggle against the French after the latter had injured them in some way or another. One such was Francisco Abad Moreno (Chaleco), a shepherd from Valdepeñas whose mother and brother were killed when the French sacked his home town in June 1808. This case is well documented, and there seems little doubt that Abad was genuinely committed to the struggle: thanks to the patronage of General Castaños, at the end of the war he was a colonel, whilst he also earned the praise even of men who were normally sceptical of the *guerrilla popular.*[28]

In other instances, however, there is room for doubt. Thus, revenge was supposedly the motivation of the Franciscan friar Lucás Rafael, the prosperous *labrador* Camilo Gómez, the post-rider Toribio Bustamente and the wealthy nobleman Ventura Jiménez (in brief, it is claimed that Rafael's father was executed by the French for refusing to swear loyalty to Joseph Bonaparte; that Gómez's wife and daughters were violated by French troops who had sacked his home and seized his livestock; that Bustamente's wife and son were murdered when the French sacked his home town of Medina de Río Seco in July 1808; and that Jiménez's wife was raped by soldiers quartered in his home). Yet how far can we trust these stories? The fact that Jiménez's own version of events makes no mention of his wife's violation is not encouraging: he rather says that he had to flee his home after acting as a guide for some passing Spanish troops.[29] Equally, the only evidence for the story relating to the murder of Rafael's father comes from a pamphlet that is couched in such exaggerated language that it is hard to take anything that it says at face value.[30] In at least two further instances, meanwhile, they can be shown to be nonsense, the first of these being that of the famous Juan Martín Díez. According to Rodríguez Solis, El Empecinado went to war to avenge the death at the hands of French troops of the son of a local *cacique*, who had shown him much favour, whilst the English seminarian Brindle has a still more dramatic story:

> On the eruption of the French, the town of Aranda de Duero suffered in common with the other places visited by the enemy, but the family of John Martin [*sic*] had a more than equal share of those sufferings. His wife was killed before his own eyes; his daughters were treated in the most brutal and shocking manner, his property was plundered and destroyed, and from a state of affluence he was reduced to the greatest want without wife or child to console him in his misfortunes.[31]

All this, alas, is invention pure and simple (aside from anything else, El Empecinado's wife survived the war). To get a plausible story we must therefore turn rather to El Empecinado's twentieth-century biographers, who are agreed that he killed a French soldier over a girl and had in consequence to take flight. Perhaps this is the truth, and, then again, perhaps it is not. Why, though, was the Frenchman killed? Was El Empecinado trying to protect the girl's honour, as his admirers suggest, or did he quarrel with the enemy soldier in a fit of jealousy? We shall, of course, never know, but it is impossible not to suspect that what actually happened is very different from the stuff of legend.[32]

Very different from the stuff of legend, too, is the real story of how Martín Javier Mina became a *cabecilla*. The son of a landowner with a seat in the provincial estates, according to Southey, Mina had been a student in Pamplona when the war broke out. Struck down by illness, he was forced to retire to his father's estates, and there he might well have remained but for the fact that one night his home was plundered by French troops. Having armed himself with a musket, he went to the nearest village and invited anyone who cared do so to join him in taking to the hills. Twelve men answered the call, and together they ambushed a small party of French artillerymen who were marching from Zaragoza to Pamplona. Yet this tale, too, is a fabrication, for Mina had been a student at Zaragoza rather than Pamplona, and is suggested to have spent the first year of the war working for a Navarrese general named Areizaga, who had supposedly been given the task of whipping up resistance in his home province by the Junta Central and eventually commissioned him to raise a *partida*. Even this may not be the whole story: according to some French sources, Mina was actually expelled from university for misconduct, after which he took up with a gang of bandits. We shall never know the truth, doubtless, but it does at least seem clear that the traditional version of events is not to be trusted.[33]

The question of official involvement in the formation of the guerrilla bands is one to which we shall return in due course, and all that needs to be noted for the time being is the extent to which the origins of the *partidas* have become shrouded in myth. In reality, like Espoz y Mina, El Mozo, as he became known, was little more than an adventurer, whilst in case after case what emerges is a picture in which patriotism plays little part. Thus, in the Condado de Niebla, Juan Santana Bolaños appears as a mere hireling taken on by the local *caciques* Vicente Letoña and Atanasio Rodríguez when the latter decided to finance and equip a *partida* in the hope of insuring themselves against charges of collaboration.[34] In other cases economic necessity was replaced by happenstance, with the *cabecillas* including a number of men who seem to have become guerrilla commanders more by accident than by design. One such was an erstwhile Guardia de Corps named Ramón de Murillo, who was dispatched to the province of Soria in the aftermath of the Spanish defeat at Gamonal in November 1808 to round up fugitives from the battle, only to find himself issued with a commission by an insurgent junta that had been established at Nájera.[35] Still another was the well-known *manchego* leader, Manuel Hernández (El Abuelo), who only took up arms when a delegation of his neighbours requested that he fill the place left vacant when Francisquete – in 1808 a fellow inhabitant of the town of Madridejos – was killed in action in 1810.[36] And a third was Juan Díaz Porlier, who became a guerrilla when he was cut off at Gamonal and found himself isolated in the mountains with a handful of fugitives.[37]

In still other instances, as with Mina and Espoz y Mina, the dominant impression that one is left with is one of opportunism. Few commanders, perhaps, were quite as blatant in their motives as a *resguardo* officer in the service of the French from Sanlúcar de Barrameda named Julián Fernández, who turned up in the Patriot zone asking for a commission as a *cabecilla* for no better reason than that he had not been paid for months.[38] But even so, self-interest was often buried only a short way beneath the surface, a case in point being that of the Aragonese *cabecilla* Fidel Mallén. Having placed himself under the orders of the newly arrived Pedro Villacampa, in November 1809 he asked if he could recruit a new *partida* from the many deserters sitting out the war in those parts of Aragón occupied by the French. So far, so good, but then came the sting in the tail: claiming that the Junta Central's guerrilla ordinances (see below, pp. 105–7) were ruining his plans, weakening his forces and limiting his powers of independent action, he demanded that they be waived. In justification of this demand he pointed out that he had seen his house destroyed, his goods confiscated and his business ruined, all of which entitled him, or so he argued, to some consideration. But in doing so, of course, he simply gave the game away: underlying the whole proposal was nothing more than a desire for plunder.[39]

What use Mallén made of the independence that he claimed we unfortunately do not know, but one figure whose misdeeds are all too well chronicled is Antonio Piloti. Of Italian origin, in 1808 Piloti was a gunsmith in Madrid.

Claiming to have handed out many weapons to the populace at the time of both the Dos de Mayo and Napoleon's assault on the capital in December 1808, in June 1809 he wrote to the Junta Central asking permission to implement a scheme that he had evolved for the establishment of bands of sharpshooters in La Mancha, Old Castile and Vizcaya with the help of a number of other gunsmiths.[40] Permission was immmediately granted, and by the late summer he had acquired a small group of followers and travelled to the vicinity of the town of Cuenca, where, on 22 September, the Junta of Aragón announced that, at the head of a band 400-strong, he had just taken prisoner a small French detachment at Perales de Tajuña.[41] Yet the reality was very different. In fact, Piloti never possessed more than seventeen men, of whom most seem to have been runaway friars, whilst he terrorised the countryside, showered commissions and appointments on all sides and engaged in suspicious contacts with the French. These the gunsmith tried to pass off as attempts to encourage desertion amongst the enemy, but it was to no avail: despite an abortive attempt on the part of his men to defend him, on 22 September he was arrested by the governor of Cuenca, the Marqués de las Atalayuelas.[42] Nothing if not resourceful, Piloti tried to talk his way out of trouble – 'My services on behalf of the Spanish nation are as patent as they are obvious . . . The desertion of the greater part of the garrison of the capital was very close, all that was needed being for me to get to Alcalá [de Henares] and give the word'[43] – and, fortunately for him secured the backing of the Duque del Infantado, a singularly vapid individual who had been one of his original sponsors.[44] What happened next is unknown, but at all events Piloti escaped punishment, for in November 1810 he turned up at El Empecinado's headquarters in Sigüenza. The reason for his visit was clear to all and sundry – that he was out to enveigle Martín into giving him some troops, and rumours immediately spread that Piloti was going to be given the command of the Tiradores de Sigüenza, one of the regiments that by now made up the latter's command. Convinced that he was about to be demoted, the unit's commander, one Nicolás María de Isidro, accosted El Empecinado in the street and shouted that he had formed the regiment himself and was not going to let anyone take it away from him. After fleeing to his quarters, the famous guerrilla was besieged by a mob of angry soldiers, whilst the erstwhile gunsmith decided to leave town in a hurry.[45] There follows another gap in the record, but in 1813 Piloti resurfaces again, this time being arrested in an inn in Ciudad Rodrigo on two charges of banditry. Even then he was not finished – there followed two dramatic gaolbreaks – but in January 1815 he finally commenced a ten-year prison sentence.[46]

Whether Piloti actually set out to become a bandit is another matter – it is, in fact, more likely that he was rather a would-be Espoz y Mina whose ambitions came to naught – but there are a number of instances where it is quite clear that a life of crime was central to the decision to become a *cabecilla*. Let us take, for example, the case of Antonio Valdivielso Morguecho. A member of the so-called 'Companía de Contrabandistas de Ayamonte', in September 1810 he suddenly went absent without leave and turned up in Cádiz with a highly dubious story to the effect that he was dissatisfied with his current unit on account of the fact that it was not doing enough to fight the French. Needless to say, he wanted to be allowed to form his own *partida*, having chosen for his area of operations the environs of Seville, where he claimed to have 'a great number of friends', whilst for good measure he also wanted to take as many men from his old band with him as could be persuaded to come along.[47] Whether all this was the attempt to rebuild some pre-war *cuadrilla* that it looks like we shall probably never know, but in Old Castile in particular we have a number of cases where banditry was certainly the mainspring in the formation of particular *partidas*. Of these the most prominent cases are those of Príncipe and Saornil.

Known as 'Borbón' on account of his service with the cavalry regiment of that name, Tomás Príncipe was in 1808 a deserter on the run from the law who had already had to turn to crime to make his living, whilst Jerónimo Saornil had actually been awaiting trial for banditry, but had been saved by the uprising of May 1808. With crime their only means of support, both men had soon gathered together bands that were in reality, exactly as the French claimed, nothing more than gangs of highway robbers. Little better, meanwhile, were the various deserters who became *cabecillas*, such as José Fombella, a cavalryman who fled his unit and, in the words of a Patriot army officer, 'set himself up as the captain of a gang, composed in part of men of his regiment whom he had incited to desert and in part of a variety of other thieves and ne'er-do-wells, at the head of which he has sacked many villages and committed the greatest atrocities'.[48]

Conscious of the need to camouflage their real aims, many self-appointed leaders were careful to obtain the sanction of the authorities: the murder of a French courier in December 1808, for example, was used by Saornil as a pretext to ask for a commission to form a guerrilla band, a ploy rewarded with confirmation of his command and the rank of *alférez*.[49] Even more enterprisingly, an infantry captain named Vicente Moreno who abandoned his regiment to strike out on his own as a *cabecilla* in the Serranía de Ronda appears to have forged orders from the Marqués de la Romana (then far away in Extremadura) to form a *partida* from the *dispersos* of the district, and then made use of these papers to secure genuine documents from the general who had been appointed as nominal head of the insurrection.[50]

But these stratagems should not fool us. Indeed, stripping bare the claims of the horde of petitioners who requested a command is often an interesting experience: one José González Cobos, for example, turns out to have been a deserter who had just been ejected from the 'Companía de Guerrilla de Ayamonte' for misconduct.[51] In a letter that he dispatched to General Castaños, meanwhile, Pablo Morillo was quite explicit as to what had been going on:

> You say, Your Excellency, that you are doubtful whether much benefit is to be obtained from the guerrillas. For my part, I would either assimilate them into the army or suppress them altogether. If you will pardon me for saying so, you have been too trusting and ingenuous: the men you have appointed to command them have included too many unknown adventurers who have got round you with a mixture of lies and false promises. One such is Félix Salmeiro, an inhabitant of Cáceres of the most irregular conduct to whom you awarded . . . all the trappings of an officer, only for him since to have attracted much censure. And, even if we set Salmeiro aside, the fact is that many of the men who came to you did so with no other aim than the devastation of this province . . . It is all very well to place one's trust in individuals of some repute such as . . . the doctor, Juan Peralta [i.e., Palarea], but giving credit to men whose criminal conduct has horrified the whole of . . . Extremadura has so increased the number of bandits that it will take a century to get rid of them.[52]

Yet in a sense such doubts are irrelevant. Whatever may have been the motivation of their commanders, one cannot deny that plenty of *partidas* sprang up without any intervention on the part of the authorities, nor wish away the numerous petitions from men eager to set themselves up as *cabecillas*. Sufficient space has already been devoted to the former phenomenon, but of the latter let us take a few examples from 1809. On 30 April Juan del Castillo, a supernumerary cavalry officer who until then had been employed rounding up deserters, approached the Junta Central with a proposal for the formation of a unit of cavalry, at the head of which he proposed to raise the whole of Catalonia in revolt.[53] On 1 June Francisco Javier de Segura, an official in the administration of the state's tobacco monopoly from Tafalla who had fought as a *voluntario distinguido* at the siege of Gibraltar in 1782, asked for a commission to return to Navarre 'with the sole aim of exciting the spirits of the inhabitants and . . . getting them to take up arms . . . against the enemy'.[54] On 30 September Manuel Jiménez Guazo, an official of the Ministry of Grace and Justice, who claimed (without much plausibility) to have distinguished himself in the first siege of Zaragoza, sought permission to form a *partida*.[55] On 27 October an inhabitant of Miraflores de la Sierra named Francisco Aznar Moreno, who claimed to have lost his father in the Dos de Mayo, asked for 'the title of *comandante* . . . and the power of being allowed, through my particular knowledge of both the inhabitants and the lands of the two Castiles, to get together a guerrilla band composed of anyone capable of carrying out the sort of actions necessary to harass the enemy . . . in the domains in which he has intruded'.[56] And, finally, towards the close of the year, a chaplain of the monastery of Santo Domingo de Silos named Policarpio Romeo petitioned the government to be allowed to form 'a 400-strong corps entitled the Legion of Extermination whose purpose would be to act as light troops throughout the Sierra de Alcañiz'.[57] And, when they were not willing to fight themselves, there were plenty of individuals who were anxious to promote the virtues of organising *partidas*, or to make use of them as a means of publicising their patriotism. Thus, in February 1809 one Luis Valero sent a memorandum on guerrilla warfare to the Junta Central, in which he wrote, 'The more the guerrillas multiply, the easier it will be to kill a lot of the enemy at little cost, and the more will they become exhausted and demoralised.'[58] And in January 1810 the Marqués de Villafranca y los Vélez issued a proclamation in Murcia calling for volunteers for a new *partida* entitled 'La Cruzada Murciana', which was to consist of sixty priests and religious aged between eighteen and forty-five whom he promised to equip in splendid uniforms consisting of helmets, brown jackets with scarlet collars and cuffs and light blue piping, white breeches and riding boots.[59]

We may, then, say that the *partidas* owed a large part of their existence to individual action – that they had, in fact, a life outside the state. But the formation of the guerrilla bands was never left solely to the ambition, energy and initiative of men such as Juan Martín Díez or Francisco Espoz y Mina. From the very beginning, indeed, the Patriot authorities took it upon themselves to organise *partidas* that could harass the enemy. Thus, the irregulars that so troubled Dupont in the weeks that preceded the battle of Bailén were in many instances in the pay of the Junta of Jaén, whilst in Old Castile General Cuesta – a commander who made himself odious to many admirers of the guerrillas by having El Empecinado arrested as a bandit in the summer of 1808 – had no sooner declared against the French than he had dispatched one of his officers to encourage guerrilla resistance amongst the inhabitants of the districts that lay between his headquarters in Valladolid and French-occupied Burgos.[60] As the French regained the upper hand in the struggle in the winter of 1808–9 following the set-back that they had suffered after Bailén, so interest in the subject gained fresh impetus. On 21 January 1809, for example, we find the Conde de Tilly, one of Seville's two representatives to the Junta Central, suggesting the revival of the Moros Mogataces de Orán, a unit of Moorish irregular cavalry that had until the 1790s been attached to the garrison of the African outpost of Orán. As he wrote:

> It is clear that their style of fighting is most appropriate for guerrilla warfare . . . whilst it would certainly be very damaging to the French: the speed of their horses, their ability to fire their muskets at the gallop, and the courage with which they face danger make them terrible opponents.[61]

If this idea was hardly practical, the Junta Central more than saw the point. Thus, on 28 December 1808 a decree appeared authorising the formation of bands of irregulars up to 100-strong under the leadership of *cabecillas* responsible to the military authorities, whilst on 25 February 1809 a second order – the so-called decree of the *corso terrestre* – stipulated that any money and other valuables seized from the French and their supporters would automatically become the property of the men who had taken it.[62] Alongside this legitimisation of highway robbery, there also appeared general calls for revolt along the lines, say, of that addressed to the population of Old and New Castile on 28 April 1809:

> Castilians! Now or never! If we all unite, then we shall all be saved. The enemy . . . are few in number, and if we all fall on them at once, they will without doubt succumb . . . What do you have to lose? Risk your lives for liberty like good men and true![63]

These decrees and proclamations, meanwhile, were backed by measures of a more practical sort. Thus, in May 1809 a captain of the Cazadores de Zafra infantry regiment named José Crivell was given thirty men and sent off to raise a company of *tiradores* in the Montes de Toledo, whilst the following month saw the erstwhile second-in-command of the *resguardo* of Navarre, Manuel Loynaz, ordered to travel to his home province and whip up popular resistance there.[64] And in both Old Castile and Aragón special commissioners were appointed whose brief included the task of raising fresh *partidas* and galvanising those that were already in existence.[65]

Government action, meanwhile, was mirrored in a series of local initiatives. Threatened by French attack, in December 1808 the Junta of Badajoz formed a number of *partidas* in an effort to stave off the French, of which one was commanded by Pablo Morillo, a sergeant in the Regimiento de Infantería de Marina and veteran of the battle of Trafalgar who had in June 1808 obtained a commission in one of the new regiments formed by the Junta of Extremadura.[66] Appointed in the same month to head the provinces of Galicia, León and Asturias, the Marqués de la Romana inaugurated his command by ordering the entire male populace to be formed into large numbers of *partidas* on the grounds that, until the Spanish armies were ready to undertake major operations, the only thing to be done was 'to harass the enemy without cease and defeat him in detail' (so strong was La Romana's interest in the subject, indeed, that one of his staff officers produced a pamphlet that set out to instruct the populace in how they might take on the French, whilst the newspaper published by his army's headquarters consistently urged the Junta Central to hold back its troops in the shelter of the chains of mountains that ringed the areas then held by the French whilst relying on the guerrillas to contain and wear down the invaders).[67] In the Levant the summer of 1809 saw the captain-general of Valencia, José Caro, transform the urban militias that had been formed throughout the region into ready-made guerrilla bands that would be ready to take the field as soon as the French made an appearance (interestingly, whilst the propertied classes were expected to serve for nothing, the peasantry were promised an allowance of 5 *reales* per day). Not satisfied with the response, meanwhile, in March 1810 he ordered the immediate enlistment with the guerrilla bands of the interior of the large number of peasants and day-labourers who had flocked to the city of Valencia in search of work, food and shelter.[68] Similar efforts to set up guerrilla bands in readiness for a French invasion were made in the province of Murcia in 1809 by a commissioner dispatched there by the Junta Central named Antonio Sáenz de Vizmanos.[69] And, finally, a succession of generals proved more than willing either to confirm existing *cabecillas* in their commands or to appoint fresh chieftains. Thus, setting aside the case of Mina (which we have already examined), in September 1809 the Conde de Cartaojal – then commander of the Army of the Centre – appointed an inhabitant of Algecilla named Manuel de la Calzada to head a new *partida* in the district known as the Alcarria, whilst in May 1810 Nicolás Mahy took Francisco Longa, who had until then been operating under the orders of the Marqués de Barriolucio, under the wing of the Army of the Left.[70] And, last but not least, in May 1812 the new *comandante general* of the province of Valencia, Francisco Copons, authorised a friar named Luis Rovira to raise a force of irregulars under the name of the División de Tiradores Honrados.[71]

So much, then, for the leadership of the guerrillas. As we have seen, driven by a variety of motives, a large number of individuals either formed *partidas* on their own initiative without involving the authorities at all, or offered themselves to the latter as prospective *cabecillas*. As for the Spanish juntas and generals, threatened with complete disaster, they gladly availed themselves of partisan warfare as a means of staving off the French and weakening their forces. What, though, was the popular response to these efforts? In the eyes of tradition, of course, moved by hatred of the French and love of *el rey deseado*, the populace rushed to join the *partidas*. According to Rodríguez Solis, for example, sixty men had joined Merino within days of his taking to the hills, whilst Palarea had only to announce his intention of forming a band for 'all the sons of the province [of La Mancha] to believe themselves obliged to second him'.[72] And, if we are to believe Espoz y Mina, 'My little army was swelled by new volunteers every day, men coming forward in no small numbers in the hope of sharing the privations and glories of the soldiers who were fighting for the honour and glory of the Fatherland at my orders.'[73] At the same time a well-known list of some twenty-two guerrilla bands put together in 1812 claims that these alone numbered some 38,520 men.[74] This is all very well, but, whilst the fact of considerable popular involvement in the *guerrilla* is impossible to deny, the vision that is thereby conjured up clearly flies in the face of the lack of interest in the war that was so evident in the unoccupied parts of the country. Why, then, did so many Spaniards enlist with the guerrillas? On the surface, the French had to do no more than appear in a district for attitudes to the war to be transformed, but, as we shall see, this was not in fact the case. Setting aside the exception of parts of Navarre and the Basque provinces, where a set of absolutely unique circumstances did produce a reaction that more or less corresponded to the traditional stereotype, we must therefore look for fresh models of popular involvement.

For those addicted to the idea of an anti-French crusade, the suggestion that the populace showed no willingness to join the guerrillas may be a shocking one, but it is nevertheless one that cannot be gainsaid. Let us take, for example, the case of the thousands of *dispersos* to be found throughout the occupied provinces. Men who had run away or become separated from their regiments and fled to their homes, they were, it was generally observed, impervious to every effort to get them to return to their duty. As two commissioners sent out by the Junta of Catalonia observed to General Lacy in 1811:

> Given the critical nature of the situation, we have no option but to inform Your Excellency . . . that the province is in a state of semi-anarchy and the people dominated by ideas of a most sinister character. Catalonia is lost unless we change our maxims. Eroles, Miláns, Mansó and all the other agents who have been sent out to collect the *dispersos* will not bring in even a tenth part of them by the military means which they have adopted. They have been working at the task for more than a month, and, for all the good that they have achieved, they might as well not have bothered. Terror is all very well, but . . . in this respect it has produced the very opposite effect to the one desired.[75]

With a great deal of effort some men were got in, such as the eighty-eight stragglers, fugitives, convalescents and deserters assembled by a Valencian captain named Reig sent out by Francisco Copons from his headquarters in Alicante in the spring of 1812.[76] But the populace as a whole generally showed little enthusiasm for the struggle. Let us take, for example, the Cantabrian district of the Liebana, which Mariano Renovales spent the winter of 1810–11 trying to galvanise in favour of his projected guerrilla army. As Renovales' replacement, José Aburruza, wrote to General Mahy after the former's arrest:

> Your Excellency writes that I should stay on here to foment and support the insurrection . . . but for the sake of truth I have no option but to tell you that everyone is living quietly at home, and that I do not believe that there will be any insurrection at all until the enemy actually appears. In so far as I can see, at no time since we arrived here has anyone done anything but work in the fields.[77]

As confirmation of this indifference to the war amongst the peasantry of the Cantabrian mountains, we might take a proclamation issued by the Junta of Asturias in September 1810, which accused the inhabitants of the province of having been taken in by the efforts of the French 'to establish a ruinous indifference . . . by means of hypocrisy and feigned benevolence'.[78] Also suggestive is the fact that, at about the same time, Porlier was complaining bitterly that he could not get the inhabitants of Asturias to carry letters for him, let alone provide him with information on the movements of the French.[79] And the problem was the same elsewhere. Appointed commandant of the district known as the Tierra de Barros in Extremadura in April 1810, Morillo found that his attempts to form a home guard amongst the populace were stymied by highly implausible claims of a want of arms.[80] From La Mancha it was claimed in March 1812 that there were sufficient *dispersos* in the provinces of Cuenca, Guadalajara, Molina de Aragón, Soria and Aragón – the very heartland of the war of Durán, El Empecinado and Villacampa – to form an army of 30,000 men.[81] From Catalonia it was being reported by 1811 that the populace was not only in a state of complete apathy, but refusing to fight in the *somatén*.[82] And at about the same time a government spy in French-occupied Seville wrote, 'In this city and its surroundings there are many *dispersos*. Much rigour is needed to deal with the problem . . . The parents of the men concerned should be held responsible, and a number of examples made amongst them.'[83]

One could continue in this vein *ad infinitum*, but rather than simply listing example after example, let us take the case of the modern-day province of Huelva. Penetrated by the French for the first time in February 1810, the area had never been in any sense a hub of the Spanish war effort. Conscription had languished, and the only sign of military activity had been the formation of a so-called 'company of guerrillas' which was largely formed of deserters and seems in practice to have been little more than the private army of the Junta of Ayamonte (alongside this there was an even more dubious force consisting of a collection of bandits and smugglers who had been hired as a kind of *Freikorps*). Enthusiasm for the struggle, meanwhile, was notable only by its absence, particularly as the local authorities appear to have been particularly corrupt in the administration of the *quinta*. On arriving in the province to take command of the handful of troops who had escaped thither from the fall of Seville,

Francisco Copons therefore encountered a depressing picture. As the chronicler of his operations wrote:

> All energy and patriotism were gone. The egoism of many landowners . . . the fear and ignorance of the mass of the people and the sagacity of the enemy, who had been both buying the hearts of the rich and . . . terrifying the spirits of the poor, ensured that many *pueblos* submitted to the yoke of the *rey intruso.* As for those places that remained free, they suffered from the same egotism, their justices acting in an arbitrary manner that recognised . . . no other law than that of their caprice . . . From this it followed that in every *pueblo* many stragglers and deserters were hidden without either the justices or, much less, their parents . . . making any attempt to get them to return to their regiments.[84]

As for Copons himself, he was close to despair. No sooner had he arrived at Ayamonte than he was complaining, 'The *pueblos* of the Condado de Niebla lack the patriotic ardour that once moved them. Although they sigh for their liberty and cry out for the enemy to be defeated, nobody is doing anything.'[85] Nor did the situation improve. Notwithstanding frequent incursions on the part of the French, there were few signs of resistance.[86] Exhorted by the Junta of Cádiz to carry the war to the French, a frustrated Copons could only stamp his feet in rage: 'Whip up revolt! Nothing is more impossible! Time goes by and yet in every *pueblo* there are men who . . . exhort their fellows to remain quiet so as not to attract the ire of the enemy.'[87] Recruitment meanwhile fell into a state of complete stagnation. To quote a report sent by Copons to the Regency in September 1810:

> Thus far . . . the only men who have left this county to defend the cause of Your Majesty have been the first class of recruits, and even then it is only the poorest that have had to go . . . Protected by their less fortunate fellows, thousands of men continue to live quietly at home, and they are seemingly quite happy to see the country lost. The second class of recruits is the one that embodies most vices: the possession of a property worth a few *reales* is quite enough to give the householders who form its backbone a way out. Their homes are valued at a price which they do not merit, and because of this whole multitudes have been exempted. Amongst them are to be found men with five sons who have managed to buy out the lot. Yet, whilst their boys sit at home, their poorest neighbours go out to fight, including many lads who have had to leave behind widowed mothers living in a state of indigence. Another problem group, meanwhile, are the many clerks in minor orders . . . who have also been exempted. Amongst them are to be found many men who are barely able to read. Many marriages have also been faked,

> and the fact is that the whole time for most people the aim is to find a shield that will protect them from the draft. And the result of all this is, first, that . . . Your Majesty is not getting the men that have been called upon to assist in the explusion of the enemy . . . and, second, that amongst the populace . . . nothing is heard but laments, not to mention complaints that only the needy have to serve Your Majesty.[88]

It was not just Copons who noted the dichotomy that almost everywhere opened between hatred of the invaders and a willingness actually to join the struggle against them. Similar comments may also be noted in British sources. To quote a diplomat who travelled with Wellington's army across northern Spain in the autumn of 1812, for example:

> The feelings of all the provinces through which I have passed are decidedly inimical to the French and favourable to the common cause . . . At the same time . . . the patriotic feelings of the lower classes are of little use to their country. It is a passive feeling which murmurs under the oppression and tyranny which it suffers without exerting itself to remove or diminish what it complains of. The people pay their contributions and deliver up their mules, grain and provisions whenever they are demanded . . . by the enemy. Of course they complain of these exactions and are happy to see the English . . . But . . . it does the enemy no harm nor us any good.[89]

Much the same point, meanwhile, was made by the British general Robert Long. Thus:

> The people, alternately in the power of friends and foes, show indifference to both. They cannot take a part without danger to themselves; they prefer consequently personal security to a display of unseasonable loyalty or patriotism. In their hearts I believe they hate the French, but they have at the same time no great love for us.[90]

And finally, when Lord Blayney landed at Fuengirola in 1810, hopes that his handful of troops would be supported by the inhabitants of the neighbouring Serranía de Ronda proved unfounded, despite the fact that the whole area had seemingly taken arms against the French. Thus:

> Previous to marching I had some conversation with Captain Miller of the Ninety-Fifth Regiment, who, with several other officers, had been latterly employed in organising the Spanish peasants. He informed me that a considerable quantity of arms and ammunition had been distributed amongst them, and consequently that I might expect a number to join me immediately. In this, however, I was entirely disappointed, not more than ten or twelve making their appearance.[91]

The civilian population was not entirely indifferent to the war. When three members of Mina's band appeared in Pamplona to hand over a group of French prisoners who were being exchanged for two of his followers who had fallen into French hands, for example, they were mobbed by a cheering crowd and plied with food and drink.[92] And there were wild celebrations in both Madrid and parts of La Mancha in late July 1809, when exaggerated reports of the French defeat at Talavera set off rumours that Joseph Bonaparte had been captured with his entire army.[93] For a few of the men who followed the *cabecillas* it is even possible that traditional stereotypes hold good. Setting aside the inhabitants of Espoz y Mina's heartlands, this is especially true of the various priests and other religious who fought with the *partidas.* 'They were already our implacable enemies', wrote Sebastian Blaze. 'Forced back into the world, they became even more dangerous. Those who were young and active hung up their habits and became . . . brigands, it being to them that we owe the formation of those bands that became most famous for their cruelty.'[94] Yet how numerous these holy warriors were it is impossible to say: although one or two bands seem to have had quite a number of clerics, the general impression one is left with is that their numbers have been exaggerated.[95] And such was the strength of popular aversion to the struggle that it is impossible to place much weight on the importance of patriotism or ideology as factors in the motivation of most recruits. The most obvious alternative is revenge. Like the leaders of the *partidas*, the rank and file of the guerrillas have often been painted as men driven by such feelings. Thus, Saturnino Abuin – an early subordinate of El Empecinado who earned the sobriquet El Manco when he lost a hand in combat – and his two brothers are supposed to have joined the struggle after their home was burned down during the sack of Tordesillas by the French in December 1808.[96] Then there is the case of one Juan Gómez, a blacksmith from Bahabón de Esgueva, who reputedly joined the *partida* of Cura Merino after strangling a French soldier whom he caught molesting his daughter.[97] But there is much to mistrust here. Abuin, for example, may have been from Tordesillas, but that is about all that is true in the story that we have just retailed: in reality he was a bandit whom the uprising found in prison awaiting trial for murder, and who, like many other men on the wrong side of the law, only became a *guerrillero* because it was the safest means of reverting to his old ways. Hence his eventual decision to abandon El Empecinado and join the French as a counter-guerrilla, Juan Martín's determination to discipline his forces obviously constituting a major obstacle to Abuin's dreams of a reign of terror.[98]

Whilst noting the possibility that some of the rank and file may have been motivated by hatred of the French (whether ideological or personal), it is therefore probably better to look for other factors when it comes to explaining why men sought out the *partidas.* One of these is a sense of adventure. Such, at least, is the tradition associated with Juan Fermín Leguía, a sergeant in Espoz y Mina's forces who on 13 March 1813 scaled the walls of the castle of Fuenterrabía at the head of a small party of men, overpowered the garrison, spiked its guns and threw all its powder and ammunition into the River Bidasoa: a peasant from Vera, we are told that, being of a somewhat wayward disposition, he simply became bored with life in his parents' *caserio* and ran off to join Espoz y Mina's men.[99] This, perhaps, is just a pious tale, but some credibility is lent to it by an incident in Madrid in August 1810 in which a scandalised father complained that his son and two other boys, all three of them aged about thirteen, had been seduced into setting off to join the forces of El Empecinado.[100]

Given the hatred that attached to military service, however, the number of children eager for some desperate glory cannot have been very great. Despite all the tales of patriotism, boyish enthusiasm and hatred of the French, it is clear that, outside Navarre, a decision to volunteer for the guerrillas was the product of more mundane factors. Let us take, for example, the case of the various bands that stemmed from the motley collection of gendarmes and customs guards known as the *resguardo* that had had the responsibility of fighting banditry and smuggling in Bourbon Spain. Accustomed to life in the wild and chasing *malhechores* of all sorts across the length and breadth of the country, the various components of this force were an obvious source of recruits for the guerrillas. Indeed, some bands seem to have come straight from its ranks, such as that commanded by Alejandro Fernández in La Mancha in 1810: in 1808 Fernández had been a police corporal, and his initial followers consisted of six of his men.[101] Once again, however, the reasons why such men fled are open to doubt. We do not know why Fernández becamme a *cabecilla*, but many of his fellows were initially quite happy to serve the *josefino* régime. As time went by, however, *el rey intruso* found it harder and harder to pay his followers, and thus it was that gaps began to appear in the ranks of the *resguardo* and, with them, new recruits for the *partidas.* Setting aside the case of Julián Fernández noted above, as one *afrancesado* official wrote from Zafra, 'Some members of the . . . *resguardo* of this town have fled to the *partidas* that have been infesting the region on the pretext that they have nothing to live on.'[102]

If lack of pay was one incentive for joining the guerrillas, another was the prospect of captivity in France, or, still worse, of being shot by the wayside as a result of being unable to keep up with the long columns of starving and disease-ridden prisoners that slowly made their way to the border in the wake of every Spanish defeat. Escaped prisoners of war were therefore an important source of recruits. One such was Pascual Ralla y Miravete, a soldier of the Regimiento de Fieles Zaragozanos, who was taken prisoner in Catalonia in

January 1810, but succeeded in escaping and eventually making his way back to his home town of Calatayud, where he fell in with the forces of El Empecinado and enlisted in their ranks, and another was Justo Prieto, a volunteer from Villaluenga de la Sagra who fled to the band of Juan Palarea after being taken prisoner at the battle of Ocaña in November 1809. Also captives of the French were the future Carlist leader Zumalcárregui and Espoz y Mina's trusted subordinate Gregorio Cruchaga, both of whom were taken by the French at Zaragoza only to slip away and enlist in the first instance in the ranks of the insurgents of the valley of the Roncal.[103] How many recruits were obtained in this fashion it is impossible to say, but the number certainly ran into many hundreds, if not thousands. Thus, in the two famous attacks that he launched on French convoys at Arlaban in May 1811 and April 1812 alone, Espoz y Mina rescued over a thousand Spanish prisoners, almost all of whom ended up in the ranks of his forces.[104] Meanwhile, actions such as that of Arlaban also tapped into a fresh source of recruits in the form of soldiers taken prisoner from the enemy. For such men joining the guerrillas was often the only chance of saving their lives – General Hugo, in fact, specifically says that many prisoners were offered the choice of enlistment or the firing squad – and this applied with still more force to Spanish soldiers who had chosen to fight for the French, such as for example, one Pedro Crespo, a sometime member of Joseph's 'Regimiento Real Irlandés', who was taken prisoner fighting with a guerrilla band in the summer of 1811.[105]

Joining the guerrillas to escape a fate that was even worse was clearly very common. Particularly if it involved French soldiers, brawling was likely to incur the harshest of penalties: hence the presence in the ranks of the *partidas* of both an ex-soldier from Lerma named Julián de Pablos, who joined Merino after a drunken spree ended in a fight with the local constables, and Espoz y Mina's henchman Félix Sarasa, who had to flee to the *partidas* after he came to blows with some French soldiers in Pamplona.[106]

Also out to escape were a variety of men who had fallen foul of the law. Amongst the men who served with Moreno in Andalucía, for example, was Francisco Herrera, a young man from Vélez Málaga who had been in gaol awaiting trial for murder when the French arrived in January 1810. Still incarcerated seven months later, on 13 July he was released when Moreno raided the town, and, naturally enough, decided to join his liberators.[107] Little better off, meanwhile, was Próspero Marco, a 24-year-old graduate who had had to flee his home in Lerma early in 1808 after a fight over a girl and for a while lived as a bandit before eventually ending up in the *partida* of Jerónimo Merino.[108] Draft evasion, too, was common: in October 1810, for example, a band appeared at Alájar under one Andrés Charlán that quickly attracted large numbers of *mozos* faced with the prospect of service in the Spanish army.[109]

And, last but not least, still other men left their homes for fear of conscription to the French forces. In contrast to many other parts of the empire, this was never imposed in Spain, but even so concerns of this sort were never far away (hence, indeed, the prominence of the issue in the great propaganda campaign that had accompanied the uprising of 1808). In consequence, even the most limited measures caused panic. Thus, when the *de facto* French viceroy of Andalucía, Marshal Soult, issued orders in May 1810 for all those *dispersos* who had been serving soldiers in 1808 to report to his headquarters in Seville on the grounds that, as members of the Spanish armed forces, they in theory owed allegiance to *el rey intruso*, the results were dramatic:

> Hearing that Marshal Victor [*sic*] was out to enlist them, the young men of Jerez and the other *pueblos* of the district abandoned their homes . . . and, rounding up as many horses as they could from farm and pasture, joined together and took up arms against their oppressors.[110]

Needless to say, such fears were ruthlessly exploited by the Patriots, a good example being events in the Serranía de Ronda, where the rising against the French appears in part to have been the work of agents who spread rumours that occupation would be followed by the conscription of the entire male populace and put it about that the invaders had brought with them whole wagon-loads of manacles for this purpose.[111]

Many of the guerrillas, then, were in essence runaways, an impression reinforced still further if we consider the linked questions of draft evasion and desertion. As the British diplomat Thomas Sydenham put it, by their very existence the *partidas* 'prevented the recruiting of the regular armies, for every Spanish peasant would naturally prefer rioting and plunder and living in free quarters to being drilled and starved with the regular army'.[112] As we have seen, meanwhile, not only did soldiers desert from the army in large numbers, but many of those concerned ended up with the *partidas* (albeit *faute de mieux*: many, it seems, would have been content to stay at home had they not been picked up by one or other of the parties of regular troops sent out to round them up and forced to make a break for it).[113] Whatever the motives of such recruits, plenty of *partidas* were composed almost entirely of men of this sort: when Vicente Moreno was captured by the French in August 1810, for example, his thirty-three men included eighteen soldiers from the Reina infantry regiment, ten from that of Vélez Málaga and two from the Walloon Guards.[114]

On occasion there may have been, as tradition claims, a determination to continue the struggle by other means than fighting and dying in the regular army. Thus, after the Spanish defeat at Alba de Tormes in November 1810 two officers of the Toro provincial militia regiment who had been cut off from their unit gathered together a group of fugitives and joined the band of Manuel

Echavarría.[115] Equally, Bartolomé Amor, a sergeant in the Burgos provincial militia regiment who escaped from the battlefield of Gamonal with Juan Díaz Porlier, seems to have been a dedicated soldier who merited the command that he eventually earned of the cavalry regiment known as the Dragones de Soria.[116] But all too often the real motive for desertion was very different. We shall never know precisely why Nicolás María de Isidro, a common soldier in one of the regiments that had been sent to Denmark under the Marqués de la Romana and a native of the province of Guadalajara, had no sooner got back to Spain than he fled to join the forces of El Empecinado.[117] But Manuel Sarasa, a veteran infantryman from Navarre who also escaped from Denmark but fought on in the ranks until he was captured at the battle of the River Gebora in March 1811, has much to say on the subject:

> Had I . . . copied the misconduct of the many men who fled the army, returned to their home provinces and joined the guerrillas, I would surely have obtained promotion and suffered a lot less. As is well known, it is much harder to distinguish oneself in a field army than it is in a guerrilla band, just as the privations suffered in the former are never experienced in the latter.[118]

Even more explicit was a report sent by an anonymous staff officer attached to the headquarters of the Fifth Army to the Chief of the General Staff in Cádiz in June 1811: 'Given that the guerrillas are always dressed in the greatest comfort and never lack fistfuls of doubloons with which to treat themselves, one really has to be the greatest of patriots to serve in the army.'[119] As this suggests, the pious tales that have come down to us of men coming to the conclusion that they could fight the invaders more effectively as irregulars than they could in the ranks of the regular army should be regarded with the utmost suspicion. Much more to the point is the story of Vicente Hernández, a soldier of the Voluntarios Imperiales de Toledo who deserted early in 1810, and fought on-and-off with the *partidas* of Isidoro Mir, Ventura Jiménez and Camilo Gómez before eventually setting up as a bandit and ending up on a French scaffold.[120]

And it was not just Spanish soldiers who deserted, for the *partidas* were also joined by many refugees from the French forces. How many such men came over to the guerrillas in this fashion it is impossible to say, but they were by no means infrequent. Large numbers certainly fought with the Navarrese insurgents: wounded in action under Espoz y Mina at Sangüesa on 5 February 1812 was a Prussian named Jochüm Flich, whilst 'the King of Navarre' was joined by a steady trickle of deserters from the garrison of Pamplona, and, on one occasion, no less than half a battalion of Italians.[121] Nor was this an isolated instance. In July 1811 El Empecinado was reported to have recruited so many

Germans that he was thinking of organising them into entire companies.[122] So numerous were the foreign components of some bands, indeed, that they at times outnumbered the Spaniards: in July 1810 no fewer than fifty-eight of the eighty-three followers of the erstwhile smuggler Ignacio Alonso were Germans or Italians.[123] Indeed, there even seem to have been bands composed of nothing but foreign deserters: travelling from Segovia to Valladolid, the convoy of which Andrew Blayney was a part was attacked by 'brigands commanded by a German captain who had deserted with his company from Santa María de Nava, of which he had been commandant'.[124]

But by far the most important positive reason for enlistment was the hope of gain. For example, even Gómez de Arteche admits that, if El Empecinado was quickly able to gather a band of men around him, it was not so much because of his charisma as because he was able to offer both a wage and the chance of booty, whilst Tone, too, is prepared to admit that it was the solid funding enjoyed by Mina that allowed him to build up his *partida* so quickly.[125] And, if it was Von Brandt's opinion that the chief reason for enlistment was 'the hope of plunder', the British observers Sydenham and Larpent saw the bands as 'regular freebooters [who] subsisted on the pillage of the country' and 'a sort of *banditti*'.[126] Let us quote, too, Luis de Villaba, an artillery officer who served in the siege of Zaragoza:

> The guerrillas who go by the name of Patriots should be exterminated: they are gangs of thieves with *carte blanche* to rob on the roads and in the villages. If some of them have brought benefits, the damage that others have wrought is one thousand times greater . . . Those who believe these bands . . . to be very useful are many, but if they meditate on the desertion from the enemy that has not occurred for fear of being murdered . . . the burnings and other disasters suffered by the villages . . . the many highwaymen and bandits who carry out their crimes under this pretext, and finally the manner in which their disorder and independence have caused all kinds of evil, they will understand how far the disdvantages outweigh the benefits.[127]

To quote a famous catch-phrase of the time, then, 'Long live Ferdinand and let's go robbing!'[128] What rendered the lure of gain all the stronger was the desperate situation into which Spain had been plunged by the war. The country, as we have seen, had always been characterised by great poverty and social inequality, and matters were not improved by the inflation, wars, natural disasters and harvest failures of the period 1796–1808. But with the French there came absolute ruin. Not only was the burden of French requisitioning and taxation extremely heavy, but the propertied classes proved only too eager to save themselves at the expense of the poor (French levies were, for example, frequently funded by imposing extra taxes on basic foodstuffs). As a further means of raising money, meanwhile, many municipalities sold off considerable amounts of common land, thereby depriving many of the humbler elements of the community of firewood, pasturage, food and raw materials (chestnuts and wild asparagus came from the commons, as did the esparto grass used in such activities as basket-weaving). As most municipalities had also rented out parts of the common lands in small parcels at reasonable rents, there also disappeared many vital tenancies. In such places as the Navarrese *montaña*, where the land was sold off in *minifundia*, this policy was softened in its effects, but all too often it went in large units for which the peasants could not compete, with the result that the oligarchy consolidated its control of the local economy still further. A good example is Guipúzcoa, where a study of nine *pueblos* has shown that 14 per cent of the 1,458 purchasers got 71 per cent of the arable land (and, still worse, that a mere twelve purchasers took almost one fifth of the properties involved). Thanks to the requisition of so many draft animals and carts by the contending armies, in many areas agriculture seems virtually to have come to a standstill, whilst nature was no more kind to Spain in the period 1808–14 than she had been in the years before the war. The harvest of 1811 was particularly disastrous and wheat prices shot up dramatically (in Burgos, for example, wheat rose from 80 *reales* a *fanega* in June 1811 to 244 *reales* by the close of the year). Yet the populace were in no condition to respond to the crisis. With the French imposing strict limits on movement and clamping down on many traditional aspects of street life, opportunities to find alternative sources of employment were limited – it was, for example, impossible for the inhabitants of poverty-stricken mountain districts such as the Serranía de Ronda to migrate in search of the seasonal work that had once been their salvation – especially as industry was at a standstill, and many *señores* unable to pay their existing retainers and domestic servants, let alone take on fresh hands. On the roads, meanwhile, little could move, whilst the French had generally only to arrive in a port for its trade to collapse. In short, hunger and despair reigned on all sides.[129]

As every account of life in the French zone makes clear, the common people were tried beyond all endurance. Thus, passing through Málaga as a prisoner of the French, Andrew Blayney found a scene of misery:

> Though [Málaga] still retains some external appearance of its former prosperity, it is but the insubstantial shadow of departed reality. The total cessation of commerce and the losses consequent on the war have produced innumerable bankruptcies and universal distress; the port . . . has lost all appearance of commercial life, some fishing boats alone being seen in movement, while a few . . . feluccas and other smaller vessels are laid up rotting. What a contrast with the former flourishing commerce of this city, whose

> annual exports were valued at half a million sterling . . . Such have been the desolating effects of the unprovoked and unjustifiable invasion of the French.[130]

In Zaragoza, too, life was grim in the extreme. As Faustino Casamayor wrote in his journal on 31 January 1812:

> This month the weather has been a continuous round of cold and ice . . . whilst foodstuffs have been so scarce and expensive that there is no one who can remember the like . . . Bread has cost just as much as it did last month, and the contributions demanded by the French have been so excessive . . . that they are not to be borne . . . As for the misery of the common people, it has been so great that in the streets one sees nothing but beggars.[131]

But for sheer horror, there was nothing to beat Madrid. Let us here quote the account of Clemente Carnicero:

> There were so many unfortunates in the streets . . . that it was impossible to walk them without the stoniest heart being wrung and saddened . . . Some people could be heard complaining that it was three o'clock in the afternoon and they had still not broken their fast; others had death clearly written in their faces; others were fainting from want; and still others had just breathed their last . . . At one spot one saw a group of abandoned children crying out for bread; at another a number of tearful widows surrounded by their little ones; and at still a third some young girls assuring passers-by that they were begging so as not to prostitute themselves. On the first corner there would be a cluster of priests humbly asking for alms, and on the second persons of the highest character . . . doing exactly the same. So many were the poor . . . that however much they wandered the streets . . . they could not get enough to get them through the day . . . Going back to their homes . . . they therefore quietly . . . lay down to die.[132]

With the city's troubles worsened by a terrible gambling epidemic that drained away money that many families desperately needed to buy food, deaths from starvation in the winter of 1811–12 alone amounted to a minimum of 20,000, and the British entered the city in August of the latter year to find the most affecting scenes. To quote George Hennell:

> The poor are very numerous here, and many are most wretched objects. In the great streets you are stopped every five or six yards, and frequently by six or seven at once . . . I have seen children five or six years of age lying on the pavement with scarcely one ounce of flesh on their bones and making a piteous moaning. After dark they lie down against a door doubled almost together . . . some sleeping, others crying.[133]

The consequences of all this are scarcely difficult to foresee. Writing from the Extremaduran district of La Serena, a *josefino* official named Juan María Ponce de León informed his superiors that the area's aspect was such as 'to move the most unfeeling man to compassion' and, further, that the local inhabitants had been reduced to such a state of 'miserable nakedness' that many were leaving their homes. As he went on to remark:

> All those who can get together a little money are crossing the River Guadiana into Portugal, leaving all those who cannot to wander about . . . and try to feed and clothe themselves from what they can take from those bold enough to travel the roads of this ruined country.[134]

For another example let us look at Valladolid. The province was hit by both particularly oppressive French requisitioning and an 'extraordinary contribution' of 1,000,000 *reales*, and by the summer of 1812 even the propertied classes had been reduced to ruin, which, as one official warned the governor, meant not just penury for all those who depended on them but also wholesale flight and with it 'more recruits for the *cuadrillas*'.[135]

Nothing, then, could be clearer. At the roots of *la guerrilla popular* lay not heroism but hunger, not daring but despair. But joining a *partida* was not the only remedy for want of food. Thus, in one respect the coming of the French had made little difference to Spanish society. Beset by chronic poverty many regions of the country had long been the haunt of bandits. In Galicia, for example, the first years of the nineteenth century were marked by the activities of such gangs as those of Manuel Carvajal, Juan Manuel Varela, Ignacio Cobas, Manuel Ventura Domínguez and José Rodríguez de Requeija, whilst in Andalucía important chieftains had included Francisco Mateos Pontón, Diego Corrientes, Pablo de Reina and Bartolomé Gutiérrez.[136] According to legend, for such men the French had only to appear for them to turn patriot. 'Never had the roads been so safe', enthused one writer. 'In echo of the clarion call to defend the fatherland, even wrongdoers and professional criminals had become men of good will.'[137] This version of events, however, is quite untrue. Bandits such as the Valencian Jaime Alfonso (El Barbudo) or the *vallesoletano* leader Vitoriano Díez (Chagarito) were happy to turn their attentions on the invaders: after all, French saddle bags contained just as much money as Spanish ones, whilst there was often much profit to be had from collaborating with the British or Spanish military authorities (in order to speed up the recruitment of enemy deserters, for instance, bounties were offered for every imperial soldier who was safely handed over to the Allied armies).

Nor were *afrancesados* likely to be spared for, generally being prominent local notables, they offered rich pickings. As a result activity that might be seen as 'anti-French' was commonplace. On the night of 7 June 1811, for example, four bandits named Manuel Camacho, Francisco Pérez, Juan de la Haza and Antonio del Arahel attacked a farm that had been acquired by an officer of the garrison of Seville named Deschamps, mistreated those of his employees who had the misfortune to be present and made off with seventy-two horses.[138] From Guadalajara, meanwhile, came complaints of bandits selling the guerrillas information or killing isolated couriers and selling the dispatches that they were carrying.[139] From Vizcaya it was reported that the older brother of one of the members of the Junta Criminal Extraordinaria had been dragged from his home at Balzola at the end of a rope by a twice-pardoned bandit named Pedro de Amorrostu, stabbed to death and then cut up with an axe.[140] From both Madrid and Vizcaya come reports of bandits murdering isolated imperial soldiers.[141] And, finally, eager for booty or unwilling to be taken without a fight, bandit gangs might even be found joining regular troops or guerrilla bands in raids against the French or defending themselves against columns of enemy troops who had managed to corner them.[142]

But to think that patriotism played any part in these men's motivation would be naive in the extreme. As Blaze wrote of Chagarito, for example, 'This chief . . . after making war upon the French, turned his arms against the Spaniards in his leisure moments to keep his hand in. He . . . struck such terror into Castile that the Spaniards . . . joined the French to endeavour to take him.'[143] Such men, indeed, were as likely to be found fighting for the French as against them: shot as 'infamous and sacrilegious thieves and traitors' were Pablo Albenagorta, Juan Ruiz and Ignacio Donato, all three of whom were *malhechores* who had been taken fighting with the French at Cuenca in October 1811, whilst one of the leading *josefino* counter-guerrillas was a Catalan bandit named José Pujol, who placed his band at the service of the invaders and was allowed to use it as the basis of a unit entitled the Cazadores Distinguidos de Cataluña.[144] And, even when bandits did not actually fight alongside the invaders, they were still not averse to preying on forces associated with the Patriot cause: in October 1810 a five-man patrol of Spanish cavalry was surprised and robbed at Lepe; in March 1813 a courier travelling from Wellington to Espoz y Mina was attacked by men under the command of the *cabecilla* Marquínez; and in June 1813 the great Aragonese heroine Agustina Zaragoza Domenech was set upon by bandits whilst riding to join the Spanish forces fighting with Wellington's army in the Vitoria campaign.[145]

Before his very eyes, then, every starving Spaniard had an alternative model of salvation. In brief, why join a force committed to fighting a war in which he had no interest, and, still worse, tolerate the pretensions of some would-be general, when it was possible to seek the same rewards in conditions of greater freedom and at little greater risk? Nor was obtaining arms a problem, for the countryside was awash with weapons that had been seized in the uprising of

1808, seized from isolated Frenchmen, thrown away in the confusion of battle or sold by starving Spanish soldiers.[146] For cover, meanwhile, there was always the war against the French: time and again we hear of gangs of marauders, and sometimes even isolated individuals, entering unsuspecting *pueblos* and demanding money, horses or rations on the pretext that that they were agents dispatched by some local general or *cabecilla*, whilst many supposed guerrilla raids turn out to have been nothing more than attempts to spring captured bandits from French captivity, the first action of any *partida* that occupied a town or village generally being to empty the local gaol.[147] In short, as the Junta Criminal Extraordinaria de Jaén proclaimed, 'The so-called guerrilla bands are in reality no more than highwaymen who pillage the towns and villages and murder their fellow countrymen, the only reason that they have adopted the garb of freedom fighters having been to disguise their crimes and give themselves greater scope for their activities.'[148]

The result of all this was that the areas occupied by the French were soon swarming not just with guerrillas but with fresh bandits. As the Junta Criminal of Guadalajara complained to Joseph's Minister of Justice in January 1812:

> The Junta . . . has no option but to inform you of the . . . fatal state of this province, inundated on all sides, as it is, by thieves who keep up a constant assault on the highways and are so confident of their strength that they are not afraid of falling on town and village as well. For some time hardly a day has gone by on which this tribunal has not received the report of some robbery or other: indeed, moved by the hope that we might finish with this plague, the local justices rush to report them. The public interest demands the erection of a scaffold that will contain these excesses: unless the malefactors responsible for them are checked by the use of the most exemplary punishment, the security of the entire province will be put at risk.[149]

Lest it be thought that this is nothing but the fruit of *afrancesamiento*, let us quote the following lines taken from a letter written by the Patriot *comisionado*, Rafael Gutiérrez:

> An enormous number of *partidas* are ranging across La Mancha. . . . They do so under the name of guerrillas, but in fact many are simply gangs of thieves and deserters given over to every type of crime. Armed with documents that have been forged or stolen . . . they infest the countryside, pillaging everything in sight and holding up every wayfarer that they encounter.[150]

In one or two instances the *cuadrillas* concerned attained a measure of both size and notoriety – the most notorious was the band known as the 'Siete Niños de

Ecija'[151] – but the most common pattern was for them to be few in membership and ephemeral in existence. That said, however, they were all-pervasive, and the number of men involved must have run into many thousands. Something of the extent of the problem may be judged from the number of bandits executed by the French. Of Granada, for example, Blayney wrote:

> In the centre of the [Plaza del Triunfo] is a large gallows, with a staircase to ascend by, and on the right a *garrote*, the mode of execution by which deserves notice. On a platform are placed a number of stools with a perpendicular post behind each; the criminal being seated on the stool, an iron collar is placed round his neck, and the executioner by the turn of a screw puts an end to his existence in a moment . . . Scarce a day passes without several similar executions.[152]

Scarce a day, indeed. Work on the issue is still in its infancy, but 178 bandits have thus far been revealed as having been executed by the French and their allies in the period 1809–12 alone. These figures, however, are but the tip of the iceberg, for not all those who came before the courts perished, whilst others were never caught at all. Much better, then, to quote the fact that in April 1812 the prison of Segovia contained no fewer than thirty-two prisoners awaiting trial on charges of banditry, or that between the 11th and 23rd of the same month the chief prison in Madrid saw the admission of forty-two men in relation to the same offence.[153] And, as need hardly be said, many of these *malhechores* were deserters. To quote a correspondent of the Junta of Catalonia:

> I cannot refrain from pointing out to Your Excellency the enormous numbers of deserters who have come together in large bands, and . . . have been robbing, killing and committing the most dreadful cruelties. There is neither traveller, muleteer, peasant, country house or hamlet that is safe, for they rob and maltreat everything alike.[154]

The populace, then, possessed interests other than the fight against the French. That this was the case is suggested very strongly by the fact that there was a constant haemorrhage of men away from the guerrilla bands. This was precipitated by a variety of factors – Toribio Bustamente, for example, found that his men began to slip away whenever he ran short of the money needed for their pay[155] – but the important point to note is that it was almost invariably linked with moves in the direction either of banditry pure and simple, or of service with the *juramentados*. Of the former tendency there is much evidence. Setting aside the case of Vicente Hernández that we have already noted, the district of Villarejo de Salvanés saw four soldiers from El Empecinado's forces commit many robberies, whilst in June 1811 several more of his men were apprehended by the *cabecilla* Juan Abril near Torrelodones after they stole 500,000 *reales* from a courier travelling from Salamanca to Madrid; in July 1811 an amnestied partisan from Usillos named José Delgado who had turned to banditry was sentenced to five years' imprisonment by the Junta Criminal Extraordinaria of Valladolid; on 2 October 1811 two deserters from the *partida* of Ugarte were sent before a firing squad after a reign of terror in which they and a number of other *malhechores* had committed numerous murders, rapes and other excesses around the town of Olabarrieta; on 29 December 1811 three of Manuel Hernández's men stole 95,000 *reales* from a resident of Chinchón named Gregorio Montero; and amongst the men executed by the French in Navarre in 1811 for banditry were two deserters from the troops of Espoz y Mina.[156] For service with the French we might recall the already cited case of Abuin, but there is in fact no need to do so: in November 1810 the second-in-command of the 'Compania de Guerrilla de Ayamonte' deserted to the French after having first helped himself to the entire contents of the unit's pay-chest; in July 1811 one Nicolás García deserted from El Empecinado's forces and was rewarded with a commission in King Joseph's army; in September 1811 a Patriot spy reported that several bands of irregulars had gone over to the French at Córdoba; in March 1812 two *madrileños* named Tiburcio Ballesteros and Diego Yebenés fled the forces of Palarea and tried to enlist in a special anti-bandit force that was then being raised in the capital; and on 19 April 1812 two members of the *partida* headed by Luis Gutiérrez appeared in Madrid and enlisted in King Joseph's cavalry.[157]

An interesting question here is whether this attempt, however inchoate, to pursue a separate agenda on the part of the populace possessed a conscious social content *à la* Hobsbawm. This, however, seems unlikely. Some areas of Spain, it is true, seem to have been more in the grip of a *jacquerie* than of a guerrilla insurrection. Nowhere is this more true than the Serranía de Ronda. The disturbances that broke out in the area after it was occupied in February 1810 aroused much hope amongst the Patriot authorities. 'The uprising of the Serranía de Ronda is a glorious affair', wrote General Castaños. 'Put on the right footing, it could be of major help to future operations.'[158] However, sent to get the *serranos* together in order to use them to assist the operations of a division that was to be disembarked from the sea under Luis Lacy, Ambrosio de la Cuadra found that 'the right footing' was not something that was to be attained with any ease. In the first place an interview with the supposed leader of the rebels proved a depressing experience:

> [Serrano] Valdenebro arrived today. He is very gloomy about the state of affairs in the Sierra, and foresees all sorts of difficulties about assembling the peasants. In a word . . . the *serranos* do not want to leave their villages, and are not doing anything of any use.[159]

As La Cuadra observed, then, 'We cannot count on any aid from the Sierra, whether in terms of men, mules or anything else.'[160] The inhabitants would defend their villages from French foraging parties and punitive expeditions, and fall upon unprotected parties of civilians, but they would not take part in formal military operations. But this was not the end of the problem. As the Spanish general continued, 'The state of anarchy that prevails amongst the inhabitants ought to alarm us rather than give us hope.'[161] As to what he meant, this is best approached through the experiences of Albert de Rocca, a young French hussar officer who formed part of the garrison of Ronda. Particularly suggestive is his account of the events that transpired when the French briefly gave up the town only a month after it had been occupied:

> The very day . . . we left Ronda, the mountaineers entered it . . . shouting with joy and discharging their pieces exultingly in the streets. The inhabitants of each village arrived together marching without order, and . . . loaded their asses with whatever they found . . . till the poor beasts were ready to sink under the weight of the booty . . . The prisons were forced, and the . . . criminals they contained ran instantly to take revenge on their judges and accusers. Debtors obtained receipts from their creditors by forcible means, and all the public papers were burned in order to annul the mortgages that the inhabitants of the town had upon the mountaineers.[162]

Nor is any of this surprising. To quote an *afrancesado* official who fell into the hands of a gang of about sixty insurgents near Antequera in May 1810, 'As I afterwards discovered, all of them were given over to dissolution, whilst many had previously been given gaol sentences.'[163]

Setting aside immediate self-defence – a factor that was as likely to lead to violence against Allied marauders as it was to violence against French ones[164] – such genuine popular involvement in the war as may be found was therefore closely linked with agrarian unrest. Yet it would be wrong to take this argument too far, and especially to pursue the mirage of the 'social bandit'. Whilst more work is certainly needed on the question of banditry in Spain in the early nineteenth century, the very few archivally based works to have been published on the subject so far do not hold out much hope in this respect. Thus, if we turn to López Morán's *Bandolerismo Gallego en la Primera Mitad del Siglo XIX*, we find that the Galician bandits of which the author writes neither stood up for the people, nor were admired by the people, nor concentrated their attacks on enemies of the people. Universally feared and loathed, indeed, they seem to have been interested in nothing more than staying alive and can never once be found to have divided up their spoils Robin-Hood fashion with the poor.[165] On occasion, indeed, an outraged populace turned on *malhechores* with the sort of ferocity that the legend reserves for the French. Thus, at Medina de Río Seco on 16 March 1811 a group of men who had been drinking in a tavern fell upon two bandits who had appeared in the town, took them prisoner and handed them over to the authorities, whilst on Christmas Day the same year three bandits named Manuel Díaz, Francisco Rodríguez and José González, who had entered a village in the province of Guadalajara to demand food, were attacked by the inhabitants and once again taken prisoner.[166] Nor should we be surprised by such incidents. More often than not the victims of the bandits were themselves humble folk – shepherds and muleteers were, for obvious reasons, regular targets – whilst the frequent use of torture and even more gratuitous forms of violence were hardly calculated to endear the robbers to the populace. Very occasionally bandits who entered a *pueblo* with the intention of robbing some local dignitary appear to have whipped up the *populacho* against them, the aim being, one presumes, to protect themselves against the possibility of the people siding with the *pudientes*.[167] With some *bandoleros* little more than psychopaths, it would not in fact be for some time – generally, in fact, not until they had been all but eradicated as an effective force by the coming of the Guardia Civil – that myths of honour and generosity began to take hold in the popular mind.[168] Becoming a bandit might have been one strategy for survival in a time of trial, then, but it was one that carried with it not just considerable danger but also a high price in terms of social solidarity.

Strong though it was, the risk of becoming an outcast was evidently not sufficient to prevent many men from embarking on *la vida a salto de mata*. In doing so, of course, they reduced the already limited pool of manpower available to the *partidas* and forced the latter to engage in a variety of measures that served only to alienate them still further from the populace. One early band, for example, seems to have been recruited entirely by trickery in that its commander, Valero Ripol, simply hired some men on the same basis as he would have done had he needed them as day-labourers, without telling them what he really wanted them for.[169] But for many of the rank and file there was no choice in the matter at all. Thus, conscription and impressment were widespread, in respect of which a variety of methods were employed. One such was economic pressure: Miguel Sarasa, for example, formed his first band on the basis of what Rodríguez Solis calls 'a number of his household servants and various labourers of the district' – in short, men who were economically dependent on him and had little option but to follow his lead.[170] Just as effective, meanwhile, was fear of the noose: whilst the ringleaders of bandit gangs suppressed by such commanders as El Empecinado and Espoz y Mina were executed or handed over to the authorities, their followers were generally given the chance of a new career as freedom fighters.[171] On occasion some recourse might be had to the regulations for conscription: in Horcajo de los Montes, José Crivell succeeded in forming a guerrilla band overnight by the simple method of assembling all those inhabitants liable for military service and threatening to march off to the army any man who did not volunteer to fight with him.[172] And finally, deserters too could with some reason expect to be pressed into service: amongst the men captured by the French with the Valencian leader Romeu in 1812 were two *dispersos* who saved their lives by proving that they had been compelled to serve by force, whilst on 14 June 1810 the *partida* of Pedro Alcalde entered Alcalá la Real and demanded a list of all the *dispersos* in the town.[173] Examples of the recruits gained by such methods are legion. From Almagro, for example, we hear of the case of one Justo Barba, a conscript who had fled back home only to be snapped up by a *partida* that also arrested his father.[174] From Morata we learn that in August 1811 fifty men in uniform descended on the town and seized one Miguel Gómez as a deserter and, in addition, the father of another man named Lucio Tominaya, whom they could not locate.[175] And from Zaragoza there is the case of Ramón Galindo, a *disperso* obliged to enlist in one of the regiments of José Joaquín Durán following the city's liberation from the French in July 1813.[176]

At least such men as Barba, Gómez and Galindo were liable to the *quinta*, and generally guilty of desertion to boot. But usually there was little in the way of either ceremony or pretext. Descending on a town, chieftains would simply round up every man that they could find and force them to enlist: having occupied Cabezón de la Sal in June 1809, for example, Porlier ordered the immediate enlistment of all males between seventeen and forty-five, whilst much the same tactics were employed by Merino when he entered Lerma in June 1809.[177] Accompanying such tactics was often the utmost brutality – attempts at resistance or flight were met by hostage-taking, floggings and even executions – and matters were made still worse by the fact that *pueblos* were frequently visited by several bands in succession, all of whom would behave in exactly the same fashion.[178] Nor was anyone spared: amongst those taken were *licenciados* – soldiers of the regular army who had served out their terms of enlistment – the medically unfit and even men in government service.[179]

It is probable that the bulk of the guerrillas' Spanish conscripts were acquired in this fashion. A single foray into Aragón in 1812, for example, was reported to have gained El Empecinado several hundred men.[180] However, when all else failed, there was always the weapon of kidnap. Thus, large numbers of men appear to have been simply seized at random as they were working in the fields or travelling from one *pueblo* to another. Press-ganged in the town of Veo, for example, were the peasants José Peris, Francisco Ballester, Vicente Bó and Bautista Martí, whilst between January and May 1812 forces belonging to El Empecinado kidnapped men at Barajas, Torrejón de Ardoz and Cubillo.[181] And, to the fury of many Spanish generals, commanders such as Porlier were not averse to forcing small detachments of regular troops that they happened to come across to take service with them as well.[182]

As we have seen, such methods could not but undermine the *partidas'* claims to be a popular movement. On the contrary, rather than serve with the guerrillas, many men fled their homes and headed for parts of Spain still in the hands of the Patriots: from both Ciudad Rodrigo and La Coruña, for example, it was reported that large numbers of *mozos* were arriving from districts in the French zone.[183] Sometimes, too, there were riots: at Navahermosa the Junta Central's agent, Crivell, found himself the target of an angry mob.[184] But most common of all was probably the response of the Castilian peasant Gregorio González Arranz, who, fearing that he would be seized by the forces of Jerónimo Merino and desiring only to be left to cultivate his smallholding, took a wife, and in addition scraped together enough money for his family to be able to buy him out of trouble should the *partidas* snap him up nonetheless (as they eventually did).[185]

But the issue was not just that of military service. Conceived in the traditional historiography as a force that lived amongst the people – indeed, in symbiosis with the people – in fact the guerrillas came more and more to lead a separate existence from the populace, and, in general, to live off the sweat of their brow: as we shall see, their requisitioning was just as ruthless as that of the French. Far from offering the civilian population any protection, meanwhile, they rather increased their danger, since a succession of French decrees threatened any *pueblo* that assisted the *partidas*, allowed itself to be plundered of men or supplies without putting up any resistance, or was found to have men serving with the guerrillas with the most dire punishment.[186] These orders permitted a variety of measures – generally speaking, heavy fines of one sort or another – but in addition French commanders often resorted to outright terrorism: in Navarre, for example, we find General Reille shooting large numbers of hostages chosen from amongst the families of the guerrillas, and the governor of Tudela threatening literally to decimate the male populace unless he received information as to the identity of the killer of a single French sentry.[187] It was, of course, Espoz y Mina's boast that this brutality had no effect whatsoever other than to increase the number of men who came forward to join his forces, but no less plausible are French claims that the reverse was true. As Marshal Suchet wrote, for example:

> The Aragonese . . . felt a growing affection for the . . . troops . . . 'Los nuestros' they always said when speaking of us . . . They considered our steady and regular occupation as a means of escaping the frequent inroads of [Espoz y] Mina and Villacampa, which, from the very circumstances of their being transitory, were attended with disorder and only left evil consequences behind them without being productive of any salutary result.[188]

This, perhaps, is to go too far but, for all that, the traditional image of the Spanish guerrillas can be seen to be very hard to sustain. Neither in their origins nor in their composition do the *partidas* conform to the stereotype, in fact. In so far as they were directed against the French at all, they were the work either of representatives of the state and its allies, or, still worse, of opportunists and adventurers who saw the crisis of 1808 as a once-in-a-lifetime opportunity that was to be seized with both hands. As for the rank and file, with certain exceptions they were but little interested in the defence of *dios*, *rey y patria*. Refugees from military service, poverty, noose or prison camp, mercenary hirelings, or unwilling conscripts who had been pressed into the ranks of some *partida* or other, their interest lay in survival and personal gain, and these were goals that could be pursued just as easily in company with the bandits who covered the face of the Peninsula as they could in company with the guerrillas. Given the choice, then, many men headed not for the *guerrilla* but the *cuadrilla*, whilst, disillusioned with a cause that offered them nothing, many others sought only to live quietly at home, hoping that the great turmoil would pass them by. To talk of some great people's crusade is therefore absurd. How, then, could Copons write of Valencia, 'Every *pueblo*, or at least the vast majority, is in a state of insurrection'?[189] There is, however, no difficulty here. What seemed at first sight to be resistance to the French was rather a state of general turmoil occasioned by a mixture of resentment, poverty and despair as the rural populace at one and the same time sought to protect itself against the demands of friends and enemies alike, pursued long-standing hatreds and struggled desperately to survive. In the process some few Frenchmen were killed, doubtless, but then so were marauders from the British, Portuguese and even Spanish armies. Equally, if some of the *señores* who were the enemies of the people perished, so did many of the bandits whom Marxist romantics have seen as their friends. And, all this being the case, it follows that we should not be surprised if the contribution of the *partidas* to the defeat of the French proves to be rather less dramatic than has often been made out to be the case.

5
The Reality of the Guerrillas

The image of the guerrillas that has emerged thus far is one that could not be more contradictory. On the one hand, we see the bands of heroic freedom fighters lauded in the traditional historiography as having sustained the fight against the French through thick and thin, causing them heavy casualties and paving the way for the eventual triumph of the Anglo-Portuguese army of the Duke of Wellington, whilst on the other we see the gangs of adventurers, *malhechores* and deserters suggested by a revisionist reading of the Spanish sources. Which of these two images is the more accurate still awaits verification, but it is quite clear that it is the latter that enjoys the greater degree of plausibility. Does this matter, however? The motivation of the *partidas* may not have been that of the patriotic legend, but they still preyed on the French: after all, money was on offer for bringing in captured dispatches and enemy prisoners, whilst the invaders' packs and saddle-bags were often bulging with plunder. Is there, in short, room to conciliate the old historiography with the new?

To answer this question, it is necessary to review the capacity and achievements of the guerrillas in military terms and, in addition, to say something more about the behaviour of the *partidas*. For as long as traditional images of the invaders – being constantly harassed by an enemy that was at once everywhere and nowhere, and supported by a populace whose only wish it was to serve their every desire – go unchallenged, the process of revision that is so sorely needed will be able to make little progress.

Let us begin, however, by examining the verdict of military theory. Shaken by their failure in the Peninsula, a number of Napoleonic veterans who produced treatises on the art of war in the years after Waterloo placed great weight on the contribution made by the guerrillas. Not the least of these was the Swiss staff officer Henri de Jomini, who, having served under Marshal Ney in Spain and Russia and later gone over to the Russians, was to dominate military thought right up until the Franco-Prussian War of 1870–71. Let us quote his most famous work, *The Art of War*:

> An invasion against an exasperated people . . . is a dangerous enterprise, as was well proved by the war in Spain . . . Each armed inhabitant knows the smallest paths . . . he finds everywhere a relative or friend who aids him. The commanders also know the country, and, learning immediately the slightest movement on the part of the invader, can adopt the best movements to defeat his projects, while the latter . . . is like a blind man: his combinations are failures, and when, after the most . . . rapid and fatiguing marches, he thinks he is about to . . . deal a terrible blow, he finds no sign of the enemy . . . so that while, like Don Quijote, he is attacking windmills, his adversary is on his line of communications . . . and carries on a war so disastrous for the invader that he must inevitably yield after a time.[1]

Jomini did not quite go so far as to imply that the whole reason for Napoleon's defeat in Spain lay with the guerrillas – on the contrary, he also laid much stress on Allied control of the sea, the geography of the theatre of operations, the existence of regular armies (both Spanish and Anglo-Portuguese) that could help and sustain the insurgents, and the failure of the French to commit sufficient troops to the Peninsula – but there were other observers who threw caution to the winds in this respect. One such was Jean Le Mière de Corvey, an officer who had fought not just in Spain but also against the Vendean insurrection of 1793, and therefore felt himself peculiarly qualified to write a study of guerrilla warfare. Published in 1823 as *Des Partisans et des Corps Irreguliers*, this was absolutely unequivocal in its admiration. Thus:

> One hundred and fifty guerrilla bands scattered all over Spain had sworn to kill thirty or forty Frenchmen a month each: that made six to eight thousand men a month for all the guerrilla bands together . . . As there are twelve months in the year, we were losing about 80,000 men a year, without [counting] any pitched battles. The war in Spain lasted seven years [*sic*], so over 500,000 men were killed.[2]

Such opinions were, it would seem, widely shared.[3] How far are the claims advanced by those who sought to make the guerrillas a central pillar of the Allied war effort justified, however? Even amongst those who had fought the irregulars opinion was mixed. Let us take, first of all, the swarms of irregular bands of no great size that are seen by many observers as the very acme of *la guerrilla*. Small groups of men lacking training and discipline, armed with a variety of different weapons ranging from muskets and bayonets to knives and fowling pieces, they could pick off the odd straggler, courier or foraging party, but they could not hope to withstand considerable parties of enemy troops, attack well-protected convoys or force the surrender of enemy garrisons. Indeed, even such attacks as they were able to launch were not always very effective. To quote Marbot, for example:

> I went on my way without incident as far as . . . Briviesca, but between that place and Burgos we saw twenty mounted Spaniards appear suddenly around a low hill. They fired several shots at us without effect; then my escort [six gendarmes], my servant and I drew our swords, and went forward without deigning to reply to the enemy, who, judging from our resolute attitude that we were the kind of people to defend ourselves vigorously went off in another direction . . . Between Palencia and Dueñas I fell in with an officer and twenty-five men of the Young Guard escorting a chest of money for the garrison at Valladolid. The . . . *guerrilleros* of the neighbourhood were just attacking the detachment. On seeing my escort galloping up . . . they stopped short . . . But one of them . . . called out that no French troops were in sight, whereupon the brigands advanced boldly towards the tempting treasure wagon. I naturally took command and bade the officer of the guard not to fire until I gave the word. Most of the enemy had dismounted . . . and . . . many had only pistols. I had placed my infantry behind the wagon, and as soon as the Spaniards were within twenty paces I made them come out and gave them the order to fire. This was obeyed with terrible precision: the leader and a dozen of his men dropped. The rest bolted at full speed towards their horses.[4]

Marbot is anything but a reliable witness. Yet such views are confirmed by the supposed leader of the insurrection in the Serranía de Ronda, José Serrano Valdenebro. Already deeply perturbed by the wayward nature of his followers, he was not much reassured by their fighting abilities. Thus:

> Although war is being waged in these mountains in the style of Viriato, flattering results cannot be expected . . . The peasants are little more than unmanageable. There is little union or regularity . . . in their movements. This is not to be surprised at: amongst troops who have not been fashioned by the strictest discipline they cannot be achieved . . . Valiant in skirmishing, they do not understand that shock action is the chief weapon on the battlefield . . . So long as troops do not realise that battles are won by the sword and bayonet, all is lost. Fire is only a chimera. . . . Advancing on the enemy with union and bravery . . . is what brings victory.[5]

And, of course, if mere gangs of armed civilians were of limited use when the French were in the open, in other circumstances they were still more helpless. If it was not already protected by medieval walls or Vauban-style fortifications, or if, as in, say, Seville, the perimeter of the existing defences was too extensive to be held by the normal garrison, every town and city that was occupied by the French was given an improvised citadel into which the garrison could retire to fight off attack or await relief. In Madrid, for example, this function was fulfilled by a large earthwork fort built around the royal porcelain factory situated on the heights occupied by the present-day Parque del Retiro; in Seville by the monastery of La Cartuja; in Teruel by the same complex of churches and convents in the centre of the city that defied the Republican forces in the Spanish Civil War; in Tudela, Burgos, Zaragoza and Jaén by convenient medieval castles; and in Salamanca by three convents that stood on the bluffs overlooking the bridge across the River Tormes. Though the various buildings concerned were all strengthened by earthworks and ditches and, where necessary, as in Salamanca, afforded a clear field of fire by the demolition of whole swathes of buildings, they were in no case strong enough to withstand a regular siege (the castle of Burgos did, in fact, succeed in defying Wellington in October 1812, but this was only because he tried to take it without a proper siege train). But against them the more irregular bands stood no chance even had they had any interest in attacking them, which they did not. As a British naval officer who fought in northern Spain observed, indeed, 'When acting offensively, they never can follow up their success as the enemy invariably retreat to and entrench themselves in the nearest village from whence they cannot be dislodged by musketry.'[6]

Yet, it would seem that the larger forces that coalesced around such figures as Juan Martín Díez, José Joaquín Durán and Francisco Espoz y Mina also had their deficiencies. Until 1813, for example, they generally had no more chance of storming the French citadels than, say, Francisquete or El Abuelo. On occasion success was achieved by the use of desperate expedients, as at Aguilar del Campóo in June 1809, when Porlier succeeded in forcing the surrender of the garrison by occupying a belfry that overlooked the convent in which it had taken refuge, heaving enormous rocks up the stairs and then dropping them through the roof of the enemy strongpoint.[7] And there was, too, scope for daring commando-style raids of the sort that in March 1813 saw a handful of Espoz y Mina's men scale the walls of the castle of Fuenterrabía, overcome the garrison and throw all the cannons and powder in the place into the River Bidasoa.[8] But in the ordinary course of events the only hope was to attempt to undermine the walls or to mount a blockade in the hope that the defenders would run out of food. Both tactics were tried from time to time, but they obviously required many days to be successful, and in consequence generally proved abortive, the French almost always being able to scrape together a relief force before too long. For a good example here, we might cite the attack mounted by Durán on the city of Soria in March 1812. A surprise attack on the walls launched from four directions at once proved too much for the defenders to cope with and they withdrew into the castle, leaving Durán free to demolish much of the outer defences and plunder the garrison's stores. But without artillery the castle was impregnable, whilst the week that it took for a relief force to appear was not sufficient to exhaust the defenders' supply of food and water, and the División de Soria therefore had no option but to withdraw.[9] And if the forces involved were not properly speaking guerrillas, but rather the regular troops of Pedro Villacampa's 'División de la Izquierda de Aragón', much the same experience was had by the Spaniards when they attacked Teruel in May 1810. As Villacampa ruefully remarked, the seminary that constituted the French citadel could not be bombarded for want of artillery, blown up for want of engineers or set alight for want of combustibles. The garrison's only weakness was that it lacked its own well, but even when the attackers cut the aquaduct that supplied water to the part of the city in which it was situated, a relief force once again arrived before the citadel was seriously inconvenienced.[10]

For a more general view of the case, let us turn to the experienced and thoughtful Heinrich von Brandt. Thus:

> As long as the guerrillas . . . constituted [an actual armament of the people], they . . . were . . . extremely dangerous to the French . . . But even in the first year of the rise of these bands, they lost this character and absurdly aped the regularity . . . of the military profession. They lost, in particular, the activity which they had shown in the earlier part of their formation and gave to their enemies . . . a thousand opportunities of combating them with success. They ceased to become the concern of whole districts, and fell into the hands of a few leaders who made such use of them as was most suitable to their own views. . . . Rendered incapable by their great numbers to conceal themselves from the observation of a vigilant enemy and suddenly to disappear from him without giving battle as they had formerly done, they were now frequently overtaken, surprised, defeated and dispersed, and disabled for a time from offering further molestation . . . One great advantage to the French was the assembling of the enemy's troops in detached parts of the country: whole districts were entirely freed from them, the communication of supplies was interrupted, and even couriers travelled without escorts. Provisions and other necessaries were regularly supplied, whilst good order prevailed in the army. Wherever the enemy was seen concentrating his troops, the French advanced on them and dispersed them, by which means . . . movements on both sides became more decisive, but not to the advantage of Spain since the tactics of the French always procured them the victory. Even the most hazardous engagements terminated in the French becoming masters of the field, *provided no infinite superiority of numbers rendered this honour a matter of doubt.*[11]

Had Von Brandt been present in Aragón and Navarre in 1812 and 1813, rather than, as was actually the case, being recalled with his regiment for service in the Russian campaign, he might have been less sanguine, for the latter years of the conflict saw guerrilla commanders such as Espoz y Mina and Durán repeatedly defeat substantial French columns. But for these defeats he had, as suggested by the last few words of the quotation we have just cited, a ready-made explanation, and, what is more, one that was entirely plausible. Having a few months earlier committed his armies to an offensive strategy designed to bring about the conquest of Valencia, at the end of 1811 Napoleon simultaneously withdrew well over 25,000 men from Spain, whilst at the same time effectively cutting off the constant stream of replacements and reinforcements that had hitherto sustained the march of French conquest in the Peninsula. Stripped to the bone, the garrisons of Navarre and Aragón found themselves quite unable to hold their own against Espoz y Mina and his fellows, especially as the latter were by now equipped with a number of artillery pieces that had been landed by the British on the coast of the Basque provinces and laboriously transported into the heartlands of *la guerrilla*.

For the French the result was that life became quite impossible. The guerrillas were now able to muster thousands of men – in this respect it greatly helped that the advance of the Anglo-Portuguese army on Burgos following the fall of Madrid in August 1812 had forced the French to concentrate most of their forces in northern Spain against Wellington, thereby allowing Espoz y Mina much greater opportunities to recruit his forces – and use conventional tactics on the battlefield. In consequence, no force could venture out to gather in supplies or relieve beleaguered garrisons that was not itself powerful enough to fight a divisional-level action. Nor, meanwhile, could garrisons that were attacked by the guerrillas trust to their walls to protect them as they always had in the past, for the *partidas* could now bring up their guns and blast holes in the defences.

There followed, then, a dramatic series of successes. Communications with France were badly disrupted, whilst in February 1813 Espoz y Mina forced the surrender of the French garrison of Tafalla, having first defeated a column of over 3,000 troops that had been sent to relieve it. An attack on the town of Sos was beaten off, but the French nevertheless decided to evacuate the garrison and almost suffered the destruction of the column sent to its relief when Espoz y Mina attacked it at Castiliscar. In response to this activity the French Army of the North launched a powerful counter-offensive. To ensure its success, its commander was authorised to draw upon the Army of Portugal (which had been watching Wellington's army in León), and five of this force's six infantry divisions were eventually sucked into the struggle. Yet the guerrillas were not destroyed. Communications with France were placed on a more secure footing, and many of the depots that Espoz y Mina had established in the shelter of the Pyrenees laid waste, but the bulk of the Spanish forces got away into Aragón and even managed to inflict considerable damage in the process, two French battalions being annihilated at Lerín. Still worse, whereas the garrison of Aragón had hitherto been holding its own, Espoz y Mina's arrival coincided with the dispatch of some of the troops stationed there to Valencia in response to fears of a fresh Allied offensive in that direction. The result was still more mayhem, with attacks both on the town of Huesca and on various convoys travelling to and from Zaragoza.[12]

All this constituted a vital contribution to Allied victory in the Peninsular War for, by pulling so many troops away from León, Espoz y Mina opened the way for Wellington to advance once more into the hinterland of Spain. What is more, this time there was no mistake: whereas in 1812 Wellington had wasted both time and troops on Madrid, in 1813 he kept his army together and concentrated on the decisive victory on the battlefield duly obtained at Vitoria on 21 June. Yet it cannot be stressed too strongly that the situation in Aragón and Navarre was wholly exceptional and, furthermore, that it stemmed not from any special virtue of the guerrillas but rather from Napoleon's decision to invade Russia, and thereby to destabilise the position of his forces in northern Spain. Indeed, if anything, the fighting that took place in Navarre in the first five months of 1813 illustrated the vulnerability of the guerrillas, for the French had only to concentrate superior forces against them for the realm of the 'King of Navarre' (as Espoz y Mina was now sometimes known) to be overrun. Many more men were needed to consolidate the French triumph than even the combined Armies of the North and Portugal could deploy, but the fact is that in its very heartlands the strongest and most enthusiastically backed *partida* in the whole of Spain had been vanquished. As Wellington wrote, indeed:

> Independent small bodies operating upon the enemy may be extremely useful when these operations are connected and carried on in concert with those of a large body of troops which . . . occupy the whole of the enemy's attention . . . but when the enemy is relieved from the pressure of the larger body, the smaller body must discontinue its operations or be destroyed.[13]

For much of the time, in fact, the more militarised *partidas* seem to have been little more of a threat than their wholly irregular counterparts. Let us here again quote Heinrich von Brandt:

> One circumstance that greatly operated to the disadvantage of the guerrillas was that the cultivation of their talents did not keep pace with the increase of their strength. During the whole war, and under all circumstances, their tactics remained unaltered . . . An ambush, placed with great caution for the

> purpose of surprising the advanced guard, opened the day. Generally, after the first attack, these *enfants perdus* . . . fell back upon the main body, which as soon as it was perceived by our troops, raised a dreadful cry and usually commenced a sharp fire without paying any regard to the distance which might separate it from us . . . When the ground favoured the operation, the French always made an impetuous charge upon their opponents, who generally retreated after a feeble resistance.[14]

This is a little exaggerated, perhaps, but even so it is clear that even the larger *partidas* were not to be relied upon in combat. The troops of which they were composed often had only a sketchy grasp of battlefield tactics and lacked the solidity of veteran soldiers, whilst their commanders were little more than amateurs: 'El Empecinado', wrote one observer, 'is possessed of more valour and energy than I can possibly express . . . but he needs instruction in how to manage his forces.'[15] Particularly if caught in the open or attacked by superior numbers, they could therefore be broken without too much difficulty.

In this respect mention has already been made of the serious reverse inflicted on Espoz y Mina's forces at Belorado in November 1810, when the División de Navarra was caught in the open on its way back to the *montaña* from an unsuccessful foray against the French stronghold of Tarrazona and suffered the loss of one third of its men. But this was not the only disaster suffered by Espoz y Mina, for in July 1811 most of his men were again caught by the French in the open, this time in the plains of southern Navarre at Lerín. Outnumbered, exhausted after a long night march, short of ammunition on account of a torrential summer storm that had soaked their cartridges and, be it said, abandoned by their commander, who clearly saw which way the wind was blowing and made off with a few companions before the battle began, the guerrillas had no chance and lost 600 casualties.[16] Nor was Espoz y Mina the only commander who experienced disaster: in an action at Torralva in January 1811 Durán and Merino were heavily defeated after the latter's cavalry broke in panic.[17] To quote Juan Díaz Porlier, then:

> We will continue . . . to find it hard to obtain any result from the troops unless they are organised as they ought to be . . . I say this on account of what happened in the last action: I would have lost half my men, had not the cavalry saved everyone. It was impossible to contain the infantry's disorder . . . or remedy their confusion and fear.[18]

None of this is especially surprising, for the *partidas* were rarely made up of good troops. General Walker, for example, described the troops of Renovales as 'a wretched rabble . . . attended by numerous corps of officers equally ignorant of military duty as the men, who were all raw recruits not exercised above eight days and the greater part not even knowing how to load and fire'.[19] Nor was it just a matter of training. To quote Walker's aide-de-camp, 'What these chiefs mostly complain of is the great want of clothing and shoes, their troops being in general very ragged and barefooted.'[20] Having been defeated, moreover, the guerrillas were as prone to scattering over the countryside as the conscripts of the regular army: many of the troops who survived the *débâcle* at Lerín appear to have deserted, whilst, defeated at Villaconejos in August 1811, El Empecinado had to send out officers in all directions with proclamations pardoning all those who had run away and calling them back to their ranks.[21]

Things were not much better when matters went well for the guerrillas. When El Empecinado occupied Cuenca in May 1812, for example, the garrison and their *afrancesado* supporters were allowed to take refuge in the castle virtually unmolested, whilst their assailants 'spent more time engaging in sack and robbery than they did in the use of their weapons'.[22] Given that there was little that the guerrillas could have achieved against the defenders in this instance, in military terms the results of this day's work were not too bad, but this was not the case when Tudela was attacked by a combined force consisting of the *partidas* of López Campillo, Alonso and Mina on 29 November 1809. Caught by surprise, the French garrison was quickly driven into the castle, whereupon the guerrillas fell to sacking the town. With their lust for plunder satisfied, by midday the attackers were on the road for Corella, but on the way the three bands fell to squabbling over the spoils. The unedifying scenes that ensued were chronicled by an official report supplied to the Junta Central:

> The arguments became so fierce that shots were exchanged . . . Being greater in number, Cuevilla's band chased that of Mina all the way to Corella, in which *pueblo* a number of men were killed and various others stripped of everything they had and taken prisoner. With things in this state of anarchy, a shout went up that the French were coming, whereupon . . . 500 enemy troops appeared and put the whole lot to flight.[23]

Nor were things much better when Porlier succeeded in briefly reoccupying Oviedo in February 1810. Opinions of Porlier amongst those who had dealings with him were less than flattering – he was variously described as 'a mere boy who is . . . ambitious and easy to deceive' and 'at the best but chief of a band of robbers who can by no means be said to be under his command'[24] – and on this occasion he appears to have behaved with great foolishness. Thus, apparently entertaining dreams that he might be nominated to command all the Spanish forces in Asturias, he failed to march in pursuit of the French, but rather prolonged his stay in Oviedo, getting up grateful deputations from amongst the citizenry and picking quarrels with the other Spanish commanders.[25] Hence in part the successful French counter-attack that we have already detailed. Yet Porlier, it seems, did not learn his lesson. A month after this affair we therefore find the Spanish staff officer Juan Moscoso writing:

> I advise you to proceed cautiously with regard to Porlier. He still has not either responded to the captain-general's dispatch or given an account of his [most recent] operations . . . A very sharp order has just arrived from the Regency with regard to the ranks which he has conceded . . . This should give him a better idea of his duty [but] . . . it is still necessary for you to impose your authority. He is badly advised, and surrounded by people who maintain his followers in liberty and disorder.[26]

Nor, it seems, did Porlier relish having his authority challenged. On 8 April, for example, an open quarrel between the guerrilla commander and Moscoso almost led to armed conflict, whilst the very next day the regular commander, Pedro de la Barcena, had to beg him to restrain himself and set aside his swollen ego: 'It is necessary . . . to keep calm . . . and work against the common enemy. In these circumstances personal quarrels damage us; for the moment Spaniards should have no enemies other than the French.'[27] As for limiting the bounds of his operations to a reasonable compass, this, too, was too much to expect: for example, the autumn of 1809 saw forces that owed him their allegiance appear in southern Logroño demanding food and clothing from the insurgent junta that had been established in Soto en Cameros before going on to take part in the attack on Tudela that we have just detailed.[28]

As was inevitable when there were such figures as Porlier in the field, there were endless disputes and jealousies between the different chieftains. 'We found them', wrote Captain Christian, 'irritable, very jealous of each other, and it required some management to prevail upon one chief to afford us any assistance in the execution of . . . orders that did not relate immediately to himself.'[29] One such area of friction was that which existed between the *manchego* leader Martínez de San Martín and El Empecinado. Thus, according to the government agent Rafael Gutiérrez, the former sought to engineer the latter's defeat in an action at Checa by failing to appear with his men as he had promised, and then deliberately snubbed El Empecinado when he brought his troops to Cuenca to join forces with Martínez's much smaller band. As a bystander wrote to Gutiérrez:

> I have always taken San Martín for a boor and a boastful good-for-nothing, but I never thought that he could be so underhanded and discourteous. The fault belongs to those who neither choose horses for courses nor tell cobblers to stick to their lasts: however hard we try, we shall never be able achieve anything with such people.[30]

Elsewhere, meanwhile, matters were even worse. In Soria and Logroño, for example, 1809 was marked by a furious dispute between forces loyal to the Marqués de Barriolucio and José Antonio Colmenares, of whom the former had been appointed to take charge of the guerrillas of Old Castile and the latter of those of southern Aragón. The details of this dispute are as complicated as they are tedious, but, in brief, carelessness in the drafting of their instructions had left it very unclear as to where the authority of one leader ended and that of the other began. Matters were not helped by the fact that the local notables to whom Barriolucio and Colmenares turned to consolidate their position were greedy for influence and prestige. As a petition sent to the Junta Central from Logroño put it, 'The various juntas that control the province all regarding themselves as being equal, they act as they see fit without agreeing any plan or system and in consequence frequently fall foul of one another.'[31] The result was chaos. Thus, with both commanders blatant empire-builders bent on establishing themselves as all-powerful provincial satraps – Colmenares, for example, appears to have exploited the confusion prevalent in the Junta Central's capital of Seville to obtain powers far greater than it had ever been intended he should be given[32] – bands of guerrillas loyal to Barriolucio and Colmenares regularly clashed with one another, arrested local officials loyal to their opponents, poached the loyalty of rival *cabecillas* or sequestered men and resources claimed by the other side.[33] Particularly serious were the scenes witnessed in the city of Logroño itself, whose temporary evacuation by the French in November 1809 was followed by violent bickering as the two guerrilla armies jockeyed for position and sought to monopolise the resources of the inhabitants.[34]

Both sides, meanwhile, traded insults and accusations thick and fast. Colmenares' men, we learn, had spent so much time enjoying the fleshpots of the provincial capital that they had earned the nickname of the 'Regimiento Fijo de Logroño' (Fixed Regiment of Logroño), whilst those of Barriolucio 'do not think of anything but . . . seizing resources that ought to belong to the whole of the nation . . . requisitioning whatever quantity of rations takes their fancy, and hanging around places far from the enemy in great crowds, oppressing the inhabitants and in many cases committing repeated disorders'.[35] To make matters still more complicated, meanwhile, on the one hand some of Colmenares' men who had penetrated the southernmost parts of Navarre found themselves challenged by Mina, whilst on the other Barriolucio arrested a group of riders sent out by Francisco Longa to seize the proceeds of the salt monopoly in the district of Miranda de Ebro.[36] Tired of the blizzard of paper that all this generated, the Junta Central eventually reprimanded both Barriolucio and Colmenares and ordered that the affairs of Soria and Logroño should be handled by a new junta made up of one representative of each of various local bodies set up by the two warring commissioners. Yet even this did not put a stop to the violence, and finding out that some of his men had deserted to join the forces which it was establishing, Jerónimo Merino – an ally of Bar-riolucio who seems to have provided him with most of his armed strength – threatened to come and get them by force.[37]

But nothing that these incessant skirmishes produced was the equal of the extraordinary events that took place at Medina de Pomar on 6 July 1810. In brief, what appears to have occurred is that Francisco Longa decided to rid himself of a rival band headed by the erstwhile smuggler Ignacio Alonso. For this there was a perfect pretext – like many other *cabecillas*, Alonso could be accused of banditry – but the real reason was revenge: in December 1809 Longa and his men had been seized by Alonso and forced to join his forces, the Vizcayan leader being beaten and publicly humiliated when he tried to escape. Eventually turned loose with a few followers who had remained loyal to him, Longa was then almost immediately attacked by French forces he believed to have been tipped off by Alonso as to his movements, losing seventeen men killed, wounded or taken prisoner and only narrowly escaping death or capture himself.[38] By now chief of far more men than he had had before, Longa was therefore delighted to encounter Alonso with fewer than 100 followers at Medina de Pomar on 2 July 1810. Having invited Alonso and his officers to a meal, he duly surrounded them with armed men and placed them under arrest. Four days later, however, there turned up another *partida* under Juan López Campillo, who had been sent by Porlier to rescue Alonso on the grounds that he had been acting at his orders. Unaware of what this new force wanted, Longa agreed to a meeting with Campillo, at which the latter maintained that all he asked was the surrender of the booty that Alonso and his men had amassed. To this Longa agreed, and even had Alonso brought out to certify that the goods being handed over were correct. Whilst this had been happening Campillo's men had managed to release Alonso's men without anyone raising the alarm, but at length a fight broke out between Campillo's adjutant and a sentry, whereupon Campillo drew a pistol and bundled Alonso out of the house. The two men left the town on horseback, but Longa's men sallied out in pursuit, and a fierce fight followed in which a number of men were killed and wounded and most of Alonso's men recaptured.[39] But this was not an end to the matter: hearing of what had gone on, a furious Porlier sent a further detach-ment of troops under the commander of his cavalry, Juan José de la Riba, to deal with Longa, and it seems clear that the only reason that the two sides did not engage in a full-scale conflict was that the commander of the Spanish forces in northern Spain, General Mahy, sent an angry letter to La Riba ordering him to desist from his activities at once.[40]

The net result of such quarrels, of course, was that operational efficiency was greatly reduced, particularly in the region that encompassed the borders of the two Castiles and Aragón, traversed as this was by the regular troops of Pedro Villacampa, the *partidas* of Durán and El Empecinado and a variety of smaller bands under such men as Martínez de San Martín. To quote Gutiérrez, for example, 'Unless something is done, things are going to go very ill. The division of Villacampa and the forces of San Martín and El Empecinado together make up almost 9,000 men, and yet . . . the rivalry that exists between them has meant that they have done no more than devastate the countryside and then go their own way.'[41] Nor was this the only problem. Thus:

> Although each commander has no more than 500 men, they do not like joining forces with anyone of higher rank, and yet they cannot achieve anything by themselves for want of numbers. The result is that their men do nothing. Bored with inaction, they loaf about, fall prey to vice and run away.[42]

These issues proved all but intractable. Though a variety of measures were taken to improve the situation, a full year later the same observer could write:

> I enclose a letter I have just received from General Bassecourt. It will inform Your Excellency of the lack of union, system and order that reigns among the various commanders . . . to be found in this region . . . Given that they have 10,000 men, many of them cavalry, it is very sad that the divisions of Bassecourt, Montijo, Villacampa, José Durán and Juan Martín have achieved so little. Indeed, far from fighting side by side, they deliberately avoid combat, all that they have done being to lay waste the countryside . . . whilst at the same time letting the enemy come and go as he will.[43]

Why all this was so is clear enough. Let us quote, for example, the Duque del Parque. As he wrote to the Minister of War in the course of his command of the Spanish forces in Old Castile in the summer and autumn of 1809:

> From the enclosed papers Your Excellency will learn of the dissension that reigns amongst the guerrillas of this province, not to mention the lack of respect which they have for their superiors . . . I have let them have all the rewards ordered by His Majesty in accordance with the services that they have rendered, and have even gone a little further than the arrangements that have been laid down for them, but they have not listened to reason and must be prevented from carrying out any more of the robberies and other outrages that they have perpetrated in our *pueblos*. Every member of the rank and file wants a band of his own, and if the Junta Suprema Gubernativa del Reino . . . does not punish those men who with this end in mind abandon the commanders who have been appointed to head the bands, all these people will in the end turn into gangs of bandits with whom it will be necessary to come to blows before they can be brought to heel.[44]

For an even more explicit view, meanwhile, we can turn to the Prussian exile Schepeler. As he wrote of the chaos that continued to bedevil Aragón:

> If Durán, Espoz y Mina and El Empecinado . . . had possessed the highest patriotic virtue – the ability to sacrifice their own ambition to the interests of the Fatherland – Aragón would have been delivered by their united forces . . . But none of the three wanted to obey an outsider, let alone one of his rivals.[45]

For a good example of the sort of thing to which this ambition and self-love led, we have only to turn to the events that took place in La Mancha and southern Aragón in the winter of 1811–12. Desperate to get the guerrillas to co-operate with one another, as commander of the Spanish Second Army – the force to which Villacampa, Durán and El Empecinado all in theory belonged – Joaquín Blake had appointed Bassecourt to act as commandant-general of all the forces in the region, and had in addition dispatched a small division under the Conde de Montijo to bolster resistance to the French. In doing so, however, he had not taken account of the pride of Villacampa, Durán and El Empecinado, none of whom was disposed either to co-operate with the others or to work with Montijo with the result, as Gutiérrez complained, that 'the countryside is being devastated by a small enemy army that is able to make a mockery of the substantial forces that are opposed to it, and could do a great deal if only their commanders would set aside their ideas of *de tanto soy yo*'.[46] Yet this they would not do. Thus, Montijo tried to get Durán and El Empecinado to co-operate with him in an attack on Soría, but neither *cabecilla* showed up at the appointed rendezvous, with the result that Montijo was defeated with the loss of 300 casualties and forced to retreat into Aragón.[47] What makes this incident significant, however, is its context. In the autumn of 1811 the French had launched a great offensive against Valencia, and it had soon become clear to Blake – the commander responsible for its defence – that the only hope of saving the city was to use the *partidas* to stir up trouble in the French rear. Some damage was done, certainly, but not enough to check the French onset, and thus it was that on 8 January 1812 Valencia fell into the hands of the invaders in what was to prove one of the most costly Spanish disasters of the entire war.

The guerrillas, though, were blind to the big picture. In the remote hills of Aragón, the main *cabecillas* continued to refuse to recognise the need to work together, with the result that the French continued to win the occasional victory even as late as the dark days of the winter of 1812–13. Thus on 25 December 1812 the Italians of General Phillippe Severoli caught Villacampa and certain elements of the division of Durán at La Almunia and inflicted heavy casualties upon them after they had failed to co-ordinate their operations.[48] And, far from accepting the principle of outside control, so determined was El Empecinado to protect his independence that he threatened the life of the local representative of the government and seized the saddle-bags of his dispatch riders.[49] It was not just on the frontiers of Old Castile, La Mancha and Aragón that such issues were a problem, however, for bad news also reached Gutiérrez from the region of Burgos, where Longa and Merino were reported to be in dispute with the commander of the Spanish Seventh Army, General Gabriel de Mendizábal (even if it should in fairness be noted that British observers claimed that Mendizábal, who was at best lacklustre, had 'entirely lost the confidence of everybody').[50] And from Asturias, Moscoso complained:

> This place is a tangle of confusions . . . No one is trying to wage war on the enemy except in accordance with his own particular hopes and aspirations . . . You can see for yourself . . . that nobody has the force that he claims he does, and that it is impossible to count on anybody or anything . . . Everybody goes about things in their own way . . . and thinks of nothing but his own interest and convenience. In short, Asturias will only ever be recovered by an army from beyond its frontiers.[51]

It was not just operational efficiency that was damaged by the endless squabbling. A further casualty was enthusiasm for the war. Let us here quote a government agent in the province of Guadalajara named Antonio de Capetillo:

> I am afraid to say that there is disunion amongst the authorities, discord amongst the generals . . . vice amongst the soldiery, and egotism in one and all, not to mention an unbridled greed for ranks and honours that are quite unmerited. Still worse, the disillusion with our forces that has stemmed from the quarrels of the commanders is spreading a decadent apathy amongst the populace. Look at Villacampa, for example. Once the terror of the enemy . . . he has completely changed, and has not won a victory [for months] with the result that his splendid division of 5,000 gallant soldiers has been reduced in strength by more than half and is now wandering from one village of this province to the next, having completely abandoned Aragón to the enemy. As for El Empecinado's division, its commander and his officers are clearly very discontented at having been placed under the command of General Bassecourt, whilst civil war is raging in its ranks with all sorts of calumnies and accusations flying about . . . All this the inhabitants regard with great displeasure, whilst they are also fed up both with the requisitioning to which they are subjected and the commanders' lack of skill . . . The *quinta* that should have been carried out two years ago is therefore still pending . . . whilst there has been no attempt to implement the one that the Commandant-General ordered to be carried out in Cuenca some months ago.[52]

Just as telling are the complaints voiced by an anonymous Aragonese. Thus:

> Everyone wants to command and none to obey. Even the soldiery and the common people have got wind of this. Nor is this surprising. All that they have to go on are the events that surround them, and these have consisted of little else but devastation, disobedience and a complete want of respect for property and authority alike . . . Hence the disorder, desertion and disaffection that we have witnessed.[53]

Mired in the petty disputes and rivalries of their home provinces as they were, the guerrillas could also not be counted on when it came to elaborating wider strategic combinations. Indeed, attempts to call upon the services of guerrilla formations outside the districts in which they were accustomed to operate generally ended in failure. In part this was because of the attitude of the local political authorities, in that they frequently regarded troops raised in their localities as having been raised for the purposes of home defence only, and in consequence struggled hard to ensure that they remained in the vicinity of their strongholds. But the real cause lay with the guerrillas themselves. More often than not the political problem could be overcome: El Empecinado, for example, had no difficulty in shrugging off the tutelage of the Junta of Guadalajara.[54] What could not be thrown off so easily was the general opposition to marching off to some other part of Spain, for this entailed all sorts of dangers. Important sources of income might be lost; unfamiliar terrain meant greater vulnerability; and there was nothing to say that the end-result would not be assimilation into the regular army. Attempts to involve guerrilla forces in wider strategic combinations could therefore lead to great tension. In April 1811, for example, a short-lived French march on Valencia caused panic in the city and led to orders being sent to El Empecinado to march his forces down to the coast. This message drove the Castilian commander to fury – 'What the devil have the Valencians been doing all this time?', he is supposed to have shouted, 'Where are all the thousands and thousands of men who have been doing nothing but laze about and eat their rations?'[55] – and he responded in the most niggardly fashion possible, taking with him a mere 300 men.[56] In the event he was not needed, and the order was cancelled, but on 11 July a second summons was received. There being no reprieve on this occasion, the result was disaster. As a government agent reported:

> The division of El Empecinado has almost entirely disintegrated. An order from General O'Donnell for it to march on Valencia threw it into confusion. It split up into rival parties in the vicinity of the *pueblo* of Torralba, shots were exchanged and it finally dispersed, all that its commander has left being some 200 men who are now with him in Cuenca . . . This is a very bad affair,

for the division was over 4,500 strong, whilst it was much feared by the French.[57]

But this was not the end of the story. In the midst of the chaos a large force of French troops turned up, and took at least 600 men prisoner at the village of Alcocer, such few troops as remained with the colours being forced to take refuge at Sigüenza.[58]

Implicit in these troubles is another problem that was inherent in the guerrillas. El Empecinado himself blamed the general lack of enthusiasm on the corruption typical of many Patriot officials. As he wrote of the commissaries whom he employed to feed his troops:

> For none of the *comisionados* . . . have I either respect or love. I have written to the government about some of them to see if I can get rid of them, whilst I have placed others under arrest . . . The vices of such men are all too clear . . . The evil is widespread, having its origins, as it does, in . . . the utter corruption of our customs produced by twenty years of the vices of Godoy. At the present time one needs a powerful telescope to find a single honest man.[59]

But the fault did not lie with just a few corrupt officials. On the contrary, the *partidas* were extremely burdensome to the populace. Little more than gangs of bandits, many oppressed the populace quite unmercifully, supporting themselves by pillage and rapine. Complaints on this score were numerous, there being reports of such cases from all over occupied Spain. Let us take, for example, the Levant. Here the autumn of 1812 saw groups of guerrillas led by Manuel Aparici and a priest named Manchón troubling the districts of Villajoyosa and Crevillente.[60] In May, meanwhile, General Copons had complained, 'Since my arrival in this province, I have received an infinity of complaints about the guerrilla bands. Their excesses are incessant: they only occupy themselves in robbery and never attack the enemy.'[61] Particularly blatant in this respect were the events that had taken place in the *pueblo* of San Juan in the present-day province of Alicante, where a *partida* headed by one Pascual Gil had frightened the populace into taking flight with tales that a large French column was heading straight for the village, and then settled down to pillaging its deserted homes.[62]

Just as telling is the situation of Navarre in the two years that passed before it was taken over by Espoz y Mina. Determined to emphasise his own importance, *el tío Francisco* did all that he could to stress the chaos that reigned in the province before he established a monopoly of force within its frontiers. Thus:

> It is simply not possible to paint an adequate picture of the horrifying want of morals that had come to characterise . . . the guerrilla bands. The only

> exception was that of my nephew [*sic*] Mina, which was a little more regular . . . In the other bands all the outsiders in the province had found protection. There were men who had fled to Navarre to avoid some problem at home, to escape from justice, or to . . . give themselves over to a life of libertinage in a place where they were not known. There were French, Swiss, Polish, Italian and German deserters . . . And on top of them were to be found many Navarrese who had either escaped from prison . . . or were known in their home villages for their evil way of life.[63]

As to what these guerrillas achieved, the picture that Espoz y Mina draws is not an encouraging one. Describing them as 'gangs of thieves and malcontents who under the guise of patriots sacrificed everything they came across to their vices', he claimed that they were typified by the band commanded by a butcher from Corella named Pascual Echeverría: later suppressed by Espoz y Mina, this force 'did nothing but wander about the province, committing a thousand disorders'.[64]

All this was very convenient for Espoz y Mina, of course, but for once the Navarrese leader was not exaggerating. Let us take, for example, the view of Navarre's representatives in the Patriot government:

> Free from the control of any army, [the guerrillas] . . . range across the province in a disorderly fashion, seizing large numbers of mules, demanding such rations as they feel like and extorting pay at a rate of 10 *reales* per day for each cavalryman and 6 *reales* per day for each foot soldier. In addition to all this, further payments have been extracted wherever they have not been given bales of cloth for the fabrication of uniforms.[65]

Also interesting in this respect is the report of the *resguardo* officer sent to Navarre by the Junta Central in the summer of 1809 to foment popular resistance:

> Who would believe that, in addition to the continual vexations that they experience at the hands of the French, these loyal . . . vassals of Your Majesty are experiencing others just as bad at the hands of . . . the so-called guerrilla bands that have been infesting this unfortunate kingdom, along with the neighbouring districts of Castile? The disorder which these men commit is such that it is impossible to portray it without feeling a sense of horror. The least they do is to demand exhorbitant rations . . . They all ride about on the horses that they have stolen from unfortunate peasants who need them for their labours. As I myself have experienced, no respectable citizen can ride from one *pueblo* to another without being robbed . . . Almost all the leaders . . . are men long known for their misconduct . . . and the consequence is that they wage war on the richest pockets.[66]

As in the Levant and Navarre, so in other parts of Spain. From the frontiers of Galicia and Old Castile, then, comes the case of Manuel María Vázquez de la Torre. Known as Salamanquino, his speciality appears to have been rounding up deserters and then charging exhorbitant ransoms for their release. As an inhabitant of Orense wrote to General Mahy, 'His sole pretension is . . . to suck the lifeblood from every town and village . . . Every *pueblo* that knows what he is like is very angry, and such is the inhabitants' desire for revenge that they are capable of almost anything.'[67] From Asturias we learn of 'Francisco Collar, alias Burracán, . . . [who] has been taking pains to make his conduct more reprehensible by the day, robbing, sacking, bullying and even killing in all the *pueblos* that he enters'.[68] From Catalonia we hear of one Feliú Rovira y Galcerán, a peasant who used the small band of irregulars that he raised to fight the French in 1808 to establish a protection racket whereby he levied tolls on convoys heading for French-occupied Barcelona.[69] And, last but not least, there was the rather more engaging case of Francisco Salazar, it supposedly being the custom of this worthy to billet himself in the house of the prettiest woman in town and then send out her husband to spy on the French.[70]

Lest it be thought that these remarks applied only to the less militarised guerrilla bands, it is quite clear that the problem was much more generalised. In fairness to the leaders of the guerrilla bands, many of them did attempt to maintain some sort of order amongst their followers and, in addition, to suppress *cuadrillas* that could be considered to be mere gangs of bandits. Thus, there are cases of guerrilla commanders handing over their own men to the *josefino* authorities for trial and execution, whilst Espoz y Mina, in particular, makes much of the ruthless manner in which he dealt with such bands as those of Echevarría, the latter being executed by firing squad at Estella on 9 July 1810 after his men had been taken by surprise and disarmed.[71] But it is impossible not to suspect that such actions were the fruit of ambition rather than altruism. The better commanders realised that looting was both bad for discipline and likely to land them in trouble with the authorities, whilst every *cabecilla* had an obvious interest in establishing a monopoly of force in his own locality. There were, however, repeated complaints with regard to the conduct of bands that are normally regarded with some respect, a particularly good example here being that of the northern leader Francisco Longa. In the words of one petitioner:

> We beg Your Excellency to come and console these aflicted *pueblos*, which you will find in the hands of the *partida* of Longa . . . Should you do so, you would find that these so-called soldiers degrade the military profession in the most horrible fashion, seeing in it no other object but the satisfaction of their sordid passions. They ride roughshod over justice, outrage humanity, act like tyrants and seize all the rights that should belong to our august

1. Louis François Lejeune, *The skirmish at Guisando, in the 'col d'Avis' mountain passage of the Guadarama in Castille on 11 April 1811*. In this picture, the *partida* of Juan Palarea strip and massacre the survivors of a French column. A few of the Spaniards appear in hussar-style busbies: as a veteran of the Peninsular War, Lejeune would have been aware of the militarisation of the *partidas,* though his treatment of the subject suggests that he was unwilling to let this get in the way of his desire to project a romantic image of the guerrillas.

2. Louis François Lejeune, *The attack by General Mina's guerrillas in France on the convoy carrying the ladies of King Joseph's court near Salinas, 25 May 1811*. Though based on a real incident, this work by Lejeune is inaccurate in almost every detail. At bottom left, Espoz y Mina is seen urging on his men, whilst on the right some British prisoners are being freed by the Spaniards. Interestingly, with a gesture of great disgust, one of them appears to be refusing the weapon he is being offered.

3. Denis Dighton, *Spanish army. General Officer of Cavalry with Guerrillas and Lancers, 1815*. Drawn from the flesh by such figures were to be found in many of the more militarised bands.

4. Denis Dighton, *The Brigand Crosa, Guerrilla Chief of Catalonia, 1813*. The archetypal guerrilla of legend, this figure typifies the ambiguity which characterises many leaders of the 'little war'.

5. Bacler d'Albe, *Scenes of action against the guerrillas in the Aoiz valley*. Head of the French army's topographical service under Napoleon, Louis Albert Bacler d'Albe accompanied Napoleon to Spain in 1808. It is not clear, however, whether the incident depicted here is anything other than the fruit of his imagination.

6. Bacler d'Albe, *Scenes of action against the guerrillas in the Aoiz valley*. Trapped at the edge of a cliff, French troops hurl themselves to their deaths rather than let themselves be taken by the guerrillas. Although this incident may be imaginary, there are documented examples of cornered imperial soldiers shooting themselves when faced by capture.

7. Bacler d'Albe, *Block-house on the road between Hernani and Tolosa*. A base of the 'gendarmerie d'Espagne', this imposing structure typifies the effort which the French had to put into keeping open their communications in Spain.

8. Felix Phillippoteaux, *General Franceschi-Delonne captured by 'El Capuchino's' gang*. The work of a well-known French illustrator born in 1815, this engraving depicts the capture of a French cavalry general by the band of El Capuchino in 1810 and is typical of traditional views of the guerrillas. Note the romanticised appearance of the Spaniards, who look as if they have stepped straight from the stage of *Carmen*.

9. Francisco de Goya, *Nobody knows the reason*. Resident in Madrid during the Peninsular War, Goya probably witnessed such a sight many times in the period 1808 to 1813. Kept in the building that is today occupied by the Spanish Foreign Ministry, malefactors such as these were led the short distance to the Plaza de la Puerta Cerrada and garrotted at the spot now marked by the Cruz de los Caidos. Death was instantaneous but the corpses were left exposed for the rest of the day with an account of their crimes and the weapons they had used hung round their necks. As the title implies, however, it was – and remains – very difficult to judge whether the victims were heroes or villains.

10. Francisco de Goya, *The same*. The rather obscure title of this engraving refers to the caption given to the preceding scene in *The Disasters of War* which is *With reason or without?* In short, who were the combatants, and why were they fighting?

law courts. The least of their members swill down between four and six *cuartillos* of wine a day, whilst they also get one and a half pounds of bread and two pounds of meat.[72]

Nor, it seems, did Longa mend his ways. Something over two years later the Regency that now ruled Spain received an anonymous representation from a group of 'loyal Castilians' making further accusations of pillage and arbitrary conduct. Thus:

From the beginning of 1810, many men deserted from the various *partidas* that had been formed in Castile after the battle of Espinosa de los Monteros so as to enlist in the one led by Longa in the belief that it offered them more freedom and less exertion. Never more than 500 strong, this band has ever since monopolised the revenues of the saltworks of Poza and Rosio . . . and the *tercios reales* payable on the estates of both the Archbishop [of Burgos] and the religious houses . . . All this ought to have been enough to . . . equip an army of 10,000 men, and yet the *partida* has still found it necessary to live off the inhabitants, whom it has treated with the greatest despotism . . . that it is possible to imagine. There has been no order: libertinage has reigned unchecked; every soldier has behaved as if he was free to demand whatever he liked; and everyone who has tried to protest . . . or failed to accede to the guerrillas' demands has been sorely punished.[73]

Not all commanders tolerated such excesses, of course, but it was not just the commanders who have to be taken into consideration. As Espoz y Mina supposedly remarked to a priest who came to plead for the life of a man who had been condemned to death for some act of violence:

You do not know the sort of people that I have under my command: I find myself, indeed, in the sad situation of having to count my existence by moments, and when I am alone am beset by the image of a dagger striking for my heart.[74]

Except when they were under the direct control of their officers, then, the rank and file simply could not be trusted. Sent out in small parties to gather supplies and recruits, they frequently ran amok and had to be hunted down by regular troops, as was the case with some of the detachments sent out by Renovales from his base at Potes in the winter of 1810–11.[75] In response to attempts to discipline them, meanwhile, they were quite capable of attempting to overthrow their *cabecillas*, or simply of running away: the Andalusian leader Jiménez found himself flung into prison on charges of treason after arresting his second-in-command on 'charges of robbery, falsification . . . lack of subordination and other excesses', whilst many of Durán's men deserted to 'various bands in which there was more freedom . . . better rations and less work'.[76]

To counter this spate of accusations, apologists for the guerrillas can make use of a number of arguments. There were, doubtless, many *afrancesados* and members of the propertied classes who possessed good reason to claim that the guerrillas were nothing more than bandits. As El Empecinado complained, for example:

> The parish priests . . . paint the activities of the soldiers who are sent out to collect the *tercios reales* . . . in the worst colours. This is not the case with all of the clergy, but you know perfectly well that selfishness is deeply engrained amongst them. Amongst the magistrates and the wealthier inhabitants, too, there are many who are quick to spot the motes in the eyes of other people, and not the beams in their own. Self-preservation leads them to give the French all they need, but love of the fatherland gets nothing out of anybody.[77]

It might, too, be objected that, operating deep inside the French zone of occupation, the guerrillas had no option but to live off the country. As Porlier put it in a letter written to General Mahy in March 1810, 'My division has very little of the resources that it needs to survive. It has not received any money for some time.'[78] Furthermore, if they behaved badly, they were no worse than the soldiers of the regular army: in the dark days of December 1808 and January 1809 the fleeing Spanish armies pillaged many towns and villages, whilst in January 1811 the commander of the Spanish forces in Asturias accused his subordinate, Francisco González de Castejón, of allowing his men to engage in a regime of pillage and rapine.[79]

But there is a problem here. Plenty of instances may be cited of even the most undisciplined guerrilla bands attacking the French. Bandit though he was, then, on 2 May 1809 Saornil led his men in an attack on a detachment of fifty French soldiers at Fuentesaúco that ended in the death of sixteen of them and the capture of thirty-four others.[80] Equally, though regarded by the military as a bandit, on 1 June 1811 the Andalucian *cabecilla* Saldivar rode into Sanlúcar de Barrameda and killed eleven Frenchmen along with a wealthy *afrancesado* who had been decorated by King Joseph for the help he had given the invaders.[81] And finally, from Ciudad Real we learn that on 15 February 1809 a party of French troops was attacked and put to flight by a gang of smugglers at Madridejos.[82]

Yet such attacks were actually rather fewer than might at first have been thought. It is, for example, significant that an ordinance issued in Asturias in May 1810 specifically laid down that each *partida* should attack the enemy at least once every four days.[83] There is, too, the fact that Porlier and his men clashed with the invaders on no more than half a dozen occasions between March 1809 and January 1810, a number of even these skirmishes only coming to pass because the guerrillas were caught by French columns and forced to turn and fight.[84] Much the same, meanwhile, appears to be true of the *manchego* leader José González de la Torre, whose copious reports submitted to the government contained hardly a mention of fighting the French.[85] As for Camilo Gómez, he spent most of the summer of 1809 enjoying the fleshpots of Seville and eventually had to be ordered to leave the city immediately.[86] This was an extreme case, perhaps, but the fact is that raids and ambushes did not figure at all highly on the agenda of many bands. What mattered was the comparatively peaceful business of requisitioning: after suddenly making an appearance in some unoccupied *pueblo*, a *partida* would strip it of such food, manpower, money and horses as it could extract from the inhabitants and then move on in search of fresh victims.[87] Also common, meanwhile, were acts that constituted little more than extortion and highway robbery: in August 1809 fifteen inhabitants of Mansilla de las Mulas were sequestered and held to ransom by Porlier, whilst in March 1810 a deputation that had been sent by the *ayuntamiento* of Alcaudete to congratulate Joseph Bonaparte on his conquest of Andalucía was held up by a group of guerrillas near Alcalá la Real and stripped of its horses.[88]

We have, then, a picture that is profoundly negative. This impression, meanwhile, is confirmed by the course of the war. For the Allies the key to victory in the Peninsular War was the survival of the Patriot cause in Spain: were Spain ever to have been conquered, it would have been hard for Wellington to hold out in Portugal, let alone carry the war across the frontier and win a decisive battle in the style of the one that actually took place at Vitoria on 21 June 1813. But, if the Spanish cause was to survive, it was essential that the Patriot government should hold on to a substantial area of territory, for only then could it hope to secure the men and money that it needed to keep the war alive. This was especially true after 1810, moreover, for in that year the outbreak of revolution in Spanish America slashed Spain's colonial revenues to the bone, whilst at the same time presenting the Patriot government with a 'second front' that it could ill afford to neglect. It will here be claimed, of course, that the guerrillas were sufficient in themselves to keep the war going in Spain or, to put it another way, that every French advance in Spain was irrelevant. Spanish armies might topple like ninepins, and Spanish fortresses be snapped up by the dozen, but the Spanish people would keep fighting and the 'Spanish mousetrap' remain as intractable as ever. This, however, is little more than nonsense. The concept of a Spanish 'people's war' is impossible to sustain, and, besides, the guerrillas could not have survived without a network of strategic bases. From these bases, too, there could operate forces of regular troops of the sort commanded by Ballesteros and Copons that could disrupt operations against the guerrillas by taking the offensive themselves (one returns here to Wellington's views on the need to support the operations of guerrilla bands with formations of regular troops).

The validity of these views can be upheld by reference to a number of episodes in the Peninsular War. As we have already seen, in the spring and early summer of 1813 Espoz y Mina was almost crushed by a massive French offensive from whose effects he was only saved by the advance of Wellington's army. The previous year, meanwhile, he had been seriously inconvenienced by the fall of Valencia. Indeed, as the Navarrese commander makes clear, this was a disaster for his forces:

> The loss of Valencia did me a great deal of damage. In this respect the worst problem was the manner in which it deprived me of a point to which I could turn for munitions, and in fact these immediately began to run short. At the same time I feared that some of the enemy troops that had taken part in the conquest of the city would . . . fall on the area in which I had been operating.[89]

Traditionally, it has been supposed that the guerrillas could always look to the Anglo-Portuguese army for salvation, but this, in fact, was not the case. Indeed, the fact that Wellington happened to save Espoz y Mina's forces from disaster in 1813 should not be taken to mean that such operations were a primary objective of British strategy. As the British commander himself said, for example, 'I cannot adopt plans to forward the operations of such a corps as that of Ballesteros or even that of Galicia.'[90]

Much, then, depended on the operations of such forces as those of Ballesteros and Copons. In Andalucía the Allies' possession of a string of coastal towns and fortresses including Cádiz, Ayamonte, Tarifa and Gibraltar allowed these commanders to operate with some degree of safety. But let us look at the contrasting case of Catalonia. Here, the fall of Tarragona in June 1811 reduced the Patriot cause to a state of near paralysis. No sooner had the fortress been taken, indeed, than the Junta of Catalonia was exuding despair:

> Catalonia has . . . lost the only port that remained to her . . . The most . . . fertile part of the principality is in possession of the enemy . . . and the mountainous parts alone must support the burden of the war . . . Thanks to the loss of its artillery and the very great want of ammunition in that part of the country which remains free, the army is incapable of undertaking military operations. As for the enemy . . . they will no doubt advance without the least delay, and very soon become masters of the whole province.[91]

If the Junta's worst fears were never realised – thanks to Napoleon's invasion of Russia, the French never had enough troops to overrun the whole of Catalonia – the Catalan war effort never recovered from the loss of Tarragona. Driven back into the interior of the province, the First Army suffered terribly: a British report of March 1813 remarked on 'much deficiency of accoutrements

. . . very bad clothing . . . and . . . a complete want of shoes', whilst in May of the same year the Lérida infantry regiment had only 220 men fit for service out of 490 present with the colours, and of these it was written that their only uniform was 'misery and nakedness combined with a complete want of cleanliness'.[92] Desertion, then, was very high, particularly as the French made a point of allowing deserters to remain quietly in their homes.[93] Had the Spaniards been capable of raiding the French zone, the situation in this respect might not have been quite so serious, but partisan activity was all but at an end, whilst, hard pressed to man the defensive positions behind which it sheltered, the army itself was too weak to spare the parties of troops needed to round up its fugitives. Indeed, it was too weak to attempt anything at all: reduced by the spring of 1813 to a force of 7,000 men, it lacked the transport it needed to take the field, whilst the soldiers were ill-armed, lacking in the most basic items of equipment and incapable of fighting in a regular fashion.[94] But from this there stemmed a vicious circle: the First Army could not attack without obtaining more resources, and yet it could not obtain more resources without attacking. In sum, then, as a British liaison officer reported, 'Without an additional force of 6,000 or 8,000 men, nothing offensive can be undertaken.'[95]

The predicament in which the First Army found itself by the beginning of 1813 is symptomatic of the relationship that existed between the guerrillas and the Spanish war effort as a whole. In this respect, the basic point at issue was made by Sir Thomas Graham:

> There are points where it is of infinite consequence . . . that there should be armies, for, useful and important as the guerrillas are, that is not enough, let them be ever so spread out over the face of the country. They can never stop the march of a considerable body of the enemy.[96]

This, alas, was all too true. Guerrillas or no guerrillas, between 1810 and 1812, with Wellington pinned down in Portugal, the French continued to expand their territories. In January 1810 the whole of Andalucía was occupied, and thereafter, one by one, Lérida, Oviedo, Astorga, Ciudad Rodrigo, Tortosa, Badajoz, Tarragona and Valencia all fell into the hands of the enemy. Spanish casualties were very heavy, and, in the end, the Patriot armies were left fit for nothing but glorified guerrilla warfare. And, so far as the guerrillas were concerned, their best efforts had proved unavailing to stop the rot. As a pamphlet that was published in Cádiz in 1810 remarked:

> As a method of waging war, popular insurrection is almost always . . . far more costly than the use of regular forces. When protected by a regular army, at the right moment the former can reinforce the latter, but otherwise the only result is momentary success avenged later with great sacrifice . . . Is it

> still doubted that the kingdom is lost if we do not raise large armies? Let us suppose that Spain becomes the tomb of 20,000 soldiers every year . . . Napoleon has to subjugate Spain or lose his reputation . . . and, now that [Austria] is quiet . . . it is not difficult for him to send 100,000 . . . It is held that our arms cannot match those of the enemy when both sides are fighting in large forces. From here stems the foolish idea that, instead of increasing our armies, we should rely solely on the use of *partidas* and the defence of towns [by their inhabitants] when the war that we are waging on the contrary demands large armies that are capable of imposing themselves on the enemy . . . It is true that Madrid was defended heroically by its own people, that La Mancha has devoured many Frenchmen without the aid of many troops, and that the enemy was expelled from Galicia by the peasantry alone. Nevertheless, Madrid is occupied by the enemy and La Mancha in reality controlled by them, whilst Galicia would also fall into their hands if there was not a large army to protect it. Little by little the French extend their dominions whilst we celebrate a riot in some village or an attack by some guerrilla band.[97]

What made all this doubly serious, of course, was that the guerrillas were one of the chief factors in the erosion of the regular armies that were, as Graham noted, the only hope of holding back the French. And, if the guerrillas could not stop the march of the French armies, they could do even less to push them back. Unable, as we have seen, to make headway against the fortresses and strong points that studded the French dominions, they were, until the last year of the war, for the most part incapable of beating even the smallest French forces in the open field. To quote Serrano Valdenebro:

> A band of patriots situated in mountains that are almost inaccessible will hold off the bravest soldiers. However, should the latter fall back to more accessible terrain, the picture changes . . . The peasant wages a petty war . . . How can this man fight in a terrain where infantry can press upon him or cavalry ride him down?[98]

How indeed? Yet this is precisely what the view that the heroic Spanish people liberated themselves from the French yoke by means of the adoption of guerrilla warfare requires us to believe. Few observers would go so far, of course, but what about the view that the Allied victory in the Peninsular War was the product of the combination of regular and irregular warfare, or, to put it another way, that Wellington made the guerrillas an integral part of his plans for the defeat of the French? Here, too, there is every reason to doubt the traditional version of events. When he advanced into Spain in both 1812 and 1813 Wellington made use of diversionary tactics to prevent the French from concentrating against him in overwhelming force, and it is often implied that the key factor in his plans was the guerrillas. This is, however, at best a half-truth. In 1812, in particular, considerable prominence was given to Gabriel de Mendizábal's Seventh Army, which consisted of such more or less militarised *partidas* as those of Porlier and Longa, but even in that year chief reliance was placed on regular formations of one sort or another. In 1813, meanwhile, even less trust was reposed in the guerrillas. Wellington, in fact, had never been a fan of the *partidas.* As he wrote to Lord Castlereagh as early as 5 September 1808, it was his view that, although 'very formidable and efficient in their own country', the Spanish insurgents could neither operate nor be 'reckoned upon' outside their home provinces, and were in want of 'arms, ammunition, money, clothing and military equipment of every description'; above all, however, 'no officer could calculate a great operation upon such a body', let alone 'estimate the effect of their efforts'.[99] As time passed, so he admittedly became more aware of the *partidas* as a factor in the war, but his planning for his first invasion of Spain – the Talavera campaign of July 1809 – took no account of the contribution that they might make to the fighting. On the contrary, despite the favourable reports that had begun to arrive of the guerrillas, his thinking was centred on conventional operations. As he wrote to the British ambassador, 'I am convinced that the French will be in serious danger in Spain only when a great force shall be assembled which will oblige them to collect their troops.'[100] The events of the campaign did nothing to change this belief for, guerrillas or no guerrillas, the French were able to concentrate against Wellington's troops in overwhelming numbers. In the long and gloomy exchange of views that followed the retreat of the British army, the *partidas* were therefore ignored: warning against any plans for further offensives in Spain, on 1 September 1809 Wellington informed his brother, Lord Wellesley, 'The enemy has it in his power to collect his whole force in Castile and Extremadura at any point north of the Tagus and can dispose of the parts of it . . . as he thinks proper.'[101]

Clearly, then, there is no sense here that the guerrillas could distract the French from turning upon Wellington's army, and in fact the British commander seems to have been bent on decrying the concept of people's war altogether. As he wrote to Lord Castlereagh, 'People are very apt to believe that enthusiasm carried the French through their revolution and was the parent of those exertions which have nearly conquered the world; but if the subject is nicely examined, it will be found that enthusiasm was the name only . . . [and] that force was the instrument which brought those great resources which first stopped the allies.'[102] The conclusion was obvious: 'I only beg that those who have to contend with the French will not be diverted from the business of raising, arming, equipping and training regular bodies by any notion that the people, when armed and arrayed, will be . . . of much use to them.'[103]

As operations of the guerrillas gathered pace in the course of the winter of 1809–10, Wellington was forced to modify his views. Thus: 'The accounts which I receive from all quarters mention the great activity of the parties of guerrillas throughout the country. Some of these accounts are certainly exaggerated, but I have no doubt that there is some foundation for them.'[104] Equally: 'I have no doubt that the spirit of resistance . . . is general throughout all the provinces [of Spain], that it breaks out into open acts of violence whenever opportunity offers, that instances of its existence have been frequent lately, and that the confidence of the Spaniards . . . in the final success of these exertions has lately become greater than it had been.'[105]

When the opportunity arose for a fresh advance into Spain in 1812, Wellington was therefore well aware of the *partidas* as a factor in operations in the Peninsula. Indeed, at first sight he was positively enthusiastic. As he wrote to Lord Liverpool:

> These parties continue to increase, and their operations become every day more important. Saornil has lately interrupted the communications of the army in Portugal in upper Castile near Medina del Campo. He took about 100 prisoners in that town, and the party of Cuesta attacked a body of French infantry which crossed the Tietar and obliged them to retire with considerable loss.[106]

Yet trust the guerrillas he could not. In 1810 all the activity of the *partidas* had not prevented the French from massing a large army against Portugal.[107] And there was, too, still the issue of what the *partidas* could actually achieve:

> I am apprehensive that I can place no reliance on the effect to be produced by these troops. The guerrillas, although active and willing, and although their operations in general occasion the utmost annoyance to the enemy, are so little disciplined that they can do nothing against the French troops unless the latter are very inferior in numbers, and if the French take post in house or church of which they only barricade the entrance, both regular troops and guerrillas are so ill-equipped . . . that the French can remain in security till relieved by a larger body.[108]

In this context the events of the summer and autumn of 1812 were a disaster. As his own forces had advanced into Old Castile following the battle of Salamanca on 22 July, Wellington discovered that, viewed in close-up, the guerrillas were not as active as he had been led to expect. As the government agent Rafael Gutiérrez complained the day before Wellington entered Madrid, for example, 'Don José Durán was in Calahorra on the sixth whilst on the ninth Don Pedro Villacampa was in Molina and Don Juan Martín between Tarancón and Cuenca, but none of them has done anything to incommode the enemy.'[109]

Eager to share in the glory of entering the capital, El Empecinado at the last minute rode for its gates, and actually managed to enter the city ahead of the Anglo-Portuguese army. But of pursuit of the enemy there was litle sign, and the British commander actually complained that the guerrillas were spending their time 'getting quietly into the large towns and amusing themselves or collecting plunder'.[110] Still worse, when the Allied troops reached Burgos in October a horde of irregulars rushed into the city and, in the words of one British officer, 'destroyed almost everything'.[111] Small wonder, then, that, by the time he had once again retired to the frontiers of Portugal in November, Wellington was writing scathingly of 'a few rascals called guerrillas [who] attack one quarter of their numbers and sometimes succeed and sometimes not'.[112] And small wonder, too, that his plans for the campaign of 1813 made almost no mention of the guerrillas. On the contrary, with Wellington now commander-in-chief of the Spanish armies, the plan was rather to rely entirely on such regular troops as the Patriot forces could field (in brief, the Spanish armies in Andalucía and the Levant would move on the French from the south, whilst their counterparts in Galicia and León advanced in company with Wellington's own Anglo-Portuguese troops to envelop the enemy's right flank and rear). Most strikingly, indeed, no attempt seems to have been made to get in touch with Espoz y Mina until the very eve of the battle of Vitoria. The general impression that one is left with therefore is that, whilst any help rendered by the guerrillas would be gratefully received, there was no intention whatsoever of trusting to their efforts. In the event, matters did not work out quite as Wellington planned, for Espoz y Mina was able to make a far greater contribution to events than the British commander ever expected, whilst the British commander found himself quite unable to make use of the Spanish armies in the manner that he had desired. But that is no justification for *ex post facto* rationalisation: by 1813 there were clearly few observers on the Allied side who had time for notions of *la guerrilla* as people's crusade.[113]

This is not to say that the guerrillas played no part in the liberation of Spain in 1813. On the contrary, setting aside the vital role played by the forces of Durán and Espoz y Mina in the French rear in the spring and early summer, Longa made up for his earlier misdeeds by distinguishing himself at the battle of Vitoria. Indeed, quite remarkably for Spanish troops, his men even succeeded in impressing some British observers with their bearing. To quote Larpent, 'I saw Longa in the streets, a stoutish man, well dressed in a sort of hussar uniform, and looking civilised enough . . . The party of cavalry were all regularly dressed, and seemed to be more regular than most of the Spanish regulars; they wore scarlet jackets and were not unlike some of our yeomanry cavalry, but they had an air of consequence that was amazing.'[114] But there is still one more problem to address. The victory of 1813 was above all a triumph for the Anglo-Portuguese army. The guerrillas had played their part, certainly, but Wellington was able to get far less use out of the Spanish regular army than he had planned: out of a total of some 167,000 Spaniards under arms, only some 23,000 were present at Vitoria. Still worse, meanwhile, when the Allied armies actually invaded France in October 1813 most of the Spanish forces had to be sent back across the frontier in disgrace.[115] Intensely humiliating as all this was for the Spanish officer corps, the result was, first, that the military coup that restored Fernando VII to the throne as absolute ruler of Spain was a resounding success and, second, that the army was given a considerable nudge in the direction of the sustained propensity towards political intervention that was ultimately to lead to the terrible civil war of 1936–39.[116]

To hold up the guerrillas as the only villains in this situation would be manifestly absurd (the doctrinaire anti-militarism of the liberals who dominated the *cortes* of Cádiz was at least as important, for example). But there is no doubt that the *partidas* did accelerate the estrangement of the regular army from the political system that was established in Patriot Spain. Setting aside the manner in which idealised guerrilla folk heroes could be set up in contradistinction to the generals of the regular army, and the guerrillas themselves eulogised as the model for a new form of military organisation, at the heart of all the army's problems in the campaign of 1813 was the question of logistics. Spain was a ruined land, and in consequence quite unable to equip its armies with the basic necessities that it needed to take the field. Once again, the general devastation could hardly be laid entirely at the door of the guerrillas, but the fact was that they had demonstrably made things far worse than might otherwise have been the case: in Old Castile, for example, they drained the countryside of what little remained of its labour.[117] And, of course, there was the question of desertion since it was widely recognised that the guerillas continued by their very existence to encourage men to flee the army.[118]

Even when the French were driven out, meanwhile, the guerrillas made it very difficult to realise the resources of the liberated territories. What made the problem still worse, however, was the complete anarchy into which the *partidas* had plunged large parts of the country. For a good example we have only to look at Aragón. Following the fall of Zaragoza in February 1809 a provincial junta had been established at Teruel, but this had been forced to lead an extremely peripatetic existence, whilst its authority had in any case been challenged by rival bodies based at Sigüenza and Molina de Aragón. At the same time, military authority in the province had been even more bitterly contested, things having eventually reached the point at which no fewer than eight independent commanders were squabbling over the region's resources whilst at the same time generally behaving as if the Aragonese were inhabitants of an enemy province. This was a low point, true – authority in the province was eventually formally divided between Espoz y Mina and Durán – but even so the result was that Aragón had been reduced to little more than a wasteland.[119]

To conclude, then, the impact of the Spanish guerrillas was much less impressive than has generally been thought to be the case. If by 'guerrillas', we mean the irregular forces that emerged from outside the ranks of the regular army and its auxiliaries – the new regiments formed in the course of the uprising in 1808 and such local militias as the Catalan *somatenes* – we find that in the case of the smaller and less militarised bands contact with the invaders was infrequent and, further, that the military capacities of such forces were very limited. Nor is this surprising: it is not going too far to suggest that the primary objective of men such as Príncipe and Saornil was not war at all, but rather robbery, pillage and extortion. Rather more effective, and certainly more dedicated to the struggle, were the larger and more organised *partidas* that emerged under the command of such figures as Juan Martín Díez, Francisco Espoz y Mina, José Joaquín Durán y Barazábal and Juan Díaz Porlier. But even here there are many problems: the rank and file frequently did not share the priorities of their leaders, whilst the latter were often as much adventurers as they were patriots, and in consequence allowed themselves to be distracted by their own private interests. On top of all this, even the most developed of the irregular forces had only a limited amount to offer in a military sense: always vulnerable to defeat in the field, they also acquired only the most limited offensive capacity. If this seems to fly in the face of the genuine achievements of the guerrillas – and, in particular, their *de facto* liberation of much of Navarre and Aragón – it should be pointed out that they were not operating in a vacuum. To put it another way, if Espoz y Mina triumphed, he did so because Napoleon invaded Russia. At the same time, the guerrillas were quite incapable of preventing either the conquest by the French of fresh territory or the concentration of overwhelming forces against the Anglo-Portuguese army of the Duke of Wellington. If anything, indeed, the irregulars appear rather as a negative influence in the Allied war effort: consuming disproportionate quantities of food, revenue and other resources, they sapped the strength of the Spanish regulars whilst increasing the discontent and alienation of the populace. To say that the *partidas* accomplished nothing would be to go to far, but even so we therefore have a picture that clearly differs vary radically from the traditional historiography.

6

The End of the Guerrillas

Having reassessed both the nature and motivation of *la guerrilla popular* and its contribution to the Spanish war effort, we now need to examine the relationship that existed between the *partidas* and the Spanish state. From everything that has gone before it will be appreciated that this was extremely ambivalent. On the one hand the civil and military authorities were anxious to foment popular resistance as an adjunct to the operations of the regular army, but on the other they were determined to ensure that it did not threaten the established social and political order or interfere with the conduct of the war. From the very beginning, then, attempts to encourage the formation of fresh *partidas* were to be inextricably entangled with attempts to regulate their conduct, and, still more so, to subordinate the *cabecillas* to the control of the generals and juntas that formally headed the resistance in the Spanish provinces. Opposed as this process was to the interests and outlook of most of the insurgent leaders, relations between the Patriot cause and its more irregular supporters were always likely to be troubled, and it is not difficult to foresee that in the end those groups that did not allow themselves to be fully assimilated with the military estate would be cast out from the fold altogether. Yet, just as the guerrillas did not operate in a military vacuum, nor did they do so in a political one. Thus, seemingly a personification of the principle of the nation-in-arms that was as effective as it was dramatic, the guerrillas were for a time able to benefit from the patronage of powerful interests within the Patriot body politic. Yet in the end, killed off by the guerrillas' own misdeeds and the changing circumstances of the war, this support fell away, whilst the *partidas* in any case soon found themselves exposed to the infinitely more hostile climate represented by the restoration of absolutism. For some fortunate individuals this was not the end, but for most of the guerrillas the choice facing them in 1814 was to be bleak indeed.

The first point to make in connection with this chapter is that at no time were the *partidas* ever envisaged as an independent force. Even in the very first days of the fighting this principle was already well enunciated. Thus, the formation of guerrilla bands was seen as the prerogative of the civil and military authorities. Supernumerary army officers, prominent local notables or men who had by one means or another managed to ingratiate themselves with the new organs of government were issued with commissions to raise groups of armed men, and held responsible for their actions. In short, they were regarded as agents of a state that in the end remained keen to enforce its monopoly of violence. By the same token, meanwhile, men who acted on their own initiative were likely to find themselves the object of at the very least great suspicion: hence the arrest of El Empecinado in the wake of the battle of Bailén by the infamous General Gregorio García de la Cuesta.[1] And it is notable, too, that in the beginning the authorities were keen to inform the populace that they were not to move against the French except via the medium of bodies that they themselves had sanctioned. On 28 May 1808, for example, the captain-general of Andalucía issued a proclamation instructing the inhabitants of Cádiz on no account to leave the city in search of Frenchmen that they might kill, but rather to remain in their homes and enlist in the units that would be established for this purpose under the command of officers appointed by the city's authorities.[2] And in June of the same year, if the Junta of Seville called for 'a war of *partidas* in which the enemy armies will constantly be embarrassed by the denial of supplies', it proclaimed its faith in the populace embracing this enterprise not only with ardour, but also 'guided in due form'.[3]

As we have seen, this attempt to keep the formation of guerrilla bands within the purview of the élites soon foundered. For one thing, the formation of *partidas* was, for whatever reason, a popular way of engaging with the war effort; for a second, the successes of the *somatenes*, in particular, provided the leaders of the Patriot cause with valuable propaganda material; and, for a third, the rapid deterioration of the military situation in the autumn and winter of 1808 encouraged a willingness both to contemplate unorthodox means of waging war and to accept the help of anyone who was prepared to take up arms in favour of the common cause. But this does not mean that the ideal of political and military control of the *partidas* was surrendered. On the contrary, nothing could be further from the truth. Thus, men who wished to take on the role of *cabecillas* were encouraged to apply to the new authorities for authorisation to do so by means of the generous exercise of patronage, whilst men who had established guerrilla bands on their own initiative had only to proffer their allegiance to the Patriot hierarchy to be confirmed in their positions and rewarded with regular commissions (in the first instance generally as cornets of cavalry). As a prime example of this process, we might cite El Empecinado, whose willingness to collaborate with the Spanish generals operating in his locality on 4 April 1809 brought him the rank of lieutenant.[4]

Hardly surprisingly, it was not long before the principles stuck to by the civil and military authorities found official enunciation. Thus, the decree of 28 December 1808 – the first attempt on the part of the Patriot government to give form to the guerrilla movement – was not just a measure aimed at encouraging the populace to take up arms against the French. Rewards of various sorts were certainly offered to anyone who was prepared either to form a guerrilla band or to enlist as a follower of one *cabecilla* or another. Thus, volunteers were promised generous wages (6 *reales* per day for a foot soldier, and 10 for a mounted one), the value of any horses that they brought with them when they joined up, a fair share in any booty that they took from the enemy and posts in government service (as doormen and the like) should they be permanently disabled as a result of action against the enemy. As for the *cabecillas*, the decree guaranteed them the rank of cornet, implied that they would have the right to appoint their own subordinates and contained a firm assurance that, providing all went well, they could in due course expect promotion. But this was not an end to the story. The object of the decree being stated as the creation of 'a new type of militia', it was clear that the aim was to assimilate irregular resistance with the rest of the armed forces, especially so as great care was taken to specify the organisation that was to be given to each *partida* (there was to be a commandant with the rank of cornet and a second commandant with the rank of first sergeant, and two sections of fifty men apiece, the one mounted and the other dismounted, each of which was to be led by a sergeant and a corporal). And, above all, whilst pious references were made to the need to allow the *partidas* as much freedom as possible, certain facts of life were made very clear:

> In so far as the relationship of one rank to another is concerned, the same rules will be observed as in the regular army, any misdemeanours in this respect being punishable in accordance with the terms of the Royal Ordinances. . . . In order to avoid disorders and facilitate operations against the enemy, every *partida* will be attached to a division of one of the field armies under the command of the corresponding general, each of whom will appoint an officer of the appropriate rank and disposition to take charge of the *partidas* assigned to his command.[5]

As early as the end of 1808, then, the pretensions of the Patriot authorities had been laid bare. This, moreover, was well before the dimensions of the problems thrown up by the issue of irregular resistance had become fully apparent: at the time that the decree was issued the number of *cabecillas* engaged in operations against the French was still relatively small, and they often commanded no more than a handful of men. Not surprisingly, as time went on, opinion hardened. To cure the problem of men deserting from established guerrilla bands and then approaching some general or junta with a proposal to form a *partida* of their own, in September 1809 the Junta Central ordered that henceforward no authority was to entertain any approach from individual partisans unless they had the sanction of their commanders.[6] And, as the Duque del Parque wrote in November 1809, 'I neither recognise, nor will I recognise Don Juan Díaz Porlier, nor any of these independent chiefs who have not subordinated themselves to me.'[7]

The anger of generals such as Del Parque was not directed just at the guerrillas. Also in the firing line were their sponsors. For a good instance of this development we might turn to Asturias, where the officer appointed to command the regular forces in the province in 1810, Francisco Javier Losada, was soon locked in battle with its ruling junta. As he complained to his superior, General Mahy:

> I have already informed you of the letter that the Junta [of Asturias] sent me when I tried to publish the proclamation concerning the collection of stragglers and deserters . . . If we tolerate these ridiculous pretensions . . . it will be impossible to discipline the soldiery, maintain a half-decent army, or put an end to the troops' habit of running away every other moment, nor still less to prevent the guerrillas from indulging their habit of constantly changing *partidas* so as to avoid punishment for the . . . scandalous excesses for which they are responsible . . . In entertaining them, the Junta has clearly had other objects than the national interest . . . In June last year it published an ordinance regulating the guerrilla bands, and yet for whatever reason it has consistently chosen commandants who afterwards have almost all turned out to merit the accusations of banditry with which the French have sought to ridicule the *partidas*. Having with the greatest indiscretion . . . conferred ranks and appointments of all sorts on every type of person . . . it has also made its interest in defending them very clear. When the incessant protests and complaints of the suffering populace forced me to arrest the *partidario* Francisco Collar, it wrote to me praising his supposed heroism . . . with such vigour that I was left with no option but to suspend my proceedings against him . . . But there are issues with regard to which the Junta has been even more remiss . . . If Your Excellency had not already been in this province, I would here have spent some time outlining not only the lack of order . . . that I found to prevail among these troops, but also their . . . want of everything that they need. The latter is the fault of the Junta, for it distributes . . . clothing, footwear and armament in accordance with nothing more than its own whims . . . The first in the queue are always the most bare-faced of the *cabecillas*, and especially those which are known to have links with

> members of the Junta . . . and they carry off the lot, whilst the men actually fighting the enemy end up with nothing. From the day I arrived here I have struggled to put an end to this scandal . . . but the Junta . . . has gone on exactly as before, and has even ordered supplies to be distributed to . . . *partidas* that I have specifically told them ought to be disbanded and forced to join the army on account of the fact that they are entirely made up of deserters . . . And by issuing supplies without any regard for whether they were actually needed and without any requirement for them to be accounted for to men of neither birth nor reputation . . . the Junta has left the army in the same state of want and nakedness as ever whilst at the same time surrounding themselves with a crowd of rogues who not only make a living but even enrich themselves from this species of robbery. Of the little there is, not a tenth part reaches the army, and the result is that it cannot fight and is in the worst state imaginable.[8]

All sorts of interesting questions are raised here with regard to the relationship that existed between the *partidas* and the local notables. What Losada appears to be suggesting, indeed, is that – as certainly occurred later on in the nineteenth century – banditry could sometimes enjoy the patronage and protection of prominent *caciques*, who in turn received a share of its profits. Such things, however, are difficult to pin down. In consequence, let us here confine ourselves to noting that the demand that some sort of control ought to be imposed on the guerrillas was not just limited to government ministers and army commanders. On the contrary, criticism of the *partidas* was a regular feature of the Patriot press. In April 1811, for example, an anonymous article in the strongly liberal *Semanario Patriótico* stated:

> The concentration of the *partidas* is an important objective. As they have by divers means acquired a multitude of fine horses, subjected to proper discipline and given good officers, they could be transformed into excellent hussar regiments. Whilst serving the cause in the same way, such units would not be prone to the evils that have so greatly diminished the utility of the guerrilla bands.[9]

A year later, meanwhile, the official mouthpiece of the newly created general staff was writing:

> The patriotic guerrilla bands are without doubt of great use, many illustrious Spaniards having covered themselves in glory in their ranks. However, it is unfortunately true that some *partidarios* have deviated from this noble path and augmented the ills of the fatherland. It is therefore necessary to reward . . . some bands and reform others, whilst placing them all under a unified system.[10]

Not surprisingly, the growing concern soon produced legislative action, whilst there were also other signs that the guerrillas no longer enjoyed the overwhelming official favour of 1808. Thus, on 22 April 1810 an investigation into the affairs of Porlier, who had just formed a number of *partidas* into the Husares de Cantabria regiment, led the newly installed regency of General Castaños to order that henceforth no mounted unit organised by the guerrillas was to consist of more than a single squadron. The point of this was to protect their manoeuvrability and at the same time prevent the accumulation of the large numbers of non-combatants associated with the proliferation of regimental headquarters.[11] Just over a month later, meanwhile, the Junta of Asturias issued a long and detailed set of regulations in which it attempted to address the worst evils of the *partidas* (it was in fact this document that Losada accused the Junta of exploiting for its own purposes). In brief, no one could assume the role of commandant without first securing the sanction of the junta; no band could stop in a settlement without officially informing the local authorities of its presence, giving them proof that it was there on official business and providing evidence of its strength; no band could leave a settlement without securing a good-conduct certificate; no commandant was to have fewer than thirty men or more than 100; bands had to attack the enemy at least once every four days; regular returns of strength were to be sent in to the local military commander; and no band was to accept deserters, draft evaders or men already serving in another *partida*.[12] Also in the north, Mariano Renovales issued a proclamation threatening to treat any villagers that gave food to 'the disorderly gangs that wander in our territory' as collaborators, and promising to punish the families of any men found to be absent with such groups.[13] And finally in Cádiz it is noticeable that the Regency proved extremely reluctant to sanction the commissions that Espoz y Mina had issued to many of his subordinates, the matter having eventually to be raised in the *cortes*.[14]

But far more important than all this was the new ordinance that the Regency brought before the *cortes* in August 1811. Curiously enough, in view of what was to follow, this was originally an initiative of the liberal deputy José Mejía, who on 6 October 1810 had proposed that the standing committee of the *cortes* that oversaw the work of the Ministry of War should elaborate a document that would encourage the formation of fresh *partidas* by laying down the precise framework under which they should operate.[15] What emerged, however, was certainly not the sort of code that Mejía had envisaged, the draft ordinance that resulted actually bidding fair to outlaw much of the guerrilla movement altogether. Thus, dividing its members into three categories – larger forces such as that of El Empecinado, small bands with a proven record of fighting the French (such as that of Juan Palarea) and small bands who were clearly no more than criminals – it suggested that the first category should be assimilated into the army, the second deprived of their autonomy and the third wiped out as enemies of society.[16]

To the liberals who had come to dominate the *cortes* of Cádiz such a document was anathema. This is not the place to discuss their views and ideology in any detail but, in so far as the conduct of the war was concerned, they were committed to doctrines that could not but place great emphasis on the guerrillas. At the same time, it had already shown much indignation at the Regency's reluctance to confirm the commissions issued by Espoz y Mina. To quote the deputy González:

> I am afraid that it seems to me as if from the beginning of our holy revolution, instead of fomenting patriotism, we have rather sought to quench it. Sadly, those who have worked hardest for our cause have been the people who have been most persecuted, or who have at least received fewest thanks. . . . Many have come here from Madrid after swearing allegiance to King Pepe . . . and have still received promotions, appointments, salaries. . . . Others have from the beginning spent the war dodging the bullets, and yet they have been decorated and given . . . higher rank than the men who have been shedding their blood for us.[17]

Not all the deputies were quite so critical – there was, for example, some recognition that commissions could not just be handed out to all and sundry – and it is noteworthy that in the end what carried the day was the argument that Espoz y Mina's forces had already been recognised as part of the regular army. That said, however, for the liberals it was axiomatic that Spain was fighting a people's war. In 1808, they argued, the Spanish people had risen not just to fight the French but to throw off centuries of despotism, and it was this process that they now claimed to be espousing. As justification for their efforts, meanwhile, they could cite the *partidas'* supposed heroism, the only possible explanation for this phenomenon in their view being the continued yearning for liberty. But the guerrillas were not just living proof of the liberals' theory of revolution. At the same time they were also the harbinger of an entirely new form of military organisation. Convinced that regular armies were of necessity the enemies of freedom, the liberals believed that Spain should in consequence rely on a national militia, or, to put it another way, on the people-in-arms.[18] And what were the guerrillas if not the Spanish people-in-arms and, still more so, an answer to those who claimed that only regular armies could save the country? As Alvaro Flórez Estrada proclaimed:

> The people swore to avenge the outrages that it had suffered from a perfidious invader; it formed a government and charged it with the formation of powerful armies. But did the latter make it desist from its first endeavour?

> Woe on us had this been the case. No: it is not the armies that have destroyed the barbarous legions of our enemies; it is not the armies that have disconcerted and upset the plans of the tyrant. It is the people. They and only they have been the . . . authors of these prodigies . . . If the *pueblos* remained tranquil, if their inhabitants resolved to accept the law of conquest, what would become of the Nation? Our war would be a cabinet war. As for our armies, they are as a general rule unable to match the consistency and vigour of their opponents. In consequence, they would sooner or later be destroyed, in which case who would replace them?[19]

But this was not the end of the fascination the guerrillas held for the liberals. Just as the *partidas* as a whole proclaimed to the world the ability of the armed people to defend the fatherland, so figures such as Juan Martín Díez and Francisco Espoz y Mina showed that birth was not a prerequisite of military prowess or leadership in society, thereby short-circuiting the desperate efforts of the forces of reaction to uphold the privileges of the nobility. For the most radical thinkers, indeed, they even provided grounds for dreams of social revolution. To quote *El Patriota*:

> The shameful madness . . . of believing that only the old generals have . . . the knowledge needed to command armies has done us the most terrible damage . . . In a new situation, everything must be new, and in consequence the only commanders we should employ are men who are formed – indeed, almost born – in the revolution. Obviously, I would not place myself wholly on the side of the new commanders, for there are men among them who are just as wretched . . . as their predecessors, but, if we take the commanders of the revolt in Catalonia, when did many of them embark on their military careers? And in what military school . . . did the immortal [Espoz y] Mina learn . . . how to maintain himself for three years in the midst of the enemy . . . almost without communication with the government? Could any of the generals of the old army have achieved as much?[20]

Not surprisingly, then, the result was a lively debate in the *cortes* when the matter was brought before the assembly on 9 August 1811, with deputy after deputy rising to warn the government that the new ordinance would be certain to ruin the guerrillas, and even that it hid a deliberate attempt to destroy them altogether. There was, true, a general willingness to accept that any band proved to have used the war as a cover for a career of banditry should be exterminated and, further, that no deserters should be allowed to serve with the guerrillas, but beyond that most of the deputies would not go, despite a staunch defence of the ordinance by the Conde de Toreno, a leading liberal who had been a member of the committee that had actually framed the document.

Whilst the arguments raised against the decree were many and varied, they basically fell into two groups. On the one hand there was the claim that any attempt to regulate the *partidas* would necessarily discourage the populace. And on the other there was the pretence that such a move would undermine the irregulars' efficacy. In this latter respect, particular emphasis was placed on the manner in which the bands were to be subordinated to the control of the regular army (many of the *partidas* were henceforth to be commanded by regular officers, whilst they were to be placed under the command of the generals responsible for the provinces in which they were operating and subjected to regular inspection by special officers appointed for the task). It was argued, first, that regular officers would be less likely to know the country than *cabecillas* raised in the district; second, that regular officers would be hamstrung in their operations by inappropriate notions of honour that might, for example, lead them to fight a superior enemy who ought rather to have been avoided; and, third, that subjecting the bands to interference on the part of distant generals and their representatives might easily cause them to miss some opportunity for striking a blow against the invaders. Also objected to in this context were the ordinance's demands that the guerrillas should surrender any horses in their possession that could be used by the regular cavalry. There was, in general, a tendency to minimise the extent of the irregulars' depredations and to pretend that the men and resources which they absorbed could never have reached the army on account of the occupation of the districts from which they stemmed by the French. Typical of the rhetoric employed was that of Joaquín Capmany:

> This ordinance tends towards the complete destruction of the guerrillas, for it threatens to annihilate the useful *partidas* with the same rules that are intended to destroy the harmful ones . . . At the same time, it will in effect place all the guerrilla bands in a state of tutelage as if they were mere novices in the art of war, when they have in reality stopped being children: they are now adults, and, what is more, adults who are much too grown up to have any need for leading reins. We are speaking, after all, of the guerrillas: men who are as honourable as they are valiant; men who have grown in number in proportion with the opportunity that they have had to fight the enemy; and men who continue every moment to pursue their heroic resolution to harass the invaders. The fluid war that they maintain in the midst of the enemy has been called disorderly, but it has to be disorderly if it is to have any chance of success . . . Subjecting these intrepid defenders of the fatherland to controls of so rigorous and narrow a nature would be to bind them hands and feet.[21]

Perhaps inevitably – he was the greatest speaker in house – the 'divine' Agustín Argüelles was also a vocal participant in the debate:

> The bands which have been the seed corn of the insurrection in the midst of the enemy – the sort of bands that conduct their operations in accordance with the circumstances of the moment without any sort of planning or preparation, are composed of . . . men completely removed from the military profession, and commanded by civilians who are driven solely by patriotism and good will – should never in my opinion by subjected to an ordinance of a type that must destroy the *partidas* that are already in existence and prevent the formation of fresh groups . . . The class of service which they perform is very important, but it is not one of a sort that can be regulated by a formal military code . . . We should not let ourselves be deluded into thinking that it is possible to obtain a perfection which is compatible with neither the nature of these forces nor their mode of operation.[22]

These arguments were augmented by the liberal army officer Evaristo Pérez de Castro. Thus:

> The good guerrillas . . . are of the greatest importance, for they are the peculiar weapon of our insurrection, and cannot be copied or counterfeited by the enemy, whose energy and martial skills will always come to grief when confronted by this singular and most original product of national sentiment . . . Such a weapon does not need much in the way of regulation. Multiply the *partidas* in such a manner that the enemy . . . finds himself constantly distracted and harassed in front, flank and rear by small groups that make surprise attacks, appear and disappear as if by magic, and that pick his men off one by one day and night . . . and Spain will in a few months become the tomb of the invader . . . In consequence, terror of the enemy as it is, let us look after this special weapon most carefully; let us attempt, indeed, to make the guerrillas as numerous as grains of sand on a beach. And, to ensure that we achieve this, let us elaborate fewer ordinances of a sort that can only quench the fires of patriotism and leave us reliant on the much slower and more difficult remedy offered by the organisation . . . of mass armies.[23]

In the face of such rhetoric, the proponents of control were helpless, and the assembly in the end voted unanimously to reject the ordinance. Yet the issue did not go away. Even the most enthusiastic supporters of the guerrillas had agreed that a more appropriate document should be elaborated in place of the one rejected by the *cortes*. At the same time, such was the situation on the ground that the loyalties even of elements whom the partisans might have regarded as their natural supporters were soon under considerable strain. Indeed, within months of the debate of August 1811 the *Semanario Patriótico* was admitting that, even though the harm wrought by the *partidas* was outweighed by the damage that they had done to the enemy, it would still be a good idea to place them under some form of inspectorate and, for good measure, to form units of *cazadores rurales* that could suppress those who refused to toe the line.[24] Just as critical, meanwhile, was the renegade cleric José Blanco White. Thus:

> In so far as the . . . guerrillas are concerned, I have always believed them to be most useful, but also most dangerous. When the bands become small divisions headed by accredited commanders such as Mina, El Empecinado and Sánchez, the advantages they bring cannot be numbered . . . but the ones that have remained mere handfuls of men headed by captains who show neither subordination nor . . . responsibility and generally act like bandit chiefs need very great reform. Because they have killed twenty or thirty Frenchmen one day, they think they have the right to burn a Spanish village and commit 1,000 disorders the next.[25]

Yet another voice raised in protest, meanwhile, was that of Luis Baccigalupi, a priest of strongly liberal views, who had fought with the *somatenes* in Catalonia and published a pamphlet that, if it did not deny the *partidas* a separate identity, still called for them to be given a regular military organisation on a nationwide scale. In brief, the bands were to be grouped into 'flying legions' consisting of a general staff, four battalions of infantry, a regiment of lancers and a company apiece of engineers and scouts. However, Baccigalupi envisaged that most of the time the 'mixed brigades' that his plan called for would fight split up into smaller units, the essence of his thinking being an attempt to retain the flexibility and high mobility associated with the guerrillas with the discipline and reliability supposed to characterise regular troops.[26]

With Blanco White going so far as to argue that those *partidas* that refused either to militarise themselves or to enlist in the ranks of one of the 'regular' bands should be suppressed as bandits, the new guerrilla ordinance finally came into force on 11 July 1812. Less drastic than it had been in its original form, this nonetheless made it quite clear that the days of freedom and tolerance were at an end. In brief, all guerrilla bands were henceforth to be subordinate to the army commander responsible for the district in which they were operating, whilst the generals concerned were each to appoint an inspector whose task it would be to keep a check on their activities, sanction all promotions within their ranks, punish individual wrongdoers, suppress those *partidas* whose behaviour did not come up to scratch, and look into all proposals for the establishment of fresh bands. No new bands would be permitted without the sanction of the authorities; prospective *cabecillas* would henceforth be expected to give proofs of their patriotism and good conduct; the recruitment of deserters and men liable to conscription was forbidden; and the guerrillas were to be subjected to military discipline. And, on top of all this, the decree was to be retrospective, in that the inspectors appointed by the generals were given the power to investigate the past conduct of each band and to strip them of any men who ought to be serving in the regular army.[27] Yet even without this decree in many parts of Spain the military had already begun to take action. Arriving in Algeciras, for example, General Ballesteros gave short shrift to the inhabitants of the Serranía de Ronda:

> The . . . guerrilla bands that infested the region were one of the objects that called for my consideration. Not only had questions been raised as to the services that they had rendered, but the *pueblos* of the district were loudly complaining of their excesses . . . I examined the truth of these representations in person . . . Convinced that the *partidas* existing in the district under my command were both militarily useless and prejudicial to the nation, I immediately ordered their disbandment.[28]

At about the same time that Ballesteros was acting in this fashion, a slightly different tack had been adopted in León, where Julián Sánchez had formed a second regiment of his Lanceros de Castilla by pressing a number of minor bands that had been active in the area.[29] Similar measures, meanwhile, had already been carried out in Old Castile and Extremadura by Juan Díaz Porlier and Pablo Morillo. Thus, in a move sanctioned by his superior, General Mahy, in September 1810 Porlier ordered the commander of his cavalry, José de la Riba, to incorporate all the independent *partidas* that he could in his Husares de Cantabria, whilst in May 1811 Morillo, who now commanded a division of the Spanish Fifth Army, arrested a guerrilla band led by one Manuel Cardenas, consisting entirely of deserters, on the grounds that it had been making extortionate demands for rations.[30] And in the Ronda area, too, they were nothing new: sent to support the insurrection with 3,000 men in 1810, Luis Lacy had eventually expelled the insurgents from his camp and arrested most of their chiefs, whilst he would doubtless have approved of the solution adopted by Ballesteros, which was to form the *serranos* into the formal home guard that we have already noted.[31]

But by far the best evidence we have for this process comes from the southern part of the province of Valencia. The French having had too few troops to occupy the area following the occupation of the capital in January 1812, it had become home to swarms of *partidas*. Based in Alicante, however, were the Spanish generals José O'Donnell and (albeit from May 1812 only) Francisco Copons, neither of whom had a good word to say for his neighbours. Bombarded with appeals for help from the local populace, the two commanders therefore launched a sustained offensive against the guerrillas. First to move was O'Donnell, who was at the head of the Spanish forces who had escaped Valencia when the city fell in January 1812. Thus, on 18 March 1812 he appointed Colonel Francisco Samper 'Interim Commandant General of the Patriotic Guerrilla Bands of the Kingdom of Valencia', and gave him the task of 'consolidating the establishment of the guerrillas whilst at the same time giving them a form that will both ensure the success of their enterprises and prevent them from becoming prejudicial to the common cause'.[32] Samper's instructions were copious: amongst other things he was to ensure that no deserters enlisted in the *partidas*, that no *cabecillas* were allowed to operate unless they had first received authorisation from the commandant-general of the province, that all the bands were to base themselves in territory occupied by the French, that any deserters or draft dodgers who had already joined the guerrillas should be surrendered forthwith, that all disorders were to be punished with the utmost severity, and that the various chieftains should submit weekly reports and maintain a minimum strength of fifty men.[33] And finally a captain of the First Regiment of Cazadores de Valencia named Fernando Reig was sent out with a handful of sergeants to round up such deserters as he could find, his task in the meantime being made somewhat easier by the fact that he was allowed to promise prospective recruits that they would be retained in the province as a security force rather than being returned to their units.[34]

On arriving in Alicante at the beginning of May, however, Copons found that matters had not much improved. As O'Donnell complained, indeed:

> Ever since I placed the . . . *partidas* under the command of . . . Samper, I have been hearing of the disorders that they have been committing, and I have in consequence never ceased to press your predecessor as commandant-general of Valencia . . . on the need to put these bands in order and subject them to the sort of discipline needed to secure the punishment of any commander who acts in an arbitrary fashion, or is responsible for disorders of any sort.[35]

Already angry at what he had seen as commandant-general of the Condado de Niebla, Copons set to work with a will. Promising O'Donnell his fullest support, he immediately ordered Samper to withdraw the commissions of a number of *cabecillas* who had been accused of banditry, appointed a Lieutenant-Colonel Juan Barrera to act as inspector of guerrillas and authorised a priest named Rovira to establish a special *partida* whose task it would be to hunt down deserters.[36] As to his intentions, he made these very clear:

> A retired lieutenant-colonel who says that he is the second-in-command of a guerrilla band has just presented himself to me. However, I did not need what he had to say to inform myself of the disorder that reigns among the *partidas*. Their wretched commanders, the sort of men from which they are recruited and the little use which they are to the fatherland in comparison

> with the harm that they inflict . . . on the inhabitants of this kingdom are all well known to me. Great evils necessitate dramatic remedies. The combination of the powers that you have been given . . . make me confident that within a matter of hours my desires will be realised. As to what these are, they are that all the commandants should be men of proven probity; that there should not be a single deserter in any of the bands; that any which are found should be sent to this city [i.e., Alicante], along with any criminals who have been released from gaol or men of ill-repute; that . . . the *partidas* should only be made up of men who are exempt from conscription; and that any horses that the guerrillas have to which they have no right . . . should be collected up and . . . sent to me here.[37]

For all Copons' good intentions, however, it was difficult to make progress. Samper, for example, was found to be at best a man of little energy, and at worst an accomplice of the *partidas*, whilst many of the *cabecillas* refused to recognise Barrera's authority and the latter complained that without an escort of armed men he would be able to achieve little.[38] Nor, meanwhile, did it help that Copons' counterpart in La Mancha, General Bassecourt, arrested Reig as a bandit when he travelled to Almansa to arrest the *cabecilla* Aparici.[39] At the same time, no sooner was the heat turned on one band or another than its members melted away: as Reig complained, it was sometimes impossible to find any guerrillas at all.[40] All the same, the campaign for the restoration of order was not without its successes. Various *partidas* were suppressed, whilst the particularly violent chieftain José Puchau was arrested after he had murdered a rival *cabecilla*.[41] This latter affair illustrated all too well the difficulties the authorities were up against: Puchau had essayed defiance – at one point, indeed, it appeared that he was about to attack Barrera – and had thrown himself on the mercy of the Aragonese commander Pedro Villacampa, who allowed himself to be enveigled into riding to his support with a detachment of troops in return for the promise of the allegiance of the Valencian *cabecilla*. In the end, Villacampa decided to back off and Puchau was duly arrested, but as he was being taken to Alicante his brother attempted to rescue him with the aid of thirty of his followers.[42]

As it happened, Puchau was very shortly recaptured and imprisoned, but the reality of dealing with the guerrillas at close quarters had not been such as to lessen the concerns of the military authorities. As Barrera wrote to Copons, indeed, 'In God's name I beg you not to allow any civilian to command a *partida* unless you are very sure of him. The *cabecillas* are the worst thieves that I have ever come across. I swear that they are driving me mad.'[43] There was, it seemed, no way forward unless they were got rid of altogether: as soon as a group of stragglers and deserters were got together, for example, they would be encouraged to take flight once again by emissaries of such leaders as Agustín Nebot (who certainly does not seem to have deserved the admiring coverage that he received in the liberal press).[44] To quote Barrera again:

> So long as there are . . . guerrilla bands commanded by men of neither scruples nor instruction with no links with the rest of society, there will be no progress with regard to the restoration of order. At the same time, public opinion will continue to be cast down, whilst wrongdoers who wish to avoid joining the army or give full rein to their passions will always find a refuge. And how can this be otherwise when the *partidas* are either commanded by men such as El Fraile and his subalterns or unworthy sergeants and corporals who have fled their colours and are the scandal of our military system?[45]

Pressing though such concerns were, annihilation was not the only policy pursued by the authorities with regard to the *partidas*. In La Mancha, for example, El Empecinado was very keen for the large number of minor bands that were swirling around his forces to be placed under his command.[46] This was in part blatant empire building, but it was also a solution favoured by other observers. Amongst the latter was the government's chief agent in the area, Rafael Gutiérrez, who suggested that the *cuadrillas* might be bribed into offering El Empecinado their allegiance.[47] As time went by, however, Gutiérrez, who had come to realise that the famous guerrilla leader was not quite the hero of legend, switched his support to the alternative plan of having a new commander sent in from outside. 'The state of these provinces', he wrote, 'would be flourishing . . . if only the government would send them the firm, wise and incorruptible officer who could give them the impulse that is needed, and, in particular, get into action the . . . thousands of men who have become disgusted at the quarrels of their leaders and used them as a pretext to return to their homes.'[48] For still other correspondents the way forward was simply to ensure that all the bands were militarised in terms of their organisation and discipline.[49]

But in a sense such nuances are irrelevant. By the end of 1812 the writing was on the wall. Unless the guerrillas surrendered their autonomy, accepted full militarisation and submitted to the norms imposed on them by the Patriot state, they could expect to be treated as outlaws. As yet, there was still some hope that those who behaved with due docility might find a permanent place in the armed forces. In the course of 1813 even those hopes were killed, however. Thanks to the campaigns of 1812 the French had been permanently ejected from Andalucía, New Castile, Extremadura and Asturias. If ever the guerrillas were to prove their devotion to the national cause, then this was the moment for them to do so. By abandoning their old haunts and closing in on the increasingly beleaguered imperial forces, the guerrillas of these provinces might have shown beyond all doubt that they were motivated by hatred of the invaders and the desire to fight for *dios, rey y patria*, but the opportunity was never grasped. In New Castile, El Empecinado seems to have spent all his time chasing the bands of such rival leaders as 'Puchas' and 'Borbón', whilst of Juan Palarea we hear that he 'has remained in a state of inactivity, and, despite the favourable nature of the country, made no exertion whatever to harass the small foraging parties which the enemy have . . . sent into the mountains'.[50] In the north, bent on personal aggrandisement, Porlier had eschewed taking any part in the fighting since the fall of Santander in August 1812, the bulk of his energies having rather been directed towards attempting to wrest control of the province from the commander of the Seventh Army, General Mendizábal.[51] And on the frontiers of Portugal the forces of Julián Sánchez were in a state of considerable disorder, large numbers of his lancers having deserted rather than accept the fact that they had become regular troops.[52] As Schaumann complained, meanwhile, the behaviour of those who remained was quite insufferable:

> They were very much feared . . . Let me give just one example of this. One of my muleteers had a young and extraordinarily pretty girl with him (whether she was his wife or not I do not know) . . . One afternoon . . . a guerrilla dashing past suddenly halted and scrutinised the group with some attention; then, calling the girl to him, he peremptorily commanded her to jump up behind him on the horse's back, and galloped away with her. The parted couple did not dare to protest against this treatment by uttering even one syllable of complaint![53]

Nor did things get very much better in the months that followed. Palarea presented himself to a Spanish divisional commander and requested permission to transform his 300 horsemen into a regiment of regular cavalry.[54] Meanwhile, Longa accepted assimilation into the ranks of the newly renumbered Spanish Fourth Army and, as we have seen, fought alongside the Anglo-Portuguese army in the campaign of Vitoria. But most of the guerrillas effectively withdrew from the struggle, and finally showed themselves in their true colours. As Wellington's forces advanced into Spain, for example, their rear elements were preyed upon incessantly which caused William Keep to complain of constantly coming across 'dead bodies . . . where misfortunes had happened or deeds of rapine by the native robbers committed on stray travellers (particularly officers' servants with baggage), and this even in the paths of so numerous a body of men'.[55] At the same time, meanwhile, thanks to the guerrillas, who had eaten up everything that had not been taken by the French, they discovered that food could only be gleaned from the countryside with great difficulty.[56] And finally, Allied couriers were waylaid and killed in a manner no different from the fate that had overtaken so many of their French counterparts.[57]

But it is not just British sources that tell the story. From all over Spain, indeed, came complaints of pillage and rapine. A band of renegades from Sánchez's forces terrorised the inhabitants of the villages between Salamanca and Avila; the *partidas* of Príncipe and Marquina ravaged the district between Salamanca and Ciudad Rodrigo; and the district around Guadalajara was plagued by hundreds of men who had fled the troops of El Empecinado.[58] As one of Wellington's correspondents put it, in short, 'Every day the guerrillas do less good and cause more damage.'[59] Given what has been revealed in the course of this study, there is nothing surprising about this statement: the *partidas*, indeed, were behaving exactly as everything that we know about their composition and motivation would lead us to expect. But the point is nonetheless an important one. According to apologists for the guerrillas, the failure to follow up the invaders was the product of a pronounced parochialism or, to put it another way, of a tendency to see the struggle solely in terms of the defence of hearth and home. To quote John Tone's discussion of the aftermath of the French evacuation of Galicia in the summer of 1809:

> Instead of following Ney and Soult as they retreated into León . . . the Galicians disbanded. The truth is that in Galicia, as in . . . every other centre of guerrilla warfare, people were not terribly committed to liberating Spain. The objective . . . was . . . to prevent requisitions, tax collections and violence by French soldiery . . . The cause likely to arouse Galicians for a fight was . . . Galicia, not Spain . . . Galicians could be made to fight only for Galicia . . . Spanish guerrillas did not fight for their nation, but for their homes, valleys, districts and, at best, provinces.[60]

But this flies in the face of reality. Setting aside the very real questions that exist as to whether most Spaniards actually fought the French at all, 1813 clearly shows the defenders of hearth and home ravaging the very hearths and homes that they are supposed to have defended.

Let us not return, however, to the issue of what the Spanish 'people's war' was about. What is clear is that the liberals were finally shaken out of their complacency. As late as February 1813 figures such as Agustín Nebot were continuing to receive enthusiastic coverage in the liberal press. On 15 January, for example, *El Conciso* described how he had raised a force of 3,000 men, established a liberated area ruled by its own local junta and set up a number of workshops to fabricate uniforms and mend weapons and equipment, whilst remitting the revenues of his district to the government and inflicting a number of important reverses on the enemy.[61] Similarly, on 11 February the *Diario de*

Gobierno de Sevilla reported that Nebot had put down a number of bandits who had pretended to be operating under his command.[62] Thereafter, however, support for the *partidas* was limited to only the most radical elements in the Patriot camp. For a good example we might turn to the mouthpiece of the leading radical Alvaro Flórez Estrada. Thus:

> The partisan warfare that is typical of our character kept up the enthusiasm of the populace at a time when neither the Spanish government, nor *la Carlota*,[63] nor the august offshoots of her family could reach them, and when misfortune had banished all hope of liberty. In the midst of French domination, love of fatherland, noble ambition and inherited valour gave birth to the *partidas* and armed them with the very arms of the enemy, whilst preserving hopes of vengeance, tying down considerable forces of the tyrant and contributing most effectively to the success of the holy cause for which we are fighting. As for the evils attributed to the *cuerpos francos*, these are to a certain extent inevitable given the sort of war that they have been fighting, whilst they are of little moment when set alongside the benefits they have conveyed. Without them, indeed, we would have had to surrender to the usurper. Let us not forget that the greater part of the *partidas* harass the enemy in the areas that he occupies, and this reflection alone ought to be enough to dispel the opposing arguments.[64]

But Flórez Estrada was now very much a lone voice. In the session of 5 October a motion had already been passed enjoining the Regency to take steps to ensure that the *ayuntamientos* fulfilled the duty imposed on them by the constitution to maintain order.[65] The pressure was now redoubled, however. The liberal press applauded vigorously when Príncipe was surprised by the French at Fuentecén with the loss of a number of prisoners, with one Granada newspaper remarking that 'the death of these soldiers means almost as much to us as does that of the troops of the enemy'.[66] On 1 April, meanwhile, an extremely forthright article printed in the radical *El Conciso* condemned the guerrillas out of hand:

> If it is true that we have a constitution, if . . . there exists a government charged with its execution, if the rights of man in society are not a chimera . . . why do we hesitate in casting aside the thick veil that has until now covered the atrocities, outrages and insatiable rapacity of these gangs of bandits who so unjustly usurp the respectable name of 'patriot'? And what is the fatherland? Is it composed only of the soil on which we tread? Perhaps so, for nothing else is respected by those who call themselves its defenders. The law, the government, the honour, life and property of their fellow citizens are for them mere playthings which they insult with the most insolent

> daring . . . Disabuse yourself, Mr Editor: all these things are incompatible with the existence of these bands, and we must therefore annihilate them or renounce our rights. There is always great indignation in Cádiz at infractions of the constitution, and yet ears are closed to the complaints made against the guerrillas. Why so? Because they kill Frenchmen? Could they not do this at less cost? For how long must we remain blind? Woe on us if our salvation must come from such a source. Did Lord Wellington liberate Portugal with the aid of *partidas*? Did he defeat Marmont with them? And what have we achieved with them but to complete our ruin, strip the provinces of their resources, set back public spirit, disorganise our armies, fill hundreds of families whose only crime was to have money or pretty daughters with shame and sorrow, and plunge entire *pueblos* into the blackest desperation. Patriots of Cádiz, to you are directed the pitiful cries of the patriots of Old Castile. Your opinion is horribly mistaken: the majority . . . of those you believe to be heroes are no more than infamous bandits without law, discipline or feeling . . . Uniting your voice with theirs, demand . . . the extermination of these executioners of our compatriots, of these bands that . . . are the shame of the nation and the scourge of humanity.[67]

According to the Marxist Pérez Garzón, all this was to be explained solely in terms of the rankest cynicism: the guerrillas had served their purpose and, as a threat to property and the social order, were now to be suppressed.[68] But, although partly true, this misses the point. The guerrillas did not represent a threat just to law and order, but also to the very authority of the state. Thanks in large part to their activities, large parts of the liberated territories were completely beyond the control of the government, whilst the need to put an end to this situation had led Wellington to insist on the imposition of rule by the army at the local level, and thus to threaten many of the principles that the liberals held most sacred. British commander As the wrote:

> We must not conceal from ourselves that there is but little authority of any description whatever in the provinces which have been occupied by the enemy, and [that] even that little depends on the exercise of military power. It is vain to expect that a gentleman called an intendant will exercise the power to realise the resources of the country . . . without the assistance of a military force . . . I am aware that it is wrong in principle to invest military men with civil powers, but when the country is in danger that must be adopted which will tend most directly to save it . . . whatever may be the constitutional principles which may be invaded by those measures.[69]

In fairness, the problem was not just the fault of the the guerrillas: across large parts of the liberated territories the rural populace was in a state of ferment over the question of feudalism. Incensed at the failure of the *cortes* either to rescue them from the clutches of the *señores* or to address the question of land reform, many peasants, indeed, were on the brink of revolution. Meanwhile, the regime's problems were complicated still further by its efforts first, to raise money through the sale of the common lands and, second, to impose a new system of taxation that, whilst ostensibly much fairer, in practice led to a huge increase in the amount of money that had to be found by many provinces. And, on top of all this, liberation meant a return to conscription, which in turn produced a fresh wave of flight and desertion. Last but not least, in a number of regions such as Galicia and the Basque provinces the interests of many local notables had been seriously affected by particular aspects of government policy, the result being that they joined reactionary elements of the Church in whipping up resistance to the *jefes políticos* and intendants appointed by Cádiz.[70]

In the context of all this the *cabecillas* were very worrying figures, especially when they proved willing to defy the writ of the regime. For a very good example of the sort of chaos that this development could inflict we have only to turn to Aragón, and in particular Zaragoza. With no regular Spanish forces in the vicinity, the only troops available to occupy the city as the armies of King Joseph fell back in the wake of the battle of Vitoria were those of Espoz y Mina and Durán. For a brief moment the garrison of General Pâris looked as if it might try to hold on to the city, but a day of fierce fighting which saw elements of the two guerrilla commanders' men advance to its very gates led the governor to think again. In consequence, the night of 8/9 July saw the bulk of Pâris' men file out over the bridge across the Ebro. A small force stayed behind in the Aljafería castle, which the French had turned into a citadel, to slow down the pursuit, but otherwise the city was the Spaniards' for the taking: at dawn, indeed, a delegation of the town council presented itself at Durán's outposts in token of surrender. From the beginning, however, things did not go well. Commander of only the northern half of Aragón, Espoz y Mina had at first been unwilling to send any troops to re-occupy Zaragoza for, positioned as it was on the southern bank of the Ebro, the city lay in the domain of Durán, who was *comandante militar* of the southern half of the province. It may have been that the Navarrese *caudillo* was hoping that his much weaker rival's men would be repulsed, leaving him to pick up the pieces and acquire all the benefits of re-taking it for himself. His hand forced by the French collapse, Espoz y Mina had in the end had no choice but to appear before the city, but he was sullen and unco-operative, giving Durán no help with the siege of the Aljafería and taking the bulk of his men off in pursuit of Pâris.[71] And there was worse to come. Shortly after Zaragoza was occupied, Durán was sent off to join the Spanish Second Army in its pursuit of the French forces that were retreating from Valencia, Espoz y Mina being given control of the whole of Aragón and allowed to strip the División de Soria of several of its best units. In late September, however, he heard that the Regency was planning to make the commander of one of the regiments concerned, Ramón Gayán, governor of the city. The results were spectacular, to say the least. In the words of Casamayor:

> 28 September: at the orders of General Don Francisco Espoz y Mina, the commander of the Cariñena infantry regiment, Don Ramón Gayán, who had been acting as interim governor of the city, was taken under arrest to the town of Egea de los Caballeros. For this purpose there came a captain . . . and 400 cavalry, the first thing that they did being to disarm such soldiers as Gayán could muster, and then take them to the castle. At the same time they occupied his house and let no one approach, let alone go inside. Sentries were posted at every street corner along the Coso, parties of cavalry were sent out to patrol the city, and the whole of the Fifth Regiment of Navarre was placed under arms. It was just as if we were under attack. Round about one o'clock in the afternoon, Gayán came out in a sedan chair escorted by an armed guard, and was taken out of the city on the Zuera road. The whole affair caused much talk among the people and gave rise to a great sensation.[72]

Extraordinary as it was, this coup was very much in keeping with Espoz y Mina's administration of his Aragonese domains. There were stories – angrily denied by the general, of course – that he had sold the effects he had captured in the castle of the Aljafería for his own benefit.[73] Complaints of his arbitrary behaviour and failure to respect the constitution of 1812, which was proclaimed in few of the towns he liberated, were numerous, and one example was a pamphlet penned by an inhabitant of the town of Barbastro. According to this observer, Espoz y Mina's accession to the command of Alto Aragón had at first been welcomed, for until then the region's only defenders had been

> Sartos, Domper, Pesoduro . . . Baella, El Malcarado, commanders who . . . were unequal to the grand task of reconquering the country and yet laid down the law as if they were sovereigns . . . fugitives who . . . abusing our credulity and imprudent simplicity, entered even fair-sized towns with a handful of men to seize those unfortunates they supposed to be rich, and then led them to desolate wildernesses, where they sacrificed anyone who could not pay the immense sums they demanded in exchange for their lives and liberty to their heathen greed.[74]

Espoz y Mina, then, had appeared as 'a Moses sent to liberate us from a slavery that was worse than Egyptian', but all was far from well:

> If the sublime code of the constitution was published in Barbastro, the events that followed have proved to us that this supposedly sacred ceremony had

> little other object than a military parade. Who would have thought that . . . at the very time that . . . the liberty of the Spanish nation was being established . . . the north of Aragón would be groaning under the harshest oppression, the Aragonese threatened with prison, confiscation and even death at the merest whim of military commandants . . . priests and magistrates arrested on frivolous pretexts and detained for long and arbitrary periods, and the respectable discharge of neither sacred ministry nor public responsibility any defence against . . . being flung in a cell or strung up from an olive tree.[75]

Little more encouraging, meanwhile, is the account of Espoz y Mina given by Augustus Schaumann, a German commissary attached to Wellington's army who had dealings with him after the battle of Vitoria. Thus:

> One day the famous General Francisco Espoz y Mina passed the town [Olite] . . . The whole town went out to meet him, and the people kissed his hands, the hem of his garment and his sword. Very much inflated with his pride at all these attentions, his behaviour all too frequently betrayed his lowly origin and his total ignorance of decent manners and decorum. Once I sent one of my convoy leaders to him with a respectful and courteous letter begging him to send one of his commissaries to see me. This man had overrun the whole country and had been guilty of many acts of violence . . . and I wished to come to an understanding with him concerning the boundaries of the districts in which we should have the right to forage. In this way I hoped to put an end to all strife. Not only, however, did the general not answer this letter, but he dismissed my convoy leader, a Spaniard, with the threat that, if he ever dared to come again with such a letter, even if it were written by Lord Wellington himself, he would lay him across a bundle of straw and have him soundly thrashed by two corporals.[76]

This story, perhaps, is exaggerated, but Espoz y Mina was certainly not prepared to tolerate the presence of rivals in his patch. Nor should any of this surprise us, for relations between the Navarrese leader and the Regency had for some time suggested that the former envisaged himself as an independent satrap. In the summer of 1812, for example, he had refused to allow the government to send an officer to his division to act as its chief-of-staff: though common practice in the army since the creation of the General Staff in 1810, such an appointment would clearly have threatened Espoz y Mina's independence.[77] At the same time he had also been deeply angered when the Regency had appointed an intendant for the whole of Aragón early in 1813, thereby once again challenging his autonomy (in September 1812 he had been given command of that part of the province north of the River Ebro).[78]

To return to Zaragoza, the behaviour of Espoz y Mina's troops proved to be appalling. In his memoirs the Navarrese commander tried hard to maintain that the trouble stemmed not from his own men but from those he had inherited from Durán, not to mention the swarms of deserters and bandits who continued to range the countryside. In this he had a point: it was apparently troops from Gayán's Regimiento de Cariñena who staged a riot in the city's theatre on 9 October in the course of which they pelted the actors with stones and other missiles and defied the representatives of the civil authorities.[79] But there is clear evidence from Sos del Rey Católico that the town had been mercilessly sacked when the 'División de Navarra' attacked it in March 1813, and as early as 29 July there had been complaints that Espoz y Mina's men were molesting women in the street.[80] Furthermore, many of the bandits of which Espoz y Mina complained were deserters from his own regiments, as witness the captain of the 'Husares de Navarra' captured at the head of a gang of fifty armed men at Herrera in late November.[81] As for what followed, it was little short of a reign of terror. For a month Espoz y Mina's forces robbed innumerable passers-by, breaking into many houses and levying tolls on anyone who attempted to introduce goods into the city from the north bank of the Ebro (they had established their chief headquarters in the transpontine suburb known as the Arabal). Despite the fact that Espoz y Mina had recently been explicitly stripped of the power that he had hitherto exercised over the *bienes nacionales* in his domains, meanwhile, his representatives brazenly sold off the properties of the Arabal's Carthusian monastery at public auction. As Casamayor recorded in his journal at the end of October:

> This month has been very vexatious for the inhabitants on account of . . . the fear and terror imposed by the soldiers of the Fifth Regiment of Navarre, who, being in garrison, every night robbed everyone they could lay their hands on and beat up anyone who resisted or proved to have no money. So bad have things become that nobody dares to go out except on the most urgent business. People have complained to the justices, but nothing has been done to contain them, and they carry on robbing just the same.[82]

Nor did the attitude adopted by Espoz y Mina himself make matters any easier. In the face of the protests sent him by the *ayuntamiento* he maintained an air of the most studied innocence, pretending that the only reason that his men were lingering in the city was that he had not received any orders for their removal, and maintaining – with tongue firmly in cheek – that the troops still in Zaragoza were habitually well behaved and under the strictest orders to cause no trouble.[83]

On 1 November some relief was obtained when, having been confirmed in his position by Wellington, Gayán returned to the city as governor, and ordered all those men belonging to Espoz y Mina's division to leave the city immediately.[84] Most complied apart from the garrison of the castle, which first hung on for a few more days and then deliberately fired the building and all its contents.[85] This, however, was the parting shot of the 'División de Navarra': on 14 November Espoz y Mina's troops finally left the Arabal and departed for the Pyrenees, where they were to spend the rest of the war blockading the petty fortress of St Jean-Pied-de-Port. In the meantime the general's political control of his dominions was weakened still further by the appointment – much to his disgust – of *jefes políticos* in both Navarre and Aragón. Deprived of the chance to lord it over Pamplona, which finally fell to the Allies after a prolonged blockade at the end of October, Espoz y Mina was left angry and frustrated: hence the famous incident in which he had a copy of the Constitution of 1812 executed by firing squad.[86] As for Navarre and northern Aragón, they remained in a state of chaos. As Espoz y Mina admitted:

> With the Allied armies gathering for the invasion of France, Napoleon ordered a levy of 500,000 men; the war, it seemed, was to go on forever. When this news reached the ears of our soldiers, desertion began to affect all the units of the army, including those of my division . . . for the men were weary of constant labour. To collect up the deserters and stragglers that resulted, it was necessary to order very severe measures to be taken, whilst the government made matters worse by ordering the conscription of all single men aged between seventeen and forty. Believing that the retreat of the French meant that the war was over, the inhabitants refused to give up the fugitives, and the officers that I had commissioned for the task were in a number of cases forced to proceed against certain local magistrates who failed to cooperate with some vigour.[87]

In Navarre, in particular, conditions were rendered still worse by the impact on the already war-torn province of the arrival of the Allied armies. 'The beautiful valleys begin to look dull', wrote the British light infantry officer George Hennell. He continued:

> All the corn is gone; the apple trees [were] stripped long ago. The walnuts were scarce ripe before all were gone and the chestnuts are going fast. You can have no idea what destruction and waste an army carries with it. We are like locusts: every place we halt at . . . bears marks of it, and, although orders and punishments abound, it is impossible to prevent pillage. If a soldier wants a piece of wood to boil his kettle, and there is beautiful peach or apple by the side of a chestnut or oak, I do not believe he would go a yard to choose. I have seen fellows knock down a peck of unripe plums for the sake of five or six.[88]

But nowhere were conditions very different, the fact being that the whole of Spain was in turmoil. As the Duke of Wellington wrote to the Minister of War, General O'Donoju, in a repeat of a lament that he had first penned a year earlier:

> The wants of the troops and the state in which the army is are to be attributed to the deficiency of public authority in the provinces . . . The fact is, Sir, that the intendants of the provinces are unable or unwilling to perform their duty. All authority has been annihilated in Spain, and at the moment the greatest exertions are required to form and maintain armies to save the state: there is no authority in existence capable of enforcing the most simple order of the government. That is the truth, and, till a remedy is applied, the evil will become worse.[89]

One might here, too, cite a petition that reached the *cortes* from Avila in January 1814, painting a dismal picture of the situation that had prevailed in the wake of the province's liberation:

> By the time that the French were driven from Avila, public morality had been reduced by the occupation to a most deplorable condition. Authority was looked upon with indifference and disobeyed with impunity; there was no respect for parish priests or the heads of religious houses; crops and farm animals were constantly being stolen . . . and there were constant infractions of both our laws and our social customs. On top of all this robbery, pillage and even murder were all common on every road, much to the suffering of the populace and the general scandal of one and all.[90]

Faced by these increasingly gloomy reports, even the most die-hard liberals accepted that action had to be taken to restore order. By no means all the more regular elements of the guerrillas had proved as unruly as the forces of Espoz y Mina – when troops from El Empecinado's division entered Madrid in June in the wake of the retreating French, for example, they behaved with the utmost decorum[91] – but it was clear that they were not be trusted. As for the rest of the *partidas*, meanwhile, they had now put themselves beyond the pale. In fact, efforts to restore order had been intensifying since at least midsummer. Such bandits as could be apprehended were shown no mercy: on 10 June, for instance, Rafael Pidilla, Antonio Toral, Francisco Martínez and Francisco del Río were shot by firing squad in Jaén as 'thieves, deserters, murderers and members of the criminal gang that has been infesting the . . . paths and roads around the *pueblos* of Quesada, Pozo Alcón, Cazorla, Hinojares and Belerda' (in this respect it helped enormously that on 10 August Wellington used his authority as commander-in-chief of the Spanish armies to order the immediate dissolution of all those bands that had not been formally incorporated into the armed forces).[92] Also arrested and put on trial was the Castilian leader Saornil, although the latter eventually succeeded in escaping justice by bribing his gaolers into turning a blind eye to his plans for a daring gaolbreak.[93] And, following the receipt of an alarming missive from the Minister of Grace and Justice that painted a graphic picture of the havoc being wrought in many provinces by the guerrillas, on 3 July a plan was laid before the assembly calling for the establishment in each municipality of an armed volunteer security force mustered at a strength of one man for every 100 inhabitants.[94] Debated in the sessions of 9 and 14 July, this plan was initially thrown out on the grounds that militias of the sort proposed by the Regency had on the whole proved worse than useless. Yet there was little attempt to defend the guerrillas *per se*, and it was therefore agreed that, whatever practical problems were thrown up by the plan, the Regency should still be authorised to take such measures as it thought fit.

In consequence, after further protests in the *cortes* at the general disorder – on 18 October, for example, the deputy Pérez Pastor proclaimed: 'In the greater part of the provinces of the interior public safety is in the most lamentable state. . . . Not only are farms, roads and country estates the scene of constant robberies, murders and other outrages, but even large towns are not free from danger, the problem having acquired such dimensions that gangs of bandits have been entering them to free the prisoners from the gaols and carry out other disorders'[95] – in November the scheme was reintroduced in full. Thus, acknowledging both 'the robberies, murders and crimes of every sort that are committed with impunity on every road' and 'the innumerable demands for the adoption of radical measures aimed at the extermination of the many bands of thieves, deserters and wrongdoers of every type that infest almost every corner of the Peninsula', the Regency announced the formation of a nationwide force of *escopeteros voluntarios* ('volunteer shotgunners'), whose task it would be to patrol the highways and generally maintain order.[96]

As yet we are not talking about a gendarmerie in the style of the Guardia Civil for the rank and file of the new force were all to remain civilians, to equip themselves at their own cost, to serve on a part-time basis, and to be responsible not to the military authorities but to the *ayuntamientos*, whilst the liberals also refused to tolerate the establishment of a police administration modelled on the one that had been set up by the government of Joseph Bonaparte, on the grounds that such a move could not but threaten civil liberty.[97] Nor is this surprising: setting aside the scruples occasioned by the prospect of copying Napoleonic models, the liberals saw law and order as the responsibility of the *ayuntamientos* and they were at the same time pinning their hopes on the establishment of the national militia also prefigured by the constitution (primarily envisaged as a bulwark of Spain's political freedom, this force also had a clear anti-bandit mandate, and it is therefore no coincidence that, after months of inaction, the *cortes* now moved to accelerate its formation).[98] In a debate held in November 1812 the *cortes* had in fact specifically rejected a proposal put forward by the Regency for the creation of three companies of *celadores* ('watchmen') in each province, on the grounds that such a force would both represent a breach of the constitution and tend to usurp the role of the national militia.[99] But the idea would not go away: not only did various individuals request commissions in such companies, should they be formed, but the idea was resurrected in a number of petitions received by the *cortes*.[100]

When finally established on 15 April 1814, the national militia was certainly put forward as an answer to banditry, the royal decree that set it up specifically stating that its duties would include hunting down deserters and other wrong-doers.[101] At this stage, however, this force could make no difference. Less than three weeks later Fernando VII was back in Madrid as absolute ruler of Spain, and it is not in fact clear that any units of the militia were ever actually embodied, nor, still less, that they caught even a single bandit. Though it might be pointed out that liberal policies with regard to the restoration of order were never fairly tested, the chief weight of the problem therefore fell upon the shoulders of the bureaucratic absolutism represented by the regime of Fernando VII. Faced as it was by a problem of enormous dimensions, it was never likely that this would act with anything other than cold ferocity. The end of the guerrillas, indeed, was not long in coming. On 26 July 1814 there duly appeared a royal decree on the subject, which was characterised by a mixture of fear, contempt and lack of generosity. In brief, any officer of the *partidas* who could prove his right to the commission that he held would be assimilated into the *milicias urbanas* – companies of town guards maintained by the old Bourbon army and now restored by Fernando VII – and it was also agreed that any member of the bands who had been wounded would be accorded the pay and status of members of the army's corps of invalids. Beyond that, however, the news was very bad: the highest rank available to any officer was that of cornet of cavalry, whilst all priests and religious were ordered to return to their normal vocations and all deserters to rejoin their regiments. In short, the *partidas* were to be broken up forthwith, and given almost nothing in the way of credit for their efforts. As for the consequences of resistance, they were at best grim: any band that tried to stay together or maintain itself in arms would be treated as a gang of bandits and put to the sword.[102] Notably absent from the provisions of the decree, however, were the 'División de Navarra', the 'División de Soria' and the other militarised *partidas*. As Best says:

> Whether they were still guerrillas or not may well be questioned. The government of their country had succeeded in their cases in doing what all gov-

ernments must wish to do, and all professional military men wished to do. It had brought society's violence-potential under its own control.[103]

Needless to say, this decree was honoured more in the breach than in the observance. With agriculture, trade and industry in ruins, their homes in many cases burned-out shells, many provinces wracked by terrible epidemics of yellow fever and other diseases and the regime likely to impose conscription to raise the men it needed to fight the rebellions that had broken out in Mexico and South America in 1810, there was little incentive for the *partidas* to lay down their arms and fade away. In consequence, banditry remained a massive problem which the regime combated without mercy, setting up many special tribunals and making use of large number of regular troops (at one stage 4,000 men were said to be pursuing the so-called 'seven boys of Ecija' alone).[104] But there is again no way that the upsurge in banditry that followed the end of the war can be regarded as in any sense a consciously political phenomenon. Indeed, the most well-known of the popular leaders to have followed this course after 1814 – the Valencian Jaime Alfonso – fought for the absolutists in the guerrilla insurrection that assailed the liberals when they once again seized power in the revolution of 1820.[105] Poverty and despair bred bandits, certainly, but, as before, *la vida a salto de mata* remained at best a survival strategy whose victims were as likely to be the poor as they were the *pudientes*. In Galicia, the only province of which we have much knowledge, the proportion of the victims of banditry represented by the clergy actually seems to have fallen slightly between 1814 and 1820, whilst the populace as a whole continued to loathe the *cuadrillas*, denouncing many of their members to the authorities and on occasion hurling themselves upon gangs who appeared in their midst with whatever weapons that came to hand.[106] And, as before, though the rich were targeted, it was simply because they were rich rather than because they were the enemies of the people: when an Italian deserter who was the chief of a small gang that operated in the vicinity of Barbastro kidnapped a wealthy local proprietor and informed his family that they would be sent a piece of his body every day until they paid a ransom of 30,000 *francs*, he was acting in the manner not of Robin Hood but of Al Capone.[107] Nor, meanwhile, is there any real evidence of 'social banditry' in Extremadura, where the 'boys of Santibañez' were joined after 1814 by the much feared 'gang of Melchor and Merino'.[108]

What little we know of the fate of the wilder fringes of *la guerrilla popular* after 1814 tends to confirm a sceptical view of the insurgents' motivation in the struggle against the French. And if this is so of the more obscure elements of the movement, it is certainly the case with their leaders. For many years it was almost an article of faith in works on nineteenth-century Spain that, having fought for national independence in the struggle against Napoleon, the guerrilla commanders were drawn ineluctably into support for the cause of liberalism after 1814. To quote Pablo Casado, for example, 'Having reached high ranks in the army thanks to their spectacular actions and the powers which the *cortes* had given them, the guerrillas were with rare exceptions opposed to the absolutist regime, in which respect we might take Espoz y Mina, Díaz Porlier or Palarea as their exemplars.'[109] Much the same idea was expressed by Gabriel Lovett: 'It has not been proven that officers with a guerrilla background who . . . harboured liberal sympathies were more numerous than those with absolutist ideas, but this is more than likely since these men had risen to high rank thanks to their deeds and not to their family background or wealth.'[110]

The exceptions to which Casado refers, however, were more numerous than he admits: setting aside the obvious example of Merino, who, as we have already seen, in later life fought as a Carlist, we might here cite Francisco Longa, who in 1814 was appointed by Fernando VII as governor of Bilbao, before going on to fight against the liberals in the civil war of 1822–3. Also on a much humbler level, out of nineteen Valencian *cabecillas* identified by Ardit, five fought for the absolutists and only two for the liberals.[111] Indeed, one might go much further here. Many of the most famous guerrilla leaders certainly sided with the liberal cause after 1814: Espoz y Mina was the first military commander to 'pronounce' against Fernando; Porlier staged a revolt in La Coruña in 1815 and died before a firing squad; Mina and Renovales both became mixed up in revolutionary politics in Latin America (like Porlier, indeed, the former was eventually executed); having been taken prisoner by the absolutists in 1823, El Empecinado was hung in Roa on 19 August 1824, though not before he had made a last-minute bid to escape from the very foot of the scaffold; and finally, having first been implicated in the plots of 1814–20 and having then fought for the liberals in 1822–3, Francisco Abad Moreno (Chaleco) went to the scaffold in Granada in September 1827. Unfortunately, however, these post-war heroics have been accorded more dignity than they deserve, for they can be explained by thwarted ambition as much as by political idealism. In this respect we might quote Stanley Payne: 'Only a few months were needed . . . to show that ex-guerrilla chiefs were viewed by the court circle as upstarts . . . Having virtually held the power of life and death in their districts for years, these young commanders would inevitably feel snubbed.'[112]

In short, we return to the issue of self-interest. Payne, however, does not go far enough. Implied in his words is an assumption that there was no place at all for the guerrillas in the Spanish military establishment after 1814, or, to put it another way, that Fernando VII was unwilling to offer them adequate recompense for their sacrifices, just as the generals of the regular army were unwilling to accept them as their equals. But this is at best only partly true. The regiments that had made up the forces of commanders such as Longa,

Durán, El Empecinado and Espoz y Mina were certainly reduced in number, but they were not wiped out. Taking infantry units alone, listed in the official almanac for 1815 are the Primer de Iberia, Segundo de Iberia, Tercero de Iberia and Cuarto de Iberia regiments from Longa's command; the Voluntarios de Rioja, Voluntarios Numantinos and Cariñena regiments from Durán's command; the Tiradores de Sigüenza, Voluntarios de Madrid, Cazadores de Cuenca and Voluntarios de Guadalajara regiments from El Empecinado's command; and the Primero Cántabro, Primero Tiradores de Cantabria, Segundo Tiradores de Cantabria and Tercero Tiradores de Cantabria regiments from Porlier's command.[113] And the guerrillas were not the only part of the armed forces to suffer since their fate was shared by the vast majority of the new regiments that had been created in the course of the war.[114] As for the guerrillas' commanders, all was far from lost. As the example of Longa shows, space for them could sometimes be found even in the straitened financial circumstances that characterised Spain's situation in the immediate post-war period (and although they are not strictly speaking guerrillas, other cases that come to mind here are those of the ex-sergeant Pablo Morillo, who commanded the expeditionary force sent to Venezuela in 1814, and Julián Sánchez, who was showered with decorations and appointed president of the 'permanent council of war'). Indeed, even more minor figures could secure generous settlements of one sort or another: the Miguel Sarasa who in 1809 raised a *partida* from his tenants and household servants was in 1817 appointed to the command of a light infantry regiment, whilst junior officers such as Manuel Alegre (the brother of the Aragonese leader El Cantarero) were given posts in the *resguardo*, the tax administration or the tobacco monopoly.[115] In short, there was no vendetta against the guerrillas as such, but rather a financial squeeze that could not but produce a number of casualties, added to a political climate that was unlikely to be favourable to anyone who could be tarred with the brush of liberalism.[116]

What follows from this is that opposition to Fernando VII amongst the guerrillas was at least as much the product of circumstance as it was that of conviction. Let us take as examples the cases of Espoz y Mina, Porlier and El Empecinado. In 1814, as we have seen, Espoz y Mina led the first of a series of military revolts against the absolutist regime that was in the end to bring about the restoration of the liberals in the revolution of 1820. But this was not for love of the constitution of 1812. On the contrary, the Navarrese commander had for some time been deeply at odds with the political leadership of Patriot Spain, and initially rallied to Fernando VII with enthusiasm. One by one, however, he found that his goals – nomination to the viceroyalty of Navarre, the survival of his division as an independent command and the perpetuation of both his powers of patronage and, by extension, the various administrative and judical organs that he had established to govern his domains – were to be denied him, whilst a particularly unfortunate episode saw him publically snubbed by Fernando VII when he visited the court to try to press his claim. Why he should have been treated in this fashion is unclear, but it is probable that the king had simply been put off by his general air of bombast, come to see him as dangerously self-serving or been influenced against him by the chaotic situation in Navarre, where the local élites were protesting bitterly at his constant demands for food and money and his troops more or less running wild. Desperate to save his position, Espoz y Mina rushed back to Navarre and sought to mobilise what remained of his forces for a coup. There was no support for the general, however. Few men rallied to his cause, and when he finally attempted to seize the citadel of Pamplona on the night of 25 September 1814 the result was a fiasco that within a few hours had him fleeing for the frontier.[117] As to what Espoz y Mina was trying to achieve, no attempt was made to proclaim the constitution of 1814, and it is probable that the affair's only goal was a show of force designed to persuade the king to recognise his claims. At all events there followed years of exile, punctuated by a fresh period of government service in the *trienio liberal* of 1820–23. In the fighting of 1822–23 the Navarrese commander showed something of his old ferocity but, for all that, his liberalism was never more than skin-deep, and his conduct in the exile community in London was marked by a repellent mixture of egotism and duplicity, and there were even fears among his fellow refugees that he was aiming at a revolutionary dictatorship.[118]

Moving on to Juan Díaz Porlier, El Marquesito was at least arrested by Fernando VII in 1814. But the fact that he was in prison does not make him a liberal: Porlier had, like Espoz y Mina, been out of favour with the liberal authorities, and his arrest seems to have been motivated by nothing more than the fact that he had married the sister of the leading liberal politician the Conde de Toreno. Nor did he give full support to the regime of the war years when he broke out of gaol and rose in revolt in 1815: the need for a *cortes* was proclaimed, certainly, but it was specifically stated that the new assembly should have the right to amend the constitution of 1812 as it thought fit.[119] And what, meanwhile, of El Empecinado? In April 1814 he had willingly rallied to the absolutist standard, whilst in October of the same year Fernando VII had rewarded his loyalty by promoting him to the rank of *mariscal de campo*. Two years later there followed decoration with the Cruz Laureada de San Fernando, and two years later again the grant of noble status for himself, his brothers (who had all fought under him) and his descendants. Although he did not have an appointment at this time, it is therefore clear that he was well thought of by the regime and he seems to have had nothing to do with the cause of revolt (a long manifesto that he is supposed to have sent to Fernando in September 1815 in protest at the king's policies is now generally reckoned to have been a forgery made up by his hagiographers). This, however, did not stop him from joining the rebellion of 1820, or being rewarded with the post of military governor of Zamora. But even an El Empecinado was helpless in the face of the calamities that assailed the liberal regime as a French army stormed across the frontier to assist the rebels who had already sprung up to fight for the absolutist cause in the interior. Captured at Olmos in the last stage of the fighting, the erstwhile partisan had therefore backed the wrong horse, and it was not long before he was, as we have seen, on trial for his life at the hands of a vengeful Fernando VII.[120]

To conclude, then, the guerrillas ended, much as they had begun, in banditry and opportunism. Always primarily the product of the poverty and social disruption brought about by the impact of war, invasion and economic collapse on a society whose resources were at the best of times very sparse, the *partidas* were motivated by what contemporary observers called 'greed' as much as they were by a desire to fight the French. To put it another way, the men who flocked to their ranks saw this action as the only means of getting bread for themselves and their families, and loyalty to Fernando VII, love of the Catholic religion and even hatred of the French counted for very little when it came to persuading them to take up arms. As for their leaders, much the same applies, except that in their case there was also a measure of ambition, such men as Francisco Espoz y Mina, Juan Martín and Juan Díaz Porlier being adventurers who appreciated that their best interests lay in forcing the bands that they had established to adopt military forms and take an active part in the struggle against the French. So long as much of Spain was under enemy occupation, these problems were camouflaged by the facts, first, that, whether they were called guerrillas or bandits, the mere existence of bands of armed civilians was enough to cause tremendous problems to the invaders, and second, that even the most nefarious of actions could easily be presented as a blow in favour of the Patriot cause. From 1812 onwards, however, the situation began to change. As province after province fell into the hands of the Allies, so it became more and more apparent that the real order of the day was not resistance and heroism but pillage and self-aggrandisement. Every step that the French retreated stripped away a little more of the glamour that had bedazzled so many observers for so long, whilst the chaos that characterised the liberated areas intensified the process of repression and control that had gradually been reducing the freedom of operation enjoyed by the *partidas* since the beginning of the war. For some time this process was resisted by liberal ideologues anxious to promote the concept of a people's war and alarmed at the threat of military despotism, but by 1812 so great was the weight of evidence against the *guerrilla popular* that the bulk of its allies had fallen away, especially as many of the liberals' heroes had emerged as threats to the constitutional order rather than bastions of its defence. As a result, except in the case of those units that had been assimilated with the rest of the armed forces, by the end of 1813 Patriot Spain was effectively at war with the guerrillas. All over the country bands were being disbanded and their members executed, and the return of Fernando VII ended the last vestiges of their existence. With many of the units that had made up the commands of the guerrilla generals also gone thanks to cuts in the size of the army, and relations with the state worsened still further by the decision of some few *cabecillas* to back the liberals in their struggle with Fernando VII – a decision that for the most part smacks still further of opportunism and frustrated ambition – the guerrillas were no more.

Conclusion

Let us recapitulate. This work has presented a highly revisionist picture of the participation of the Spanish people in the Peninsular War of 1808–14. At the same time it has shed fresh light on the popular guerrillas that remain the most famous aspect of Spain's war effort. As a starting-point in this process, the historiography relating to the guerrillas was shown to have contained many ambiguities. On the whole it is favourable to them – so much so, indeed, that it verges on the hagiographic – but a succession of writers nonetheless expressed concerns that were suggestive of an alternative approach to the question. However, the pursuit of this alternative approach was immediately confronted by serious problems. Thus, the idea that the defeat of the French in Spain was the product of a combination of regular and irregular warfare has remained a constant that remains alive to this day.[1] At the same time, like it or not, the French were never able to conquer the Peninsula despite the application of overwhelming numbers of troops, and they themselves paid tribute to the importance of the Spanish guerrillas in their defeat. How, then, was it possible to take views seriously that argued, in effect, that the 'people's war' had been a phenomenon whose importance had been greatly overestimated and, further, that the guerrillas had in many respects been damaging to the Spanish war effort?

The answer was to approach the question as one of definition. 'Little war' – the ambushes, raids, skirmishes and minor operations of all sorts known in the eighteenth century as the *guerre des postes* – had clearly been of immense importance in the defeat of the French, but to what extent had its achievements in fact been the work of bands of armed civilians? Not very much, it seems. In most cases, the key figure was rather the regular soldier. Much aided by the geography of the Iberian Peninsula, in Catalonia, Asturias, Galicia and Andalucía, Spanish troops were able to cling on in the face of French conquest and mount a series of damaging *coups de main*. In Aragón and León units of regular troops – the supposed *partidas* of Julián Sánchez, Felipe Perena and Pedro Villacampa – actually operated as guerrilla bands. Along the Portuguese frontier troops of the Anglo-Portuguese army of the Duke of Wellington regularly sallied forth to attack isolated detachments of French soldiers or eliminate important strongpoints. And from the ports of Cádiz and La Coruña bodies of troops that ranged in size from a few hundred men to entire divisions were embarked on ships and sent along the coast to disembark behind enemy lines and generally cause fear and confusion in their ranks. Supplementing these troops in some parts of Spain, meanwhile, were a variety of militias and home guards that might on occasion engage in guerrilla-style operations but must yet be regarded as part of the armed forces of the state. This is not to say, of course, that traditional guerrilla bands – defined in this respect as independent groups of armed civilians – did not exist. On the contrary, in Navarre, Aragón, the Basque country, Asturias, the two Castiles, Extremadura, Andalucía and the Levant they at the very least enjoyed a high profile. But it does mean that it is possible to address the subject in a different light, and, in particular, to reassess the doings of the *partidas*.

That this is a necessary exercise we need be in no doubt, for the traditional view of a great crusade in favour of *dios*, *rey y patria* has become ever harder to sustain. In the first place, the picture that has emerged of Bourbon Spain in the years leading up to the Peninsular War – a society that was desperately poor, riven by social and economic unrest and shattered by the impact of war – is difficult to reconcile with a vision of an urban and rural poor eager to immolate itself in defence of the *antiguo régimen*. In the second, there is substantial evidence to suggest that the populace were, in fact, deeply hostile to the war against the French. And in the third, a growing weight of historical writing has made it clear that popular resistance is a subject that is open to general reassessment. Thus, taking an example from outside Europe, Harry Ward has shown that in the American War of Independence many of the partisans who fought for each side were roving bands of robbers who ravaged the civilian populace without mercy.[2] Meanwhile, if we look at Napoleonic Italy, the American authors Grab and Finley have shown that banditry was central to the 'people's war' intermittently faced by the French. Thus, for Grab, in the domains of the Milan-based Kingdom of Italy, banditry and opposition to the Napoleonic ruler were one and the same: 'Brigandage constituted . . . the most extreme form of resistance of the Italian countryside to the growing power of the Napoleonic state, its increasing intrusiveness and mounting pressure, particularly in the realms of taxation and conscription. Indeed, many of the brigands were deserters who were afraid to go home and survived by robbing and smuggling.'[3] Equally, for Finley, 'The Calabrian guerrillas . . . were simply brigands.'[4]

But all this serves to deepen the difficulty. For one thing, any identification of the guerrilla bands with brigandage cannot but echo and, in a sense, substantiate the constant Napoleonic claim that the Spanish *partidas* were in the end nothing but bandits motivated solely by their lust for plunder. And, for another, if the guerrillas were indeed bandits, then great doubts must surface with regard to their contribution to the struggle. And what, too, are the implications for those such as Jean-Réné Aymes, who have tended to see the guerrilla bands as a force that consciously stood outside the norms of state and army? For example, 'The chieftains known by their real names . . . are less numerous than those referred to by their nicknames . . . Whilst placing commanders and soldiers on the same level, these nicknames . . . do not in any sense imply an absence of respect, what they stand for being rather the formal rejection of the traditional military hierarchy.'[5]

In many ways, then, pressure has been mounting for a reassessment of the guerrillas. Who, though, do we mean when we use this term? Certainly not regular soldiers or militiamen who found themselves temporarily fighting in the 'little war'. By 'guerrilla', then, we have here meant civilians who took up arms and became members – and sometimes leaders – of semi-permanent groups of combatants that, whilst sometimes adopting military forms and being assimilated into the ranks of the regular army, had their origins outside the forces of the Spanish state, whether regular or auxiliary. Such a definition may well be deemed rather narrow, but it is the only way to make a reassessment of the *guerrilla popular* a practical possibility. And it is certainly one that coincides with popular practice. To quote Gabriel Lovett:

> When we think of the Spanish guerrillas of 1808–1813, we have in mind mainly those bands of men that arose in several areas of Spain almost from the start of the conflict under the leadership of fearless civilians who . . . settled accounts with Napoleon's armies in their own manner.[6]

The need to strip away 'false' guerrillas is not the only difficulty, however. The combatants we are talking about were, in the majority at least, very far from being an élite group, and it is probable that most of them came from small towns and villages rather than cities such as Madrid, Barcelona, Seville or Zaragoza. From this it follows that they were on the whole illiterate: in 1808 no more than 20 per cent of the population were even marginally lettered. Even amongst literate Spaniards, meanwhile, there seems to have been little of the impulse to record their experiences of the war against Napoleon that produced the vast numbers of journals, memoirs and collections of letters that eventually came to chronicle the Anglo-French picture of the struggle. In consequence, we therefore simply do not have the wonderful sources that have recently allowed Alan Forrest to produce a detailed study of motivation and morale in the French army.[7]

From this there arises the question of bias. Setting aside a mere handful of memoirs, most of which date from long after the fighting had become a thing both of distant memory and great romanticisation, and the often problematic correspondence of the guerrilla commanders themselves, we are therefore forced back on documents that originated outside the ranks of the *partidas*. But this, too, presents us with many problems. For many members of the Church and the propertied classes and, by extension, many of the political and military leaders of Patriot Spain, the idea that the populace might take up arms independently of the authorities was a nightmare that carried with it the spectre of wholesale anarchy. Though not opposed to popular resistance *per se*, it is therefore arguable that they were only too ready to 'talk up' stories of pillage and rapine in the hope that this would push the regime into acting against the *partidas* and reasserting the state's monopoly of force. In the case of generals and other regular officers, meanwhile, there was also both a certain degree of jealousy and a natural desire to camouflage the inadequacies of the Spanish army. As for British and French observers of the guerrillas, neither could view irregular combatants who scorned the normal rules of warfare without a measure of repulsion, whilst for the French it was also necessary both to explain away their defeat and to back the accepted nostrums of the Napoleonic empire (of which one, as we have seen, was to portray any civilian who fought the emperor as a bandit, and another was to attribute all popular resistance to the superstition and fanaticism of the Catholic Church).

To return to the question of our knowledge of the guerrillas themselves, when it comes to the question of identities, it has to be admitted that our information is fragmentary in the extreme. With the exception of a few well-known *cabecillas*, most of the guerrillas whose personal details we know something about are encountered in no more than a single document. Even then, details are often scanty: trial reports, for example, generally provide brief accounts of the crimes with which the men concerned had been charged, but often tell us little more than the names of the accused. Building up a coherent picture of the *partidas* is therefore hardly an easy task. Also worth pointing out, meanwhile, is the fact that even when information is more plentiful, it is by no means always reliable, as witness, for example, the numerous myths, legends and downright inventions that have crept into the stories of men such as Martín Javier Mina and El Empecinado.

And finally there is the question of ambiguity. On 31 December 1809, we are told, the guerrilla leader Juan Tapia sent the government a copy of a proclamation he had just issued in the town of Alcaraz in La Mancha. 'It is not enough to say, "I am a good Spaniard" to save Spain', the handbill announced. 'It is also necessary to dispense with one's most cherished possessions.'[8] As an admirer of the guerrillas, Gabriel Lovett tells this story with great approval, but he seems blind to the fact that it can be read in quite another sense. Under the cover of such demands, Tapia and the rest of the *cabecillas* could milk the populace unmercifully without anyone being any the wiser. And certainly fortunes were made. To quote General Castaños, 'As I have not been a guerrilla, I do not have any money, but rather only debts.'[9] Also described by Lovett, meanwhile, is an incident in Málaga in which a wealthy landowner organised a banquet for a number of enemy generals after the French arrived in 1810, only to find a little while afterwards that his country estate had been attacked and much of his crops ruined.[10] Was this the work of a guerrilla band? If so, was it a political act – the just and fitting punishment of a collaborator – or an expression of social unrest? Or was it again simply the fruit of the coincidental visitation of some gang of bandits? And, if it was, indeed, the work of bandits, were they motivated by nothing more than love of pillage or were they really 'primitive rebels' out to avenge the ills of rural society? On these matters and others like them, historians have not been slow to offer their opinions. 'Guerrilla warfare . . . was a rural phenomenon, like Carlism an aspect of peasant hatred for urban civilization . . . It had undertones of social war', wrote Raymond Carr.[11] For Burdiel, too, 'The guerrilla phenomenon was not driven solely by anti-French phobia and the pressure of ecclesiastical ideology . . . There were guerrilla bands . . . who . . . mixed guerrilla activity with the traditional conflict against the owners of the land.'[12] More sceptical, at least on the question of banditry, is Geoffrey Best: 'Spain, in fact, was not rich in the "Robin Hood" type social bandits who became national resistance leaders in the Balkans and southern Italy. It is significant that, of the enduringly famous [guerrilla] leaders, none had begun as a bandit.'[13] Well, perhaps. But we cannot be certain, and in the end can do no more than speculate.

This is a problem, of course, that has not been lost on historians. Yet it has not prevented even the most honest amongst them from offering the most positive assessments of the guerrillas. Let us take Aymes (who, for what it is worth, rejects the argument that the guerrillas were motivated by the struggle against the propertied classes with precisely the same vigour as Carr and Burdiel put it forward). Contained in his *Guerra de la Independencia* is a more or less traditional hymn of praise to these forces. Thus:

> The further removed the mass of the population was from political affairs, the more fully it participated in the struggle against the invaders . . . Unlike the French, who concentrated on dominating the cities, the guerrillas ranged rapidly across the countryside and launched surprise attacks on the French . . . The guerrillas also unleashed a war of attrition that ground down the

> enemy's economic potential . . . Aside from a few greedy or ambitious *cabecillas*, the civilian guerrillas did not seek to enrich themselves, their religious sentiment serving to moderate their actions.[14]

As with all such descriptions of the guerrillas, one cannot say that this view is either right or wrong, and this is not in fact something that preoccupies the author in question. As he continues: 'In reality it does not matter how far the guerrillas corresponded to this warm description. What matters is that, thanks to the guerrillas, the War of Independence ennobled the name of the people.'[15]

This, however, is not good enough. The material on the guerrillas available in the archives may be skewed, inadequate and ambiguous, but it cannot just be ignored, particularly as it is extremely copious. And, however uncomfortable his findings may be, it is the job of the historian to produce a view of the subject that takes it into account. What has emerged in the pages of this work is obviously a vision of the *partidas* that is diametrically opposed to the one that has been put forward by Aymes and the tradition in whose footsteps he has followed. Indeed, it is one that will be virtually unrecognisable to many observers. Far from appearing as the fruit of a great popular upsurge against the French, the guerrillas are seen rather to have been an artificial creation. In part this was the work of agents of the state (or at least the ruling authorities), supplemented by that of a variety of individuals whose sectional interests were bound up with the defence of the *antiguo régimen*. But in part, too, it was the work of opportunistic, ambitious and unscrupulous adventurers whose only redeeming feature was the recognition by some of their number that their goals were best served by adopting the approach of the regular soldier and, in short, becoming professionals themselves. As for the rank and file, voluntary enlistment was limited to deserters, draft evaders and men who had been rescued from French captivity or were in trouble with the authorities, not to mention the hungry and desperate. Patriotism, meanwhile, is notable only by its absence: the bulk of those who served with the *partidas*, indeed, were almost certainly forced to enlist at gunpoint, and the only areas where this was not so were parts of Navarre and the Basque provinces, where peculiar local conditions had created a contented rural populace whose economic interests were clearly threatened by French rule. And even these exceptions must be questioned: critical work on the response of Navarre to absolutist military mobilisation in the post-war period has suggested the devotion to the old order highlighted by Tone and other historians has been exagerrated.[16]

Co-existing with the guerrillas was the phenomenon of banditry. Already on the increase in 1808 thanks to the economic disruption of the pre-war years, this problem was converted by the arrival of the French into a phenomenon of epidemic proportions. How far, however, was it connected with resistance to the invaders? This is another question that is almost impossible to answer, but it is clear that, although the complete identification of the guerrilla with the bandit that is one of the major themes of the French memoir literature is unfounded, the two were nonetheless very closely linked. Many *cuadrillas* continued to ply their trade regardless of the French invasion, but in the process they saw no reason not to attack isolated Frenchmen or churchmen, officials and proprietors connected with the occupation authorities, and in that sense became a part of the guerrilla struggle. At the same time a variety of men who had been imprisoned or on the run in 1808 found refuge with the guerrillas or even established guerrilla bands of their own. Despite romantic claims that in 1808 Spain's bandits turned Patriots overnight, this course of action meant nothing other than that *la vida a salto de mata* was henceforth to be coated with a veneer of respectability and, what is more, a veneer of respectability that was tested to destruction as soon as the wave of French conquest receded. And, turning to the *partidas*, we find that there were also links working in the opposite direction, in that many of their recruits clearly only joined them in the expectation that by doing so they would be guaranteed easy opportunities for plunder. Nor was their commitment to the cause anything other than conditional, meanwhile: should their hopes in any sense be betrayed, whether through the sudden imposition of military discipline or the failure of their leaders to provide adequate booty, they were quick to join bands that had no pretensions to be anything other than bandits or simply to set up as bandits on their own account.

None of this is to say that no irregular ever pulled a trigger against a Frenchmen. Although there is considerable evidence that many bands saw action on only a very infrequent basis, it cannot be denied that, taking such groups as a whole, they took part in many fights and skirmishes. Indeed, the more committed leaders – the men who saw that their long-term advancement depended on carving out a name for themselves as successful soldiers – waged war on the French with unremitting ferocity. Yet the lack of motivation evident amongst much of the movement, not to mention the poor armament, insufficient training and want of solidity of many of its adherents, could not but reduce its impact. Setting aside the many bands that were mere parasites that appear to have existed solely to feed themselves at the expence of the populace, all the efforts of those *partidas* that were willing to fight the French could not halt the march of Napoleonic conquest, still less roll it back. When success was achieved, as it was in 1812 and 1813, it was only thanks to mistakes on the part of Napoleon – in particular, his foolhardy invasion of Russia – whilst all the evidence suggests that the Duke of Wellington relied far less heavily on the guerrillas' ability to distract the French than has often been claimed. No one would claim that the irregulars caused the French no difficulties at all: one might here place particular emphasis on the supply difficulties in which they involved the invaders, not to mention the growing demoralisation and fear visible amongst the officers and men sent to the Peninsula. Yet the general impression is highly negative. In brief, the guerrillas can be seen to have undermined the Spanish army whilst putting nothing in its place. At the same time, it is even possible to question the role of the guerrillas in keeping up the spirit of resistance that was supposedly so important to the struggle. Far from living amongst the populace, the guerrillas lived off it, terrorising it mercilessly and bringing down endless woes on its head.

In fact, few scholars would now give the same weight to the guerrillas in analyses of the struggle as was once the case. It is agreed that the guerrillas were important, certainly, but there is at least now a clear recognition that in the last resort they were a secondary factor in the Allied triumph. 'The liberation of Spain', writes Rothenberg, 'was the result of Wellington's victory, one to which they had contributed much.'[17] In some quarters, indeed, there is a willingness to go even further:

> In the Tyrol and Calabria . . . popular revolts had in time been smothered through the application of overwhelming military power. By 1812 the imperial forces had come very close to achieving this in Spain, too; despite heavy losses in their attritional contest with the partisans, they had made considerable headway, and the Spaniards were palpably feeling the strain.[18]

Let us here cite, too, Stuart Woolf:

> Spanish historiography has long interpreted this dramatic episode in the country's history as a nationalist war; for conservative writers, it is usually also regarded as a Catholic crusade for Church and altar. . . . But the evidence of this prolonged struggle . . . argues against any identity of view between the guerrillas . . . and either the constitutionalists or the Church . . . As the considerable number of . . . peasants and fishermen who habitually practised contraband were joined by soldiers from the former Spanish armies . . . deserters from the French armies . . . outlaws of all types, the blurring of the distinction between collective resistance and brigandage upheld by the French became ever more realistic. Indiscipline, desertions and highly personal motivations were intrinsic to the . . . bands, whose presence was often far from welcome to local villagers.[19]

The conclusion that we have reached, then, is not one that is out of line with current historical writing on the Napoleonic period. That said, however, honesty dictates the admission of a number of serious problems. We return here, above all, to the question of ambiguity. As has already been pointed out, much of the evidence that has been put forward in support of traditional discussions of the guerrillas is susceptible to interpretations that are diametrically opposed to those in whose cause they are advanced. Nor, clearly, can much reliance be placed on many of the documents and memoirs on which they are based. René Chartrand, for example, describes the memoirs of Espoz y Mina as 'a primary document in the study of the Spanish guerrillas which established [Espoz y] Mina's claims to have pinned down tens of thousands of troops which would otherwise have been deployed against Wellington,' when it is clear that they are at best partial and at worst a tissue of lies.[20] But the very same objections can be made to the evidence put forward in support of the revisionist view. To every document found in the archives complaining of sons conscripted by roving guerrilla bands, it may rightly be objected that submitting such a document was an obvious way of staving off retribution on the part of the authorities, whether French or Spanish. By the same token, every complaint of pillage and rapine on the part of some *partida* may just as plausibly be answered by the argument that such protests are not to be trusted on account of the fact that they were the equally obvious resort of *afrancesados* punished for their treason or army officers anxious to defend the prerogatives of the military. There is, too, the issue of libel: whilst ferocious attacks on Espoz y Mina may have been uncovered in the archives in Zaragoza, say, there is nothing to show that they were not the fruit of personal vendettas. And finally, if Espoz y Mina ruthlessly suppressed a number of rival *cabecillas*, why should we immediately assume that his objective was self-aggrandisement rather than accepting his claims that all he was trying to do was to save the populace from the threat of banditry?

To these arguments there is no real answer, no way that the evidence can be made to stick in favour of either side. In consequence, the thesis advanced in this book must be recognised to be as artificial in its construction as the arguments that it has been put forward to challenge. That said, however, it does seem that there are issues which the traditional view of the guerrillas simply does not address. Most prominent here is the question of popular engagement with the struggle. Whilst there are many matters about which we cannot be certain, the one issue on which there can be no doubt at all is the refusal of the Spanish people to rally to the war against Napoleon. Thus, after the very special circumstances of the summer of 1808, on all sides there was nothing to be seen but draft evasion, desertion and anti-conscription riots. Amply recorded in both British and Spanish sources, this simply cannot be wished away, and it is no good trying to explain the problem in terms of the localism talked of by Tone and others since precisely the same problem is visible with regard to the Catalan *migueletes* and *somatenes*, even though they were never required to serve beyond the frontiers of their home province. What is needed, then, is an explanation of the guerrillas that seeks to mould itself to this reality rather than airily proclaiming its faith in a people's crusade which never existed. Needless to say, it is precisely this need that the current work attempts to address.

To conclude, what impact did the guerrillas have on the future of Spain? In so far as this subject is concerned, there has been a general willingness to draw a direct line from the events of 1808–14 to the terrible civil wars that ravaged Spain between 1822 and 1876 and then again between 1936 and 1939. To quote Lovett, for example, 'The . . . Spanish people acquired the habit of . . . taking to the hills, a habit that was to become an ingrained national characteristic. Henceforward a favourite reaction to an unwelcome political situation would be . . . *echarse al monte* [take to the hills].'[21] This, however, is too facile an extrapolation, for, as Jeremy Black has shown, the irregular band was nothing new in Spain, *partidas* of armed civilians having taken an active role in the War of the Spanish Succession of 1701–14.[22] The most that can be said in this respect is that rebel forces – and by this one means primarily the Carlists – unable to establish control of sufficient territory to wage regular campaigns against the government, were provided with an alternative model of military organisation that allowed them at least to keep their cause alive. In this they were aided in the wars of 1822–3, 1827 and 1833–9 by the presence of many combatants who had actually fought with the guerrillas either as *cabecillas* – Jerónimo Merino, Jaime Alfonso – or as members of the rank and file – Tomás de Zumalacarregui (in reply to which it could be said that the liberals had their own War-of-Independence weapon in the form of the national militia). But Carlist strategy was always in essence a regular one based on the formation of field armies, whilst there is little evidence that the legacy of the *partidas* was of much importance in stirring up popular revolt amongst the Carlist rank and file.

More work is needed here, but it is not clear that popular movements on the left looked back to the struggle against the French for their inspiration when it came to asserting themselves against the establishment either. In this respect, one would have to disagree with Alexander Grab, who has argued that in Italy the peasant unrest of the late nineteenth century, and ultimately the rural wing of the Italian labour movement, was the direct descendant of the brigandage of the Napoleonic Wars.[23] Very occasionally, radical or even republican *partidas* may be encountered in histories of Spanish revolutionary movements in the nineteenth century, but the guerrilla band was not to become a tool of the left until the aftermath of the Spanish Civil War. For radicals, in fact, the traditional weapon was rather the urban rising and, above all, the barricade (which is not to say that the war against the French was not devoid of symbols that could be made use of by the progressive camp: one thinks here of the Dos de Mayo and the sieges of Zaragoza). Nor, indeed, did the guerrillas ever constitute anything more than an escape route for the most desperate so far as the populace was concerned. As we have seen, there was little identification between *partida* and *pueblo*, whilst out-and-out bandits were often fallen upon by lynch mobs or denounced to the authorities: one returns here to the belief of Best and López Morán that the *bandoleros* were anything but the champions of the commonalty dreamed of by romantic Marxists such as Hobsbawm. If the Spanish War of Independence has any links at all with the future Spanish left, then, it is rather in the revolt against feudalism of 1813–14, when hundreds of villages either physically attacked their *señores* or sought to challenge their privileges in the courts.[24] Also important here was the resistance to the sale of the common lands ordered by the *cortes* as a means of paying for the war: in November 1813, for example, the *ayuntamiento* of Cartaya complained that its disamortisation of the lands concerned was being challenged by two of the peasants who had formally rented them out.[25]

If some of the more obvious ways in which the guerrillas could have made their mark on the later development of Spanish history can therefore be ruled out, this is not to say that they are of no relevance whatsoever to later developments. On the contrary, to the extent to which the guerrilla struggle greatly fuelled banditry – between 1800 and 1810 there were 153 cases of banditry in Galicia, whereas between 1810 and 1820 there were 305[26] – the insurgents are of immense importance. By plunging the countryside into anarchy, they set Spain on the road to the creation in 1844 of the militarised police force known as the Guardia Civil, which was be one of the chief factors in the polarisation of society that ultimately led to the civil war of 1936–39: modelled on the Napoleonic Gendarmerie d'Espagne, the Guardia Civil was originally even uniformed in the style of its imperial predecessor.[27] At the same time and, in some ways, still worse, the guerrillas also intensified the army's tendency to intervene in politics. In this they were not the only factor – there were in fact many ways in which the War of Independence encouraged the officer corps to conflate the national interest with its own desires and aspirations – but the *partidas* constituted a particularly painful memory. Thus, not only had their much vaunted triumphs, many of them exaggerated or even non-existent, humiliated the military estate and provided ammunition for its enemies, but they had sapped the army of men, horses and money and thereby directly contributed to its prostration. With these sins compounded by the later identification of guerrilla warfare with the Carlists, the army in consequence became fixated by the need to maintain law and order and deeply opposed to all forms of social unrest in the countryside. Again the guerrillas were not the only factor in this process, but in this respect they may be said to have played an important role in conquering the army for social conservatism. Indeed, so strong was the military's hatred for the concept of the people in arms that it is not going too far to say that the victims of the firing squads of 1936 were in some respects paying for the sins of the *partidas* of 1808–14.[28]

And last but not least, it must be noted that the guerrillas or, more broadly, popular resistance to Napoleon, ushered in a new age. The experiences of 1808–14 did not in themselves politicise the people of Spain, any more than they imbued them with an inherent urge to take to the hills. In this respect, Burdiel's claims that the conflict was 'a powerful mechanism of political apprenticeship for the population as a whole, the lessons of which were not easily forgotten' are in the short term nonsense.[29] But they did establish them as a political presence, and to return to Aymes' remarks, 'ennoble' them. This latter concept should not be interpreted in any literal sense: as we have seen, the guerrilla struggle was a murky affair characterised by as much vice as virtue. However, no longer could the populace simply be swept aside as the *populacho* or the *canalla vil*. In contrast, whatever politicians and generals might think of them in private, they were now a force to which it was necessary to pay lip-service and to whom competing political movements could appeal for legitimacy. Even before the war had ended, the liberals had set themselves up as veritable tribunes of the people, whilst after 1814 it was a key part of the absolutist case that their enemies had usurped the people's sovereignty and governed in despite of the popular will rather than in accordance with its dictates. 'In effect', proclaimed one diatribe, 'from the moment that the ordinary *cortes* was established [the liberals] made a complete mock of the people, whom they called sovereign, and obliged them to obey their orders, however much they were contrary to the will of the greater part of the nation.'[30] This is hardly to say, of course, that Spain was in any sense democratised by the war. But for liberals and absolutists, as later for conservatives and progressives, there was a strong sense that the 'real' people of Spain had spoken, and that, given the appropriate formula, they could be brought to speak once more.

So much for the legacy of partisan warfare. Let us, however, return to the central point at issue. We have here a new analysis of the Spanish guerrillas. Rather than the freedom-fighters of legend, they appear rather as a highly complex phenomenon whose military impact has been greatly exaggerated by a combination of muddled thinking, political bias and failure to make use of the full range of primary sources that is available to the historian. Nor have matters been helped by an over-concentration on the highly atypical example of Navarre at the expense of the far more helpful examples constituted by such provinces as Aragón and La Mancha. To claim that this work is the last word on the subject would be foolish – a great wealth of material remains to be tapped in municipal archives all over Spain – but it is at least the product of a substantial programme of research. Whilst it will certainly be challenged, the issues that it has raised will not go away. The debate, then, will go on, but it will most assuredly not go backwards.

Abbreviations

BHS	*Bulletin of Hispanic Studies*
BUM	*Boletín de la Universidad de Madrid*
CHJ	*Cambridge Historical Journal*
CIH	*Cuadernos de Investigación Histórica*
CREP	*Consortium on Revolutionary Europe Proceedings*
EHQ	*European History Quarterly*
EHR	*English Historical Review*
EM	*España Moderna*
ESR	*European Studies Review*
HAHR	*Hispanic American Historical Review*
HJ	*The Historical Journal*
HT	*History Today*
IHR	*International History Review*
JEH	*Journal of Economic History*
JLAS	*Journal of Latin American Studies*
JMH	*Journal of Modern History*
JSAHR	*Journal of the Society for Army Historical Research*
QJE	*Quarterly Journal of Economics*
RHM	*Revista de Historia Militar*
RP	*Review of Politics*

Notes

1 The Guerrillas in History

1. A reproduction of Lejeune's painting may be found in J. Tulard (ed.), *L'Histoire de Napoléon par la Peinture* (Paris, 1991), p. 239.
2. Padre Maestro Salmón, *Resumen Histórico de la Revolución de España* (Cádiz–Madrid, 1812–14), II, pp. 16–17, Servicio Histórico Militar, Colección Documental del Fraile (hereafter SHM. CDF.) CMXXXIII–IV.
3. *Ibid.*, pp. 18–19.
4. *Ibid.*, III, pp. 226–7.
5. *Ibid.*, II, pp. 20–4.
6. *Ibid.*, p. 26.
7. *Ibid.*, p. 234.
8. Anon., *Historia de la revolución de España o sea rapida ojeada sobre los principales sucesos de la península desde fines de 1807 hasta septiembre de 1812 y perdida de los franceses en ella* (Valladolid, 1812), Colegio de Santa Cruz (Valladolid), 65/3914.
9. Salmón, *Resumen Histórico*, III, p. 249.
10. *Cit.* E. Rodríguez Solis, *Los Guerrilleros de 1808: Historia Popular de la Guerra de la Independencia* (Madrid, 1887), II, ii, p. 27.
11. F. Alonso y Ruiz de Canizares, *Resumen histórico militar de los principales y mas gloriosos hechos del Señor Brigadier Don Juan Martín, Comandante de la Quinta División del Segundo Ejército desde fines de junio de mil ochocientos ocho hasta abril de ochocientos once* (México, 1811), Biblioteca Nacional, Colección Gómez Imaz (hereafter BN. CGI.) R820673, pp. 6–10.
12. Cf. *Diario de Sesiones de las Cortes Generales y Extraordinarias* (Cádiz, 1810–13; hereafter *DC*), 11 March 1811. The real name of this commander was Francisco Espoz Ilundaín, but, for reasons that will become clear, in 1810 he adopted the name Espoz y Mina, although he is often referred to simply as 'Mina'. For the sake of familiarity, and to avoid confusing him with his distant relative Martín Javier Mina y Larrea, he will be referred to throughout this account as Espoz y Mina.
13. J. C. Carnicero, *Historia Razonada de los Principales Sucesos de la Gloriosa Revolución de España* (Madrid, 1814), III, pp. 62–3, SHM. CDF. CMXLII.

14. R. Brindle, 'Memoirs: a brief account of travels, etc., in Spain' (MS), p. 8, Real Colegio de San Albano, Valladolid.
15. S. Cassels (ed.), *Peninsular Portrait, 1811–1814: the Letters of Captain William Bragge, Third (King's Own) Dragoons* (London, 1963), p. 114.
16. J. Page (ed.), *Intelligence Officer in the Peninsula: Letters and Diaries of Major the Honourable Edward Charles Cocks, 1786–1812* (Tunbridge Wells, 1986), pp. 134–5.
17. J. Queipo de Llano (Conde de Toreno), *Historia del Levantamiento, Guerra y Revolución de España*, ed. Biblioteca de Autores Españoles (Madrid, 1954), p. 349.
18. Cf. Rodríguez Solis, *Guerrilleros de 1808*, II, xi, pp. 39–47 *passim*; details of the author's life and politics may be found in E. Rodríguez Solis, *Memorias* (Madrid, 1930).
19. Rodríguez Solis, *Guerrilleros de 1808*, I, ii, p. 27.
20. *Ibid.*, I, ii, p. 29.
21. R. Southey, *History of the Peninsular War* (London, 1823–32), I, p. 266.
22. *Ibid.*, p. 270.
23. *Ibid.*, pp. 371–2.
24. *Ibid.*, p. 710.
25. *Ibid.*, pp. 739–46 *passim.*
26. *Ibid.*, II, pp. 104–40.
27. *Ibid.*, pp. 167–70, 204–7.
28. *Ibid.*, pp. 328–9.
29. *Ibid.*, p. 332.
30. *Ibid.*, pp. 364–6. An example of one of these wooden cannon may be viewed in the Army Museum in Madrid.
31. *Ibid.*, pp. 383–92.
32. *Ibid.*, p. 383.
33. *Ibid.*, p. 394.
34. *Ibid.*, pp. 503–4.
35. *Ibid.*, pp. 504–5; *ibid.*, III, pp. 43–59 *passim.*
36. *Ibid.*, pp. 42–5.
37. *Ibid.*, pp. 42–3.
38. *Ibid.*, pp. 51–2, 55, 62.
39. *Ibid.*, pp. 65–7, 259–77, 338–45, 476–7, 602–5.
40. W. Napier, *History of the War in the Peninsula and in the South of France from the Year 1807 to the Year 1814* (London, 1828–40), V, pp. 38–9.
41. Chief exponent of the theory of the 'indirect approach' was Basil Liddell Hart. For an example of his thinking on the Peninsular War, cf. B. Liddell Hart, *The Decisive Wars of History: a Study in Strategy* (London, 1929), pp. 104–16.
42. Cf. C. Oman, *A History of the Peninsular War* (Oxford, 1902–30), VI, pp. 252–74.
43. *Ibid.*, III, pp. 488–92.
44. E. Longford, *Wellington: the Years of the Sword* (London, 1969), pp. 247–8.
45. R. Humble, *Napoleon's Peninsular Marshals* (London, 1974), p. 70.
46. Cf. L. Borkenau, *The Spanish Cockpit: an Eye-Witness Account of the Political and Social Conflicts of the Spanish Civil War* (London, 1937), pp. 3–4.
47. D. Chandler, 'Wellington at war: regular and irregular warfare', *International History Review*, XI, no. 1 (February, 1989), p. 9.
48. *Times Literary Supplement* (4 July 1986), p. 742.

49. G. Lovett, *Napoleon and the Birth of Modern Spain* (New York, 1965), II, pp. 665–7.
50. D. Alexander, *Rod of Iron: French Counter-Insurgency Policy in Aragón during the Peninsular War* (Wilmington, Delaware, 1985), pp. 239–41.
51. J. Tone, *The Fatal Knot: the Guerrilla War in Navarre and the Defeat of Napoleon* (Chapel Hill, North Carolina, 1994), p. 5.
52. M. Artola, *Historia de España Alianza Editorial, V: la Burguesia Revolucionaria, 1808–1874* (Madrid, 1990), p. 33.
53. M. Espadas Burgos and J. R. de Urquijo Goitia, *Historia de España Gredos, XI: Guerra de la Independencia y Epoca Constitucional, 1808–1939* (Madrid, 1990), pp. 21–2.
54. J. R. Aymes, *La Guerra de la Independencia en España, 1808–1814* (Madrid, 1975), p. 56.
55. G. Dufour, *La Guerra de la Independencia* (Madrid, 1999), p. 96.
56. R. Hocquellet, *Résistance et Révolution durant l'Occupation Napoléonnienne en Espagne, 1808–1812* (Paris, 2001), p. 176.
57. Cf. R. Farias, *Memorias de la Guerra de la Independencia Escritas por Soldados Franceses* (Madrid, 1919), pp. 317–20.
58. Cf. J. R. Aymes, 'La guerrilla española en la literatura testimonial francesa', in J. A. Armillas (ed.), *La Guerra de la Independencia: Estudios* (Zaragoza, 2001), pp. 23–4.
59. *Gazeta de Sevilla* (7 January 1812), p. 8, Hemeróteca Municipal de Madrid (hereafter HMM.) RVP.20.
60. For a detailed discussion of these issues, cf. R. Holtman, *Napoleonic Propaganda* (Baton Rouge, 1950).
61. Southey, *Peninsular War*, II, p. 336.
62. *Ibid.*, III, p. 41.
63. *Ibid.*, pp. 42–3.
64. *Ibid.*, pp. 52–3.
65. *Ibid.*, pp. 53–4, 65.
66. *Ibid.*, p. 68.
67. Napier, *Peninsular War*, II, p. 142.
68. J. Muñoz Maldonado, *Historia Política y Militar de la Guerra de la Independencia de España contra Napoleón Bonaparte* (Madrid, 1833), II, p. 270.
69. *Ibid.*, I, p. 312.
70. *Ibid.*, III, p. 106.
71. For Muñoz Maldonado's remarks on Galicia, cf. *ibid.*, II, pp. 176–83.
72. *Ibid.*, III, pp. 307–8, 395.
73. J. Gómez de Arteche y Moro, *Guerra de la Independencia: Historia Militar de España de 1808 a 1814* (Madrid, 1868–1903), II, p. 97.
74. E.g. *ibid.*, VII, pp. 462–3; *ibid.*, VIII, pp. 221–2.
75. *Ibid.*, VIII, pp. 195–7.
76. *Ibid.*, VIV, pp. 360–1.
77. *Ibid.*, VIII, pp. 185–88.
78. *Ibid.*, VII, p. 9.
79. E.g. *ibid.*, XIV, p. 354.
80. *Ibid.*, VII, p. 67.
81. *Ibid.*, XIV, p. 354.

82. *Ibid.*, VII, pp. 6–7.
83. *Ibid.*, p. 7.
84. *Ibid.*, XIV, pp. 366–8.
85. T. Sydenham to H. Wellesley, 10 October 1812, University of Southampton, Wellington Papers (hereafter US.WP.) 1/361.
86. In brief, a succession of historians has struggled to establish whether the armed gangs that terrorised much of rural France in the 1790s and early 1800s were *brigands royaux* rather than just *brigands*. No firm conclusion has been reached – the pattern, indeed, is one of great ambiguity – but in the south and west in particular there seems little doubt that the unrest was at least in part an expression of popular alienation from the Revolution. For a brief overview, cf. D. Sutherland, *France, 1789–1815: Revolution and Counter-Revolution* (London, 1985), pp. 286–92. Local studies include: G. Lewis, 'Political brigandage and popular disaffection in the south-east of France, 1795–1804' in G. Lewis and C. Lucas (eds), *Beyond the Terror: Essays in French Regional and Social History, 1794–1815* (Cambridge, 1983), pp. 195–31; D. Sutherland, *The Chouans: the Social Origins of Popular Counter-Revolution in Upper Brittany, 1770–1796* (Oxford, 1982); and G. Daly, *Inside Napoleonic France: State and Society in Rouen* (Aldershot, 2001), pp. 65–80.
87. Cf. M. Artola, 'La guerra de guerrillas', *Revista de Occidente*, X (1964), pp. 12–43, and J. R. Aymes, 'La guérilla dans la lutte espagnole pour l'indépendance, 1808–14: amorce d'une théorie et avatars d'une pratique', *Bulletin Hispanique*, XCVIII, nos 3–4 (July–December, 1976), pp. 325–49.
88. For early writings of the author on the subject, cf. C. Esdaile, 'Heroes or villains? The Spanish guerrillas in the Peninsular War', *History Today*, XXXVIII, no. 4 (April 1988), pp. 29–35; C. Esdaile, '"Heroes or villains" revisited: fresh thoughts on *la guerrilla*', in I. Fletcher (ed.), *The Peninsular War: Aspects of the Struggle for the Iberian Peninsula* (Staplehurst, 1998), pp. 93–114. On all this Hocquellet's only comment is a two-line footnote: cf. Hocquellet, *Résistance et Révolution*, p. 176.
89. M. de Avesty, *La Vida a Salto de Mata: Guerrilleros, Bandoleros y Contrabandistas* (Barcelona, 1962), pp. 17–22.
90. A good example of this linguistic confusion is offered by a treatise sent to the Spanish general Joaquín Blake in June 1809 by one M. Delcastel. Entitled 'Instrucción provisional para la guerrilla', it begins by defining the word *guerrilla* as meaning 'the methodical deployment of a body of troops in open order, whether it is to fight in broken terrain where close-order formations cannot operate, to cover the advance of a body of men formed in close order, or to act as pickets for a column of troops on the march'. Cf. Servicio Histórico Militar, Colección General Blake (hereafter SHM. CGB.) 2/14.
91. J. S. Pérez Garzón, *Milicia Nacional y Revolución Burguesa: el Prototipo Madrileño, 1808–1874* (Madrid, 1978), p. 80.
92. E. Hobsbawm, *The Age of Revolution, 1789–1848* (London, 1977), p. 107. For general statements of Hobsbawm's views on banditry and agrarian unrest, cf. E. Hobsbawm, *Primitive Rebels: Studies in Archaic Forms of Social Movement in the Nineteenth and Twentieth Centuries* (Manchester, 1959), and E. Hobsbawm, *Bandits* (London, 1969). In neither, however, is any attention given to Napoleonic Spain.

2 The Guerrillas at War

1. For two discussions of the impact of the war of 1793–95, cf. R. Herr, *The Eighteenth-Century Revolution in Spain* (Princeton, 1958), pp. 297–315, and J. R. Aymes, 'La "Guerra Gran" (1793–95) como prefiguración de la "Guerra del Francés" (1808–14)' in J. R. Aymes (ed.), *España y la Revolución Francesa* (Madrid, 1989), pp. 311–66. Information on the local militias of the pre-war period is scanty, but for some details of the Galician example, cf. Rodríguez Solis, *Guerrilleros de 1808*, I, v, pp. 35–40.
2. For an excellent introduction to the military geography of the Iberian Peninsula at the beginning of the nineteenth century, cf. Oman, *Peninsular War*, I, pp. 72–88.
3. Gómez de Arteche, *Guerra de la Independencia*, II, pp. 214–18; Muñoz Maldonado, *Guerra de la Independencia*, I, pp. 293–5, 312–13; Rodríguez Solis, *Guerrilleros de 1808*, I, ii, pp. 10–11; Anon., 'Memoria sobre la entrada de los franceses en Andalucía' (MS.), Archivo Histórico Nacional, Sección de Estado (hereafter AHN. Estado) 52–F, no. 404.
4. Muñoz Maldonado, *Guerra de la Independencia*, I, p. 313; L. F. Gille, *Mémoires d'un Conscrit de 1808*, ed. P. Gilles (Paris, 1893), pp. 75–84; J. de Haro, *Guerra de la Independencia: Bailén – Diarios y Memorias* (Ciudad Real, 1999), pp. 196–200.
5. Gómez de Arteche, *Guerra de la Independencia*, II, pp. 85–123, 589–636 *passim*; Muñoz Maldonado, *Guerra de la Independencia*, I, pp. 231–4; *ibid.*, II, pp. 68–71; Rodríguez Solis, *Guerrilleros de 1808*, I, ii, pp. 3–9; memorial of F. Rovira, 21 November 1814, Servicio Histórico Militar, Colección de la Guerra de la Independencia (hereafter SHM. CGI.) 4/8.
6. Gómez de Arteche, *Guerra de la Independencia*, VII, pp. 14–15; Rodríguez Solis, *Guerrilleros de 1808*, I, ii, pp. 31–8; Muñoz Maldonado, *Guerra de la Independencia*, II, p. 266–9; A. Cassinello, *Juan Martín, 'El Empecinado', o el Amor a la Libertad* (Madrid, 1995), pp. 51–7; for an early account of the operations of Juan Martín Díez at this time, cf. Anon., *Apuntes de la Vida y Hechos Militares del Brigadier Don Juan Martín Díez, El Empecinado, por un Admirador de Ellos* (Madrid, 1814), pp. 6–9, Servicio Histórico Militar, Depósito de la Guerra (hereafter SHM. DG.) 1811/5.
7. *Informe* of D. Argüero, 5 July 1810, Archivo General de Simancas, Sección de Gracia y Justicia (hereafter AGS. GJ.) 1076.
8. Memorial of F. Mallén, 19 November 1809, AHN. Est. 61–N, no. 317.
9. J. M. Iribarren, *Espoz y Mina, el Guerrillero* (Madrid, 1965), pp. 50–1.
10. Muñoz Maldonado, *Guerra de la Independencia*, I, pp. 281–4; *ibid.*, II, pp. 68–70; Rodríguez Solis, *Guerrilleros de 1808*, I, iii, pp. 43–4.
11. Rodríguez Solis, *Guerrilleros de 1808*, I, v, p. 20.
12. Petition of P. Morillo, 6 February 1810, *cit.* A. Rodríguez Villa, *El Teniente General Don Pablo Morillo, Primer Conde de Cartagena, Marqués de la Puerta (1778–1837): Estudio Biográfico* (Madrid, 1908), II, pp. 8–11.
13. T. Simmons (ed.), *Memoirs of a Polish Lancer: the Pamietniki of Dezydery Chlapowski* (Chicago, 1992), p. 47.
14. M. de Marbot, *The Memoirs of Baron de Marbot, late Lieutenant General in the French Army*, ed. A. Butler (London, 1892), I, pp. 335–45.
15. J. M. Codón, *Biografía y Crónica del Cura Merino* (Burgos, 1986), pp. 27–30; P. Marco, *El Cura Merino, 1808–1813: Memorias de un Contemporáneo* (Madrid, 1899), pp. 9–12.

16. Arteche, *Guerra de la Independencia*, VII, pp. 40–1; Rodríguez Solis, *Guerrilleros de 1808*, I, v, pp. 18–22; J. Sánchez Fernández, *¡Nos Invaden! Guerrilla y Represión durante la Guerra de la Independencia Española, 1808–1814* (Valladolid, 2000), p. 30. For Lucas Rafael, cf. *Relación de los hechos de los méritos y proezas de Fray Lucas Rafael, religioso Sacerdote de San Francisco, Teniente-Capitán de los reales ejércitos, y juntamente comandante de una partida de guerrilla* (Seville, 1809), BN. CGI. R62302.
17. Rodríguez Solis, *Guerrilleros de 1808*, I, vi, pp. 22–5; *ibid.*, viii, pp. 27–30; *ibid.*, ix, pp. 40–1.
18. *Ibid.*, I, viii, pp. 16–18; Iribarren, *Espoz y Mina, el Guerrillero*, pp. 308–11.
19. For details on most of these figures, cf. R. Guirao, *Guerrilleros y Patriotas en el Alto Aragón, 1808–1814* (Huesca, 2000), pp. 54–96.
20. Rodriguez Solis, *Guerrilleros de 1808*, I, viii, pp. 12–14; F. Rovira to Junta of Catalonia, 6 June 1810, Archivo de la Corona de Aragón, Sección Junta Superior de Cataluña (hereafter ACA. JSC.) 76.
21. Iribarren, *Espoz y Mina, el Guerrillero*, pp. 62–8; M. Ortuño, *Xavier Mina: Guerrillero, Liberal, Insurgente* (Pamplona, 2000), pp. 42–69.
22. In the absence of a general military history of the guerrillas, these details have been obtained from Rodríguez Solis, *Guerrilleros de 1808*, I, v–viii *passim*. For some accounts of individual *partidas*, cf. Cassinello, *Juan Martín*, pp. 73–87; Ortuño, *Xavier Mina*, pp. 69–84; Codón, *Cura Merino*, pp. 33–8; R. de Barthèlemy, *'El Marquesito': Juan Díaz Porlier, General que Fue de los Ejércitos Nacionales, 1788–1815* (Santiago de Compostela, 1995), I, pp. 94–160.
23. A. Miot, *Mémoires du Comte Miot de Melito, Ancien Ministre, Ambassadeur, Conseilleur d'Etat et Membre de l'Institut* (Paris, 1858), III, pp. 56–8.
24. H. von Brandt, *The Two Minas and the Spanish Guerrillas* (London, 1825), pp. 54–8.
25. A. de Rocca, *Memoirs of the War of the French in Spain*, ed. P. Haythornthwaite (London, 1990), p. 89.
26. Suchet's own account of the fighting in Aragón in the second half of 1809 and the first months of 1810 may be found in L. G. Suchet, *Memoirs of the War in Spain from 1808 to 1814* (London, 1829), I, pp. 42–109; for a detailed modern account, cf. Alexander, *Rod of Iron*, pp. 21–41.
27. A. Bigarré, *Mémoires du Général Bigarré, Aide-de-Camp du Roi Joseph, 1775–1813* (Paris, 1903), pp. 284–7.
28. For the growth of guerrilla resistance in Andalucía, cf. Rodríguez Solis, *Guerrilleros de 1808*, I, x, 1–11; *ibid.*, I, xi, pp. 9–17. For Valencia, cf. M. Ardit, *Revolución Liberal y Revuelta Campesina: un Ensayo sobre la Desintegración del Régimen Feudal en el País Valenciano, 1793–1840* (Barcelona, 1977), pp. 211–17.
29. F. Espoz y Mina, *Memorias del General Don Francisco Espoz y Mina, Escritas por El Mismo*, ed. J. M. de Vega (Madrid, 1851), I, pp. 16, 39–40.
30. L. Picado Franco, *Historia del origen, acontecimientos y acciones de guerra de la Sexta División del Segundo Ejército (o sea de Soria) durante nuestra sagrada lucha al mando del Excmo. Señor Don José Joaquín Durán y Barazábal, Mariscal de Campo de los reales ejércitos* (Madrid, 1817), I, pp. 44–6, Biblioteca del Senado, Colección Gómez de Arteche (hereafter BS. CGA.) 039809.
31. *Cit. El Redactor General* (25 October 1811), p. 513, HMM. 6/3. According to an undated memorandum in the papers of General Castaños, Espoz y Mina's cavalry – the Husares de Navarra – wore blue dolmans with red collars and cuffs, grey

pelisses trimmed with grey fur and white frogging, grey overalls with a red stripe, and bell-topped shakos adorned with red cockades, loops, cords and pom-poms. For some good depictions of the sort of uniforms adopted by units such as those of Espoz y Mina, cf. J. M. Bueno, *Uniformes Militares de la Guerra de Independencia* (Madrid, 1989), pp. 157–9.

32. Tone, *Fatal Knot*, pp. 106–7; for some acute remarks on the greater vulnerability of larger and more elaborate *partidas* to French attack, cf. Von Brandt, *The Two Minas*, p. 59.
33. Espoz y Mina, *Memorias*, I, p. 87.
34. *Ibid.*, I, p. 90; those wishing to contrast the tactics used by Espoz y Mina at Aibar with the practice of Wellington's army will find much of use in P. Griffith (ed.), *Forward into Battle: Fighting Tactics from Waterloo to Vietnam* (Chichester, 1981), pp. 12–42.
35. These issues are discussed at greater length in Esdaile, 'Heroes or Villains', p. 33. For some examples of the desire of at least some guerrillas to acquire the status of regular troops, cf. Picado Franco, *Sexta División*, II, pp. 53–4; F. Longa to Lord Wellington, 20 October 1813, US. WP.1/378. In view of the behaviour of some regular officers, their eagerness is perfectly comprehensible: when the *cabecilla* Saornil dined at Wellington's headquarters in February 1813, General O'Lalor 'treated him like a child [and] told him what to eat': G. Larpent (ed.) *The Private Journal of Judge-Advocate F. S. Larpent, Attached to Lord Wellington's Headquarters, 1812–14* (London, 1853), I, p. 81.
36. Gómez de Arteche, *Guerra de la Independencia*, XII, pp. 402–13; for a partial account of these operations, cf. F. Durán to Wellington, 18 and 28 August 1812, US. WP. 1/349. An example of the sort of cannon supplied to the guerillas may be found in the Army Museum in Madrid.
37. Cf. Mina, *Memorias*, I, pp. 19–51 *passim*; Tone, *Fatal Knot*, pp. 99–125 *passim*.
38. Anon. to J. F. Caballero, 29 May 1811, AHN. Est. 3146. Espoz y Mina's own account of this affair may be found in Espoz y Mina, *Memorias*, I, pp. 124–7, and may be contrasted with Iribarren, *Espoz y Mina, el Guerrillero*, pp. 256–70.
39. For the campaigns of Espoz y Mina in the latter part of the war, cf. Tone, *Fatal Knot*, pp. 131–45; Alexander, *Rod of Iron*, pp. 189–220.
40. These nicknames are not always easy to translate. Perhaps the worst case is that of El Empecinado. The word from which the nickname comes – *pecina* – is the name given to a particularly black and sticky type of mud associated with the district from which Juan Martín Díez hailed, and it has often been assumed that a comparison was intended with the guerrilla commander's rather swarthy complexion – hence some sources' use of 'Inky Face'. However, comparison with the rather similar case of Julián Sánchez suggests a different rendition. Thus, Sánchez was known as El Charro, a term applied to all the inhabitants of the province of Salamanca. But a *charro* is also a rustic, a boor or a backwoodsman – hence 'Stick-in-the-Mud' for El Empecinado.
41. Brindle, 'Memoirs', pp. 46–7.
42. Anon. to R. Gutiérrez, 12 February 1811, AHN. Est. 3146.
43. For a reproduction of this picture, which is housed in the Royal Collection, cf. Esdaile, 'Heroes or Villains', p. 29. This, however, should be contrasted with the Goya portait of El Empecinado shown in the same work on p. 31, this clearly illustrating the way in which fashions of dress had often changed by 1814.

44. Espoz y Mina, *Memorias*, I, p. 41.
45. *Cit.* Salmón, *Resumen Histórico*, III, pp. 246–7.
46. Cf. V. Malibrán to E. Bardaji, 22 March 1811, AHN. Est. 3146.
47. For a contemporary depiction, cf. H. Lachouque and others, *Napoleon's War in Spain: the French Peninsular Campaigns, 1807–1814* (London, 1982), p. 115.
48. For the formation of the Guipúzcoa coastguards, cf. decree of F. Amoros, 26 April 1809, AGS. GJ. 1076, whilst the *gendarmes d'Espagne* are covered in J. Elting, *Swords around a Throne: Napoleon's Grande Armée* (New York, 1988), pp. 415–16.
49. J. Echegaray to P. Chevalier, 31 December 1809, AGS. GJ. 1076.
50. Southey, *Peninsular War*, III, pp. 46–9. For a detailed account of the rising in the Serranía de Ronda, cf. Anon., *Villa de Casares, año de 1813: expediente que comprobará los heroicos servicios hechos a la patria por la villa de Casares en la gloriosa sublevación de la sierra contra los franceses desde el año de 1810 hasta el presente* (Algeciras, 1813), Servicio Histórico Militar, Colección de la Guerra de la Independencia (hereafter SHM. CGI.) 2/2; for the Roncal, meanwhile, cf. Anon., *Relación remitido al gobierno desde el Reino de Navarra que manifiesta los descalabros que allí han sufrido los enemigos por aquellos naturales al mando del Bgdr. Don Mariano de Renovales desde principios de mayo hasta principios de septiembre del presente año* (Seville, 1809), AHN. Est. 33–B, no. 182.
51. Rocca, *Memoirs*, p. 154.
52. Anon., *Villa de Casares*, pp. 5–6; Rodríguez Solis, *Guerrilleros de 1808*, I, xi, pp. 9–12.
53. *Ibid.*, pp. 32–5.
54. For all this, cf. Junta of Badajoz to Junta Central, 20 April 1809, AHN. Est. 41–B, no. 8; J. D. Pacheco to M. de Garay, 24 April 1809, AHN. Est. 41–E, no. 183.
55. Rodríguez Solis, *Guerrilleros de 1808*, I, viii, pp. 4–12 *passim*; for the attack on Marshal Augereau, cf. *Gazeta Militar y Política del Principado de Catalunya* (26 December 1809), AHN. Est. 38–D, no. 44.
56. Rodríguez Solis, *Guerrilleros de 1808*, II, i, pp. 34–5.
57. J. Clarós, *Representación del Coronel de los reales ejércitos y gobernador militar y político interino del corregimiento de Gerona, Don Juan Clarós, a S.A. el Consejo de la Regencia sobre la exposición que contra el hizo el Marqués de Castroverde* (Vich, 1812), p. 26, SHM. DG. 1811/4.
58. Southey, *Peninsular War*, I, pp. 648–9. The name *miguelete* is a reference to a band of mercenaries commanded by a sixteenth-century Catalan soldier named Miguel de Prats. Confusingly, the same name was also applied to the regular home guard that operated in the Basque provinces.
59. Oman, *History of the Peninsular War*, III, p. 53; for a contemporary account of O'Donnell's exploits in the autumn of 1809, cf. 'Diario de operaciones de las unidades a las ordenes del General Enrique O'Donnell' (MS.), SHM. CGB. 3/5.
60. Arteche, *Guerra de la Independencia*, VIII, pp. 219–49; Muñoz Maldonado, *Guerra de la Independencia*, II, pp. 315–24.
61. For Enrique O'Donnell's own account of operations in Catalonia in the wake of the battle of Vich, cf. E. O'Donnell to F. Eguía, 27 March 1810, SHM. CGI. 2/10.
62. *Cit.* Arteche, *Guerra de la Independencia*, IX, p. 252.
63. Rodríguez Solis, *Guerrilleros de 1808*, I, ix, pp. 26–30.
64. Oman, *Peninsular War*, III, pp. 497–9.
65. L. Lacy to Junta of Catalonia, 6 October 1811, SHM. CGI. 4/23.

66. Arteche, *Guerra de la Independencia*, VIII, pp. 120–44; Barthèlemy, *El Marquesito*, I, pp. 164–78.
67. Cf. J. Díaz Porlier to N. Mahy, 1 July 1810, Servicio Histórico Militar, Colección Duque de Bailén (hereafter SHM. CDB.) 17/21/67.
68. Oman, *Peninsular War*, III, pp. 485–7; Gómez de Arteche, *Guerra de Independencia*, IX, pp. 424–6; Barthèlemy, *El Marquesito*, I, pp. 185–237 *passim*.
69. Muñoz Maldonado, *Guerra de la Independencia*, III, pp. 105–6.
70. Oman, *Peninsular War*, III, pp. 465–72; Gómez de Arteche, *Guerra de la Independencia*, IX, pp. 410–14.
71. Anonymous report, n.d., AHN. Est. 2994.
72. Proclamation of Marshal Soult, 8 May 1810, *cit. Gazeta Extraordinaria de Sevilla* (10 May 1810), pp. 317–19, AHN. Est. 2994.
73. Proclamation of B. de Aranza, 8 May 1810, *cit. ibid.*, pp. 314–17.
74. Gómez de Arteche, *Guerra de la Independencia*, VIII, pp. 185–7; Oman, *Peninsular War*, III, pp. 214–15, 326–30; for a modern account of the campaigns of Ballesteros and Copons, cf. M. A. Peña, *El Tiempo de los Franceses: La Guerra de la Independencia en el Suroeste Español* (Huelva, 2000), pp. 24–31.
75. *Gazeta Extraordinaria de la Regencia* (30 August 1810), p. 595, Real Academia de Historia (hereafter RAH.) 9:6968.
76. Salmón, *Resumen Histórico*, III, pp. 108–9.
77. M. de Alzega to F. Copons, 21 August 1810, RAH. 9:6968.
78. Oman, *Peninsular War*, III, pp. 330–5, 337–8.
79. Rodríguez Solis, *Guerrilleros de 1808*, I, xi, pp. 9–12.
80. Oman, *Peninsular War*, III, pp. 335–7; A. Blayney, *Narrative of a Forced Journey through Spain and France as a Prisoner of War in the Years 1810 to 1814* (London, 1814), I, pp. 1–36.
81. Oman, *Peninsular War*, V, pp. 550–7.
82. *Ibid.*, IV, pp. 599–605.
83. *Ibid.*, V, pp. 314–32.
84. *Ibid.*, pp. 274–6, 521–2. An interesting account of the action at Villafranca de los Castillejos is contained in F. Ballesteros to Lord Wellington, 27 January 1811, US. WP.1/342.
85. T. Bunbury, *Reminiscences of a Veteran, being Personal and Military Adventures in Portugal, Spain, France, Malta, Norfolk Island, New Zealand, Anderman Islands and India* (London, 1861), I, pp. 111–12.
86. P. Morillo to La Romana, 9 May 1810, *cit.* Rodríguez Villa, *Pablo Morillo*, pp. 56–8.
87. P. Morillo to Marqués de la Romana, 20 May 1810, *cit. ibid.* pp. 62–4.
88. P. Morillo to Marqués de la Romana, 27 May 1810, *cit. ibid.* pp. 64–5.
89. P. Morillo to Marqués de la Romana, 29 June 1810, *cit. ibid.* pp. 68–70.
90. P. Morillo to Marqués de la Romana, 9 September 1810, *cit. ibid.* pp. 76–80.
91. N. Horta-Rodríguez, *D. Julián Sánchez, 'El Charro', Guerrillero y Brigadier* (Ciudad Rodrigo, 1986), pp. 28–64 *passim*.
92. Anon. report, 26 April 1811, SHM. CGI. 3/33. For an account stemming from one of Sánchez's own subordinates, cf. 'Parte dado por la Primera Legión de Castilla', 12 April 1811, US. WP.1/346.
93. Cassells, *Peninsular Portrait*, p. 57; C. Boutflower, *The Diary of an Army Surgeon during the Peninsular War* (Manchester, 1912), p. 54.
94. Marbot, *Memoirs*, II, p. 162.

95. Horta Rodríguez, *Julián Sánchez*, pp. 67–93 *passim.*
96. Proclamation of L. Bassecourt, 15 March 1810, AHN. Est. 2994.
97. Proclamation of P. Villacampa, n.d., AHN. Est. 2994.
98. Guirao, *Guerrilleros y Patriotas*, pp. 74–6.
99. *Ibid.*, pp. 41–4, 83–4; for an eyewitness account of this affair, cf. J. North (ed.), *In the Legions of Napoleon: the Memoirs of a Polish Officer in Spain and Russia, 1808–1813* (London, 1999), pp. 73–4.
100. A. de Rojas to E. Bardaji, 12 April 1811, AHN. Est. 3146.
101. J. Skerret to W. Cooke, 8 November 1811, PRO. WO.1/252, ff. 544–5.

3 The Guerrillas in Context

1. *Regeneración de España* (Seville, n.d.), n.p., BN. CGI. R60292–3.
2. Lovett, *Napoleon and the Birth of Modern Spain*, pp. 329–30.
3. For some examples of revisionist writing, cf. E. Canales Gil, 'La deserción en España durante la Guerra de la Independencia', *Bi-centenari de la Revolució Francesa (1789–1989): Le Jacobinisme* (Barcelona, 1990), pp. 211–30; E. Canales, *Patriotismo y Deserción durante la Guerra de la Independencia en Cataluña* (Coimbra, 1988); C. Esdaile, 'Rebeldía, reticencia y resistencia: el caso gallego de 1808', *Trienio*, no. 35 (May, 2000), pp. 57–80.
4. For discussions of events in La Mancha and Zaragoza, cf. J. de Haro, *Guerra de la Independencia: La Mancha, 1808 – Diarios, Memorias y Cartas* (Alcázar de San Juan, 2000), pp. 95–117, and R. Rudorff, *War to the Death: the Sieges of Saragossa, 1808–1809* (London, 1974), pp. 87–96. For a contemporary account of the action at El Bruch, cf. F. Solá Montaña (ed.), *Els Manresans al Bruch: Relacions del Capdill en Maurici Carrió Referents a la Batalla del Bruch, 6 de Juny de 1808* (Barcelona, 1908), pp. 35–6.
5. R. Carr, *Spain, 1808–1975* (Oxford, 1982), p. 88.
6. F. Casamayor, 'Años políticos y históricos de las cosas mas particulares occuridas en la imperial, augusta y siempre heróica ciudad de Zaragoza', XXV (1808), f. 33, Biblioteca de la Universidad de Zaragoza (hereafter BUZ.), MS.131. As with a number of other documents relating to Zaragoza, I owe my knowledge of Casamayor's chronicle to my good friend and colleague Francisco-Javier Maestrojuan of the University of Navarre, whose help in this respect I am delighted to acknowledge.
7. Anon., *Manifiesto de las ocurrencias más principales de la plaza de Ciudad Rodrigo desde la causa formada en el real sitio del Escorial al Serenísimo Señor Príncipe de Asturias, hoy nuestro amado soberano, hasta la evacuación de la plaza de Almeida por los franceses en el dia 1º de octubre de 1808* (Salamanca, 1808), AHN. Est. 65–G, no. 264, pp. 9–10, 27.
8. M. S. Foy, *History of the War in the Peninsula under Napoleon* (London, 1827), II, p. 200. Both shrines were of immense significance in the context of 1808: Covadonga was regarded as the birthplace of the reconquest of Spain from the Moors, whilst Saint James was known as the 'Moorkiller' thanks to a legend that he had appeared in a battle against the Moors and led the Spaniards to victory.
9. Casamayor, 'Años políticos y históricos', XXV (1808), ff. 35–6, BUZ. MS.131; the palm tree was a symbol of purity, and, by extension, one of the mother of Christ as well.

10. Solá, *Manresans al Bruch*, p. 33.
11. S. Blaze, *Mémoires d'un Apothécaire sur la Guerre d'Espagne pendant les Années 1808 à 1814* (Paris, 1828), I, pp. 72–3.
12. For a representative collection of Patriot propaganda, cf. S. Delgado (ed.), *Guerra de la Independencia: Proclamas, Bandos y Combatientes* (Madrid, 1979), whilst horror stories of the Dos de Mayo may be found in Anon., *Resumén de los hechos mas notables que fijan la conducta del ejército francés durante su existencia en la capital de España y relación circunstanciada de todo lo ocurrido en la escena del dia dos de mayo* (Madrid, 1808), BN. R60398–2.
13. P. Girón, *Memorias de la Vida de Don Pedro Agustín Girón*, ed. A. Berazaluce (Pamplona, 1978), I, p. 217; M. de Cova to Junta of Galicia, 11 June 1808, AHN. Est. 74–C, no. 314^2; F. de León to Junta of Galicia, 10 June 1808, *ibid.*, no. 322; M. A. Belo to Junta of Galicia, 13 June 1808, *ibid.*, no. 337; Junta of Ribadeo to Junta of Galicia, 20 June 1808, *ibid.*, 74–A, no. 116.
14. Memorial of S. Riggi, 6 March 1810, AGS. GJ. 1078; M. García del Barrio, *Sucesos de Galicia en 1809 y operaciones en la presente guerra del Coronel D. Manuel García del Barrio, comisionado del gobierno para la restauración de aquel reino y electo Comandante General por las patriotas gallegos* (Cádiz, 1811), pp. 8–12, Servicio Histórico Militar (hereafter SHM. CDF.) CIX.
15. Petition of J. Schumacher, 22 February 1810, AGS. GJ. 1078; Anon., *Causa contra el Canónigo Calvo* (Valencia, 1808), BN. CGI. R60087–11.
16. J. Blanco White, *Cartas de España*, ed. V. Llorens and A. Garnica (Madrid, 1972), p. 321.
17. R. Gras y de Esteva, *Zamora en la Guerra de la Independencia, 1808–14* (Madrid, 1913), pp. 126–36.
18. Peña, *Tiempo de los Franceses*, p. 62; M. López Pérez and I. Lara, *Entre la Guerra y la Paz: Jaén, 1808–1814* (Jaén, 1993), p. 272.
19. For the students of Santiago, cf. Anon., *Colección general de interesantes e instructivos discursos literarios publicados en el reino de Galicia, donde se incluye lo ocurrido en las activas y prontas disposiciones dadas por el dicho reino para el armamento del ejército y sus diferentes posiciones contra el enemigo del mundo* (Madrid, 1808), pp. 104–8, BN. CGI. R60624; for Salgado, cf. petition of José Salgado, 19 August 1809, AHN. Est. 77–A, no. 67; for Zumalacárregui, cf. B. Jarnés, *Zumalacárregui: el Caudillo Romántico* (Madrid, 1972), p. 22. For Calvo, cf. J. J. Marcén (ed.), *El Manuscrito de Matías Calvo: Memorias de un Monegrino durante la Guerra de la Independencia* (Zaragoza, 2000), p. 105; finally, the case of Mina is discussed below.
20. Junta of Vigo to Junta of Galicia, 21 July 1808, AHN. Est. 74–A, no. 191.
21. B. Spencer to Lord Castlereagh, 21 June 1808, Public Record Office, War Office Papers (hereafter PRO. WO.) 1/226, f. 478.
22. Casamayor, 'Años políticos y históricos', XXV (1808), f. 99, BUZ. MS.131.
23. E. Iglesias to A. Filanghieri, 6 June 1808, AHN. Est. 74–B, no. 238.
24. 'Resumen de la exposición que desde Moya dirigió a la Junta Central el Teniente Coronel del Segundo Batallón de Barcelona, Don Miguel de Haro, dando cuenta del estado de las cosas en Barcelona', AHN. Est. 80–T, no. 261; proclamation of the Junta of Seville, 12 June 1808, BN. CGI. 60034–11; J. Rico, *Memoria histórica sobre la revolución de Valencia* (Cádiz, 1811), p. 110, BN. CGI. 61075.
25. Junta of Orense to Junta of Galicia, 8 June 1808, AHN. Est. 75–E, no. 309.

26. For some examples of these regulations, cf. proclamation of Junta of Granada, 6 June 1808, SHM. CDF. DCCCLXIV, no. 50; proclamation of Junta of Santander, 16 August 1808, PRO. WO.1/229, ff. 55–7.
27. Proclamation of Junta of Galicia, 4 June 1808, AHN. Est. 74–A, no. 9.
28. Royal Decree, 7 October 1808, AHN. Est. 46–A, f. 2.
29. M. de Godoy, *Cuenta dada de su Vida Política por Don Manuel de Godoy, Principe de la Paz, o sea Memorias Críticas y Apolegéticas para la Historia del Reinado del Señor Carlos IV de Borbón* (Madrid, 1836–46), I, p. 136.
30. For some examples of what was done on the occasion of the installation of the Junta Central in September 1808, cf. T. de Morla to Conde de Floridablanca, 11 October 1808, Archivo del Congreso de Diputados, Serie General (hereafter ACD. SG.), 1, no. 4; *Ayuntamiento* of La Coruña to Conde de Floridablanca, 12 October 1808, *ibid.*, no. 5.
31. J. Girón y Montezuma to M. de Garay, 7 August 1809, AHN. Est. 61–T, no. 420.
32. E.g. Anon., *El templo del heroismo consagrado a nuestro muy amado monarca, Fernando VII, y a la valiente fidelísima nación española* (Málaga, 1808), p. 18, BN. CGI. R60124–2; pastoral letter of the Bishop of León, 22 September 1808, BN. CGI. R60378.
33. Salmón, *Resumen Histórico*, I, p. 100, SHM. CDF. CMXXXII.
34. Anon. to Junta Central, n.d., AHN. Est. 52–G, no. 312.
35. Conde del Pinar to M. de Garay, 16 April 1809, AHN. Est. 30–E, no. 79.
36. Petition of *ayuntamiento* of El Ferrol, 25 June 1808, AHN. Est. 74–A, no. 60.
37. Junta of Santiago to Junta of Galicia, 12 June 1808, AHN. Est. 74–A, no. 140.
38. Petition of Marqués de Usategui, 27 March 1809, AHN. Est. 83–N, no. 395.
39. Anon. to Conde de Floridablanca, 12 November 1808, AHN. Est. 52–A, no. 85.
40. For a discussion of these issues, cf. C. Esdaile, *From Constitution to Civil War: Spain in the Liberal Age, 1808–1939* (Oxford, 2000), pp. 4–10; C. Crowley, '*Luces* and *Hispanidad*: Nationalism and Modernization in Eighteenth-Century Spain', in M. Palumbo and W. Shanahan (eds), *Nationalism: Essays in Honour of Louis L. Snyder* (Westport, Connecticutt, 1981), pp. 87–102; and B. Barreiro, 'La conflictividad social durante el reinado de Carlos IV' in P. Molas (ed.), *La España de Carlos IV* (Madrid, 1991), pp. 81–9. M. García Ruipérez, *Revueltas Sociales en la Provincia de Toledo: la Crisis le 1802–1805* (Toledo, 1999), is a helpful regional study, whilst the example of Valencia is discussed in Ardit, *Revolución Liberal y Revuelta Campesina*, pp. 77–119. Meanwhile, general discussions of the nature of Spanish society may be found in Carr, *Spain*, pp. 1–37, and J. Lynch, *Bourbon Spain* (Oxford, 1989), pp. 198–246.
41. Cf. R. Herr, 'Good, evil and Spain's rising against Napoleon', in R. Herr and H. Parker (eds), *Ideas in History: Essays Presented to Louis Gottschalk by his Former Students* (Durham, North Carolina, 1965), pp. 157–81.
42. J. Kincaid, *Adventures in the Rifle Brigade* (London, 1909), p. 86.
43. Anon. report, 3 September 1810, AGS. GJ. 1076.
44. F. Jiménez de Gregorio, *Murcia en los dos primeros años de la Guerra de la Independencia* (Murcia, 1947), pp. 14–15; *Manifiesto de las ocurrencias mas principales de la plaza de Ciudad Rodrigo*, pp. 36–8; Gras, *Zamora en la Guerra de la Independencia*, p. 51. For a general discussion of the membership of the juntas, cf. Hocquellet, *Résistance et Révolution*, pp. 145–54.
45. The *sevillano* Tap y Núñez, for example, was a smuggler who had just been released from prison, and the Valencian Juan Rico a friar who had fled his convent.

46. Cf. petition of B. Pena, 5 July 1808, AHN. Est. 74–A, no. 91; Junta of Ribadeo to Junta of Galicia, 16 June 1808, Est. 74–A, no. 115.
47. Memorandum of Junta of Lugo, 12 September 1808, AHN. Est. 75–C, no. 176; decree of the Junta of Galicia, 15 July 1808, AHN. Est. 75–B, no. 63; decree of Junta of Granada, 24 June 1808, AHN. Est. 78–A, no. 4; Rico, *Memoria Histórica*, pp. 71–2.
48. E.g. Junta of Betanzos to Junta of Galicia, 17 and 18 June and 9 July 1808, AHN. Est. 75–A, nos 7, 8, 9.
49. Real Orden, 18 November 1808, SHM. CDF. DCCCLXIV, p. 69; Real Orden, 3 February 1809, AHN. Est. 31–C, no. 78.
50. J. de Miranda to M. de Garay, 19 March 1809, AHN. Est. 16–3[2], f. 58.
51. Proclamation of Junta of Cádiz, 16 January 1809, BN. CGI. R60002–4.
52. Proclamation of Vicario Capitular of Cádiz, 6 March 1809, AHN. Est. 62–G, no. 272.
53. Proclamation of Alcalde Mayor of Cádiz, 28 February 1809, BN. CGI. R60002–11.
54. Proclamation of Comisario General of Isla de León, 18 July 1809, BN. CGI. R60002–29.
55. L. Gómez Romero to M. de Garay, 18 April 1809, AHN. Est. 16–7, f. 37.
56. J. de San Miguel to Marqués de Astorga, 22 June 1809, AHN. Est. 81–R, no. 242.
57. Junta Central to A. Cornel, 14 June 1809, AHN. Est. 82–C, no. 356.
58. Anon. to Junta Central, 11 November 1808, AHN. Est. 52–A, no. 111; anon. to Junta Central, 18 November 1808, AHN. Est. 52–A, no. 114; memorial of J. Ovalle, 31 December 1808, AHN. Est. 15–2[3], ff. 42–5; P. de Mendoza to Conde de Floridablanca, 29 October 1808, AHN. Est. 52–A, no. 97; anon. to Junta Central, 1 August 1809, AHN. Est. 52–F, no. 275.
59. Anon. to Junta Central, AHN. Est. 52–G, no. 306.
60. Anon. to Junta Central, AHN. Est. 52–A, no. 13; for a somewhat similar view of the Junta of Mallorca, cf. anon. to M. de Garay, 18 July 1809, AHN. Est. 62–B, no. 78.
61. For all this, cf. *Real Ordenanza en que S.M. establece las reglas que inviolablemente deben observarse para el re-emplazo del ejército*, 27 October 1800, BS. CGA. 039950.
62. *Ayuntamiento* of Murcia to Junta Central, 22 July 1809, AHN. Est. 83–A, no. 22; petition of L. Palou, 5 July 1809, ACA. JSC. 74.
63. Cf. Junta Central to A. Cornel, 27 February 1809, AHN. Est. 82–C, no. 302.
64. Anon. to Junta Central, 9 March, 1809, AHN. Est. 52–E, no. 266; petition of M. Caval and others, 28 June 1808, AHN. Est. 74–A, no. 207; 'El verdadero español' to Junta Central, n.d., AHN. Est. 52–E, no. 218.
65. For the cost of exemption in Granada, cf. anon. to Junta Central, n.d., AHN. Est. 52–G, no. 353.
66. Junta of Molina to Junta Central, 31 January 1809, AHN. Est. 80–N, no. 170; *Diario de las Cortes Generales y Extraordinarias de España* (Cádiz, 1810–13; hereafter DC.), II, p. 1491.
67. C. La Hoz to Junta Central, n.d., AHN. Est. 52–D, no. 186; anon. to Junta Central, n.d., AHN. Est. 52–A, no. 110.
68. Petition of J. Ginesta, M. Riera and J. Puig, 8 December 1809, ACA. JSC. 71; report of M. de Garay, 6 March 1809, AHN. Est. 82–C, no. 310.

69. Petitions of J. Viladerau, F. Felíu and F. Aragonés, 30 November 1808, 13 August 1809 and 27 August 1811, ACA. JSC. 71; Viladerau was a prosperous merchant, Feliu was the son of a landowner, and Aragonés an official of the state lottery.
70. Anon. to Junta Central, 11 November 1808, AHN. Est. 52–A, no. 111.
71. Anon. to Junta Central, n.d., AHN. Est. 52–G, no. 403; for some concrete examples from Jimena de la Frontera, cf. anon. to Conde de Altamira, 8 January 1809, AHN. 52–E, no. 257.
72. Anon. to Junta Central, 1 August 1809, AHN. Est. 52–F, no. 275.
73. L. Gómez Romero to M. de Garay, 25 March 1809, AHN. Est. 16–7, f. 12.
74. Junta of Ayamonte to Junta Central, 11 August 1809, AHN. Est. 61–T, no. 426; cf. also M. Galindo to Junta Central, 14 April 1809, AHN. Est. 81–N, no. 315. At the time that the Junta of Ayamonte, a town in the most remote corner of southwest Spain, made its boast the nearest Frenchmen lay on the River Tagus, whilst no enemy forces had ever come closer to the junta than Badajoz.
75. Anon. to Junta Central, n.d., AHN. Est. 52–A, no. 27.
76. Anon. to the Junta Central, n.d., AHN. Est. 52–G, no. 367; cf. also to Junta Central, n.d., *ibid.*, no. 104.
77. Proclamation of commanding officer of the Voluntarios Distinguidos de Cádiz, 18 January 1809, BN. CGI. R60002–5; proclamation of V. Escalante, 12 September 1809, BN. CGI. R60002–32; proclamation of F. Venegas, 27 November 1809, BN. CGI. R60002–40; proclamation of Junta of Cádiz, 22 September 1810, BN. CGI. R60002–71.
78. A. Toribio Sánchez to Junta Central, 25 February 1809, AHN. Est. 62–A, no. 3; anon. to Junta Central, 30 July 1809, AHN. Est. 40–A, no. 25. For an example of the objections of the propertied classes to service in the *milicias honradas*, cf. anon. to Junta Central, AHN. Est. 52–E, no. 230.
79. Anon. to Junta Central, n.d., AHN. Est. 52–A, no. 128.
80. Accounts of this affair may be found in J. Mackenzie to J. Cradock, 24 February 1809, PRO. WO.1/240, ff. 41–6; Marqués de Villel to M. de Garay, 22 February 1809, AHN. Est. 31–C, no. 39[8]; F. Jones to M. de Garay, 22 and 24 February 1809, Est. 31–C, nos 39[1] and 43[2]; Marqués de Villel to T. Reding, 28 February 1809, ACA. JSC. 4.
81. E.g. Junta of Manresa to Junta of Catalonia, 4 October 1809, ACA. JSC. 71.
82. 'Lista de los Quintos que han Caído en el actual Sorteo en este Corregimiento de Manresa', 24 March 1810, ACA. JSC. 76; Blayney, *Narrative of a Forced Journey*, I, pp. 124–5.
83. Anon. report, 25 September 1812, ACA. JSC. 43.
84. M. Galindo to M. de Garay, 14 April 1809, AHN. Est. 81–N, no. 315.
85. For a brief summary of Colley's argument, cf. L. Colley, *Britons: Forging the Nation, 1707–1837* (New Haven, Connecticut, 1992), pp. 364–75.
86. Cf. M. Broers, *Europe under Napoleon, 1799–1815* (London, 1996), pp. 103–4.
87. For a discussion of the state of popular nationalism at the time of the war against Napoleon and, more to the point, of the manner in which Spanish nationalism was a product of the struggle, rather than its motor, cf. J. Alvarez Junco, *Mater Dolorosa: la Idea de España en el Siglo XIX* (Madrid, 2002), pp. 119–49, and Hocquellet, *Résistance et Révolution*, pp. 117–40. For a more traditional view,

cf. E. Goodman, 'Spanish nationalism in the struggle against Napoleon', *Review of Politics*, XX, no. 2 (July 1958), pp. 330–46.

88. Cf. M. Galindo to M. de Garay, 14 April 1809, AHN. Est. 81–N, no. 315; A. de Cortabarría to M. de Garay, 11 April 1809, AHN. Est. 16–3[1], ff. 22–3; F. Gil de la Parra to Junta Central, 18 June 1809, AHN. Est. 62–E, no. 167.
89. A. de Cortabarría to M. de Garay, 11 April 1809, AHN. Est. 16–3[1], ff. 22–3.
90. Petition of Junta of Llerena, 30 August 1809, AHN. Est. 80–D, no. 44.
91. L. Gómez Romero to M. de Garay, 10 April 1809, AHN. Est. 16–7, ff. 25–6.
92. F. Ballesteros to N. Mahy, 2 August 1809, SHM. CDB. 7/10/26; M. Pinto to M. de Garay, 24 July 1809, AHN. Est. 62–F, no. 168; C. O'Donnell to Junta Central, 29 October 1808, AHN. Est. 62–H, no. 368.
93. For some examples of despair at the performance of the Spanish generals, cf. anon. to Junta Central, 29 November 1808, AHN. Est. 52–A, no. 40; anon. to Junta Central, AHN. Est. 30–E, 13 January 1809, no. 237; B. Monzón to M. Serra, 12 January 1809, AHN. Est. 40–A, no. 6[2].
94. Cf. C. Esdaile, *The Duke of Wellington and the Command of the Spanish Army, 1812–14* (London, 1990), p. 89.
95. J. Walker to Lord Liverpool, 18 September 1810, PRO. WO.1/261, f. 42; cf. also proclamation of the Junta Central, 11 March 1809, BN. CGI. R60002–15); J. Díaz Porlier to N. Mahy, 25 March 1811, SHM. CDB. 25/35/24; *El Redactor General* (23 August 1811), p. 267, HMM. 6/3.
96. Lord Wellington to H. Wellesley, 14 May 1812, US. WP.12/1/5.
97. Anon. to Junta Central, 25 November 1808, AHN. Est. 52–A, no. 37.
98. Marqués de Lazán to J. Blake, n.d., SHM. CDB. 2/19.
99. Anon. report, 26 March 1811, AHN. Est. 3146; anon. report, 16 June 1811, AHN. Est. 3010; anon. report, 23 August 1811, AHN. Est. 3146. For the disputes underlying these garbled stories, Esdaile, *Duke of Wellington and the Command of the Spanish Army*, pp. 16-19 *passim*. Good examples of the sort of anti-British propaganda that had begun to circulate include Anon., *Carta de un valenciano amigo de su país a sus compatriotas* (Valencia, 1813), AHN. Est. 3010, and Anon., *Representación de las damas españolas a Jorge Tercero, Rey de Inglaterra, sobre los vagos rumores acerca de la conducta del gobierno inglés y de sus ejércitos en la guerra de España* (Cádiz, 1811), SHM. CDF. CXII.
100. For a discussion of popular attitudes to conscription in Spain in the reigns of Carlos III and Carlos IV, cf. C. Esdaile, *The Spanish Army in the Peninsular War* (Manchester, 1988), pp. 9–13. Cf. also C. Borreguero, *El Reclutamiento Militar por Quintas en la España del Siglo XVIII: Orígenes del Servicio Militar Obligatorio* (Valladolid, 1989), pp. 317–28.
101. Anon. to Junta Central, n.d., AHN. Est. 52–A, no. 82.
102. Anon. to Junta Central, n.d., AHN. Est. 52–G, nos 303, 315, 334. Brindle, 'Memoirs', f. 12. It is interesting to note that in the course of the uprising in Valladolid in 1808 rioters had threatened the seminarians of the English college with death unless they too joined the army.
103. Anon. to Floridablanca, 30 December 1808, AHN. Est. 52–E, no. 256.
104. For some Catalan examples of pleas for exemption, cf. petitions of V. Cendra, J. Morera and J. Lazaro, 30 November 1808 and 5 and 24 January 1809, ACA. JSC. 71.
105. J. Patterson, *The Adventures of Captain John Patterson* (London, 1837), p. 216; anon. to Junta Central, n.d., AHN. Est. 52–G, no. 403.

106. T. García to Junta of Catalonia, 18 August 1811, ACA. JSC. 88.
107. Junta of Santiago to Junta of Galicia, 16 December 1808, AHN. Est. 74–B, no. 272. Cf. also. P. de Burgos to Junta of Galicia, 9 November 1808, AHN. Est. 77–C, no. 140.
108. Junta of Ecija to Junta of Seville, 13 June 1809, AHN. Est. 82–C, no. 335.
109. 'Lista de los mozos de Paymogo en quienes se ha advertido colusión y por cuya causa se desertaron los quarenta y tantos mozos alistados', AHN. Est. 16–17, ff. 20–1.
110. No cases of this phenomenon have been encountered in the archives, but the prevalence of the practice in other states makes it safe to assume that it also took place in Spain.
111. F. Ribas to Junta of Catalonia, 16 December 1809, ACA. JSC. 71.
112. 'Estado general de todos los solteros, viudos sin hijos, casados y viudos con hijos existentes en este partido de marina [i.e. Arens de Mar]', 12 June 1811, ACA. JSC. 16.
113. Junta Central to Junta of Seville, 13 May 1809, AHN. Est. 82–C, no. 329.
114. J. Claros to Junta of Cataluña, 29 June 1811, ACA. JSC. 16.
115. Junta of Mesía to Junta of Santiago, 11 June 1808, AHN. Est. 74–A, no. 112[2]; petition of G. Menéndez de la Vega, 9 June 1808, AHN. Est. 74–B, no. 247; R. Clausell and J. Vila to Junta of Catalonia, 6 October 1811, ACA. JSC. 16.
116. J. Onate to Junta Central, 28 December 1808, AHN. Est. 80–U, no. 262; F. de León to Junta Central, 27 January 1809, AHN. Est. 31–G, no. 150; J. Castro de Lavalle to T. Reding, 18 January 1809, ACA. JSC. 4; Junta of Catalonia to Junta Central, 15 February 1809, AHN. Est. 31–F, no. 136; Anon. *Noticias de Lérida* (Lérida, 1809), BN. CGI. R60292–7; J. Mergelina to Junta Central, 28 February 1809, AHN. Est. 31–E, no. 127; Junta of Jerez de la Frontera to Junta Central, 1 March 1809, AHN. Est. 31–E, no. 129; C. de Campos to Junta Central, 3 and 7 January 1809, AHN. Est. 31–H, nos 172–3; J. M. de Retamosa to Junta Central, 7 January 1809, AHN. Est. 31–H, no. 183.
117. Rodríguez Solis, *Guerrilleros de 1808*, I, v, p. 17.
118. E. O'Donnell to Junta Central, 28 January 1810, SHM. CGB. 3/18; Marqués de Portazgo to J. Jorda, 27 December 1809, ACA. JSC. 76.
119. Junta of Mataró to Junta of Catalonia, 24 January 1809, ACA. JSC. 4.
120. F. Rovira to Junta of Manresa, 19 January 1810, ACA. JSC. 76; J. Blake to Junta of Catalonia, 15 September 1809, AHN. Est. 38–E, no. 386[8].
121. 'Memorial de las justicias de los pueblos del Valles', 29 August 1809, ACA. JSC. 71.
122. J. Blake to Junta Central, 16 September 1809, SHM. CGB. 3/4; J. Roset to Junta of Catalonia, 31 December 1809, ACA. JSC. 74.
123. F. Guervos to his parents, 18 November 1808, RAH. 11:9003.
124. B. Spencer to Lord Castlereagh, 17 June 1808, PRO. WO.1/226, f. 464; F. García Marín, *Memorias para la Historia Militar de la Revolución Española* (Madrid, 1817), pp. 26–7, BS. CGA. 040731; Alvarez Valdés, *Memorias*, pp. 55–6.
125. For evidence of self-inflicted wounds, cf. J. Encinas Lago to Junta Central, 25 November 1809, AHN. Est. 33–A, no. 97.
126. Proclamations of the Junta of Seville, 31 May, 12 June and 4 July 1808, SHM. CDF. DCCCLXIV, no. 45; BN. CGI. R60034–11/12; Gras, *Zamora en la Guerra de la Independencia*, p. 67.

127. J. M. Carvajal to N. Mahy, 22 January 1809, SHM. CDB. 5/8/3; J. Mascareñas to N. Mahy, 10 March 1809, SHM. CDB. 5/8/9; J. Gómez de la Torre to M. de Garay, 16 April 1809, AHN. Est. 16–18, ff. 76–7; 'Lista de los Desertores que el Resguardo de este Capital ha Capturado', AHN. Est. 80–F, no. 108; M. Valbuena to N. Mahy, 8 May 1809, SHM. CDB. 7/10/25; J. de San Miguel to Marqués de Astorga, 22 June 1809, AHN. Est. 81–R, no. 342.
128. For some examples of soldiers trying to remain in their home provinces, cf. F. Ballesteros to N. Mahy, 4 and 28 August 1809, SHM. CDB. 7/10/26. Figures for the desertion of Catalan soldiers are discussed in Canales, *Patriotismo y Deserción*, pp. 277–9.
129. E.g. P. Morillo to Marqués de la Romana, 9 April 1810, *cit.* Rodríguez Villa, *Morillo*, II, pp. 37–8; J. González de la Torre to P. Rivero, 24 November 1809, AHN. Est. 40–F, no. 235.
130. J. González de la Torre to P. Rivero, 26 November 1809, AHN. Est. 40–E, no. 187.
131. E.g. Lord Wellington to Lord Wellesley, 8 August 1809, US. WP. 1/274.
132. E.g. *Gazeta del Gobierno* (27 January 1809) HMM. AH17–2 (2925bis); Duque del Infantado, *Manifiesto de las operaciones del Ejército del Centro* (Seville, 1809), pp. 83–4. For the penalties laid down for desertion, cf. proclamation of Junta Central, 3 January 1809, BN. CGI. 60002–2.
133. E.g. F. Adam to J. Murray, 24 March 1813, US. WP.1/368.
134. For a general discussion of the conditions endured by the Spanish army in the Peninsular War, cf. Esdaile, *Spanish Army*, p. 140.
135. S. Rodríguez to M. de Garay, 16 February 1809, AHN. Est. 46–B, no. 56; J. Espina to Junta of Galicia, 16 September 1808, AHN. Est. 75–B, no. 69.
136. Petition of M. de la Herrera, J. del Campo and J. Navarrete, 19 March 1810, AGS. GJ. 1078.
137. Junta of Villafranca to Junta of Catalonia, 29 March 1810, ACA. JSC. 76.
138. Bishop of Ciudad Rodrigo to G. M. de Jovellanos, 10 February 1809, AHN. Est. 65–G, no. 287.
139. Cf. J. Lefevre to J. Leith, 25 October 1808, PRO. WO.1/229, f. 451; Junta of Molina to J. Ovalle, 26 December 1808, AHN. Est. 15–2[3], ff. 22–5; report of A. Sáenz Vizmanos, n.d., AHN. 15–7[1], ff. 38–9; Junta of Mallorca to Junta Central, 10 December 1808, AHN. Est. 62–B, no. 24; petition of *ayuntamiento* of La Coruña, 6 June 1808, AHN. Est. 74–A, no. 30; Junta of Ayamonte to F. Copons, RAH. 9:6967; Junta of Galicia to F. J. Caro and M. M. Avalle, 31 December 1808, AHN. Est. 72–B, no. 209.
140. E.g. Anon. to Junta Central, n.d., AHN. Est. 52–G, no. 343; Junta of Mallorca to Junta Central, 10 December 1808, AHN. Est. 62–B, no. 24; J. Pinto y Palacios to M. de Garay, 24 July 1809, AHN. Est. 62–F, no. 168; J. O'Donnell to N. Mahy, 18 February 1809, SHM. CDB. 5/8/9; M. Modet to M. de Garay, 4 April 1810, AHN. Est. 16–9, ff. 29–30.
141. Proclamations of Junta of Seville, 6 and 30 June 1808, SHM. CDF. DCCCLXIV, ff. 50, 63; Gras, *Zamora en la Guerra de la Independencia*, p. 67.
142. Gras, *Zamora en la Guerra de la Independencia*, p. 109.
143. E.g. R. Gómez Aguado to N. Mahy, 1 May 1809, SHM. CDB. 5/8/9; F. de León to Junta Central, 27 February 1809, AHN. Est. 31–G, no. 158.
144. E.g. M. Modet to M. de Garay, 4 April 1810, AHN. Est. 16–9, ff. 29–30.

145. M. Núñez to N. Mahy, n.d., SHM. CDB. 7/10/25; L. Gómez Romero to M. de Garay, 10 April 1809, AHN. 16–17, ff. 23–4.
146. Lord Burghersh to Lord Wellington, 18 October 1809, *Supplementary Despatches, Correspondence and Memoranda of Field Marshal Arthur, Duke of Wellington*, ed. Second Duke of Wellington (London, 1858–72), VI, p. 406.
147. A. Ludovici (ed.), *On the Road with Wellington: the Diary of a War Commissary in the Peninsular Campaigns* (New York, 1925), pp. 79–80.
148. For some examples of this thinking, cf. *El Observador* (27 July 1810), p. 63, SHM. CDF. CX; *Diario Redactor de Sevilla* (9–11 December 1812), SHM. CDF. CXXXII; *El Tribuno del Pueblo Español* (9 March 1813), p. 179, HMM. AH1–4 (no. 121); *El Español* (30 April 1810), p. 14, HMM. AH4–2 (no. 710).
149. E. de Bardaji to F. Abadia, 8 July 1810, AHN. Est. 2994; proclamation of J. O'Donnell, 21 March 1812, RAH. 9:6971.
150. Royal Decree, 13 March 1814, ACD. SG. 1/60. For a general assessment of the social policy of the *cortes*, cf. C. Esdaile, *The Peninsular War: a New History* (London, 2002), pp. 403–5, 438–9.

4 The Origins of the Guerrillas

1. For all this, cf. Tone, *The Fatal Knot*, pp. 9–41 *passim*. The impact of proximity to France on notions of identity with relation to the rather different Catalan district of La Cerdaña is discussed in P. Sahlins, *Boundaries: the Making of France and Spain in the Pyrenees* (Berkeley, California, 1989). For the impact of *émigré* religion, cf. Herr, *Eighteenth-Century Revolution in Spain*, pp. 298–302.
2. Cf. Tone, *Fatal Knot*, pp. 166–8.
3. J. North (ed.), *In the Legions of Napoleon: the Memoirs of a Polish Officer in Spain and Russia, 1808–1813* (London, 1999), p. 89.
4. Von Brandt, *The Two Minas*, p. 29.
5. In arriving at these figures the greatest problem was what to do with the fifteen men whose occupations were given as *labradores* or *ganadores*. The meaning of these terms being simply 'farmer' (in the former case arable, and in the latter pastoral), in the absence of additional information it is impossible to assess their social standing with any certainty. Although the words were applied to men of a wide range of income, they have in this instance all been classified as peasants – in other words, tenants or owner-occupiers working plots of land with, for most of the time, no more aid than that of their immediate family. This slightly underestimates the number of members of the 'establishment' that have been positively identified: the number of *pudientes* should probably be raised to at least 206. The information on which these figures are based is in due course to be published in electronic form as part of a much larger data base that is currently being elaborated with the aid of funding received from the Arts and Humanities Research Board and the British Academy.
6. For the case of Pascual y Casas, a prosperous landowner from Badalona who raised a guerrilla band at his own cost in 1808, cf. petition of E. Pascual y Casas, 26 October 1809, AHN. Est. 65–A.
7. For Crespo and Uriz, cf. J. M. Iribarren, *Espoz y Mina, el Liberal* (Madrid, 1967), pp. 127–33; for Mayor, cf. Anon., *Apuntes de la vida y hechos militares del*

Brigadier Don Juan Martín, el Empecinado (Madrid, 1814), p. 29, SHM. DG. 1811/5. To round off Uriz's story, be it said that, after a murky period as an absolutist double agent in which he collaborated with the almost equally unsavoury Mariano Renovales in securing the collapse of an expedition to Mexico, he reappeared in Spain in 1820 in the guise of an ardent liberal and attempted to blackmail Espoz y Mina into securing a government post for him. For Temprano's defence of his actions, cf. A. Temprano to Junta Central, 22 September 1809, AHN. 41–C, no. 69.

8. Codón, *Cura Merino*, pp. 23–30; Marco, *Cura Merino*, pp. 8–9; Rodríguez Solis, *Guerrilleros de 1808*, I, ii, pp. 33–6. For an example of the sort of complaints that were voiced at the conduct of clerical guerrillas, cf. M. Traggia to P. Rivero, AHN. Est. 41–C, no. 73.
9. A. Jiménez, *Queja de un patriota al supremo consejo nacional en que manifiesta la alevosía conque se persigue a las partidas de guerrilla y a los defensores mas celosos de la patria* (Cádiz, 1811), BN. CGI. R61148.
10. Muñoz Maldonado, *Guerra de la Independencia*, II, p. 267; Rodríguez Solis, *Guerrilleros de 1808*, I, ii, pp. 36–7; *ibid.*, I, viii, p. 17.
11. E.g. Memorial of F. Rovira, 21 November 1814, SHM. CGI. 4/8.
12. For an account of Mina's captivity, cf. J. R. Aymes, *La Déportation sous le Premier Empire: les Espagnols en France, 1808–1814* (Paris, 1983), pp. 353–6.
13. M. Renovales to N. Mahy, 7 September 1810, SHM. CDB. 16/20/58.
14. Cf. F. Losada to N. Mahy, 16 November 1810, SHM. CDB. 16/20/58; J. Aburruza to Mahy, 28 March 1811, SHM. CDB. 16/20/58.
15. For details of Renovales' career in the latter years of the war and afterwards, cf. Iribarren, *Espoz y Mina, el Liberal*, p. 132; Aymes, *La Déportation sous le Premier Empire*, pp. 342–3.
16. Espoz y Mina, *Memorias*, I, pp. 7–11.
17. *Ibid.*, p. 25.
18. Anon., 'Algarabía, o noticia al público de un pozo sin suelo, boca de una mina de oro y plata, dada a luz quien la ha observado atentamente y penetrado sus interiores' (MS.), pp. 13–15, Archivo Municipal de Zaragoza (hereafter AMZ.) 27–22. For Von Brandt's views on Espoz y Mina's character, cf. Von Brandt, *The Two Minas*, p. 25.
19. For this affair, cf. Iribarren, *Espoz y Mina, el Guerrillero*, pp. 214–16.
20. For the doings of the man whom Espoz y Mina insultingly refers to as 'Don Fulano de Miguel', cf. Espoz y Mina, *Memorias*, I, pp. 54–7. Whilst it is probably true that Miguel was a pompous and self-seeking incompetent who alienated all those with whom he came into contact and fled at the first sign of the French, it is quite clear that Espoy y Mina turned the troops against him and effectively engineered his downfall.
21. Espoz y Mina, *Memorias*, I, p. 181. Despite his claims, Espoz y Mina was not Mina's uncle, but rather a distant cousin, the former's great-aunt being the latter's great-grandmother.
22. For a contemporary example of rumours that Mina was betrayed, cf. Salmón, *Resumen Histórico*, II, p. 277.
23. 'Algarabía', pp. 2–9.
24. J. Sherer, *Recollections of the Peninsula* (London, 1825), p. 248.
25. Blayney, *Narrative of a Forced Journey*, I, p. 139.

26. P. Haythornthwaite (ed.), *Life in Napoleon's Army: the Memoirs of Captain Elzéar Blaze* (London, 1995), p. 194.
27. Salmón, *Resumen Histórico*, III, p. 277.
28. Haro, *La Mancha*, p. 102; A. Merlo, 'El 6 de junio de 1808 en Asturias' in J. García Prado and others, *Estudios de la Guerra de la Independencia* (Zaragoza, 1964–7), p. 51.
29. Petition of V. Jiménez, n.d., AHN. Est. 41–E, no. 162.
30. *Relación de los méritos y proezas de Fray Lucas Rafael.*
31. Brindle, 'Memoirs', p. 44; for Rodríguez Solis's version of events, cf. Rodríguez Solis, *Guerrilleros de 1808*, I, i, pp. 55–6.
32. For the story that El Empecinado became a guerrilla after killing a French soldier in a quarrel, cf. F. Hernández Girbal, *Juan Martín, El Empecinado, terror de los franceses* (Madrid, 1985), pp. 72–3.
33. Ortuño, *Xavier Mina*, pp. 42–59; Von Brandt, *The Two Minas*, pp. 8–11. For the traditional version of events, cf. Southey, *Peninsular War*, II, pp. 392–3.
34. Peña, *Tiempo de los franceses*, p. 49.
35. Petition of R. de Murillo, 7 January 1810, AHN. Est. 15^1, f. 46.
36. Rodríguez Solis, *Guerrilleros de 1808*, II, iii, pp. 43–5.
37. Barthèlemy, *El Marquesito*, I, pp. 42–4.
38. Anon. report, 15 November 1811, AHN. Est. 3146.
39. Petition of F. Mallén, 19 November 1809, AHN. Est. 61–N, no. 317.
40. Petition of A. Piloti, 23 June 1809, AHN. Est. 41–E, no. 188.
41. Proclamation of the Junta of Aragón, 22 September 1809, AHN. Est. 61–N, no. 263.
42. Marqués de las Atalayuelas to M. de Garay, 22 September 1809, AHN. Est. 41–E, no. 193; cf. also A. Cornel to M. de Garay, 20 October 1809, AHN. Est. 41–E, no. 200.
43. A. Piloti to M. de Garay, 30 September 1809, AHN. Est.41–E, no. 195.
44. Duque de Infantado to M. de Garay, 31 December 1809, AHN. Est. 41–E, no. 202. Infantado's frivolity and want of common sense are well recorded. For some examples, cf. H. R. Holland, *Foreign Reminiscences*, ed. H. E. Holland (London, 1857), p. 110; J. García de León y Pizarro, *Memorias de la Vida del Excmo. Sr. D. José García de León y Pizarro Escritas por El Mismo*, ed. A. Alonso (Madrid, 1894), I, p. 229.
45. 'Noticia puntualizada de la ocurrencia que en la tarde de 26 de noviembre de 1810 acaeció en esta ciudad de Sigüenza con los oficiales, comandantes de partidas y batallón de infantería que hasta ahora han obrado bajo las ordenes del Brigadier D. Juan Martín Díez, El Empecinado', n.d., AHN. Est. 3010.
46. I owe this information on the latter half of Piloti's career to the generosity of my good friend Jorge Sánchez Fernández.
47. Petition of A. Valdivielso Morguecho, 29 September 1810, RAH. 9:6968.
48. *Cit.* F. Carantoña, *La Guerra de la Independencia en Asturias* (Oviedo, 1983), pp. 168–9. For Príncipe and Saornil, cf. Sánchez Fernández, *Nos Invaden!*, pp. 32–6.
49. Rodríguez Solis, *Guerrilleros de 1808*, I, v, p. 20.
50. Cf. report of Junta Criminal Extraordinaria de Granada, 10 August 1810, AGS. GJ. 1086. For a highly coloured version of Moreno's career based largely on the claims made by his wife after his execution in August 1810 in the hope of obtaining compensation from the *cortes*, cf. R. Fernández de Castro, *Apuntes*

Histórico-Biográficos del Insigne Patriota, Capitán de Infantería, Don Vicente Moreno, Héroe de la Independencia (Melilla, 1908), pp. 61–159.
51. Junta of Ayamonte to F. Copons, 22 July 1810, RAH. 9:6967.
52. P. Morillo to F. J. Castaños, n.d., *cit.* Rodríguez Villa, *Morillo*, II, pp. 156–8.
53. Petition of J. del Castillo, 30 April 1809, ACA. JSC. 74.
54. Memorial of F. J. de Segura, 1 June 1809, AHN. Est. 15–2^{4}, f. 52.
55. M. Jiménez Guazo to M. de Garay, 30 September 1809, AHN. Est. 41–E, no. 167.
56. Petition of F. Aznar Moreno, 27 October 1809, AHN. Est. 41–E, no. 188.
57. Junta General Militar to A. Cornel, 11 December 1809, AHN. Est. 61–N, no. 352.
58. L. Valero to Junta Central, 8 February 1809, AHN. 52–D, no. 203.
59. Proclamation of Marqués de Villafranca y los Vélez, 23 January 1810, SHM. CDB. 3/28.
60. García del Barrio, *Sucesos de Galicia*, p. 8; López Pérez and Lara, *Entre la Guerra y la Paz*, pp. 85–90.
61. Conde de Tilly to M. de Garay, 21 January 1809, AHN. Est. 39–D, no. 254.
62. Royal Decree, 28 December 1808, *cit. Gazeta del Gobierno* (3 February 1809), pp. 82–7, HMM. AH17–2(2925bis); Royal Decree, 25 February 1809, *cit. Diario de Badajoz* (10 March 1809), pp. 261–2, HMM. AH14–1(2457).
63. Proclamation of M. de Garay, 28 April 1809, AGS. GJ. 1147.
64. A. Cornel to J. Crivell, 12 May 1809, AHN. Est. 16–5^{2}, f. 4; M. de Garay to C. Areizaga, 15 June 1809, AHN. Est. 15–2^{4}, f. 55.
65. Cf. B. Hermida to J. A. Colmenares, 13 May 1809, AHN. Est. 61–N, no. 229.
66. A. de Arce to M. de Garay, 3 December 1808, AHN. Est. 38–C, no. 129; petition of P. Morillo, 6 February 1809, *cit.* Rodríguez Villa, *Morillo*, II, pp. 8–11.
67. Proclamation of Marqués de la Romana, n.d., AHN. Est. 17–7, ff. 3–4; Marqués de la Romana to J. Blake, 26 September 1810, SHM. CGB. 3/25; J. Moscoso, *Reflexiones sobre la guerra de España e instrucciones para la guerra de partidas o de paisanos* (Cádiz, 1809) BS. CGA. 040325; *Memorial Militar y Patriótico del Ejército de la Izquierda*, 6 April 1810, pp. 2–3, HMM. AH3–3(no. 536bis).
68. Muñoz Maldonado, *Guerra de la Independencia*, II, p. 265; anon. to Junta Central, n.d., AHN. Est. 52–A, no. 25; proclamation of José Caro, 7 March 1810, Archivo Municipal de Zaragoza, Colección General Palafox (hereafter AMZ. CGP.) 08174/19–8/15.
69. A. Sáenz de Vizmanos to M. de Garay, 22 June 1809, AHN. Est. 15^{1}–7, ff. 44–7.
70. Duque de Infantado to M. de Garay, 5 September 1809, AHN. Est. 41–E, no. 149; proclamation of N. Mahy, 27 May 1810, SHM. CDB. 17/21/65.
71. Cf. proclamation of F. Copons, 17 June 1812, RAH. 9:6971.
72. Rodríguez Solis, *Guerrilleros de 1808*, I, v, p. 20; *ibid.* I, vi, p. 11.
73. Espoz y Mina, *Memorias*, I, p. 53.
74. *Diario Redactor de Sevilla* (5 November 1812), SHM. CDF. CXXXII.
75. E. Pages and J. Battle to L. Lacy, 6 August 1811, ACA. JSC. 88.
76. F. Reig to F. Copons, 20 May 1812, RAH. 9:6971.
77. J. Aburruza to N. Mahy, 28 March 1811, SHM. CDB. 16/20/58.
78. Proclamation of the Junta of Asturias, 3 September 1810, SHM. CDB. 19/23/90.
79. J. Díaz Porlier to N. Mahy, 18 and 25 July 1810, SHM. CDB. 16/20/60.
80. P. Morillo to Marqués de La Romana, 12 April 1810, *cit.* Rodríguez Villa, *Morillo*, II, p. 42.
81. R. Gutiérrez to Regency, 4 March 1812, AHN. Est. 3010.

82. J. Battle to E. Pages, 24 July 1811, ACA. JSC. 16; J. Ciervo to Junta of Catalonia, 28 July 1811, *ibid.*
83. Anon. report, 22 July 1811, AHN. Est. 3146.
84. J. Ibáñez, *Diario de operaciones de la división del Condado de Niebla que mandó el Mariscal de Campo, Don Francisco de Copons y Navía, desde el dia 14 de abril de 1810, que tomó el mando, hasta el 24 de enero de 1811, que pasó este general al Quinto Ejército* (Faro, 1811), pp. 3–4, SHM. CDF. CCCXLII.
85. F. Copons to F. Eguía, 14 April 1810, RAH.9:6966; in view of the lacklustre performance of the Condado de Niebla hitherto, the reference to patriotic ardour may seem puzzling, but Copons was probably referring not to the Napoleonic period but to that of *los reyes católicos*, many towns in the district having played a leading role in the voyages of Christopher Columbus.
86. E.g. F. Copons to *ayuntamiento* of Trigueros, 7 May 1810, RAH. 9:6966.
87. F. Copons to Junta of Cádiz, 18 May 1810, RAH. 9:6966.
88. F. Copons to Junta of Regency, 20 September 1810, RAH. 9:6968.
89. T. Sydenham to H. Wellesley, 12 September 1812, US. WP.1/361.
90. T. McGuffie (ed.), *Peninsular Cavalry General: the Correspondence of Lieutenant General Robert Ballard Long* (London, 1951), pp. 96–7; for further examples of British complaints at the passivity of the populace in the occupied regions, cf. T. Pakenham (ed.), *The Pakenham Letters, 1800 to 1815* (London, 1914), p. 111; W. Thompson (ed.), *An Ensign in the Peninsular War: the Letters of John Aitchison* (London, 1981), p. 162.
91. Blayney, *Narrative of a Forced Journey*, I, pp. 13–14. NB. according to Blayney the presence of Miller and the other officers, of whom the most prominent appear to have been two lieutenant-colonels named Basset and Warrington, was the work of the Duque del Infantado, the latter having prevailed on the British government to send a number of British officers to organise the *serranos. Ibid.*, pp. 26–7.
92. Report of Junta Criminal Extraordinaria de Pamplona, AGS. GJ. 1085.
93. Report of Junta Criminal Extraordinaria de Guadalajara, 1 August 1809, AGS. GJ. 1081; Carnicero, *Historia Razonada*, II, pp. 78–80.
94. Blaze, *Mémoires*, II, pp. 86–7.
95. For evidence of a band in which clerical participation was strong, cf. petition of L. de Nájera, 5 November 1809, AHN. Est. 41–E, no. 98; however, cf. also Tone, *Fatal Knot*, pp. 150–1.
96. Rodríguez Solis, *Guerrilleros de 1808*, I, iv, p. 24.
97. Codón, *Cura Merino*, p. 28.
98. For Abuin, cf. Sánchez Fernández, *Nos Invaden!*, pp. 24–6.
99. Iribarren, *Espoz y Mina, el Liberal*, pp. 44–5.
100. Report of A. Revenga, 29 August 1810, AGS. GJ. 1148.
101. Rodríguez Solis, *Guerrilleros de 1808*, I, x, p. 37.
102. J. M. Ponce de León to Marqués de Almenara, 12 March 1810, AGS. GJ. 1163.
103. Rodríguez Solis, *Guerrilleros de 1808*, I, x, pp. 22, 25; Barnés, *Zumalacárregui*, pp. 24–5; Tone, *Fatal Knot*, p. 75.
104. Tone, *Fatal Knot*, pp. 120, 135.
105. L. Guimbaud (ed.), *Mémoires du Général Hugo* (Paris, 1934), p. 180; G. O'Farrill to P. Romero, 18 August 1811, AGS. GJ. 1083.

106. Rodríguez Solis, *Guerrilleros de 1808*, I, iii, pp. 19–20; Espoz y Mina, *Memorias*, I, pp. 35–6.
107. L. Guerrero to M. Romero, 25 January 1811, AGS. GJ. 1082.
108. Marco, *Cura Merino*, pp. 8–9.
109. Junta of Ayamonte to F. Copons, n.d., RAH. 9:6167.
110. Anon. report, n.d., AHN. Est. 2994; for the caution of the *josefino* administration with regard to any mention of military service, cf. circular of G. O'Farrill, 24 March 1810, AGS. GJ. 1163.
111. *Informe* of M. J. Martínez Valcarcel, 4 August 1810, AGS. GJ. 1078; anon. *informe*, 29 August 1810, *ibid.*
112. T. Sydenham to H. Wellesley, 10 October 1812, US. WP.1/361.
113. E.g. H. Balsa to J. Elío, 19 September 1810, AMZ. CGP. 08174/19–8/70.
114. E.g. F. Castaño to F. Copons, 5 July 1810, RAH. 9:6967; report of Junta Criminal Extraordinaria of Granada, 10 August 1810, AGS. GJ. 1086.
115. F. Taboada to N. Mahy, 27 June 1810, SHM. CGB. 17/24/98.
116. Rodríguez Solis, *Guerrilleros de 1808*, I, v, p. 27.
117. *Ibid.*, I, vi, p. 23.
118. J. M. Sarasa, *Vida y Hechos Militares del Mariscal de Campo, Don Juan Manuel Sarasa, Narrados por El Mismo*, ed. J. del Burgo (Pamplona, 1952), p. 16.
119. Anon. report, 28 June 1811, SHM. CGI. 3/34.
120. *Informe* of Junta Criminal Extraordinaria de Toledo, n.d., AGS. GJ. 1082.
121. F. Espoz y Mina to G. de Mendizábal, 7 February 1812, AHN. Est. 3010; Tone, *Fatal Knot*, pp. 170–1.
122. R. Gutiérrez to E. Bardaji, 17 July 1811, AHN. Est. 3146.
123. 'Inventario de Todos los Efectos Hecho por el Sr. Longa a la Partida Llamada de Voluntarios de Castilla', 3 July 1810, SHM. CDB. 17/21/61.
124. Blayney, *Forced Journey*, I, p. 354.
125. Cf. Arteche, *Guerra de la Independencia*, VII, p. 14; Tone, *Fatal Knot*, p. 75.
126. Von Brandt, *The Two Minas*, p. 54; T. Sydenham to H. Wellesley, 10 October 1812, US. WP.1/361; Larpent, *Private Journal of Judge-Advocate F. S. Larpent*, I, p. 132.
127. L. Gonzaga de Villaba, *Zaragoza en su segundo sitio* (Palma de Mallorca, 1811), p. 77, SHM. DG. 1811/6.
128. A. von Schepeler, *Histoire de la Révolution d'Espagne et de Portugal ainsi que de la Guerre qui en Résulta* (Liège, 1829–31), II, p. 430.
129. The social history of the War of Independence remains to be written. However, helpful regional texts include P. Fernández Albadalejo, *La Crisis del Antiguo Regimen en Guipúzcoa, 1766–1833: Cambio Económico e Historia* (Madrid, 1975) and F. Miranda, *La Guerra de la Independencia en Navarra: la Acción del Estado* (Pamplona, 1977).
130. Blayney, *Forced Journey*, I, pp. 57–8.
131. Casamayor, 'Años políticos', XXIX, f. 22, BUZ. MS.135.
132. Carnicero, *Historia Razonada*, III, pp. 121–2.
133. M. Glover (ed.), *A Gentleman Volunteer: the Letters of George Hennell from the Peninsular War* (London, 1979), p. 52.
134. J. M. Ponce de León to Marqués de Almenara, 28 April 1810, AGS. GJ. 1163.
135. Petition of M. Ortiz Ortáñez, 18 May 1812, AGS. GJ. 1079.
136. B. López Morán, *El Bandolerismo Gallego en la Primera Mitad del Siglo XIX* (La

Coruña, 1995), pp. 32–4; J. Santos, *El Bandolerismo en Andalucía, I: Sevilla y su Antiguo Reino* (Seville, 1991), pp. 149–97 *passim*.

137. J. Ortega, *Historia de las Escuadras de Cataluña: su Origen, sus Proezas, sus Vicisitudes Intercalada con la Vida y Hechos de los Mas Célebres Ladrones y Bandoleros* (Barcelona, 1968), p. 192.
138. Proclamation of M. J. Solano, 11 January 1812, AGS. GJ. 1080.
139. Cf. report of R. Moyano, 19 February 1812, AGS. GJ. 1087.
140. Petition of S. de Bernaola, 12 November 1811, AGS. GJ. 1082.
141. Report of Ministerio General de Policia, 16 February 1810, AGS. GJ. 1078; Z. J. Garrido to Junta Criminal Extraordinaria de Vizcaya, 5 December 1809, AGS. GJ. 1076.
142. E.g. proclamation of Junta of Aragón, 1 December 1809, AHN. 61–N, no. 322; F. Reig to F. Copons, 7 May 1812, RAH. 9:6971.
143. Haythornthwaite, *Life in Napoleon's Army*, p. 57.
144. A. Bassecourt to N. Mahy, 18 October 1811, SHM. CDB. 24/33/0; Santos, *Bandolerismo en España*, pp. 210–11.
145. A. Caballero to F. Copons, 5 October 1810, RAH. 9:6167; F. Espoz y Mina to F. J. de Castaños, 12 March 1813, US. WP.1/368; J. Donaldson, *Recollections of the Eventful Life of a Soldier* (Edinburgh, 1852), pp. 206–7.
146. E.g. J. Moscoso to N. Mahy, 25 February 1810, SHM. CDB. 16/20/52; Conde de Noroña to P. de Rivero, n.d., AHN. Est. no. 77–A, no. 106.
147. E.g. report of F. Martínez, 24 May 1811, AGS. GJ. 1081; report of F. de Echavarri, 12 March 1812, AGS. GJ. 1087; G. Valdés to P. Romero, 15 August 1811, AGS. GJ. 1083.
148. Proclamation of the Junta Criminal Extraordinaria of Jaén, 13 August 1811, AGS. GJ. 1083.
149. Junta Criminal Extraordinaria de Guadalajara to P. Romero, 5 January 1812, AGS. GJ. 1087; for some Patriot complaints in similar vein, cf. Junta of Mataró to Junta of Catalonia, 11 September 1809, ACA. JSC. 71; Junta of Vich to Junta of Catalonia, 5 December 1811, ACA. JSC. 16.
150. R. Gutiérrez to Regency, 30 April 1811, AHN. Est. 3146.
151. Cf. Santos, *Bandolerismo en Andalucía*, pp. 216–25.
152. Blayney, *Narrative of a Forced Journey*, I, pp. 73–4.
153. Report of A. Picatoste, 6 April 1812, AGS. GJ. 1087; various reports, AGS. GJ. 1151.
154. F. Mesone to Junta of Catalonia, 26 June 1811, ACA. JSC. 16.
155. T. Bustamente to M. de Garay, 7 May 1809, AHN. Est. 80–L, no. 164.
156. Report of J. C. López, n.d., AGS. GJ. 1145; Rodríguez Solis, *Guerrilleros de 1808*, II, p. 44; report of P. García Triguero, 3 May 1812, AGS. GJ. 1087; report of J. R. de Zamalloa, 2 October 1811, AGS. GJ. 1084; report of J. Sánchez Mendoza, 9 January 1812, AGS. GJ. 1150; Espoz y Mina, *Memorias*, I, p. 178.
157. J. Heredia to F. Copons, 21 December 1810, RAH. 9:6967; R. Gutiérrez to I. de la Pezuela, 13 August 1812, AHN. Est. 3010; anon. report, 25 September 1811, AHN. Est. 3146; report of A. Amat de la Fortuna, 24 March 1812, AGS. GJ. 1145; report of J. Ibarrola, 21 April 1812, AGS. GJ. 1151.
158. F. J. de Castaños to J. Blake, 28 March 1810, SHM. CGB. 3/25.
159. A. de la Cuadra to J. Blake, 13 June 1810, SHM. CGB. 4/12.
160. A. de la Cuadra to F. Abadia, 13 June 1810, *ibid.*

161. *Ibid.*
162. Rocca, *Memoirs*, pp. 150–1.
163. R. de Mazariegos to A. Romero Valdés, 19 May 1810, AGS. GJ. 1086.
164. For some examples of attacks on British soldiers, cf. C. O'Neill, *The Military Adventures of Charles O'Neill, who was a Soldier in the Army of Lord Wellington during the Memorable Peninsular War and the Continental Campaigns from 1811 to 1815* (Worcester, Massachusetts, 1851), pp. 139, 145; W. Hay, *Remniscences under Wellington, 1808–1815*, ed. S. Wood (London, 1901), p. 70; Ludovici, *On the Road with Wellington*, p. 88; E. Costello, *The Adventures of a Soldier, or Memoirs of Edward Costello, K.S.F.* (London, 1841), pp. 220–1.
165. López Morán, *Bandolerismo Gallego*, pp. 357–70.
166. Report of F. Martínez, 24 May 1811, AGS. GJ. 1081; report of R. Moyano, 25 January 1812, AGS. GJ. 1180.
167. E.g. proclamation of Junta Criminal Extraordinaria de Sevilla, 30 January 1813, AGS. GJ. 1079.
168. For an example of a bandit with clear psychopathic tendencies, cf. Ortega, *Escuadras de Cataluña*, pp. 195–297.
169. Rodríguez Solis, *Guerrilleros de 1808*, I, v, p. 5.
170. *Ibid.*, I, vii, p. 15.
171. E.g. J. Martín Díez to Marqués de Zayas, 25 July 1811, AHN. Est. 3010; Espoz y Mina, *Memorias*, I, p. 48.
172. J. Crivell to M. de Garay, 5 September 1809, AHN. Est. 16–5^2, f. 40.
173. Rodríguez Solis, *Guerrilleros de 1808*, II, v, p. 20; report of G. Valdés, 17 June 1810, AGS. GJ. 1076.
174. Petition of M. García, 7 December 1811, AGS. GJ. 1080.
175. Report of Ministerio de Policía General, 5 August 1811, AGS. GJ. 1146.
176. Petition of M. Soribas, 22 August 1813, Archivo Municipal de Zaragoza, Serie General (hereafter AMZ. SG.) 869.
177. P. Palurcio to T. García Galindo, 7 June 1809, AGS. GJ. 1147; R. Santillán, *Memorias de Don Ramón Santillán (1808–1856)*, ed. A. Berazluce (Madrid, 1996), p. 50.
178. D. Martínez to J. Martín Díez, 13 April 1811, AHN. Est. 3010; J. R. Ruiz y Darmengol to M. Romero, 28 June 1811, AGS. GJ. 1082; P. Darripe to P. Arribas, 5 January 1812, AGS. GJ. 1151; P. Darripe to P. Arribas, 6 March 1811, AGS. GJ. 1146.
179. Cf. anon. to R. Gutiérrez, 1 April 1812, AHN. Est. 3010; A. Begines de los Ríos to A. González Salmón, 10 July 1811, AHN. Est. 3146; petition of F. Mateo, 21 June 1812, RAH. 9:6971.
180. Anon. to R. Gutiérrez, 23 March 1812, AHN. Est. 3010.
181. Petition of P. Cortes, 10 September 1812, AGS. GJ. 1080; petition of J. Coronado, 15 January 1812, AGS. GJ. 1150; petition of J. Martín, 27 January 1812, *ibid*; report of Junta Criminal Extraordinaria de Guadalajara, 31 May 1812, AGS. GJ. 1080. For some earlier cases, cf. petition of M. J. Micha, 9 July 1811, report of P. de Mora, 3 September 1811, AGS. GJ. 1150, and report of P. García Triguero, 3 May 1812, AGS. GJ. 1087.
182. E.g. F. Flevia to N. Mahy, 17 November 1809, SHM. CDB. 7/10/27.
183. Cf. Junta of Ciudad Rodrigo to Junta Central, 30 January 1809, AHN. Est. 41–E, no. 223; M. Renovales to the Junta of La Coruña, 24 August 1810, SHM. CDB. 16/20/58.

184. J. Miguel and others to M. de Garay, 5 October 1809, AHN. Est. 16–5[3], ff. 4–5.
185. E. Alonso (ed.), *Memorias del Alcalde de Roa, Don Gregorio González Arranz, 1788–1840* (Roa, 1995), pp. 23–4.
186. For some examples, cf. proclamation of General Kellermann, 12 February 1811, SHM. CDB. 19/23/83; Royal Decree, 7 August 1811, AGS. GJ. 1084; proclamation of General Dorsenne, 24 November 1811, BN. CGI. R60002–105.
187. Espoz y Mina, *Memorias*, I, pp. 147–55; Captain Berry to *Ayuntamiento* of Tudela, 9 July 1809, Archivo Municipal de Tudela, Sección de Cartas Históricas, 1809:5C–17.
188. Suchet, *Memoirs*, I, pp. 272–4. Cf. also Guimbaud, *Mémoires du Général Hugo*, p. 179.
189. F. Copons to J. O'Donnell, 10 May 1812, RAH. 9:6971.

5 The Reality of the Guerrillas

1. *Cit.* G. Chaliand, *The Art of War in World History: from Antiquity to the Nuclear Age* (Berkeley, California, 1994), pp. 733–4.
2. *Cit. ibid.*, pp. 664.
3. E.g. Bigarré, *Mémoires*, p. 278; Rocca, *Memoirs*, p. 89; Miot, *Mémoires* (Paris, 1858), III, pp. 56–8.
4. Marbot, *Memoirs*, II, pp. 70–1.
5. J. Serrano Valdenebro to J. M. Carvajal, 4 April 1811, *cit. Diario de Algeciras* (24 April 1811), pp. 357–61, HMM. AH227.
6. H. Christian to C. Cotton, 26 August 1811, PRO. WO.1/261, ff. 386–7.
7. Barthélemy, *El Marquesito*, I, pp. 75–6.
8. Tone, *Fatal Knot*, pp. 142–3.
9. J. A. Pérez-Rioja, 'Soria en la Guerra de la Independencia', in García Prado, *Estudios de la Guerra de la Independencia*, I, pp. 261–2.
10. D. Gascón, *La Provincia de Teruel en la Guerra de la Independencia* (Madrid, 1908), pp. 241–5.
11. Von Brandt, *The Two Minas*, pp. 56–67 *passim*. Author's italics.
12. For all this, cf. Espoz y Mina, *Memorias*, II, pp. 10–46; Alexander, *Rod of Iron*, pp. 203–23; Oman, *Peninsular War*, VI, pp. 252–74; Tone, *Fatal Knot*, pp. 141–5.
13. Lord Wellington to J. Villiers, 20 November 1809, PRO. WO.1/242, ff. 420–2.
14. Von Brandt, *The Two Minas*, pp. 68–9.
15. R. Gutiérrez to E. de Bardaji, 1 October 1811, AHN. Est. 3146.
16. Tone, *Fatal Knot*, p. 123.
17. Picado Franco, *Sexta División*, I, p. 70.
18. J. Díaz Porlier to N. Mahy, 25 March 1811, SHM. CDB. 25/36/24.
19. G. Walker to Lord Liverpool, 1 November 1810, PRO. WO.1/261, f. 114.
20. J. Johnston to G. Walker, 6 September 1811, PRO. WO.1/261, ff. 415–16; cf. also H. Douglas to Lord Liverpool, 7 September 1811, PRO. WO.1/261, f. 436.
21. Proclamation of El Empecinado, 14 August 1811, AGS. GJ. 1082.
22. A. Castillo to Minister of Police, 11 May 1812, AGS. GJ. 1080.
23. J. A. Colmenares to M. de Garay, n.d., AHN. Est. 16–2[3], f. 88.
24. J. Moscoso to N. Mahy, 14 February 1810, SHM. CDB. 16/20/52; G. Walker to Lord Liverpool, 1 November 1810, PRO. WO.1/261, ff. 115–16.
25. J. Moscoso to N. Mahy, 14 February 1810, SHM. CDB. 16/20/52.

26. J. Moscoso to N. Mahy, 11 March 1810, SHM. CDB. 16/20/52.
27. J. Moscoso to N. Mahy, 8 May 1810, SHM. CDB. 16/20/52; P. de la Barcena to J. Díaz Porlier, 9 April 1810, AMZ. CGP. 08187/26–1/545.
28. J. A. Colmenares to P. Rivero, 25 November 1809, AHN. Est. 41–E, no. 120.
29. H. Christian to C. Cotton, 26 August 1811, PRO. WO.1/261, f. 386.
30. R. Gutiérrez to E. Bardaji, 1 March 1811, AHN. 3146; anon. to R. Gutiérrez, 28 February 1811, *ibid.*
31. P. del Canto and B. Bonifaz to Junta Central, 4 December 1809, AHN. Est. 41–E, no. 127.
32. Cf. A. Cornel to M. de Garay, 30 August 1809, AHN. Est. 61–N, no. 206.
33. For some examples, cf. Junta of Quintana de la Sierra to Junta Central, 9 September 1809, AHN. Est. 65–G, no. 313; G. M. Ortiz de Nájera y Córdoba to Junta of Soto en Cameros, 8 November 1809, AHN. Est. 41–E, no. 105; J. B. Guergués to J. A. Colmenares, 2 November 1809, AHN. Est. 41–E, no. 107[1]; J. Arbizu to Marqués de Barriolucio, 20 November 1809, AHN. Est. 41–E, no. 114.
34. Cf. Report of E. López Blanco, 12 November 1809, AHN. Est. 41–E, no. 109; J. A. Colmenares to P. Rivero, 12 November 1809, AHN. Est. 41–E, no. 108.
35. 'Oficio sobre los excesos cometidos por la comisión de Soto y sus subdelegados' (MS.), AHN. Est. 41–E, no. 116[2]; Junta of Soto en Cameros to J. A. Colmenares, 14 November 1809, AHN. Est. 41–E, no. 110.
36. Cf. P. M. Garcés de los Fayos to J. A. Colmenares, 18 November 1809, AHN. Est. 41–E, no. 112; J. A. Colmenares to P. Rivero, 23 November 1809, AHN. Est. 41–E, no. 122.
37. P. Rivero to F. Saavedra, 14 and 17 December 1809, AHN. Est. 82–F, nos. 362–3; Picado, *Sexta División*, I, p. 17.
38. For all this, cf. petition of F. Longa, 11 July 1810, SHM. CDB. 14/19/41.
39. 'Villarcayo: información hecha por instancia del Sr. D. Francisco de Longa, comandante de la partida de voluntarios de Castilla autorizado por el Excmo. Sr. D. D. Nicolás Mahy, Teniente General de los reales ejércitos, sobre los acaecimientos en dicha villa con la partida al mando del titulado Campillo' (MS.), SHM. CDB. 4/19/41; I. Alonso to J. J. de la Riba, 2 July 1810, SHM. CDB. 17/21/62.
40. J. J. de la Riba to F. Longa, 21 July 1810, SHM. CDB. 17/21/62; N. Mahy to J. J. de la Riba, 3 August 1810, *ibid.*
41. R. Gutiérrez to E. de Bardaji, 12 February 1811, AHN. Est. 3010.
42. R. Gutiérrez to Regency, 8 August 1811, AHN. Est. 3146.
43. R. Gutiérrez to E. de Bardaji, 27 February 1812, AHN. Est. 3010.
44. *Cit.* A. Cornel to M. de Garay, 24 September 1809, AHN. Est. 41–C, no. 70.
45. Schepeler, *Histoire de la Révolution Espagnole*, III, p. 464.
46. R. Gutiérrez to Regency, 4 March 1812, AHN. Est. 3010. 'De tanto soy yo' defies translation: the literal meaning is 'how great I am'.
47. Pérez-Rioja, 'Soria en la Guerra de la Independencia', pp. 260–1.
48. Suchet, *Memoirs*, II, p. 281; Picado Franco, *Sexta División*, VI, pp. 130–5.
49. R. Gutiérrez to J. García de León y Pizarro, 30 May 1812, AHN. Est. 3010.
50. R. Gutiérrez to I. de la Pezuela, 7 July 1812, AHN. Est. 3010; H. Popham to Lord Wellington, 10 October 1812, US. WP.1/262. For these problems, cf. also Schepeler, *Histoire de la Révolution Espagnole*, III, p. 338.
51. J. Moscoso to N. Mahy, 8 May and 16 June 1810, SHM. CDB. 16/20/52.

52. A. de Capetillo to E. de Bardaji, 6 March 1811, AHN. Est. 3010.
53. Anon. to Rafael Gutiérrez, 23 March 1812, AHN. Est. 3010.
54. E.g. J. Martín Díez to Marqués de Zayas, 22 July 1811, AHN. Est. 3010.
55. F. M. Guerra to R. Gutiérrez, 6 April 1811, AHN. Est. 3010.
56. Anon. *The Military Exploits of Don Juan Martín Díez, the Empecinado, who first Commenced and then Organised the System of Guerrilla Warfare in Spain* (London, 1823), pp. 85–6, BS. CGA. 032589.
57. A. de Capetilla to E. de Bardaji, 16 July 1811, AHN. Est. 3010.
58. R. Gutiérrez to E. de Bardaji, 17 July 1811, *ibid; El Redactor General* (2 August 1811), p. 183, HMM. 6/3.
59. J. Martin Díaz to R. Gutiérrez, 23 April 1811, AHN. Est. 3146; cf. also petition of M. Ibarra, J. C. López and F. Martínez, 21 August 1811, *ibid.*
60. Marqués de Vivot to F. de Copons, 21 October 1812, RAH. 9:6972; D. O'Daly to F. de Copons, 1 November 1812, *ibid.*
61. F. Copons to J. O'Donnell, 2 May 1812, RAH. 9:6971.
62. F. Reig to F. Copons, 27 April 1812, RAH. 9:6971.
63. Espoz y Mina, *Memorias*, I, pp. 23–4.
64. *Ibid.*, pp. 12, 19.
65. Petition of M. de Valenza and C. Amatria, 18 October 1809, AHN. Est. 41–D, no. 78.
66. M. Loynaz to P. Rivero, 22 November 1809, AHN. Est. 15–2[4], ff. 70–4. It is worth comparing both these remarks and the ones that precede them with the complaints received by the French authorities; cf. petition of the *ayuntamiento* of Estella, 28 October 1809, AGS. GJ. 1078.
67. J. Moscoso to N. Mahy, 20 January 1811, SHM. CGB. 24/33/7; cf. also Junta of Orense to N. Mahy, 27 February 1811, *ibid.*
68. F. J. Losada to Junta of Asturias, 12 November 1810, SHM. CDB. 14/19/42.
69. Junta of Villafranca to Junta of Catalonia, 29 March 1810, ACA. JSC. 76.
70. Rodríguez Solis, *Guerrilleros de 1808*, I, viii, p. 33.
71. E.g. memorandum of P. Arribas, 7 April 1812, AGS. GJ. 1079; report of P. A. Calva, 2 January 1812, AGS. GJ. 1150; J. Sanjurjo to P. Arribas, 5 May 1812, *ibid*; for the execution of Echevarría, cf. Espoz y Mina, *Memorias*, I, p. 48.
72. G. de Bustamente and others to J. J. de la Riba, 14 July 1810, SHM. CDB. 17/21/62; cf. also Junta of Villarcayo to J. J. de la Riba, 15 July 1810, SHM. CDB. 17/21/62.
73. 'Manifiesto de los leales castellanos', 9 November 1812, US. WP.1/364; cf. also Lord Wellington to F. Longa, 20 January 1813, US. WP.1/364.
74. *Cit.* Iribarren, *Espoz y Mina, el Guerrillero*, p. 158.
75. E.g. F. Taboada to N. Mahy, 1 January 1810, SHM. CDB. 19/24/98.
76. Jiménez, *Queja de un patríota*; Picado, *Sexta División*, I, pp. 59–60.
77. J. Martín Díez to R. Gutiérrez, 23 April 1811, AHN. Est. 3146.
78. J. Díaz Porlier to N. Mahy, 23 March 1810, SHM. CDB. 16/20/56.
79. F. J. Losada to N. Mahy, 28 January 1811, SHM. CDB. 24/33/6.
80. Rodríguez Solis, *Guerrilleros de 1808*, I, v, p. 21.
81. Anon. report, 3 June 1811, AHN. Est. 3146.
82. A. Sáenz to Junta of Ciudad Real, 15 February 1809, AHN. Est. 40–A, no. 21.
83. 'Ordenanza que se había de observar en el principado de Asturias por todos los comandantes de partidas sueltas a quienes habilite el gobierno de el para obrar ofensivamente sobre el enemigo', 29 May 1810, SHM. CDB. 19/23/31.

84. Barthélemy, *El Marquesito*, pp. 76–160.
85. Cf. AHN. Est. 40–C, no. 61–263.
86. M. de Garay to A. Cornel, 30 September 1809, AHN. Est. 41–E, no. 154.
87. For some examples, cf. report of G. Valdés, 17 June 1810, AGS. GJ. 1046; report of P. de Mora, 6 April 1811, AGS. GJ. 1150; report of P. de Mora, 24 September 1811, AGS. GJ. 1146; report of Comisario General de Policia of Toledo, 19 June 1812, AGS. GJ. 1146; report of J. Paulón, 26 July 1812, AGS. GJ. 1149.
88. M. de Garano to P. Arribas, 23 August 1809, AGS. GJ. 1147; petition of T. J. Nuceta, 14 March 1810, AGS. GJ. 1163.
89. Espoz y Mina, *Memorias*, I, p. 237.
90. Lord Wellington to H. Wellesley, 10 March 1812, US. WP. 12/1/5.
91. Junta of Catalonia to C. Cotton, 6 July 1811, US. WP.1/343.
92. F. Adam to J. Murray, 24 March 1813, US. WP.1/368; memorandum of A. Puig, 4 May 1813, RAH. 9:6973.
93. Memorandum of C. Zehnpfenning, 1 January 1813, US. WP.1/368.
94. F. Copons to L. Wimpffen, 13 March 1813, RAH. 9:6973; Barón de Eroles to Lord Wellington, 5 February 1813, US. WP.1/366.
95. C. Zehnpfenning to Lord Wellington, 17 March 1813, US. WP.1/367.
96. T. Graham to H. Bunbury, 27 October 1810, PRO. WO.1/247, f. 629.
97. Anon., *Medios de salvar el reino* (Cádiz, 1810), pp. 5–9, BS. CGA. 038158.
98. J. Serrano Valdenebro to J. M. Carvajal, 4 April 1811, *cit. Diario de Algeciras* (24 April 1811), pp. 357–61, HMM. AH227.
99. Lord Wellington to Lord Castlereagh, 5 September 1808, US. WP.1/214.
100. Lord Wellington to J. H. Frere, 24 April 1809, US. WP.1/257; for an example of the sort of news that was being received of the guerrillas by the British in the summer of 1809, cf. J. H. Frere to G. Canning, 26 June 1809, Public Record Office, Foreign Office Papers 72/73, ff. 247–53.
101. Lord Wellington to Lord Wellesley, 1 September 1809, US. WP.1/277.
102. Lord Wellington to Lord Castlereagh, 25 August 1809, US. WP.1/275.
103. Memorandum of Lord Wellington, 11 November 1809, PRO. WO.1/242, ff. 416–22.
104. Lord Wellington to Lord Liverpool, 11 April 1810, PRO. WO.1/244, f. 62.
105. Lord Wellington to Lord Liverpool, 19 April 1810, PRO. WO.1/244, ff. 69–71.
106. Lord Wellington to Lord Liverpool, 19 February 1812, US. WP.12/1/5; cf. also Lord Wellington to Lord Liverpool, 13 May 1812, US. WP.12/1/5.
107. Cf. Lord Wellington to Lord Liverpool, 11 July 1810, PRO. WO.1/245, ff. 61–2.
108. Lord Wellington to Lord Liverpool, 18 June 1812, US. WP.1/347.
109. R. Gutiérrez to I. de la Pezuela, 11 August 1812, AHN. Est. 3010; for a less jaundiced view, cf. Marqués de Monsalud to Lord Wellington, 28 July 1812, US. WP.1/345.
110. Lord Wellington to H. Wellesley, 23 August 1812, US. WP.1/347.
111. I. Fletcher (ed.), *For King and Country: the Letters and Diaries of John Mills, Coldstream Guards, 1811–14* (Staplehurst, 1995), p. 231; Muñoz Maldonado, *Guerra de la Independencia*, III, pp. 308–10.
112. Lord Wellington to W. Cooke, 25 November 1812, US. WP.1/351.
113. For two discussions of these matters, cf. Esdaile, *The Duke of Wellington and the Command of the Spanish Army*, pp. 74–134 *passim*; C. Esdaile, 'Wellington and the

Spanish guerrillas: the campaign of 1813', *Consortium on Revolutionary Europe Proceedings*, XXI (1991), pp. 298–306.

114. Larpent, *Journal*, I, p. 234.
115. For this affair, cf. Esdaile, *The Duke of Wellington and the Command of the Spanish Army*, pp. 161–3.
116. For a discussion of these issues, cf. Esdaile, *Spanish Army*, pp. 177–200 *passim.*
117. 'Manifiesto de los leales castellanos', 9 November 1812, US. WP.1/364.
118. E.g. 'Informe de la Regencia anterior a las Cortes sobre la deserción', 5 March 1813, US. WP.1/382.
119. 'Exposición dirigida a las Cortes Generales y Extraordinarias sobre el estado de Aragón en junio de 1813', *cit. El Tribuno del Pueblo Español* (29 October 1813), HMM. AH1–4 (no. 123).

6 The End of the Guerrillas

1. For this affair, cf. *Military Exploits of Don Juan Martín Díez*, pp. 11–12.
2. Proclamation of Marqués del Socorro, 28 May 1808, SHM. CDF. DCCCLXIV.
3. Proclamation of Junta of Seville, n.d., SHM. CDF. DCCCLXIV.
4. Cassinello, *Juan Martín*, pp. 70–1.
5. Royal Decree, 28 December 1808, SHM. CDF. DCCLXXXVIII.
6. A. Cornel to M. de Garay, 24 September 1809, AHN. Est. 41–C, no. 70.
7. Duque del Parque to N. Mahy, 4 November 1809, SHM. CDB. 5/8/4.
8. F. J. Losada to N. Mahy, 25 November 1811, SHM. CDB. 14/19/45.
9. *Semanario Patriótico* (11 April 1811), HMM. AH1–6 (no. 197).
10. *El Periódico Militar del Estado Mayor General*, no. 13, *cit. El Redactor General* (9 April 1812), p. 1176, HMM. 6/3. Hussar regiments were traditionally used for such duties as skirmishing, raiding and reconnaissance.
11. Cf. *El Redactor General* (15 December 1812), HMM. 6/3.
12. 'Ordenanza que se había de observar en el Principado de Asturias por todos los comandantes de partidas sueltas a quienes habilite el gobierno de el para obrar ofensivamente sobre el enemigo', 29 May 1810, SHM. CDB. 19/23/81.
13. Proclamation of M. Renovales, n.d., AGS. GJ. 1146.
14. *DC*, 2 and 7 March 1811; for Espoz y Mina's own version of this affair, cf. Espoz y Mina, *Memorias*, I, pp. 108–17.
15. *DC*, 6 October 1810.
16. Cf. *ibid.*, 2 August 1811.
17. *Ibid.*, 2 March 1811.
18. For the liberals' views on the Spanish army and the need for people's war, cf. Esdaile, *Spanish Army*, pp. 158–9, 168–70.
19. *El Tribuno del Pueblo Español* (22 December 1812), pp. 206–7, HMM. AH1–4 (no. 120).
20. *El Patriota*, no. 1, HMM. AH.1–5 (no. 158).
21. *DC*, 10 August 1811.
22. *Ibid.*
23. *Ibid.*
24. *Semanario Patriótico* (31 October 1811), pp. 337–49, HMM. AH.1–6 (no. 198).
25. *El Español* (30 March 1812), HMM. AH4–2 (no. 713).

26. L. Baccigalupi, *Indicaciones acerca de la organización de las columnas volantes* (Cádiz, n.d.), BS. CGA. 041970.
27. 'Reglamento para las partidas de guerrilla', 11 July 1812, SHM. DG. 1812/4.
28. F. Ballesteros, *Respetuosos descargos que el Teniente General Don Francisco Ballesteros ofrece a la generosa nación española en contestación a los cargos que S.A. la Regencia del Reino se ha servido hacerle en su manifiesto del 12 de diciembre del año pasado de 1812 dirigido a la misma para su inteligencia* (Cádiz, 1813), pp. 21–2, SHM. CDF. CLIV.
29. 'Creación de nuevos cuerpos de caballería' (MS.), SHM. CDB. 3/4/31; for a protest at actions of this sort, cf. *El Redactor General*, HMM. 6/3.
30. Proclamation of N. Mahy, 3 July 1810, SHM. CDB. 17/21/62; J. Díaz Porlier to J. de la Riba, 12 September 1810, SHM. CDB. 19/23/87; P. Morillo to Consejo Permanente de Guerra, 4 June 1811, SHM. CDB. 3/6/34.
31. Oman, *Peninsular War*, III, p. 328; *Villa de Casares*, p. 32.
32. J. O'Donnell to F. Samper, 18 March 1812, RAH. 9:6971.
33. 'Instrucción que debera observar bajo la mas estrecha posibilidad las partidas de guerrillas', n.d., *ibid.*
34. Cf. F. Reig to F. Copons, 20 May 1812, *ibid.*
35. J. O'Donnell to F. Copons, 3 May 1812, *ibid.*
36. F. Copons to J. O'Donnell, 6, 10 and 14 May 1812, *ibid.*
37. F. Copons to J. J. Barrera, 20 May 1812, *ibid.*
38. J. J. Barrera to F. Copons, 5 June 1812, *ibid.*
39. F. Reig to F. Copons, 23 June 1812, *ibid.*
40. F. Reig to F. Copons, 17 July 1812, *ibid.*
41. J. J. Barrera to F. Copons, 29 June and 18 July 1812, *ibid.*
42. J. J. Barrera to F. Copons, 22 July 1812, *ibid.*
43. J. J. Barrera to F. Copons, 8 August 1812, *ibid.*
44. J. J. Barrera to F. Copons, 14 September 1812, *ibid.*
45. J. J. Barrera to F. Copons, 13 September 1812, *ibid.*
46. E.g. J. Martín Díez to R. Gutiérrez, 16 March 1811, AHN. Est. 3146.
47. R. Gutiérrez to Regency, 30 April 1811, AHN. Est. 3146.
48. R. Gutiérrez to E. de Bardaji, 4 March 1812, AHN. Est. 3010.
49. E.g. M. Cano to E. de Bardaji, 4 April 1812, AHN. Est. 3010.
50. *Military Exploits of Don Juan Martín Díez*, pp. 135–6; A. Leith-Hay to R. Hill, 24 January 1813, US. WP.1/364.
51. Barthélemy, *El Marquésito*, I, pp. 329–35.
52. E. Mejía to Lord Wellington, 7 December 1812, US. WP.1/354; Lord Wellington to J. M. de Carvajal, 11 December 1812, US. WP.1/363.
53. Ludovici, *On the Road with Wellington*, p. 324.
54. Conde de Penne Villemur to Lord Wellington, 28 February 1813, US. WP.1/366.
55. I. Fletcher (ed.), *In the Service of the King: the Letters of William Thornton Keep at Home, Walcheren and in the Peninsula, 1808–1814* (Staplehurst, 1997), p. 144.
56. Cf. Junta of Burgos to Lord Wellington, 9 June 1813, US. WP.1/371.
57. E.g. F. Espoz y Mina to F. J. Castaños, 12 March 1813, US. WP.1/368.
58. R. Escobeda to Lord Wellington, 8 March 1813, US. WP.1/367; A. Guillén to Lord Wellington, 27 February 1813, US. WP.1/382; *Diario de Gobierno de Sevilla* (22 March 1813), pp. 769–70, SHM. CDF. CXL.
59. R. Escobeda to Lord Wellington, 12 March 1813, US. WP.1/367.

60. J. Tone, 'The Peninsular War', in P. Dwyer (ed.), *Napoleon and Europe* (London, 2001), pp. 240–1.
61. *El Conciso* (15 January 1813), HMM. AH.2–5 (no. 348).
62. *Diario de Gobierno de Sevilla* (11 February 1813), SHM. CDF. CXXXIX.
63. 'La Carlota' was the nickname of Fernando VII's elder sister Carlota Joaquina, who was married to the heir to the throne of Portugal, Prince João, and in consequence possessed the title Princess of Brazil. A bitter opponent of revolution, she became the chief hope of the enemies of the liberal cause in Spain, and was much favoured by them as the head of a reactionary regency that could steer the Patriot cause in a direction opposed to the one which it had taken since 1810.
64. *El Tribuno del Pueblo Español* (23 March 1813), HMM. AH.1–4 (No. 121).
65. *DC* (5 October 1812).
66. *Diario Crítico y Erúdito de Granada* (10 March 1813), pp. 37–8, HMM. AH5–5 (no. 1046); *El Redactor General* (12 March 1813), p. 2561, HMM. 6/3.
67. *El Conciso* (1 April 1813), pp. 3–5, HMM. AH2–5 (no. 351).
68. Pérez Garzón, *Milicia Nacional y Revolución Burguesa*, p. 80.
69. Lord Wellington to J. M. de Carvajal, 4 December 1812, US. WP.1/355.
70. For the situation of Spain in the winter of 1812–13, cf. Esdaile, *Peninsular War*, pp. 431–9.
71. For all this, cf. L. Picado Franco, *Memorias sobre la reconquista de Zaragoza, conservación de la plaza y rendición de su castillo por las tropas españolas en julio de 1813, donde se evidencia lo mucho que se equivocó el autor de la comedia titulada 'Zaragoza reconquistada por Don Francisco Espoz y Mina', como también otros autores que han dado toda la gloria a este general* (Madrid, 1815), pp. 31–65, BUZ. 52/1037; Picado Franco, *Sexta División*, II, pp. 192–8.
72. Casamayor, 'Años Políticos y Históricos', XXX (1813), f. 255, BUZ. MS.136.
73. Espoz y Mina, *Memorias*, II, pp. 73–9.
74. Anon., *Resumen Histórico de los Sacrificios y Desgracias de Aragón, Principalmente en su Orilla Izquierda del Ebro desde la Rendición de Zaragoza hasta su Reconquista* (Zaragoza, 1813), pp. 12–15 *passim*, AMZ. G5757.
75. *Ibid.*, pp. 18–27 *passim*.
76. Ludovici, *On the Road with Wellington*, pp. 386–7.
77. Espoz y Mina, *Memorias*, I, pp. 292–3.
78. *Ibid.*, II, pp. 15–16.
79. Cf. AMZ. Ayto. Actas del Ilustrísimo Ayuntamiento de Zaragoza, Vol. 119 (July–December, 1813), f. 170; Ayuntamiento de Zaragoza to J. M. Colubri, 11 October 1813, AMZ. Ayto. Serie General, Caja 869.
80. Cf. Anon. *Relación de los sucesos ocurridos en Sos del Rey Católico durante la Guerra de la Independencia*, n.d., AMZ. CGP. 08145/1–10/6; AMZ. Ayto. Actas, Vol. 119, f. 96.
81. Iribarren, *Espoz y Mina, el Liberal*, pp. 156–7.
82. Casamayor, 'Años Políticos e Históricos', XXX, f. 272.
83. F. Espoz y Mina to *ayuntamiento* of Zaragoza, 21 Ocotber 1813, AMZ. Ayto. 869.
84. *Ibid.*, f. 273; L. Wimpffen to Lord Wellington, 26 October 1813, US. WP.1/389.
85. Casamayor, 'Años políticos e históricos', XXX (1813), f. 278, BUZ. MS.136.
86. Iribarren, *Espoz y Mina, el Liberal*, pp. 193–6.
87. Espoz y Mina, *Memorias*, II, p. 102.
88. Glover, *Gentleman Volunteer*, p. 133.

89. Lord Wellington to J. O'Donoju, 7 December 1813, US. WP.1/381.
90. Petition of J. L. Fernández, 31 December 1813, ACD. SG. 19, No. 35.
91. F. Diz to J. O'Donoju, 15 June 1813, SHM. CGI. 4/32.
92. Proclamation of the commandant-general of Jaén, 15 June 1813, BN. CGI. R60016–23.
93. Sánchez Fernández, *Nos Invaden!*, pp. 34–6.
94. *DC* (3 July 1813).
95. *DC* (18 October 1813).
96. Royal Decree, 26 November 1813, *cit. El Imparcial: Diario Político y Militar de la Ciudad de Alicante* (27–29 December 1813), SHM. CDF. CCLV.
97. M. Ballbé, *Orden Público y Militarismo en la España Constitucional, 1812–1983* (Madrid, 1985), p. 57.
98. For the formation of the National Guard, cf. Esdaile, *Spanish Army*, p. 173; Pérez Garzón, *Milicia Nacional y Revolución Burguesa*, pp. 81–4.
99. *DC* (24 November 1812).
100. E.g. petitions of F. Sánchez Tercero and A. Carabantes, 13 March 1813, ACD. SG. 17, no. 38[13]; petitions of J. Guerra and A. Luque, 14 February 1813, ACD. SG. 17, no. 38[14]; petition of *ayuntamiento* of Carmona, 21 February 1813, ACD. SG. 17, no. 38[15].
101. Royal Decree, 15 April 1814, ACD. SG. 1, No. 60/III–73.
102. Royal Decree, 28 July 1814, *cit.* Espoz y Mina, *Memorias*, II, pp. 158–61.
103. Best, *War and Society in Revolutionary Europe*, p. 174.
104. M. Pintos Vieites, *La Política de Fernando VII entre 1814 y 1820* (Pamplona, 1958), pp. 256–7.
105. Ardit, *Revolución Liberal y Rebeldía Campesina*, pp. 229–40.
106. López Morán, *Bandolerismo Gallego*, pp. 55–7, 173–209 *passim.*
107. C. García Rodríguez, *Historias de Bandoleros Aragoneses* (Huesca, 2000), p. 33.
108. F. Flores, *El Bandolerismo en Extremadura* (Badajoz, 1992), pp. 15–42, 141–51 *passim.*
109. P. Casado, *Las Fuerzas Armadas en el Inicio del Constitucionalismo Español* (Madrid, 1982), p. 90.
110. Lovett, *Napoleon and the Birth of Modern Spain*, p. 720.
111. L. Fernández Martín, *El General Don Francisco de Longa y la Intervención Española en Portugal, 1826–27* (Bilbao, 1954), p. 42; Ardit, *Revolución Liberal y Rebeldía Campesina*, pp. 213–17.
112. S. Payne, *Politics and the Military in Modern Spain* (Stanford, California, 1967), p. 17.
113. 'Estado militar de España; año de 1815' in *Kalendario Manual y Guia de Forasteros en Madrid para el Año de 1815* (Madrid, 1815), BS. CGA. 016638.
114. *Ibid.*
115. For Sarasa and Alegre, cf. Guirao, *Guerrilleros y Patriotas*, pp. 66–7, 119–20.
116. For a discussion of the financial problems faced by the regime of Fernando VII, cf. J. Fontana, *La Quiebra de la Monarquía Absoluta, 1814–1820: la Crisis del Antiguo Régimen en España* (Barcelona, 1971), pp. 51–70.
117. Tone, *Fatal Knot*, pp. 172–6; for some interesting contemporary remarks, cf. A. Berazaluce (ed.), *Memorias de la Vida de Don Pedro Agustín Girón* (Pamplona, 1978), II, pp. 14–17; F. Whittingham (ed.), *A Memoir of the Services of Lieutenant General Sir Samuel Ford Whittingham* (London, 1868), p. 367.

118. For an excellent discussion of Espoz y Mina's role in the exile community, cf. I. Castells, *La Utopia Insurreccional del Liberalismo: Torrijos y las Conspiraciones Liberales de la Década Ominosa* (Barcelona, 1989), pp. 113–65 *passim*.
119. Barthélemy, *El Marquesito*, I, pp. 375–424; *ibid.*, II, pp. 427–90; E. González López, *Entre el Antiguo y el Nuevo Régimen: Absolutistas y Liberales – el Reinado de Fernando VII en Galicia* (La Coruña, 1980), pp. 38–56 *passim*.
120. Cassinello, *Juan Martín*, pp. 253–310 *passim*.

Conclusion

1. For some up-to-the-minute examples, cf. G. Rothenberg, *The Napoleonic Wars* (London, 1999), pp. 154–5; J. Black, *Western Warfare, 1775–1882* (London, 2001), pp. 48–9; Tone, 'The Peninsular War', pp. 235–42.
2. Cf. H. Ward, *Between the Lines: Banditti of the American Revolution* (London, 2002).
3. A. Grab, 'State power, brigandage and rural resistance in Napoleonic Italy', *European History Quarterly*, XXV, no. 1 (January, 1995), p. 40.
4. M. Finley, *Most Monstrous of Wars: the Napoleonic Guerrilla War in Southern Italy, 1806–1811* (Columbia, South Carolina, 1994), p. 147.
5. Aymes, *Guerra de la Independencia* (Madrid, 1975), p. 57.
6. Lovett, *Napoleon and the Birth of Modern Spain*, II, p. 672.
7. Cf. A. Forrest, *Napoleon's Men: the Soldiers of the Revolution and Empire* (London, 2002).
8. Cf. Lovett, *Napoleon and the Birth of Modern Spain*, II, p. 677.
9. F. J. Castaños to Lord Wellington, 27 June 1813, US. WP.1/371.
10. Lovett, *Napoleon and the Birth of Modern Spain*, II, p. 691.
11. Carr, *Spain, 1808–1975*, p. 109.
12. I. Burdiel, 'The liberal revolution, 1808–1843' in J. Alvarez Junco and A. Shubert (eds), *Spanish History since 1808* (London, 2000), p. 20.
13. Best, *War and Society in Revolutionary Europe*, pp. 175–6.
14. Aymes, *Guerra de la Independencia*, pp. 56–63 *passim*.
15. *Ibid.*, p. 64.
16. Cf. R. del Río, *Los Orígenes de la Guerra Carlista en Navarra, 1820–1824* (Pamplona, 1987), pp. 57–65.
17. Rothenberg, *Napoleonic Wars*, p. 155.
18. D. Gates, *The Napoleonic Wars, 1803–1815* (London, 1996), p. 190.
19. S. Woolf, *Napoleon's Integration of Europe* (London, 1991), pp. 233–5.
20. For Chartrand's remarks, cf. R. Chartrand, 'The guerrillas: how Wellington underestimated the role of irregular forces', in P. Griffith (ed.), *A History of the Peninsular War, IX: Modern Studies of the War in Spain and Portugal, 1808–1814* (London, 1999), p. 162.
21. Lovett, *Napoleon and the Birth of Modern Spain*, II, p. 720; cf. also Carr, *Spain*, p. 109.
22. J. Black, *European Warfare, 1660–1815* (New Haven, Connecticut, 1994), pp. 232–3.
23. E.g. Grab, 'State power, brigandage and rural resistance', p. 64.
24. Cf. F. J. Hernández Montalbán, *La Abolición de los Señorios en España, 1811–1837* (Valencia, 1999), pp. 161–81; Ardit, *Revolución Liberal y Revuelta Campesina*, pp.

219–25; A. Bernal, *La Lucha por la Tierra en la Crisis del Antiguo Régimen* (Madrid, 1979), p. 118; S. de Moxo, *La Disolución del Régimen Señorial en España* (Madrid, 1965), pp. 56–60.

25. Petition of *ayuntamiento* of Cartaya, 6 November 1813, ACD. SG. 15/59.
26. López Morán, *Bandolerismo Gallego*, p. 173.
27. Ballbé, *Orden Público y Militarismo*, p. 141.
28. For a discussion of the impact of the War of Independence on the political outlook of the Spanish army, cf. Esdaile, *Spanish Army*, pp. 194–200.
29. Burdiel, 'Liberal revolution', p. 19.
30. Anon., *Observaciones sobre los atentados de la Cortes Extraordinarias de Cádiz contra las leyes fundamentales de la monarquía española y sobre la nulidad de la constitución que formaron* (Madrid, 1814), p. 15, BS. CGA. 041437.

Glossary

afrancesado	literally, 'frenchified one'; supporter of Joseph Bonaparte
afrancesamiento	literally, 'frenchification'; sympathy with, or an attempt to implement, French models, especially those of the Napoleonic empire
alarma	Galician home guard
alcalde mayor	local magistrate
alférez	ensign
alistados	recruits
amo	landlord; boss
antiguo régimen	*ancien régime*; old order
apodo	nickname
apostólicos	hardline traditionalists (post 1823)
ayuntamiento	town hall; town council; municipality
bienes nacionales	literally, 'national properties'; property expropriated from the Church, the municipalities or, more rarely, political opponents
cabecilla	bandit or guerrilla chieftain
cacique	landowner or other local notable possessed of sufficient economic power to be able to exert political influence in his locality
campesino	literally, 'countryman'; in practice, a generic term used to describe all those sectors of the rural lower classes engaged in agriculture
canalla vil	scum; rabble
caudillo	leader; commander
cazadores rurales	literally, 'country riflemen'; one of many terms used by the French to describe their irregular Spanish auxiliaries
cédula de crédito	credit bond issued under Joseph Bonaparte
comandante de armas	military commandant

comisario regio	royal commissioner
comisionados	agents; commissioners
consejo	council (usually administrative)
contribución única	literally, 'the single contribution'; new system of taxation introduced by the *cortes* of Cádiz
corregidor	city governor-cum-chief magistrate appointed by the monarch prior to 1808
cortes	parliament
cuadrilla	gang, especially of bandits
desamortización	expropriation and/or sale of entailed land
dispersos	stragglers
fuero militar	privileges enjoyed by Bourbon officer corps prior to 1808
fueros	traditional rights/privileges/codes of justice
gaditano	inhabitant of/pertaining to Cádiz
godoyismo	term of abuse associated with the royal favourite, Manuel de Godoy; corruption; decadence; vain-glory
guerrilla, la	literally, 'little war'; the guerrilla struggle against the French
guerrillero	guerrilla
hacendados	landowners; used colloquially, the rich in general
herederos	property owners
jefe político	literally, 'political head'; provincial governor appointed under the constitution of 1812
josefino	supporter of Joseph Bonaparte; pertaining to Bonaparte Spain
junta	committee of government or administration
junta militar	advisory council of generals established by the Junta Central
juramentado	literally, 'sworn one'; Spanish official or, more usually, soldier in the service of Joseph Bonaparte
labrador	landowner; prosperous tenant farmer
licenciados	graduates
madrileño	inhabitant of/pertaining to Madrid
malagueño	inhabitant of/pertaining to Málaga
malhechor	literally, 'wrongdoer'; criminal bandit
mariscal de campo	major-general (often mistranslated as field marshal)
migueletes	in Catalonia, volunteer infantry regiments raised by the provisional junta in 1808; in the Basque provinces, an irregular local home guard
milicias honradas	urban militia recruited solely from the propertied classes by order of the Junta Central
minifundia	very small farms typical of Galicia
montaña	literally, 'the mountain'; the name given to northern Navarre

mozo	young unmarried man of military age
partida	guerrilla band
partidarios	alternative term for guerrillas
personalismo	politics resting wholely on clientage or personal ambition
poderoso	literally 'powerful one'; bigwig; local notable
populacho	literally, 'the mob'; the lower classes
pretendiente	office-seeker
pudiente	local notable; *cacique*
pueblo	town or village, but also the people
quinta	conscript; levy of conscripts
real	basic unit of Spanish currency prior to 1870
regidor perpetuo	hereditary town councillor for life
resguardo	locally organised pre-1808 anti-bandit security forces
rey deseado, el	literally, 'the desired king'; i.e., Fernando VII
rey intruso, el	literally, 'the intrusive king'; i.e., Joseph Bonaparte
ribera	literally, 'the riverside'; that part of Navarre lying in the Ebro valley
señorialismo	Spanish feudal system
serranía	mountainous district
serrano	literally, 'mountaineer'; term applied to the inhabitants of the Serranía de Ronda
sevillano	inhabitant of/pertaining to Seville
siempre, los de	literally, 'the same ones as always'; i.e., the established local oligarchy
somatén	Catalan home guard
sorteo	ballot for military service
tercios reales	literally, 'royal thirds'; share of the title claimed by the Spanish state
valenciano	inhabitant of/pertaining to Valencia
vallesoletano	inhabitant of/pertaining to Valladolid
vecino	literally, 'neighbour'; propertied tax-payer
vecinos honrados	literally, 'honourable inhabitant'; householder
vida a salto de mata	literally, 'a life of jumping out from behind bushes'; a life of crime
voluntario distinguido	literally, 'distinguished volunteer'; recruit funding the cost of his own uniform and weapons
yunteros	landless labourer possessed of a yoke of oxen or mules
zaragozano	inhabitant of/pertaining to Zaragoza

Bibliography

A. Archival Sources

Archivo del Congreso de Diputados, Madrid

Serie General, Legajos 1, 15, 17, 19, 30
Serie de Papeles Reservados de Fernando VII, Vol. 52

Archivo de la Corona de Aragón, Barcelona

Sección de la Junta Superior de Cataluña, Legajos 4, 16, 43, 68, 71, 74, 76, 88

Archivo General de Simancas

Sección de Gracia y Justicia, Legajos 1076–87, 1145–51, 1163

Archivo Histórico Nacional, Madrid

Sección de Estado, Legajos 5, 15–17, 30–1, 33, 38–41, 46, 52, 60, 62, 65, 70, 72, 74–5, 77, 80–3, 2959, 2994, 3010, 3146, 3566

Archivo Municipal de Tudela

Sección de Cartas Históricas, 1809:5C-17

Archivo Municipal de Zaragoza

Actas Municipales, Vol. 119
Serie General, Cajas 27, 868–70
Colección General Palafox 08145, 08147, 08165, 08174, 08179, 08187

Biblioteca Nacional, Madrid

Colección Gómez Imaz, Vols R60002, R60034, R60124, R60129, R60140, R62280, R63078, R63928

Biblioteca del Senado, Madrid

Colección Gómez de Arteche, Vols 011166, 011634, 011867, 011961, 016544, 017057, 028477, 029083, 031030, 032589, 032605, 032675, 035255, 038158, 039809, 039854, 040126, 040270, 040325, 040458, 040733, 041437, 041478, 041970, 041996, 042062, 042070, 042092, 042094, 043523

Biblioteca de la Universidad de Zaragoza

F. Casamayor, 'Años políticos y históricos de las cosas mas particulares occuridas en la imperial, augusta y siempre heróica ciudad de Zaragoza', MSS. 106–42

British Library, London

Additional MSS. 37286–9, 37291–3, 37314, 38243–4, 38246–7, 38249–55, 64131

Public Record Office, Kew

(a) War Office Papers, Series 1, Vols 226–7, 229–52, 260–1
(b) Foreign Office Papers, Series 72, Vols 71, 73, 75, 108, 112, 121, 128, 131–3, 142–7, 150–5, 159–60

Real Academia de Historia, Madrid

Legajos 9:6964–73; 11:9003

Real Colegio de San Albano, Valladolid

R. Brindle, 'Memoirs: a Brief Account of Travels, etc., in Spain' (MS)

Servicio Histórico Militar, Madrid

(a) Colección Documental del Fraile, Vols XXVII, XXXII–XLI, CX, CXIV–CXVII, CXXXII–CLXIV, CXCI, CCLX, CCLIII–CCLXVIII, CCCXXXVI–CCCLI, CDLII–CDLXVII, DXL, DCXLVII–DCCLXIII, DCCLXXXIX, DCCXCI, DCCCLXIV, CMVIII, CMXXII
(b) Colección Duque de Bailén, Carpetas 1/2/2, 1/2/8, 3/2/4, 3/4/23–4, 3/4/28, 3/4/32, 3/6/34, 4/2/10, 4/7/25, 5/8/1–10, 7/10/25–7, 12/16/11, 13/17/29–30, 14/10/41–5, 14/18/38, 16/20/51–3, 16/20/56, 16/20/58, 16/20/60, 17/21/61, 17/21/65, 17/21/67, 18/22/71–9, 19/23/81,

19/23/83, 19/23/85, 19/23/87, 19/23/89–90, 19/24/94, 19/24/96, 19/24/98, 24/33/0, 24/33/6–8, 25/34/24, 32/49/21, 32/49/23, 33/53/59, 34/52/53, 36/54/1
(c) Colección General Blake, Carpetas 1/19, 2/14, 2/21, 2/23–4, 3/2–4, 3/12, 3/18, 3/25, 3/28, 4/12, 4/17, 4/26
(d) Colección Guerra de la Independencia 2/1–3, 2/10, 3/30–4, 4/8, 4/22–3, 4/28, 4/32–4, 4/36–43

University of Southampton

Wellington Papers, Vols 1/205, 1/207–14, 1/216, 1/264–7, 1/269, 1/274–7, 1/284, 1/290–5, 1/297–8, 1/311, 1/315, 1/331–2, 1/341–56, 1/358–83, 1/387–420, 1/439–45, 1/447, 12/1/1–3, 12/1/5, 12/2/3

B. Published Contemporary Sources

(a) Official Publications, Documentary Collections, etc.

Constitución Política de la Nación Española (Cádiz, 1812)
Correspondance de Napoléon I publiée par ordre de l'Empéreur Napoléon III (Paris, 1858–69)
The Croker Papers: the Correspondence and Diaries of the Right Honourable John Wilson Croker, LL.D, F.R.S., Secretary to the Admiralty from 1809 to 1830, ed. L. Jennings (London, 1884)
Diario de las Sesiones y Actas de las Cortes Generales y Extraordinarias (Cádiz, 1810–13)
The Dispatches and Correspondence of the Marquess Wellesley during his Mission to Spain as Ambassador Extraordinary to the Supreme Junta in 1809, ed. M. Martin (London, 1838)
The Dispatches of Field Marshal the Duke of Wellington during his various Campaigns in India, Denmark, Portugal, Spain, the Low Countries and France from 1789 to 1815, ed. J. Gurwood (London, 1852)
Estados de la Organización y Fuerza de los Ejércitos Españoles Beligerantes en la Península durante la Guerra de España contra Napoleón Bonaparte Arreglados por la Sección de Historia Militar en 1821 (Barcelona, 1822)
Guerra de la Independencia: Proclamas, Bandos y Combatientes, ed. S. Delgado (Madrid, 1979)
Kalendario Manual y Guía de Forasteros en Madrid (Madrid, 1807, 1815)
Mémoires et Correspondance Politique et Militaire du Roi Joseph, ed. P. du Casse (Paris, 1853–4)
Ordenanzas de S.M. para el Régimen, Disciplina, Subordinación y Servicio de sus Ejércitos (Madrid, 1768)
Supplementary Despatches, Correspondence and Memoranda of Field Marshal Arthur, Duke of Wellington, ed. Second Duke of Wellington (London, 1858–72)

(b) Newspapers, Gazettes, etc

Atalaya de la Mancha en Madrid (Madrid, 1813–14)
Correo de Murcia (Murcia, 1809)
Correo de Valencia (Valencia, 1811)
Diario Crítico y Erudito de Granada (Granada, 1813)
Diario de Badajoz (Badajoz, 1808–9)
Diario de Gobierno de Sevilla (Seville, 1812–13)
Diario de Granada (Granada, 1808–9)
Diario de la Tarde (Cádiz, 1813)
Diario de Málaga (Málaga, 1808–9)
Diario Mercantil de Cádiz (Cádiz, 1813)
Diario Redactor de Sevilla (Seville, 1812–13)
El Censor General (Cádiz, 1812)
El Ciudadano por la Constitución (La Coruña, 1813)
El Conciso (Cádiz, Madrid, 1812–14)
El Duende de los Cafées (Cádiz, 1813)
El Español (Cádiz, London, 1810–14)
El Español Libre (Cádiz, 1813)
El Fanal (Seville, 1812)
El Imparcial (Alicante, 1813)
El Patriota (Cádiz, 1812–13)
El Redactor General (Cádiz, 1811–14)
El Tío Tremendo o los Críticos del Malecón (Cádiz, 1813)
El Tribuno del Pueblo Español (Cádiz, 1812–13)
Gazeta de La Coruña (La Coruña, 1808)
Gazeta de la Junta Superior de la Mancha (Cuenca, 1811–12)
Gazeta de la Regencia de España e Indias (Cádiz, Madrid, 1810–14)
Gazeta del Gobierno (Madrid, Seville, 1808–10)
La Abeja Española (Cádiz, 1812–13)
Los Amigos de Ballesteros (Isla de León, 1813)
Los Ingleses en España (Seville, 1813)
Memorial Militar y Patriótico del Ejército de la Izquierda (Badajoz, 1810)
Semanario Patriótico (Madrid, Seville, Cádiz, 1808–12)
Semanario Político, Histórico y Literario de La Coruña (La Coruña, 1809–10)

(c) Memoirs, Diaries and Contemporary Accounts

A. Alcaide, *Historia de los Dos Sitios que Pusieron a Zaragoza en los Años de 1808 y 1809* (Madrid, 1830)
A. Alcalá Galiano (ed.), *Memorias de D. Antonio Alcalá Galiano* (Madrid, 1886)
A. Alcalá Galiano, *Recuerdos de un Anciano* (Madrid, 1907)
E. Alonso (ed.), *Memorias del Alcalde de Roa, Don Gregorio González Arranz, 1788–1840* (Roa, 1995)

A. Alvarez Valdés, *Memorias del Levantamiento de Asturias en 1808*, ed. M. Fuertes Acevedo (Oviedo, 1889)
Anon., *The Military Exploits of Don Juan Martín Díez, the Empecinado* (London, 1825)
Anon., *Memoirs of a Sergeant Late in the Forty-Third Light Infantry Regiment, previously to and during the Peninsular War* (London, 1835)
A. Argüelles, *La Reforma Constitucional de Cádiz*, ed. J. Longares (Madrid, 1970)
C. Atkinson (ed.), 'A Light Dragoon in the Peninsular War: extracts from the letters of Captain Lovell Badcock, Fourteenth Light Dragoons, 1809–14', *JSAHR*, XXXIV, no. 138, pp. 70–9
C. Atkinson (ed.), 'A Peninsular brigadier: letters of Major General Sir F. P. Robinson, K.C.B., dealing with the campaign of 1813', *JSAHR*, XXXIV, no. 140, pp. 153–70
G. Bankes (ed.), *The Autobiography of Sergeant William Lawrence, a Hero of the Peninsular and Waterloo Campaign* (London, 1886)
R. Batty, *Campaign of the Left Wing of the Allied Army in the Western Pyrenees and the South of France in the Years 1813 and 1814 under Field Marshal the Marquess of Wellington* (London, 1825)
M. de Baudus, *Etudes sur Napoléon* (Paris, 1841)
G. Bell, *Rough Notes of an Old Soldier*, ed. B. Stuart (London, 1956)
N. Bentley (ed.), *Selections from the Reminiscences of Captain Gronow* (London, 1977)
A. Berazaluce (ed.), *Recuerdos de la Vida de Don Pedro Agustín Girón* (Pamplona, 1978)
A. Bigarré, *Mémoires du Général Bigarré, Aide de Camp du Roi Joseph, 1775–1813* (Paris, 1903)
J. Blanco White, *Cartas de España*, ed. V. Llorens and A. Garnica (Madrid, 1972)
A. Blayney, *Narrative of a Forced Journey through Spain and France as a Prisoner of War in the Years 1810 to 1814* (London, 1814)
S. Blaze, *Mémoires d'un Apothécaire sur la Guerre d'Espagne pendant les Années 1808 à 1814* (Paris, 1828)
C. Boutflower, *The Journal of an Army Surgeon during the Peninsular War* (Manchester, 1912)
H. von Brandt, *The Two Minas and the Spanish Guerrillas* (London, 1825)
E. Buckham, *Personal Narrative of Adventures in the Peninsula during the War in 1812–1813 by an Officer late in the Staff-Corps Regiment of Cavalry* (London, 1827)
R. Buckley (ed.), *The Napoleonic War Journal of Captain Thomas Henry Browne* (London, 1987)
T. Bunbury, *Reminiscences of a Veteran, being Personal and Military Adventures in Portugal, Spain, France, Malta, Norfolk Island, New Zealand, Anderman Islands and India* (London, 1861)
C. Cadell, *Narrative of the Campaigns of the Twenty-Eighth Regiment since their Return from Egypt in 1802* (London, 1835)

J. Canga Argüelles, *Observaciones sobre la Historia de la Guerra de España que Escribieron los Señores Clarke, Southey, Londonderry y Napier* (Madrid, 1833–6)

J. C. Carnicero, *Historia Razonada de los Principales Sucesos de la Gloriosa Revolución de España* (Madrid, 1814)

F. Carr Gomm (ed.), *Letters and Journals of Field Marshal Sir William Maynard Gomm, G.C.B., Commander-in-Chief of India, Constable of the Tower of London, etc., etc., from 1799 to Waterloo, 1815* (London, 1881)

S. Cassels (ed.), *Peninsular Portrait, 1811–1814: the Letters of Captain William Bragge, Third (King's Own) Dragoons* (London, 1963)

J. Cooper, *Rough Notes of Seven Campaigns in Portugal, Spain, France and America during the Years of 1809–10–11–12–13–14–15* (London, 1869)

E. Costello, *The Adventures of a Soldier, or Memoirs of Edward Costello, K.S.F.* (London, 1841)

J. Dellard, *Mémoires Militaires du Général Baron Dellard* (Paris, n.d.)

J. Donaldson, *Recollections of the Eventful Life of a Soldier* (Edinburgh, 1852)

R. Douglas (ed.), *From Valmy to Waterloo: Extracts from the Diary of Captain Charles François, a Soldier of the Revolution and Empire* (London, 1906)

F. Espoz y Mina, *Memorias del General Don Francisco Espoz y Mina, Escritas por El Mismo*, ed. J. M. de Vega (Madrid, 1851)

W. Fernyhough, *Military Memoirs of Four Brothers (Natives of Staffordshire) Engaged in the Service of their Country as well in the New World and Africa as on the Continent of Europe by the Survivor* (London, 1829)

I. Fletcher (ed.), *For King and Country: the Letters and Diaries of John Mills, Coldstream Guards, 1811–14* (Staplehurst, 1995)

I. Fletcher (ed.), *In the Service of the King: the Letters of William Thornton Keep* (Staplehurst, 1997)

M. Foy, *History of the War in the Peninsula under Napoleon* (London, 1827)

J. García de León y Pizarro, *Memorias de la Vida del Excmo. Señor D. José García de León y Pizarro Escritas por El Mismo*, ed. A. Alonso Castrillo (Madrid, 1894)

L. Gille, *Les Prisonniers de Cabrera: Mémoires d'un Conscrit de 1808* (Paris, 1893)

G. Gleig, *The Subaltern* (London, 1825)

M. Glover (ed.), *A Gentleman Volunteer: the Letters of George Hennell from the Peninsular War, 1812–13* (London, 1979)

W. Grattan, *Adventures of the Connaught Rangers from 1808 to 1814* (London, 1847)

J. Green, *The Vicissitudes of a Soldier's Life, or a Series of Occurrences from 1808 to 1815* (London, 1815)

L. Guimbaud (ed.), *Mémoires du Général Hugo* (Paris, 1934)

J. Hale, *Journal of James Hale, late Sergeant in the Ninth Regiment of Foot* (London, 1826)

B. Hall, *Corcubión*, ed. J. Alberich (Exeter, 1975)

J. Harley, *The Veteran, or Forty Years in the British Service, comprising Adventures in Egypt, Spain, Portugal, Belgium, Holland and Prussia* (London, 1838)

P. Hawker, *Journal of a Regimental Officer during the Recent Campaigns in Portugal and Spain under Viscount Wellington* (London, 1810)
W. Hay, *Reminiscences under Wellington, 1808–1815*, ed. S. Wood (London, 1901)
P. Haythornthwaite (ed.), *Life in Napoleon's Army: the Memoirs of Captain Elzéar Blaze* (London, 1995)
P. Hayward (ed.), *Surgeon Henry's Trifles: Events of a Military Life* (London, 1970)
R. Herr (ed.), *Memorias del Cura Liberal, Don Juan Antonio Posse, con su Discurso sobre la Constitución de 1812* (Madrid, 1984)
C. Hibbert (ed.), *The Recollections of Rifleman Harris* (London, 1985)
C. Hibbert (ed.), *A Soldier of the Seventy-First* (London, 1975)
C. Hibbert (ed.), *The Wheatley Diary: a Journal and Sketchbook kept during the Peninsular War and the Waterloo Campaign* (London, 1964)
E. Holland, *The Spanish Journal of Elizabeth, Lady Holland*, ed. Earl of Ilchester (London, 1910)
H. R. Holland, *Foreign Reminiscences*, ed. H. E. Holland (London, 1850)
D. Horward (ed.), *The French Campaign in Spain and Portugal: An Account by Jean Jacques Pelet* (Minneapolis, 1973)
Lady Jackson (ed.), *The Diaries and Letters of Sir George Jackson* (London, 1872)
W. Jacob, *Travels in the South of Spain* (London, 1811)
B. Jones (ed.), *Napoleon's Army: the Military Memoirs of Charles Parquin* (London, 1987)
L. Junot, *Mémoires du Madame la Duchesse d'Abrantes* (Paris, 1831–5)
J. Kincaid, *Adventures in the Rifle Brigade* (London, 1909)
L. Knowles (ed.), *The War in the Peninsula: Some Letters of Lieutenant Robert Knowles of the Seventh, or Royal, Fusiliers, a Lancashire Officer* (Bolton, 1913)
G. Larpent (ed.), *The Private Journal of Judge-Advocate F. S. Larpent, attached to Lord Wellington's Headquarters, 1812–14* (London, 1853)
J. Leach, *Rough Sketches in the Life of an Old Soldier* (London, 1831)
A. Leith-Hay, *Memoirs of the Late Lieutenant General Sir James Leith, G.C.B., with a Précis of Some of the Most Remarkable Events of the Peninsular War* (London, 1818)
L. Lejeune, *Memoirs of Baron Lejeune, Aide-de-Camp to Marshals Berthier, Davout and Oudinot*, ed. A. Bell (London, 1897)
G. L'Estrange, *Recollections of Sir George L'Estrange* (London, 1873)
H. Lewin, *The Life of a Soldier: a Narrative of Twenty-Seven Years' Service in Various Parts of the World* (London, 1834)
B. Liddell Hart (ed.), *The Letters of Private Wheeler, 1809–1828* (London, 1951)
J. Llorente, *Memorias para la Historia de la Revolución Española* (Paris, 1814)
A. Ludovici (ed.), *On the Road with Wellington: the Diary of a War Commissary in the Peninsular Campaigns* (New York, 1925)

E. Macdonald, *Recollections of Marshal Macdonald, Duke of Tarentum*, ed. C. Rousset (London, 1892)

T. McGuffie (ed.), *Peninsular Cavalry General: the Correspondence of Lieutenant General Robert Ballard Long* (London, 1951)

H. Mackinnon, *A Journal of the Campaign in Portugal and Spain containing Remarks on the Inhabitants, Customs, Trade and Cultivation of those Countries from the Year 1809 to 1812* (Bath, 1812)

J. Marcén (ed.), *El Manuscrito de Matías Calvo: Memorias de un Monegrino durante la Guerra de la Independencia* (Zaragoza, 2000)

P. Marco, *El Cura Merino, 1808 a 1813: Memorias de un Contemporáneo* (Madrid, 1899)

J. Maurice (ed.), *The Diary of Sir John Moore* (London, 1904)

M. de Mesonero, *Memorias de un Setentón* (Madrid, 1880)

A. Miot, *Mémoires du Comte Miot de Melito, Ancien Ministre, Ambassadeur, Conseilleur d'Etat et Membre de l'Institut* (Paris, 1858)

S. Monick (ed.), *Douglas's Tale of the Peninsula and Waterloo* (London, 1997)

W. Napier, *History of the War in the Peninsula and in the South of France from the Year 1807 to the Year 1814* (London, 1828–40)

A. Neale, *Letters from Portugal and Spain comprising an Account of the Operations of the Armies under Their Excellencies Sir Arthur Wellesley and Sir John Moore from the Landing of their Troops in Mondego Bay to the Battle at Corunna* (London, 1809)

J. North (ed.), *In the Legions of Napoleon: the Memoirs of a Polish Officer in Spain and Russia, 1808–1813* (London, 1999)

C. Ompteda, *In the King's German Legion: Memoirs of Baron Ompteda, Colonel in the King's German Legion during the Napoleonic Wars* (London, 1894)

J. Page (ed.), *Intelligence Officer in the Peninsula: Letters and Diaries of Major the Honourable Edward Charles Cocks, 1786–1812* (Tunbridge Wells, 1986)

T. Pakenham (ed.), *The Pakenham Letters, 1800 to 1815* (London, 1914)

J. de Palafox, *Memorias*, ed. H. Lafoz (Zaragoza, 1994)

J. Patterson, *The Adventures of Captain John Patterson* (London, 1837)

V. Pina, *Páginas de 1808: Memorias de un Patriota* (Zaragoza, 1959)

R. Porter, *Letters from Portugal and Spain Written during the March of the British Troops under Sir John Moore* (London, 1809)

M. de Pradt, *Mémoires Historiques sur la Révolution d'Espagne* (Paris, 1816)

J. Queipo de Llano (Conde de Toreno), *Historia del Levantamiento, Guerra y Revolución de España* (Madrid, 1835–7)

A. de Rocca, *Memoirs of the War of the French in Spain*, ed. P. Haythornthwaite (London, 1990)

P. Rodríguez Fernández (ed.), *La Guerra de Independencia en Asturias: Correspondencia de General Bonet, 1809–1812* (Gijón, 1991)

I. Rousseau (ed.), *The Peninsular War Journal of Sir Benjamin D'Urban* (London, 1930)

R. Roy (ed.), 'The memoirs of Private James Gunn', *JSAHR*, XLIX, no. 198, pp. 90–120

E. Sabine (ed.), *Letters of Colonel Sir Augustus Simon Frazer, K.C.B., Commanding the Royal Horse Artillery in the Army under the Duke of Wellington Written During the Peninsular and Waterloo Campaigns* (London, 1859)

L. Saint-Cyr, *Mémoires* (Paris, 1831)

E. de Saint-Hilaire, *Souvenirs Intimes du Temps de l'Empire* (Paris, 1860)

L. de Saint Pierre (ed.), *Les Cahiers du Général Brun* (Paris, 1953)

Padre Maestro Salmón, *Resumen Histórico de la Revolución de España* (Cádiz–Madrid, 1812–14)

R. Santillán, *Memorias de Don Ramón Santillán (1808–1856)*, ed. A. Berazluce (Madrid, 1996)

J. Sarrazin, *History of the War in Spain and Portugal from 1807 to 1814* (London, 1815)

A. von Schepeler, *Histoire de la Révolution d'Espagne et de Portugal ainsi que de la Guerre qui en Résulta* (Liège, 1829–31)

J. Sherer, *Recollections of the Peninsula* (London, 1825)

E. Shore (ed.), *An Engineer Officer under Wellington in the Peninsula: the Diary and Correspondence of Lieutenant Rice Jones, R.E., during 1808–9–10–11–12* (Cambridge, 1986)

T. Simmons (ed.), *Memoirs of a Polish Lancer: the Pamietniki of Dezydery Chlapowski* (Chicago, 1992)

F. Solá Montaña (ed.), *Els Manresans al Bruch: Relacions del Capdill en Maurici Carrió Referents a la Batalla del Bruch, 6 de Juny de 1808* (Barcelona, 1908)

R. Southey, *History of the Peninsular War* (London, 1823–32)

M. Spurrier (ed.), 'Letters of a Peninsular War commanding officer: the letters of Lieutenant Colonel, later General, Sir Andrew Barnard, G.C.B.', *JSAHR*, XLVII, no. 191, pp. 131–48

Earl of Stanhope, *Notes of Conversations with the Duke of Wellington, 1831–1851* (London, 1889)

C. Steevens, *Reminiscences of my Military Life from 1795 to 1818*, ed. N. Steevens (Winchester, 1878)

W. Stothert, *A Narrative of the Principal Events of the Campaigns of 1809, 1810 and 1811 in Spain and Portugal* (London, 1812)

J. Sturgis (ed.), *A Boy in the Peninsular War: the Services, Adventures and Experiences of Robert Blakeney, Subaltern of the Twenty-Eighth Regiment* (London, 1899)

L. Suchet, *Memoirs of the War in Spain from 1808 to 1814* (London, 1829)

W. Swabey, *Diary of the Campaigns in the Peninsula for the Years 1811, 12 and 13*, ed. F. Whinyates (London, 1984)

D. Thiébault, *The Memoirs of Baron Thiébault (late Lieutenant General in the French Army)* (London, 1896)

W. Thompson (ed.), *An Ensign in the Peninsular War: the Letters of John Aitchison* (London, 1981)

J. Tomkinson (ed.), *The Diary of a Cavalry Officer in the Peninsular and Waterloo Campaigns, 1809–1815* (London, 1894)
C. Vaughan, *Narrative of the Siege of Saragossa* (London, 1809)
A. Viesse de Marmont, *Mémoires du Maréchal Marmont, Duc de Raguse, de 1792 à 1841* (Paris, 1857)
R. Verner (ed.), *Reminiscences of William Verner, 1782–1871* (London, 1965)
W. Verner (ed.), *A British Rifleman: Journals and Correspondence [of George Simmons] during the Peninsular War and the Campaign of Waterloo* (London, 1899)
J. Villanueva, *Mi Viaje a las Cortes* (Madrid, 1860)
J. Villanueva, *Vida Literaria de Don Joaquín Lorenzo Villanueva*, ed. G. Ramírez Aledón (Alicante, 1996)
C. Vivian (ed.), *Richard Hussey Vivian, First Baron Vivian: a Memoir* (London, 1897)
F. Wellesley (ed.), *The Diary and Correspondence of Henry Wellesley, First Lord Cowley, 1790–1846* (London, 1930)
V. Wellesley (ed.), *The Conversations of the First Duke of Wellington with George William Chad* (Cambridge, 1956)
F. Whinyates (ed.), *Letters Written by Lieutenant General Thomas Dyneley, C.B., R.A., while on Active Service between the Years 1806 and 1815* (London, 1895)
F. Whittingham, *A Memoir of the Services of Lieutenant General Sir Samuel Ford Whittingham* (London, 1868)
R. Wollocombe (ed.), *With the Guns in the Peninsula: the Peninsular War Journal of Captain William Webber, Royal Artillery* (London, 1991)
G. Wood, *The Subaltern Officer: a Narrative* (London, 1825)
L. Woodford (ed.), *A Young Surgeon in Wellington's Army: the Letters of William Dent* (Old Woking, 1976)
H. Wylly (ed.), *A Cavalry Officer in the Corunna Campaign, 1808–1809: the Journal of Captain Gordon of the Fifteenth Hussars* (London, 1913)

C. Secondary Sources

Anon., *Historia de la Guerra de la Independencia Española: Años de 1808 a 1814* (Madrid, 1879)
R. Abella, *La Vida y Epoca de José Bonaparte* (Barcelona, 1997)
R. Aldington, *Wellington* (London, 1946)
D. Alexander, 'The impact of guerrilla warfare in Spain on French combat strength', *CREP*, V (1975), pp. 91–8
D. Alexander, *Rod of Iron: French Counter-Insurgency Policy in Aragón during the Peninsular War* (Wilmington, Delaware, 1985)
M. Alonso, *El Ejército en la Sociedad Española* (Madrid, 1971)
J. Alvarez Junco, *Mater Dolorosa: la Idea de España en el Siglo XIX* (Madrid, 2002)
M. Ardit, *Revolución Liberal y Revuelta Campesina: un Ensayo sobre la Desintegración del Régimen Feudal en el País Valenciano, 1793–1840* (Barcelona, 1977)

J. A. Armillas (ed.), *La Guerra de la Independencia: Estudios* (Zaragoza, 2001)
M. Arriazu (ed.), *Estudios sobre Cortes de Cádiz* (Pamplona, 1967)
M. Artola, *Los Afrancesados* (Madrid, 1976)
M. Artola, *Historia de España Alianza Editorial, V: la Burguesia Revolucionaria, 1808–1874* (Madrid, 1990)
M. Artola, *La España de Fernando VII* (Madrid, 1999)
M. Artola, 'La guerra de guerrillas', *Revista de Occidente*, X (1964), pp. 12–43
M. Artola, *Los Orígenes de la España Contemporánea* (Madrid, 1959)
M. de Avesty, *La Vida a Salto de Mata: Guerrilleros, Bandoleros y Contrabandistas* (Barcelona, 1962)
J. Aymes, *La Déportation sous le Premier Empire: les Espagnols en France, 1808–1814* (Paris, 1983)
J. Aymes, *La Guerra de la Independencia en España, 1808–1814* (Madrid, 1975)
J. Aymes, 'La guérilla dans la lutte espagnole pour l'independence, 1808–14: amorce d'une théorie et avatars d'une pratique', *Bulletin Hispanique*, XCVIII, nos 3–4 (July–December, 1976), pp. 325–49
J. Aymes, *España y la Revolución Francesa* (Madrid, 1989)
M. Ballbé, *Orden Público y Militarismo en la España Constitucional, 1812–1983* (Madrid, 1985)
R. Barahona, *Vizcaya on the Eve of Carlism: Politics and Society, 1800–1833* (Reno, Nevada, 1989)
R. Barahona, 'The Napoleonic occupation and its political consequences in the Basque provinces, 1808–1813', *CREP*, XV (1985), pp. 101–16
R. G. de Barthèlemy, *'El Marquesito': Juan Díaz Porlier, General que fue de los Ejércitos Nacionales, 1788–1815* (Santiago de Compostela, 1995)
R. Bayod, *Suministros Exigidos al Pueblo Aragonés para el Ejército Napolénico-Francés* (Zaragoza, 1979)
R. Bayod, *El Reino de Aragón durante el Reino Intruso de los Napoleón* (Zaragoza, 1979)
E. Becerra and F. Redondo, *Ciudad Rodrigo en la Guerra de la Independencia* (Ciudad Rodrigo, 1988)
N. Benavides and J. Yaque, *El Capitán General D. Joaquín Blake y Joyes, Regente del Reino y Fundador del Cuerpo de Estado Mayor* (Madrid, 1960)
A. Berkeley (ed.), *New Lights on the Peninsular War: International Congress on the Iberian Peninsula, 1780–1840* (Lisbon, 1991)
A. Bernal, *La Lucha por la Tierra en la Crisis del Antiguo Régimen* (Madrid, 1979)
A. Bernal, *La Propiedad de la Tierra y las Luchas Agrarias Andaluzas* (Barcelona, 1974)
G. Best, *War and Society in Revolutionary Europe, 1770–1870* (London, 1982)
J. Black, *European Warfare, 1660–1815* (New Haven, Connecticut, 1994)
J. Black, *Western Warfare, 1775–1882* (London, 2001)
A. Blanch, *Historia de la Guerra de la Independencia en el Antiguo Principado* (Barcelona, 1861)

R. Blanco, *Rey, Cortes y Fuerza Armada en los Orígenes de la España Liberal, 1808–1823* (Madrid, 1988)
C. Borreguero, *El Reclutamiento Militar por Quintas en la Espana del Siglo XVIII: Orígenes del Servicio Militar Obligatorio* (Valladolid, 1989)
M. Broers, *Europe under Napoleon, 1799–1815* (London, 1996)
A. Bryant, *The Age of Elegance, 1812–22* (London, 1950)
A. Bryant, *The Great Duke, or the Invincible General* (London, 1971)
A. Bryant, *Years of Victory, 1802–1812* (London, 1944)
J. M. Bueno, *Uniformes Militares de la Guerra de la Independencia* (Madrid, 1989)
W. Callahan, *Church, Politics and Society in Spain, 1750–1874* (Cambridge, Massachusetts, 1984)
W. Callahan, 'The origins of the conservative Church in Spain, 1789–1823', *ESR*, X, no. 2 (April, 1980), pp. 199–223
C. Cambronero, *El Rey Intruso: Apuntes Históricos Referentes a José Bonaparte y a su Gobierno en España* (Madrid, 1909)
E. Canales, 'La deserción en España durante la Guerra de la Independencia', *Bi-centenari de la Revolució Francesa (1789–1989): Le Jacobinisme* (Barcelona, 1990), pp. 211–30
E. Canales, *Patriotismo y Deserción durante la Guerra de la Independencia en Cataluña* (Coimbra, 1988)
F. Carantoña, *Revolución Liberal y Crisis de las Instituciones Tradicionales Asturianas* (Gijón, 1989)
F. Carantoña, *La Guerra de la Independencia en Asturias* (Oviedo, 1983)
P. Casado, *Las Fuerzas Armadas en el Inicio del Constucionalismo Español* (Madrid, 1982)
A. Cassinello, *Juan Martín, 'El Empecinado', o el Amor a la Libertad* (Madrid, 1995)
I. Castells, *La Utopia Insurreccional del Liberalismo: Torrijos y las Conspiraciones Liberales de la Década Ominosa* (Barcelona, 1989)
I. Castells and A. Moliner, *Crisis del Antiguo Régimen y Revolución Liberal en España, 1789–1845* (Barcelona, 2000)
C. de Castro, *La Revolución Liberal y los Municipios Españoles, 1812–1868* (Madrid, 1979)
J. Cepeda, *El Ejército en la Política Española, 1787–1843: Conspiraciones y Pronunciamientos en los Comienzos de la España Liberal* (Madrid, 1990)
M. Chamorro, *1808/1936: Dos Situaciones Históricas Concordantes* (Madrid, 1973)
D. Chandler, *The Campaigns of Napoleon* (London, 1966)
D. Chandler (ed.), *Napoleon's Marshals* (New York, 1987)
D. Chandler, *On the Napoleonic Wars: Collected Essays* (London, 1994)
D. Chandler, 'Wellington at war: regular and irregular warfare', *IHR*, XI, no. 1 (February, 1989), pp. 2–13
E. Christiansen, *The Origins of Military Power in Spain, 1800–1854* (Oxford, 1967)
J. M. Codón, *Biografía y Crónica del Cura Merino* (Burgos, 1986)
O. Connelly, *The Gentle Bonaparte: Biography of Joseph, Napoleon's Elder Brother* (New York, 1968)

O. Connelly, *Napoleon's Satellite Kingdoms* (New York, 1965)
C. Crowley, '*Luces* and *hispanidad*: nationalism and modernization in eighteenth-century Spain', in M. Palumbo and W. O. Shanahan, *Nationalism: Essays in Honour of Louis L. Snyder* (Westport, Connecticut, 1981), pp. 87–102
N. Cruz, *Valencia Napoleónica* (Valencia, 1968)
J. Cuenca, *La Iglesia Española ante la Revolución Liberal* (Madrid, 1971)
G. Desdevises du Dézert, *L'Espagne de l'Ancien Régime* (Paris, 1897–1904)
A. Domínguez Ortiz, *Sociedad y Estado en el Siglo XVIII Español* (Barcelona, 1976)
G. Dufour, *La Guerra de la Independencia* (Madrid, 1999)
P. Dwyer (ed.), *Napoleon and Europe* (London, 2001)
G. Ellis, *The Napoleonic Empire* (London, 1991)
J. Elting, *Swords around a Throne: Napoleon and his Grande Armée* (New York, 1988)
C. Esdaile, *The Duke of Wellington and the Command of the Spanish Army, 1812–14* (London, 1990)
C. Esdaile, 'The Duke of Wellington and the Spanish revolution, 1812–14', in C. Woolgar (ed.), *Wellington Studies, II* (Southampton, 1999), pp. 163–87
C. Esdaile, *The French Wars* (London, 2001)
C. Esdaile, 'Heroes or villains? The Spanish guerrillas in the Peninsular War', *HT*, XXXVIII, no. 4 (April, 1988), pp. 29–35
C. Esdaile, *The Peninsular War: a New History* (London, 2002)
C. Esdaile, 'Rebeldía, reticencia y resistencia: el caso gallego de 1808', *Trienio*, no. 35 (May, 2000), pp. 57–80
C. Esdaile, *The Spanish Army in the Peninsular War* (Manchester, 1988)
C. Esdaile, 'War and politics in Spain, 1808–1814', *HJ*, XXXI, no. 2 (April 1988), pp. 295–317
C. Esdaile, *The Wars of Napoleon* (London, 1995)
C. Esdaile, 'Wellington and the military eclipse of Spain, 1808–1814', *IHR*, XI, no. 1 (February, 1989), pp. 55–67
C. Esdaile, 'Wellington and the Spanish guerrillas: the campaign of 1813', *CREP*, XXI (1991), pp. 298–306
M. Espadas and J. R. de Urquijo, *Historia de España Gredos, XI: Guerra de la Independencia y Epoca Constitucional, 1808–1939* (Madrid, 1990)
A. Espinar, *Málaga durante la Primera Etapa Liberal, 1812–1814* (Málaga, 1994)
R. Farias, *Memorias de la Guerra de la Independencia Escritas por Soldados Franceses* (Madrid, 1919)
P. Fernández Albaladejo, *La Crisis del Antiguo Régimen en Guipúzcoa, 1766–1833: Cambio Económico e Historia* (Madrid, 1975)
F. Fernández Bastarreche, *El Ejército Español en el Siglo XIX* (Madrid, 1978)
V. Fernández Benítez, *Carlismo y Rebeldia Campesina: un Estudio sobre la Conflictividad Social en Cantabria durante la Crisis Final del Antiguo Régimen* (Madrid, 1988)
V. Fernández Benítez, *Burguesia y Revolución Liberal: Santander, 1812–1840* (Santander, 1989)

L. Fernández Martín, *El General Don Francisco de Longa y la Intervención Española en Portugal, 1826–27* (Bilbao, 1954)
R. Fernández de Castro, *Apuntes Histórico-Biográficos del Insigne Patriota, Capitán de Infantería, Don Vicente Moreno, Héroe de la Independencia* (Melilla, 1908)
E. Fernández de Pinedo and others, *Centralismo, Ilustración y Agonía del Antiguo Régimen, 1715–1833* (Barcelona, 1980)
M. Figueroa, *La Guerra de la Independencia en Galicia* (Vigo, 1992)
I. Fletcher (ed.), *The Peninsular War: Aspects of the Struggle for the Iberian Peninsula* (Staplehurst, 1998)
F. Flores, *El Bandolerismo en Extremadura* (Badajoz, 1992)
J. Fontana, *La Quiebra de la Monarquía Absoluta, 1814–1820: la Crisis del Antiguo Régimen en España* (Barcelona, 1971)
A. Fugier, *La Junta Superior de Asturias y la Invasión Francesa* (Gijón, 1989)
L. García Guijarro, *La Guerra de la Independencia y el Guerrillero Romeu* (Madrid, 1908)
P. García Gutiérrez, *La Ciudad de León en la Guerra de la Independencia* (León, 1991)
J. García Mercadel, *Palafox, Duque de Zaragoza, 1775–1847* (Madrid, 1948)
J. García Pérez and others, *Historia de Extremadura* (Badajoz, 1985)
J. García Prado and others, *Estudios de la Guerra de la Independencia* (Zaragoza, 1964–7)
C. García Rodríguez, *Historias de Bandoleros Aragoneses* (Huesca, 2000)
M. García Ruipérez, *Revueltas Sociales en la Provincia de Toledo: la Crisis de 1802–1805* (Toledo, 1999)
D. Gascón, *La Provincia de Teruel en la Guerra de la Independencia* (Madrid, 1908)
N. Gash, *Wellington: Studies in the Military and Political Career of the First Duke of Wellington* (Manchester, 1990)
D. Gates, *The Napoleonic Wars, 1803–1815* (London, 1996)
D. Gates, *The Spanish Ulcer: a History of the Peninsular War* (London, 1986)
G. Girod de l'Ain, *Joseph Bonaparte, le Roi Malgré Lui* (Paris, 1970)
M. Glover, *Legacy of Glory: the Bonaparte Kingdom of Spain* (New York, 1971)
M. Glover, *The Peninsular War: a Concise Military History* (London, 1974)
M. Glover, *Wellington as Military Commander* (London, 1968)
J. Gómez de Arteche, *Guerra de la Independencia: Historia Militar de España de 1808 a 1814* (Madrid, 1868–1903)
M. Gómez Bajo, *La Guerra de la Independencia en Astorga, 1808–1814* (Astorga, 1986)
E. González López, *Entre el Antiguo y el Nuevo Régimen: Absolutistas y Liberales – el Reinado de Fernando VII en Galicia* (La Coruña, 1980)
E. Goodman, 'Spanish nationalism in the struggle against Napoleon', *RP*, XX, no. 3 (July, 1958), pp. 330–46
R. Gras, *Zamora en la Guerra de la Independencia, 1808–14* (Madrid, 1913)
A. Grasset, *Málaga, Provincia Francesa, 1811–1812* (Málaga, 1996)

P. Griffith (ed.), *Forward into Battle: Fighting Tactics from Waterloo to Vietnam* (Chichester, 1981)
P. Griffith (ed.), *A History of the Peninsular War, IX: Modern Studies of the War in Spain and Portugal, 1808–1814* (London, 1999)
P. Griffith (ed.), *Wellington-Commander: the Iron Duke's Generalship* (Chichester, 1986)
P. Guedalla, *The Duke* (London, 1931)
R. Guirao, *Guerrilleros y Patriotas en el Alto Aragón, 1808–1814* (Huesca, 2000)
R. Guirao and L. Sorando, *El Alto Aragón en la Guerra de la Independencia* (Zaragoza, 1995)
M. L. Guzmán, *Mina el Mozo, Héroe de Navarra* (Madrid, 1932)
E. Hamilton, 'War and inflation in Spain, 1780–1800', *QJE*, LIX, no. 1 (November, 1944), pp. 36–77
E. Hamilton, *War and Prices in Spain, 1651–1800* (Cambridge, Massachusetts, 1947)
B. Hamnett, *La Política Española en una Epoca Revolucionaria* (México City, 1985)
J. de Haro, *Guerra de la Independencia: Bailén – Diarios y Memorias* (Ciudad Real, 1999)
J. de Haro, *Guerra de la Independencia: La Mancha, 1808 – Diarios, Memorias, Cartas* (Alcázar de San Juan, 2000)
P. Hayman, *Soult: Napoleon's Maligned Marshal* (London, 1990)
F. Hernández Girbal, *Juan Martín, el Empecinado, Terror de los Franceses* (Madrid, 1985)
F. Hernández Montalbán, *La Abolición de los Señorios en España, 1811–1837* (Valencia, 1999)
R. Herr, *The Eighteenth-Century Revolution in Spain* (Princeton, 1958)
R. Herr, 'Good, evil and Spain's uprising against Napoleon', in R. Herr and H. Parker (eds), *Ideas in History: Essays Presented to Louis Gottschalk by his Former Students* (Durham, North Carolina, 1965), pp. 157–81
R. Herr, *Rural Change and Royal Finances in Spain at the End of the Old Régime* (Berkeley, California, 1989)
C. Hibbert, *Wellington: a Personal History* (London, 1997)
E. Hobsbawm, *The Age of Revolution, 1789–1848* (London, 1977)
E. Hobsbawm, *Bandits* (London, 1969)
E. Hobsbawm, *Primitive Rebels: Studies in Archaic Forms of Social Movement in the Nineteenth and Twentieth Centuries* (Manchester, 1959)
R. Hocquellet, *Résistance et Révolution durant l'Occupation Napoléonienne en Espagne, 1808–1812* (Paris, 2001)
R. Holtman, *Napoleonic Propaganda* (Baton Rouge, 1950)
N. Horta Rodríguez, *D. Julián Sánchez, 'El Charro', Guerrillero y Brigadier* (Ciudad Rodrigo, 1987)
R. Humble, *Napoleon's Peninsular Marshals* (London, 1974)
J. M. Iribarren, *Espoz y Mina, el Guerrillero* (Madrid, 1965)
J. M. Iribarren, *Espoz y Mina, el Liberal* (Madrid, 1967)
L. James, *The Iron Duke: a Military Biography of Wellington* (London, 1992)

B. Jarnés, *Zumalacárregui: el Caudillo Romántico* (Madrid, 1972)

F. Jiménez de Gregorio, *Murcia en los Dos Primeros Años de la Guerra por la Independencia* (Murcia, 1947)

H. Lachouque and others, *Napoleon's War in Spain: the French Peninsular Campaigns, 1807–1814* (London, 1982)

H. Lafoz, *La Guerra de la Independencia en Aragón: del Motín de Aranjuez a la Capitulación de Zaragoza* (Zaragoza, 1996)

H. Lafoz, *José Palafox y su Tiempo* (Zaragoza, 1992)

B. Liddell Hart, *The Decisive Wars of History: a Study in Strategy* (London, 1929)

E. Longford, *Wellington: the Years of the Sword* (London, 1969)

B. López Morán, *El Bandolerismo Gallego en la Primera Mitad del Siglo XIX* (La Coruña, 1995)

M. López Pérez and I. Lara, *Entre la Guerra y la Paz: Jaén, 1808–1814* (Granada, 1993)

L. Lorente, *Agitación Urbana y Crisis Económica durante la Guerra de la Independencia, 1808–1814* (Cuenca, 1993)

L. Lorente, 'Coyuntura económica y presión social en la España ocupada: el modelo tributario francés en Toledo, 1811–1813', in E. de Diego and others (eds), *Repercusiones de la Revolución Francesa en España* (Madrid, 1990), pp. 403–19

L. Lorente, *Poder y Miseria: Oligarcas y Campesinos en la España Señorial, 1760–1868* (Madrid, 1994)

G. Lovett, *Napoleon and the Birth of Modern Spain* (New York, 1965)

G. Lovett, 'The Spanish guerrillas and Napoleon', *CREP*, V (1975), pp. 80–90

J. Lynch, *Bourbon Spain, 1700–1808* (Oxford, 1989)

J. Marshall-Cornwall, *Massena* (Oxford, 1965)

E. Martínez Quinteiro, 'Coyuntura económica y liberalismo, 1788–1810', *Hispania*, XLIII, no. 155 (September, 1983), pp. 581–98

E. Martínez Ruiz (ed.), *II Seminario Internacional sobre la Guerra de la Independencia: Madrid, 24–26 de Octubre de 1994* (Madrid, 1995)

J. Mercader, *Catalunya i l'Imperi Napoleònic* (Montserrat, 1978)

J. Mercader, *José Bonaparte Rey de España, 1808–13: Historia Externa del Reinado* (Madrid, 1971)

J. Mercader, *José Bonaparte, Rey de España, 1808–13: Estructura del Estado Español Bonapartista* (Madrid, 1983)

F. Miranda, *La Guerra de la Independencia en Navarra: la Acción del Estado* (Pamplona, 1977)

P. Molas (ed.), *La España de Carlos IV* (Madrid, 1991)

A. Moliner, 'La conflictividad social en la Guerra de la Independencia', *Trienio*, no. 35 (May, 2000), pp. 81–115

A. Moliner, 'La peculiaridad de la revolución española de 1808', *Hispania*, no. 166 (May, 1987), pp. 632–46

A. Moliner, 'Las juntas corregimentales de Cataluña en la Guerra del Frances', *Hispania*, no. 158 (September, 1984), pp. 549–82

A. Moliner, *Revolución Burguesa i Movimiento Juntero en España* (Lérida, 1997)
R. Montes, *El Bandolerismo en la Región de Murcia durante el Siglo XIX* (Murcia, 1998)
M. Morán, *Poder y Gobierno en las Cortes de Cádiz* (Pamplona, 1986)
M. Morán, *Revolución y Reforma Religiosa en las Cortes de Cádiz* (Madrid, 1994)
I. Morant, *El Declive del Señorio: los Dominios del Ducado de Gandía, 1705–1837* (Valencia, 1984)
M. Moreno, *Los Españoles durante la Ocupación Napoleónica: la Vida Cotidiana en la Voragine* (Málaga, 1997)
M. Moreno, *Sevilla Napoleónica* (Seville, 1995)
S. de Moxo, *La Disolución del Régimen Señorial en España* (Madrid, 1965)
F. Moya and C. Rey, *El Ejército y la Armada en las Cortes de Cádiz* (Cádiz, 1913)
J. Muñoz Maldonado, *Historia Política y Militar de la Guerra de la Independencia contra Napoleón Bonaparte desde 1808 a 1814* (Madrid, 1833)
B. Narbonne, *Joseph Bonaparte, le Roi Philosophe* (Paris, 1949)
A. Ollero, *Palencia durante la Ocupación Francesa, 1808–1814: Repercusiones Sociales y Económicas* (Valladolid, 1983)
C. Oman, *A History of the Peninsular War* (Oxford, 1902–1930)
J. Ortega, *Historia de las Escuadras de Cataluña: su Origen, sus Proezas, sus Vicisitudes Intercalada con la Vida y Hechos de los Mas Célebres Ladrones y Bandoleros* (Barcelona, 1968)
M. Ortuño, *Xavier Mina: Guerrillero, Liberal, Insurgente* (Pamplona, 2000)
A. Pacho, *Del Antiguo Régimen a la España Moderna: Manuel Traggia (de S. Tomás) OCD, Protagonista e Interprete del Tránsito* (Burgos, 1979)
P. Pascual, *Curas y Frailes Guerrilleros en la Guerra de la Independencia: las Partidas de Cruzada Reglamentadas por el Carmelita Zaragozana, P. Manuel Traggia* (Zaragoza, 2000)
D. Pastor, *El Bandolerismo Social en España: Cinco Siglos de Desequilibrio Social y de Bandolerismo* (Barcelona, 1979)
S. Payne, *Politics and the Military in Modern Spain* (Stanford, California, 1967)
M. A. Peña, *El Tiempo de los Franceses: la Guerra de la Independencia en el Suroeste Español* (Huelva, 2000)
J. Pérez Garzón, *Milicia Nacional y Revolución Burguesa: el Prototipo Madrileño, 1808–1874* (Madrid, 1978)
M. Pérez Regordán, *El Bandolerismo Andaluz, I: desde los Orígenes a la Muerte de Tragabuches* (Arcos de la Frontera, 1987)
M. Pintos, *La Política de Fernando VII entre 1814 y 1820* (Pamplona, 1958)
J. Priego, *Como fue la Guerra de la Independencia* (Madrid, 1936)
J. Priego, *Guerra de la Independencia, 1808–1814* (Madrid, 1972–2000)
P. Prieto, *El Grande de España, Capitán General Castaños, Primer Duque de Bailén y primer Marqués de Portugalete* (Madrid, 1958)
M. Ramisa, *Els Catalans i el Domini Napoleonic* (Montserrat, 1995)
M. Ramisa (ed.), *Guerra Napoleònica a Catalunya, 1808–1814: Estudis i Documents* (Montserrat, 1996)
J. Read, *War in the Peninsula* (London, 1977)

R. del Río, *Los Orígenes de la Guerra Carlista en Navarra, 1820–1824* (Pamplona, 1987)
C. Rodríguez López-Brea, *Frailes y Revolución Liberal* (Toledo, 1996)
E. Rodríguez Solis, *Los Guerrilleros de 1808: Historia Popular de la Guerra de la Independencia* (Madrid, 1887)
A. Rodríguez Villa, *El Teniente General Don Pablo Morillo, Primer Conde de Cartagena, Marqués de la Puerta (1778–1837): Estudio Biográfico* (Madrid, 1908)
M. Ross, *The Reluctant King: Joseph Bonaparte, King of the Two Sicilies and Spain* (London, 1976)
G. Rothenberg, *The Napoleonic Wars* (London, 1999)
R. Rudorff, *War to the Death: the Sieges of Saragossa, 1808–1809* (London, 1974)
P. Sahlins, *Boundaries: the Making of France and Spain in the Pyrenees* (Berkeley, California, 1989)
S. Saiz, 'Lerma en el levantamiento guerrillero de la Guerra de la Independencia', *RHM*, no. 63 (July, 1987), pp. 161–77
J. Sánchez Fernández, 'El Ejército contra las guerrillas: la jefatura militar frente al fenómeno guerrillero durante la Guerra de la Independencia', *RHM*, no. 87 (July, 1999), pp. 149–74
J. Sánchez Fernández, *La Guerrilla Vallesoletana, 1808–1814* (Valladolid, 1997)
J. Sánchez Fernández, 'Las Juntas Criminales Extraordinarias en el reinado de José Bonaparte en España: el caso vallesoletano', *Aportes: Revista de Historia Contemporánea*, no. 40 (February, 1999), pp. 31–7
J. Sánchez Fernández, *¡Nos Invaden! Guerrilla y Represión en Valladolid durante la Guerra de la Independencia Española, 1808–1814* (Valladolid, 2000)
J. Santos, *El Bandolerismo en Andalucía, I: Sevilla y su Antiguo Reino* (Seville, 1991)
J. Santos, *El Bandolerismo en España: una Historia Fuera del Ley* (Madrid, 1995)
S. M. de Soto (Conde de Clonard), *Historia Orgánica de la Armas de Infantería y Caballería Españolas* (Madrid, 1851–62)
J. Tone, *The Fatal Knot: the Guerrilla War in Navarre and the Defeat of Napoleon* (Chapel Hill, North Carolina, 1994)
J. Tone, 'Napoleon's uncongenial sea: guerrilla warfare in Navarre during the Peninsular War, 1808–14', *EHQ*, XXVI, no. 3 (July, 1996), pp. 355–81
J. Tone, 'The pacification of Navarre', in W. D. Phillips and C. R. Phillips (eds), *Marginated Groups in Spanish and Portuguese History* (Minneapolis, 1989), pp. 111–26
J. Tulard (ed.), *L'Histoire de Napoléon par la Peinture* (Paris, 1991)
A. Uffindell (ed.), *On Wellington: the Duke and his Art of War by Jac Weller* (London, 1998)
R. Vidal, *Historia de la Guerra de la Independencia en el Campo de Gibraltar* (Cadiz, 1975)
P. Vilar, *Hidalgos, Amotinados y Guerrilleros: Pueblo y Poderes en la Historia de España* (Barcelona, 1999)
J. Weller, *Wellington in the Peninsula, 1808–14* (London, 1962)
S. Woolf, *Napoleon's Integration of Europe* (London, 1991)

Index

NOTE: Compound Spanish surnames appear under the first element. Prefixes in a name are transposed, e.g. Cuadra, Ambrosio de la, apart from a definite article alone, e.g. La Mière de Corvay, Jean. Page numbers followed by *n* and a number refer to information in the Notes.